EVIDENCE-BASED PRACTICE IN THE FIELD OF SUBSTANCE ABUSE

EVIDENCE-BASED PRACTICE IN THE FIELD OF SUBSTANCE ABUSE

A Book of Readings

Katherine van Wormer
University of Northern Iowa

Bruce A. Thyer
Florida State University

EDITORS

SAGE

Los Angeles | London | New Delhi
Singapore | Washington DC

For information:

SAGE Publications, Inc.
2455 Teller Road
Thousand Oaks, California 91320
E-mail: order@sagepub.com

SAGE Publications Ltd.
1 Oliver's Yard
55 City Road
London EC1Y 1SP
United Kingdom

SAGE Publications India Pvt. Ltd.
B 1/I 1 Mohan Cooperative Industrial Area
Mathura Road, New Delhi 110 044
India

SAGE Publications Asia-Pacific Pte. Ltd.
33 Pekin Street #02-01
Far East Square
Singapore 048763

Printed in the United States of America

Library of Congress Cataloging-in-Publication Data

Evidence-based practice in the field of substance abuse: a book of readings/[edited by] Katherine Van Wormer, Bruce A. Thyer.

   p. cm.
Includes bibliographical references and index.
ISBN 978-1-4129-7577-3 (pbk.)

   1. Substance abuse—Treatment. 2. Evidence-based social work. I. Van Wormer, Katherine S. II. Thyer, Bruce A.

HV4998.E95 2010
362.29′132—dc22   2009025273

This book is printed on acid-free paper.

09   10   11   12   13   10   9   8   7   6   5   4   3   2   1

Acquisitions Editor:	Kassie Graves
Editorial Assistant:	Veronica K. Novak
Production Editor:	Brittany Bauhaus
Typesetter:	C&M Digitals (P) Ltd.
Proofreader:	Laura Webb
Cover Designer:	Glenn Vogel
Marketing Manager:	Stephanie Adams

CONTENTS

PREFACE

Alcohol and other drug abuse are issues of major concern to the society in terms of loss of health and life and productivity, and to all mental health professionals who deal with the legacy of pain from substance abuse on a daily basis. Given the high social and economic costs associated with chemical dependency, and the associated policy and treatment issues, the need for empirical research is paramount.

A paradigm shift is taking place in addiction treatment in the United States today. This shift is related to the continuing theoretical advancement of a field with a unique and proud history, a field peopled by workers with a commitment to helping that exceeds that found anywhere in the treatment industry. Traditionally counselors in addiction treatment have been schooled in the hard knocks of life and dedicated to bringing what they had learned through personal experience and recovery to their clients. The fervor that they brought to their work was truly extraordinary. So whatever changes take place and whatever the future holds, let us not lose sight of the contributions of the men and women—so many lives saved, so many lives turned around.

So it is with a recognition of the contributions of pioneers in the field that we turn our attention toward science—what the evidence shows concerning the efficacy and effectiveness of treatment interventions. Among the research questions addressed are whether a particular intervention is effective for diverse populations and whether diverse treatments are equally effective for the general population. Or, in other words, what kinds of strategies work best for whom under what circumstances and conditions? And is a treatment that works for alcoholism equally effective when applied to other addictions such as addiction to heroin or methamphetamines?

A model that integrates practice wisdom that has stood the test of time with evidenced-based strategies likely will be the most effective in treating alcohol and other drug use disorders (Zweben, 2008). It is not only the effectiveness of treatment that is at stake, however, but the public perception that treatment is effective that is important. We are talking here about the readiness of clients to enter treatment, the regular referral by the medical community to agencies that provide the treatment, and the ready support of third party funding sources for the agencies. Whether the agencies are fighting to avoid budget cuts in difficult economic times or competing for generous federal funds, accountability is of the essence. Evidence-based and cost-effective practice, in fact, are being pushed at every level from the federal government to state and local funding sources to insurance companies that stress accountability for the money spent. Politically, as we anticipate change with the appointment of a new drug czar working under a new administration, the climate is ripe to support treatment innovations both experimentally and of demonstrated effectiveness.

The Substance Abuse Mental Health and Services Administration, which is under the auspices of the U. S. Department of Health and Human Services at www.mentalhealth.samhsa.gov has stated its strong commitment to funding research evaluations of model programming, identifying best practices, and linking services to evidence-based findings. This special collection of research articles contributes to that mission. Together, the selections identify such practices and help us move toward the goal of advancing human understanding of substance use.

Within this economic context, the publication of a collection of empirically-based research articles describing "best practices" is timely. A major advantage of such a collection is that the readings, taken as a whole, are interdisciplinary, and organized from the vast wealth of research material that is scattered throughout the literature. This presentation in one place of diverse information, allows for a resource that is both convenient and thought-provoking.

The previously published journal articles that are chosen for inclusion in this book were selected by the editors on the basis of topic relevance, ability to stimulate classroom discussion, and the significance of the findings to policy practice and treatment design. *Evidence-Based Practice in the Field of Substance Abuse* is designed for use as a general or supplementary text in courses on substance abuse, for general practice seminars, and for courses on evidence-based research. Educators might find that this collection can serve as a gateway to introduce students (advanced undergraduates and graduate students) to the importance of consulting research findings as an ongoing practice in the mental health profession. To enhance critical thinking about themes of professional interest, critical thinking questions are included at the conclusion of each article.

To enhance the teaching effort and promote excitement in this field, we have selected articles that cover a range of topics of interest to practitioners, namely, assessment, work with clients with co-occurring disorders, gender-specific programming, and treatment innovations that are controversial but pragmatic. Many of these selections, in fact, are at the cutting edge of treatment innovation. The reader will find here research on such issues as the effectiveness of gender specific treatment and a discussion of experiments in providing housing to the alcoholic and drug-using homeless. Harm reduction strategies are explored in terms of their viability, and motivational enhancement techniques, derived from basic truths of social psychology, are described. The book concludes with an empirical evaluation of drug courts.

For organizational purposes, this volume is organized around five major sections. At the beginning of each section is a major overview to guide the reading. The section headings by topic are: introduction to evidence-based practice, assessment, gender- and culturally-based interventions, treatment issues and innovations, and policy considerations. Throughout the readings, attention is paid to interventions geared toward different age groups, genders, and multicultural populations. Our hope is that these selections will stimulate thought, help promote acceptance of the burgeoning paradigm shift in the field, perhaps even generate treatment innovation, and, above all, lead to questioning of some taken-for-granted assumptions that are without any scientific merit. The adoption of treatment modalities consistent with empirical research will help move the substance abuse field forward and enhance the reputation of the men and women who engage so tirelessly in the frontline work.

All the contributions that follow share a common theme of the desire to reduce the suffering and social harms stemming from alcohol and other drug problems and the desire to help us think in fresh and imaginative ways about the nature of these problems and their remedies.

ACKNOWLEDGMENTS

The authors and SAGE gratefully acknowledge the contributions of the following reviewers:

David J. Carter, *University of Nebraska at Omaha*

Katherine Dooley, *Mississippi State University*

Cynthia Glidden-Tracey, *Arizona State University*

Michael D. Loos, *University of Wyoming*

Oliver J. Morgan, *University of Scranton*

Frank Norton, *Bowie State University*

Leslie W. O'Ryan, *Western Illinois University-Quad Cities*

Brock Reiman, *Malone College*

REFERENCE

Zweben, A. (2008, winter). Integrating research and clinical wisdom: Social work in addictions. Columbia University School of Social Work: *Spectrum*, 8–9.

PART I

INTRODUCTION TO EVIDENCE-BASED PRACTICE

This section of the book consists of two readings to provide you with a general introduction to the topic of evidence-based practice (EBP). The first, by this volume's, two editors, provides a general outline of the five step process of EBP, and tries to make clear what this model does say, versus what it is not about. The latter is emphasized because despite the newness of EBP, it is subject to numerous misrepresentations in our professional literature, misrepresentations that can result in discouraging human service professionals from learning more about this model. This is why we emphasize locating and reading the primary source materials on EBP, rather than relying on second- or third-hand interpretations. We discuss the existence of numerous systematic reviews based on the substance abuse treatment and assessment literature, and most highly recommend those to be found on the websites of the Campbell and Cochrane Collaborations as having high credibility. All substance abuse counselors should acquaint themselves with these extremely relevant documents and become familiar with their conclusions.

The review article by Gambrill (2006) (see entire Chapter 2) presents a much more encompassing review of EBP, a field she prefers to call evidence-informed practice, since EBP is actually grounded in much more than purely scientific considerations when it comes to selecting assessment methods and interventions. Gambrill clearly points out that EBP is a framework for thinking about how decisions should be made, and is not a fan of the preparation of 'lists' of so-called evidence-based treatments created on the basis of research evidence alone. She describes the great importance of client considerations in the decision-making process, and of the different types of questions that EBP deals with (e.g., effectiveness, prevention, risk prognosis, and assessment). Too often EBP is seen as being exclusively focused on reviewing effectiveness questions, to the exclusion of these other issues of importance to practice. She critiques the using of the term evidence-based practice without the substance behind it, of, in effect, putting old wine in new bottles.

Gambrill also stresses the *transparency* of the EBP process—transparency in describing exactly how systematic reviews were undertaken, and transparency in sharing information (and our lack of credible information) with our clients. She reviews the compilation of hierarchies of evidence, and cautions

1

us against the possibility of prematurely concluding that something is well supported because it meets some arbitrary research standard. For example, one well-known standard claims that an intervention can be considered as empirically based if it is supported by two well-designed randomized controlled trials (RCTs). The peril of such a standard is that it fails to take into account that the same intervention may also be the focus of many more RCTs with *negative results!* You can see how it would be misleading, in the case of a treatment that has been tested in 10 RCTs, eight of which yielded negative results and two positive, to then claim that that treatment is empirically supported (because it meets the two positive RCT benchmark). This is not a theoretical issue. Recently Feinstein (2008) published a so-called systematic review on a treatment called 'energy psychology' and concluded that it was a probably efficacious treatment. Feinstein's (2008) review was both incomplete and misleading, and he omitted citing and discussing several RCTs with negative outcomes of energy psychology (Pignotti & Thyer, 2009). Most readers of Feinstein (2008) will not become aware of Pignotti and Thyer's (2009) subsequent critique of his review, and thus have the potential to be misled by considering these so-called energy psychologies for their clients.

These two readings, Thyer and van Wormer, and Gambrill, represent only an introduction to the topic of evidence-based practice. Readers are encouraged to pursue the topic further on their own.

REFERENCES

Feinstein, D. (2008). Energy psychology: A review of the preliminary evidence. *Psychotherapy: Theory, Research Practice Training, 45,* 199–213.

Gambrill, E. (2006). Evidence-based practice and policy: Choices ahead. *Research on Social Work Practice, 16,* 338–357.

Pignotti, M. & Thyer, B. A. (2009). Some comments on "Energy Psychology: A Review of the Preliminary Evidence": Premature conclusions based on incomplete evidence? *Psychotherapy: Theory, Research, Practice, Training 49,* 257–261.

1

Evidence-Based Practice in the Area of Substance Abuse

Katherine van Wormer

University of Northern Iowa

Bruce A. Thyer

Florida State University

You probably abuse substances such as alcohol and other drugs. A dictionary in our office provides one definition of abuse as "To use so as to injure or damage." By this standard, the hangover following excessive alcohol consumption indicates abuse. Actually, when one of the authors (Thyer) has more than just a couple of drinks, he gets a headache. Abuse. On several occasions during his lengthy life, he has ingested so much alcohol that he became physically sick to his stomach. Abuse. Other similar episodes could be presented, but you get the point. Many of us abuse some sort of substance on occasion, but for most of us, this abuse does not cause significant difficulties in our interpersonal relationships, our ability to work, or to otherwise negotiate the demands of life. For some individuals however, their use of substances rises to the level of abuse to such an extent that significant problems do emerge. The nosology (e.g., scientific classification) of substance abuse problems is an arcane art, incorporating much myth, clinical lore, and a modest amount of credible research. We can quibble about the distinctions among terms such as abuse, dependence, addiction, disorders, and the like. How client functioning and problems related to substance abuse are described will not be satisfactorily resolved in the near future, so in this chapter, and elsewhere in the volume, a variety of terms and classifications will be employed. Which are the 'best' or most 'accurate' is not for us to say. We are confident in presuming that people do develop problems related to substance abuse. We are less confident in asserting which language or terms used to describe these problems is the closest to nature's truth. Just like Pluto exists, regardless of whether or not astronomers agree on calling it a planet, so too do substance problems exist. Distance exists in nature, but

3

how we measure it—miles, kilometers, cubits or furlongs—are conventions arrived at by human beings. So does time exist. Time marches on and pays no attention to the national shifts back and forth from daylight savings time, or whether our clocks read in 12 hour or 24 hour increments, or if the Pope decrees a shift in the calendar.

We do believe that individuals providing substance abuse counseling, prevention, and treatment services, should be familiar with the most common language and terms used to define substance abuse, and this language is found in the fourth edition, text revision, of the *Diagnostic and Statistical Manual of Mental Disorders* (American Psychiatric Association, 2000). A few of the more common terms are reproduced in Table 1.1. Most so-called diagnoses are grouped by specific substances (alcohol, cocaine, amphetamine, caffeine, cannabis, etc.), with various subtypes involving intoxication, abuse, dependence or withdrawal, and full or partial remission. Keep in mind, these classifications are agreed upon conventions, like how we categorize objects in

space, time, or distance. Each new edition of the DSM brings many changes, but the problems themselves are not altered. There are also alternative nosological systems, such as the *International Classification System of Diseases,* each with its own merits and flaws. However it makes no sense to claim that we have squared the circle and arrived at a complete and accurate classification scheme for any of these approaches. The DSM is the most widely used system, which is why we highlight it here.

In this volume we have collected some readings which we judge to represent fairly sound contemporary research on the topics of assessing and treating individuals with substance abuse problems, and on policy applications of such research. We have done this to further what can be generally labeled as the approach called evidence-based practice, a model of practice in the human services that very explicitly is grounded, in part, on such research findings. It is important at this point to present the evidence-based practice model, so we are clear from the outside what this approach entails.

Table 1.1   Common Terminology Used in the Field of Substance Abuse as Defined in the *Diagnostic and Statistical Manual of Mental Disorders* (APA, 2000).

- "Substance Abuse is a maladaptive pattern of substance use manifested by recurrent and significant adverse consequences related to the repeated use of substances . . . There may be repeated failure to fulfill major role obligations, repeated use in situations in which it is physically hazardous, multiple legal problems, and recurrent social and interpersonal problems." (p. 198)

- "Substance Dependence is a cluster of cognitive, behavioral, and physiological symptoms indicating that the individual continues use of the substance despite significant substance-related problems. There is a pattern or repeated self-administration that can result in tolerance, withdrawal, and compulsive drug-taking behavior." (p. 192)

- "Tolerance is the need for greatly increased amount of the substance to achive intoxication (or the desired effect) or a markedly diminished effect with continued use of the same amount of the substance." (p. 192)

- "Withdrawal is a maladaptive behavioral change, with physiological and cognitive concomitants, that occurs when blood or tissue concentrations of a substance declined in an individual who maintained prolonged heavy use of the substance. After developing unpleasant withdrawal symptoms, the person is likely to take the substance to relieve or avoid those symptoms." (p. 194)

EVIDENCE-BASED PRACTICE: WHAT IT IS

The evidence-based practice model emerged in the early 1990s from the field of medicine. It was made possible through the emergence of a number of concurrent developments, including the rise of email and Internet, which greatly speeds up communication and the dissemination of new research findings; the rapid development of empirically-based approaches to assess and treat clients with much greater effectiveness than in the past; and an increasing sense of professional accountability, an ethical awareness that to some extent, we as professionals have an obligation to offer clients as first-choice options, methods of assessment and treatment which are more likely to help them (Myers & Thyer, 1997).

The EBP model was first comprehensively outlined in the little book *Evidence-Based Medicine: How to Practice and Teach EBM* (Sackett, Richardson, Rosenberg, & Haynes, 1997), now in its third edition (Straus, Richardson, Glasziou, & Haynes, 2005). Anyone wishing to be informed on what EBP really is should read this volume first. It is not wise to rely on third, fourth or fifth hand regurgitations. For example, Webb (2001) presented the first article discussing EBP in the prestigious *British Journal of Social Work*. Unfortunately he failed to cite a single primary source from the EBP literature in his misguided critical analysis. The only quote he had was from a webpage of a British organization. He then proceeded to mischaracterize the entire EBP process with a series of straw man attacks. The best protection against absorbing straw-man portrayals of EBP is to read primary sources yourself.

Here is an accurate definition of EBP: EBP " . . . requires the integration of the best research evidence with our clinical expertise and our patient's unique values and circumstances' (Straus et al., 2005, p. 1). Additional definitions go on to describe best research evidence as valid and clinically relevant research, clinical expertise means one's ability to use our clinical skills and past experience in our working with new clients, patient values refer to the unique preferences, concerns and expectations clients bring to us, and circumstances involve the individual's clinical state and the service setting. The process of EBP consists of five steps (from Straus et al., 2005, pp. 3–4):

1. Convert our need for information into an answerable question (see Gambrill & Gibbs, 2009, for a social work perspective on this step).

2. Track down the best available evidence pertaining to answering that question (see Rubin & Parrish, 2009).

3. Critically evaluate the evidence we locate in terms of its validity and applicability to our client (see Bronson, 2009).

4. Integrate this critical appraisal with our clinical expertise and our client's unique values and circumstances (see Gambrill, 2009).

5. Evaluate our effectiveness and efficiency in completing steps 1–4 (see Thyer & Myers, 2007, 2009).

Note that locating and applying research evidence is one critical piece, but this is not to accord more importance than the other critical features, such as clinical skills, or the client's values and preferences. And of course, in common with all good practice, professional ethics inform our decisions as well. The recent edition of the *Social Worker's Desk Reference* (Roberts, 2009, pp. 1115–1182) now includes a special section on EBP as it applies to social work, and is an excellent resource that was edited for its general adherence to the original EBP model. The literature on EBP does tend to focus on more of the research issues related to this topic, since these are often accorded considerably less attention in the educational curricula of the human service professions. These emphasize the acquisition of clinical skills, socialization in one's field, professional ethics, and not much on the utilization of meta-analyses versus randomized controlled trials, hence the EBP literature tries to fill this gap.

This process of reviewing the pertinent high quality research literature bearing on your answerable question can be conducted using either a bottom-up or top-down approach. In the bottom-up approach, the individual social worker personally searches the literature, retrieves relevant studies, carefully reads them, critically appraises their methods and conclusions, and arrives at a judgment about the answer (e.g., Does research evidence suggest that a given treatment is effective? Does research evidence suggest that a given assessment method is clinically useful and psychometrically sound?). While this can be a time-consuming process, once completed for a particular question (e.g., Does assertive community treatment better help prevent relapse, compared to standard care, among persons diagnosed with schizophrenia?'), future updates will be less demanding of time and effort.

An alternative to this approach is to seek out well-crafted systematic reviews completed by competent research terms and see what they have concluded. There are two major organizations explicitly devoted to this process of preparing systematic reviews about the types of answerable questions formed as a part of the EBP process. The first is known as the Cochrane Collaboration (www.cochrane.org) and focuses on the preparation of systematic reviews in the broad area of health care, and the second is the Campbell Collaboration (www.campbellcollaboration.org), with a focus on social welfare, criminal justice, and education. If you go to these websites you will find comprehensive handbooks on the methodologies used to

Table 1.2   Selected Systematic Reviews on Substance Abuse Treatment Available through the Cochrane Collaboration (www.cochrane.org) and Campbell Collaboration (www.campbellcollaboration.org). There are many additional completed reviews. This list is just a sampling.

From the Cochrane Collaboration

- Alcoholics Anonymous and other 12-Step Programmes for Alcohol Dependence

- Auricular Acupuncture for Cocaine Dependence

- Case Management for Persons with Substance Disorders

- Interventions for Drug Using Offenders in the Courts, Secure Establishments and the Community

- Primary Prevention for Alcohol Misuse in Young People

- Interventions for Prevention of Drug Use by Young People Delivered in Non-School Settings

- Psychosocial Interventions for Cocaine and Psychostimulant Amphetamines Related Disorders

- Psychosocial Interventions for Women Enrolled in Alcohol Treatment During Pregnancy

- Therapeutic Communities for Substance Related Disorder

- Psychosocial Treatment for Opiate Abuse and Dependence

From the Campbell Collaboration

- Incarceration-Based Drug Treatment: Effectiveness on Criminal Behavior

- Street-Level Drug Law Enforcement

develop systematic reviews, and these represent about the highest quality standards to be found anywhere on the preparation of systematic reviews. Of even greater value, is the posting of several thousand (Cochrane) and over 50 (Campbell) completed systematic reviews. Thus, if you as a practitioner can locate a completed systematic review that really does pertain to the answerable question you are seeking answers for, this can be an immense savings of time. Table 1.2 lists a few examples of completed systematic reviews to be found on the Cochrane and Campbell websites pertaining to substance abuse. There are many more, and the reader is urged to regularly consult this evolving and updated resource. These can be a great savings of time and effort in completing that aspect of the EBP process dealing with locating and critically appraising relevant research studies. If you are fortunate to find a relevant systematic review, it is enough a good idea at that point to undertake an updated review on your own of work published since the systematic review you located was posted.

Evidence-Based Practice: What It Is Not

Evidence-Based Practice Does Not Tell Social Workers What to Do

Evidence-based practice does not provide practitioners with lists of so-called *approved* assessment methods or interventions from which you are expected to select.

Keep in mind that EBP represents the process of *integrating* the best available scientific findings *with* other equally important factors such as acceptability to clients, ethical appropriateness, your own clinical expertise, feasibility and time constraints, and so on. Thus the *process* of EBP is violated by any intimation that you are engaging in EBP if asked to choose treatments from any kind of listing. The very idea is absurd. For example, suppose it were scientifically proven that amputating the hands

of thieves exerted a deterrent effect on crime among the general population. Despite any scientific support this intervention would have, in contemporary North America the ethical objections to such an approach would deem it an unsuitable option. Or suppose (and this is true) that cognitive-behavior therapy has been shown to be a pretty effective intervention for clients suffering from major depression. This may well be true, but if your client has a developmental disability, s/he may not possess the intellectual requisites needed to effectively engage in this form of treatment, and CBT would not be a first choice treatment for him/her, regardless of what any 'list' of effective treatments may indicate.

Hopefully readers of the present chapter and of primary sources on the EBP model, will not be deceived by misrepresentations such as those of Webb, when he erroneously claimed "According to this view, social work decisions should rest solely on evidence leading to effective outcomes." (Webb, 2001, p. 62).

Also, some practitioners confuse the development and propulgation of practice guidelines (PG) with the EBP movement. These are two distinct initiatives, and the use of PGs are nowhere to be found or advocated within the primary EBP literature. Practice guidelines are:

" . . . recommendations for clinical care based on research findings and the consensus of experienced clinicians with expertise in a given practice area. Practice protocols, standards, algorithms, options, parameters, pathways, and preferred practice patterns are nuanced terms broadly synonymous with the concept of *clinical practice guidelines.*" Howard & Jensen, 1999, p. 285, emphasis in original)

Practice guidelines *do* tell clinicians what to do. Have a client who meets the criteria for Bipolar Disorder? Then consult, for example, the American Psychiatric Association's practice guideline on this topic. These are eschewed in EBP because

EBP is a process to aid in helping clinicians make decisions, but it does not directly tell them what to do. Also, practice guidelines, unlike systematic reviews, typically contain a strong element of clinical consensus, something EBP tends to avoid.

Evidence-Based Practice Is Primarily a Managerial Tool

EBP is not a tool for managers to cut costs. In fact, by engaging in the EBP process it may emerge that first choice treatments to help clients may turn out to be *more* expensive than the conventional methods of therapy. EBP did not emerge at all from the ranks of administrators and managers; it arose from the combined efforts of an international group of clinicians and researchers, with plenty of consumer input.

Evidence-Based Practice Is Simply Disguised Behaviorism

EBP is not derived from behaviorism, contrary to Webb's assertion that EBP leads to " . . . an evidence-based infrastructure derived solely from a behaviourist worldview and an empirically generated methodology." (2001, p. 60). Behaviorally-oriented professionals had very little to do with the development of EBP, which, as stated earlier, originated in the field of medicine. As it turns out, behavioral practices may well be represented among the approaches which practitioners select, but this is a function of their research support and ethical appropriateness, not some sort of epistemological hegemony. Quite literally *any* approach to social work services can be promoted within the EBP process.

There is Not Enough Evidence in Social Work to Apply Evidence-Based Practice

Another misconception is that social work lacks a sufficient body of solid evidence to be able to apply the EBP process.

This misconception is based on the idea that only the highest quality scientific evidence can be incorporated into the process of choosing assessment methods and interventions. The reality is that EBP encourages the practitioner to locate and critically evaluate the very best *available* evidence. It only makes sense that if an approach is rejected by several high-quality published randomized controlled studies, by a well-conducted meta-analysis or a Cochrane Systematic Review, that such evidence will be accorded greater weight than several anecdotal case histories described by colleagues over the dinner table. But if no systematic review, meta-analyses, or randomized controlled trials are available, then the best evidence may be quasi-experimental studies. If these are not available, then the best evidence may be pre-experimental studies. The practitioner continues to drill down through searching the literature, in keeping with the EBP principle of locating the best *available* knowledge. At the lower end are sources such as single-subject designs, narrative case histories, qualitative studies, theory, or informed clinical opinion. But there is *always* evidence to consult, even if it is to be found at the lower end of the hierarchy.

It is unwise to assume that little or no evidence exists regarding the answers to the practice question relevant to your clinical situation until you have completed a thorough electronic review of the literature. Such a search increasingly is feasible via university and public library Internet portals. Table 1.2 lists a sampling of completed systematic reviews addressing substance abuse which you can download from the website of the Cochrane Collaboration. Interested in alcoholism? The review on the effectiveness of AA will surely be of interest. Interested in prevention of alcohol misuse among the young? There is a systematic review of such interventions on that topic as well. Psychosocial treatments for cocaine abuse? That is covered in Cochrane as well.

Evidence-Based Practice is Only Applicable to Clinical Services

You may believe that EBP is only applicable to clinical practice, and since you engage in macro, administrative or policy practice that this new model has little relevance to you. You may believe that but you would be wrong. There is large and exponentially growing literature on the applications of the EBP model, with adaptations, to macro-level practice (see Thyer, 2008, for a recent review). A search of the phrase "evidence-based government" will turn up a surprising amount of literature, which largely seems to have escaped the attention of academic social workers. The September 2003 issue of the *Annals of the American Academy of Political and Social Science* was devoted to the topic of evidence-led policy, with Sherman's (2003, p. 226) essay titled *Experimental Evidence and Governmental Administration* suggests that " . . . there is a growing nonpartisan interest, across the range of ideologies, in gaining better evidence about achieving results in the private sector." He asserts that "If we stop viewing government as a contest between two sides claiming to have the best capacity to govern, and start to view it as a matter of learning what works to solve problems, we may stop rewarding good luck and start rewarding good practice." (Sherman, 2003, p. 228). This experimentalist sentiment was echoed by President Obama in his inauguration speech:

"The question we ask today is not whether our government is too big or too small, but *whether it works*—whether it helps families find jobs at a decent wage, care they can afford, a retirement that is dignified. Where the answer is yes, we intend to move forward. Where the answer is no, the programs will end." (Barack Obama, 20 January 2009).

The September 2008 issue of the *Journal of Evidence-Based Social Work* was devoted to the applications of the EBP model to macro-level social work practice, and its articles cover topics such as organizational and community practice, neighborhood-based work, university-community partnerships, and other domains. In short, the principles of the EBP process have application at all levels of social intervention, from assessing the individual drug abuser, to establishing drug abuse prevention programs, to creating national policies for health and social care. EBP is more developed at the clinical level, but corresponding applications at the macro level are expanding rapidly.

Evidence-Based Practice Supports a Cookbook Approach to Social Work

It has been contended that EBP promotes a cookbook-like approach to service delivery. A cookie-cutter approach to practice tends to apply one intervention promiscuously to different clients with a wide array of problems (e.g., insight-oriented psychotherapy, Alcoholics Anonymous). Since each client presents with a different constellation of values and preferences, and EBP requires that these be integrated into decision making, each client is freshly appraised, and individualizing the assessment and treatment process is actually enhanced through use of the EBP process model (see Straus, 2002).

EBP is not business as usual. It is not usual for social workers to routinely consult the highest quality available research to assist them in making important practice decisions with their clients. Doing so will require the acquisition of new literature search skills. A good search does not consist of perusing the latest issue of *Social Work* or even of *Research on Social Work Practice*. It requires access to major electronic databases such as PsycINFO or Web-of-Science, and skills at selecting the most relevant search terms and inclusionary and exclusionary criteria. You may not have been taught this in graduate school. If not, then Straus et al. (2005) and Rubin and Parrish (2009) will be good professional reading for you. You may not have been taught very much about how to critically evaluate high quality and sophisticated studies. If not, then to become truly adept at EBP you must acquire these skills. Bronson (2009) should be next on your reading list. And you may learn that certain psychosocial interventions are particularly useful for helping clients like those you often see in your practice. In which case you will need to learn these new skills, via continuing education programs, conference workshops, or institutes. This may all be quite new and represent a lot of work on your part. Welcome to the world of evidence-based practice.

SUMMARY

The process of EBP practice has a good deal to offer practitioners, agency administrators and policy-makers about effective prevention, assessment, and intervention in the field of substance abuse. There is already a large and growing literature on the topic, covering both prevention and treatment (e.g., Eliason, 2007; Emmelkamp & Vedel, 2006; Haug, Shopshire, Tajima, Gruber, & Guydish, 2008; Leukefeld, Gullotta, & Staton-Tindall, 2009; Waldron & Turner, 2008). EBP has been widely adopted at the federal level, whose agencies are vigorously promoting it (e.g., Squires, Gumbley & Storti, 2008). The articles comprising the balance of this book reflect readings which, we believe, exemplify some of the better approaches to psychosocial research in this important domain. Such research findings are an important, but not sole, component of undertaking EBP. It is too soon to claim at EBP is going to revolutionize substance abuse prevention and treatment services but it is certainly one of the more promising developments to have occurred within the past several decades.

REFERENCES

American Psychiatric Association. (2000). Diagnostic and statistical manual of mental disorders, (4th ed., text revision). Washington, DC: Author.

Bronson, D. E. (2009). Critically appraising studies for evidence-based practice. In A. R. Roberts (Ed.). *Social worker's desk reference* (2nd ed., pp. 1137–1141). New York: Oxford University Press.

Eliason, M. J. (2007). *Improving substance abuse treatment: An introduction to the evidence-based practice movement.* Thousand Oaks, CA: Sage.

Emmelkamp, P. M. G. & Vedel, E. (2006). *Evidence-based treatments for alcohol and drug abuse: A practitioner's guide to theory, methods, and practice.* New York: Routledge.

Gambrill, E. (2009). Integrating evidence from diverse sources in evidence-based practice. In A. R. Roberts (Ed.). *Social worker's desk reference* (2nd ed., pp. 1163–1169). New York: Oxford University Press.

Gambrill, E. & Gibbs, L. (2009). Developing well-structured questions for evidence-informed practice. In A. R. Roberts (Ed.). *Social worker's desk reference* (2nd ed., pp. 1120–1126). New York: Oxford University Press.

Haug, N. A., Shopshire, M., Tajima, B., Gruber, V., & Guydish, J. (2008). Adoption of evidence-based practices among substance abuse treatment providers. *Journal of Drug Education, 38,* 181–192.

Howard, M. O. & Jenson, J. M. (1999). Clinical practice guidelines: Should social work develop them? *Research on Social Work Practice, 9,* 283–301.

Leukefeld, C. G., Gulotta, T. P., & Staton-Tindall, M. (2009). *Adolescent substance abuse: Evidence-based approaches to prevention and treatment.* Thousand Oaks, CA: Sage.

Myers, L. L. & Thyer, B. A. (1997). Should social work clients have the right to effective treatment? *Social Work, 42,* 288–298.

Roberts, A. R. (Ed.) (2009). *Social worker's desk reference* (2nd ed.). New York: Oxford University Press.

Rubin, A. & Parrish, D. (2009). Locating credible studies for evidence-based practice. In A. R. Roberts (Ed.). *Social worker's desk reference* (2nd ed., pp. 1127–1136). New York: Oxford University Press.

Sackett, D. L., Richardson, W. S., Rosenberg, W., & Haynes, R. B. (1997). *Evidence-based medicine: How to practice and teach EBM.* London: Chuchill Livingston.

Sherman, L. W. (2003). Experimental evidence and governmental administration. *Annals of the American Association of Political and Social Science, 589,* 226–233.

Squires, D. D., Gumbley, S. J. & Storti, S. A. (2008). Training substance abuse treatment organizations to adopt evidence-based practices: The Addiction Technology Transfer Center of New England Science to Service Laboratory. *Journal of Substance Abuse Treatment, 34,* 293–301.

Straus, S. E. (2002). Individualizing treatment decisions: The likelihood of being helped or harmed. *Evaluation and the Health Professions, 25,* 210–224.

Straus, S. E., Richardson, W. S., Glasziou, P., & Haynes, R. B. (2005). *Evidence-based medicine: How to practice and teach EBM.* New York: Elsevier.

Thyer, B. A. (2008). Evidence-based macro practice: Addressing the challenges and opportunities. *Journal of Evidence-based Social Work, 5*(3–4), 453–472.

Thyer, B. A. & Myers, L. L. (2007). *A social worker's guide to evaluating practice outcomes.* Alexandria, VA: Council on Social Work Education.

Thyer, B. A. & Myers, L. L. (2009). N = 1 experiments and their role in evidence-based practice. In A. R. Roberts (Ed.). *Social worker's desk reference* (2nd ed., pp. 1176–1182). New York: Oxford University Press.

Waldron, H. B., & Turner, C. W. (2008). Evidence-based psychosocial treatments for adolescent substance abuse. *Journal of Clinical Child and Adolescent Psychology, 37,* 238–261.

Webb, S. A. (2001). Some considerations on the validity of evidence-based practice in social work. *British Journal of Social Work, 31,* 57–79.

2

Evidence-Based Practice and Policy

Choices Ahead

Eileen Gambrill

University of California, Berkeley

Choices about how to view evidence-based practice (EBP) are being made by educators, practitioners, agency administrators, and staff in a variety of organizations designed to promote integration of research and practice such as clearinghouses on EBP. Choices range from narrow views of EBP such as use of empirically based guidelines and treatment manuals to the broad philosophy and evolving process of EBP, envisioned by its originators, that addresses evidentiary, ethical, and application issues in a transparent context. Current views of EBP and policy are reviewed, and choices that reflect the adopted vision and related indicators are described. Examples include who will select the questions on which research efforts are focused, what outcomes will be focused on, who will select them and on what basis, how transparent to be regarding the evidentiary status of services, how clients will be involved, and whether to implement needed organizational changes. A key choice is whether to place ethical issues front and center.

Keywords: evidence-based practice; choices; ethics; transparency

Author's Note: Portions of this article were presented as a keynote address at the Leadership Symposium on Evidence-Based Practice in the Human Services, sponsored by the California Social Work Education Center and the Child and Family Institute of California, Sacramento, California, July 14th, 2005. This article was invited by the editor. Correspondence concerning this article should be addressed to Eileen Gambrill, PhD, School of Social Welfare, Haviland Hall, University of California, Berkeley, Berkeley, CA 94720-7400; e-mail: gambrill@berkeley.edu.

SOURCE: "Evidence-Based Practice and Policy: Choices Ahead" by Eileen Gambrill. In the 2006 issue of *Research on Social Work Practice*, *16*(3), 338–357. Used with permission.

Choices about how to view evidence-based practice (EBP) are being made not only by educators, practitioners, and agency administrators but also by staff in a wide variety of organizations designed to promote the integration of research and practice. There are many such organizations including the Millbank Memorial Fund, which recently published *Evidence-Based Mental Health Treatments and Services* (Lehman, Goldman, Dixon, & Churchill, 2004), the Urban Institute, and the Rand Corporation. Regional organizations include the Bay Area Social Services Consortium (BASSC) and the recently formed California Child Welfare Clearinghouse for Evidence-Based Practice. The latter "exists to promote a quality practices framework for California's child welfare service system to ensure that children are safe and stable in families that can nurture them and assure their well being" (California Child Welfare Clearinghouse for Evidence-Based Practice, 2005). Such an organization may influence how educators, administrators, clients, and practitioners view EBP. What view of EBP will staff in such organizations embrace? Will they define this narrowly as basing decisions on practice-related research or using practice guidelines? Will they use the name but not the substance—continue business as usual? These questions are of vital importance because these organizations have an impact on the decisions made by educators and agency administrators, which in turn influence the decisions of practitioners and clients. Indeed, the very purpose of some is to advise administrators what services should be used. Consider the following:

> The Clearinghouse will provide guidance on selected evidence-based practices to statewide agencies, counties, public and private organizations, and individuals in simple straightforward formats reducing the "consumers" need to conduct literature searches, review extensive literature, or understand and critique research methodology. The

Clearinghouse, using both a state advisory committee and a national panel of scientific advisors, will identify areas of priority interest and establish a set of criteria to select highly relevant evidence based practices to be included in the Clearinghouse database for dissemination. (California Child Welfare Clearinghouse for Evidence-Based Practice, 2005, n.p.)

What criteria will be used to identify "highly relevant evidence based practices"? The report from the Milbank Memorial Fund (Lehman et al., 2004) lists multisystemic therapy (MST) as an EBP, as does the aforementioned clearinghouse. Is there evidence that it is effective? Choices made reflect different views of EBP and policy that have been evident in the professional literature for some time. Choices and indicators that can be used to reveal them are described in this article.

DIFFERENT VIEWS OF EBP AND POLICY

Descriptions of EBP differ greatly in their breadth and attention to ethical, evidentiary, and application issues and their interrelationships ranging from the broad, systemic philosophy and related evolving process initiated by its originators (Sackett, Richardson, Rosenberg, & Haynes, 1997; Sackett, Rosenberg, Gray, Haynes, & Richardson, 1996; Sackett, Straus, Richardson, Rosenberg, & Haynes, 2000) to narrow views (using empirically supported interventions that leave out the role of clinical expertise, attention to client values, and preferences and application problems) to total distortions of the original idea (redubbing authoritarian practices such as appeal to consensus as evidence based; Gambrill, 2003). In considering the different views and related choices, we should keep in mind ethical obligations described in professional codes of ethics: beneficence, avoiding harm, informed consent, and maximizing autonomy and self-determination. I suggest that only by taking the broad systemic view can we honor these ethical obligations.

EBP as Described by Its Originators

The process and philosophy of EBP as described by its originators is a new educational and practice paradigm for closing the gaps between research and practice to maximize opportunities to help clients and avoid harm (Gray, 1997, 2001a, 2001b; Sackett et al., 1997, 2000). It is assumed that professionals often need information to make important decisions, for example, concerning risk assessment or what services are most likely to help clients attain outcomes they value. It has not "been around for decades," as suggested in the *Guide for Child Welfare Administrators on Evidence-Based Practice* (Wilson & Alexandra, 2005, p. 5). Saying there is nothing new about a paradigm shift is one way to continue business as usual (e.g., authoritarian practices such as ignoring important uncertainties regarding decisions that must be made). Indeed, many related publications suggest that this systemic approach to integrating ethical, evidentiary, and application concerns that emphasize transparency regarding the uncertainties involved in helping clients may be rejected in favor of a view of EBP likely to promote continuation of the very style of decision making EBP was designed to avoid, such as failure to involve clients as informed participants, hiding flaws in practice and policy-related research, and promoting ineffective services.

Evidence-based decision making arose as an alternative to authority-based decision making in which decisions are based on criteria such as consensus, anecdotal experience, or tradition.

EBP is "the integration of best research evidence with clinical expertise and [client] values." (Sackett et al., 2000, p. 1)

"It is the conscientious, explicit, judicious use of current best evidence in making decisions about the care of individual [clients]." (Sackett et al., 1997, p. 2)

Evidence-based health care refers to "use of the best current knowledge as a basis for decisions about groups of patients or populations." (Gray, 2001b, p. 20)

EBP is an evolving process. It describes a philosophy and process designed to forward effective use of professional judgment in integrating information regarding each client's unique characteristics, circumstances, preferences, and actions and external research findings (see Figure 1). "It is a guide for thinking about how decisions should be made" (Haynes, Devereaux, & Guyatt, 2002, p. 36). EBP describes a process and a new professional education format (problem-based learning) designed to help practitioners to link evidentiary, ethical, and application issues. Many components of EBP are designed to minimize biases such as jumping to conclusions, for example, by using quality filters when reviewing external research findings related to a question. Recently, more attention has been given to the gap between client actions and their stated preferences because what clients do (e.g., carry out agreed-on tasks or not) so often differs from their stated preferences, and helper estimates of participation are as likely to be inaccurate as accurate (Haynes et al., 2002; see Figure 1). Clinical expertise includes use of effective relationship skills and the experience of individual helpers to rapidly identify each client's unique circumstances, characteristics, and "their individual risk and benefits of potential interventions and their personal values and expectations" (p. 1). Clinical expertise is drawn on to integrate information from various sources. As Archie Cochrane (1972) noted, "Outcome is not the whole story, the manner in which services are provided, including kindliness and ability to communicate," (p. 95)

Clinical Characteristics and Circumstances

Figure 1   An Updated Model for Evidence-Based Decisions

SOURCE: Haynes, Devereaux, and Guyatt (2002).

matters also. Client values refers to "unique preferences, concerns and expectations each [client] brings to an . . . encounter and which must be integrated into . . . decisions if they are to serve the [client]" (Sackett et al., 2000, p. 1).

EBP as viewed by its originators is as much about the ethical obligations of educators and researchers to be honest brokers of knowledge and ignorance as it is about the obligations of practitioners and administrators to honor ethical obligations described in professional codes of ethics; for example, to integrate practice and research and honor informed-consent obligations. It is essentially a way to handle uncertainty in an honest and informed manner, sharing ignorance and knowledge. Transparency (honesty) regarding the evidentiary status of services is a hallmark of this philosophy. A quote that illustrates this appeared on the back of *Clinical Evidence* (7th edition, June issue,

2002): "The purpose of this book is to share knowledge, ignorance and uncertainty about each of the conditions described therein." (*Clinical Evidence* is continually updated and is distributed free of charge to all physicians throughout the U.K.) There is a willingness to say, "I don't know." The uncertainty associated with decisions is acknowledged, not hidden. EBP requires considering research findings related to important practice or policy decisions and sharing what is found (including nothing) with clients. Critical thinking values are integral to this systemic views of EBP:

Courage: Critically appraise claims regardless of negative reactions.

Curiosity: An interest in deep understanding and learning.

Intellectual empathy: Accurately understanding and presenting the views of others.

Humility: Awareness of the limits of knowledge including our own; lack of arrogance (e.g., promoting bogus claims of effectiveness).

Integrity: Honoring the same standards of evidence to which we hold others.

Persistence: Willingness to struggle with confusion and unsettled questions (Paul, 1993).

In addition to a philosophy of practice and policy emphasizing attention to ethical issues and the vital importance of addressing application problems, a unique process that includes the following five steps is suggested:

1. Converting information needs related to practice decisions into well-structured answerable questions.

2. Tracking down, with maximum efficiency, the best evidence with which to answer them.

3. Critically appraising that evidence for its validity, impact (size of effect), and applicability (usefulness in practice).

4. Applying the results of this appraisal to practice and policy decisions. This involves deciding whether evidence found (if any) applies to the decision at hand (e.g., Is a client similar to those studied? Is there access to services described?) and considering client values and preferences in making decisions and other application concerns.

5. Evaluating our effectiveness and efficiency in carrying out Steps 1 to 4 and seeking ways to improve them in the future (Sackett et al., 2000, pp. 3–4).

Although the steps in this list may seem simple, they are challenging to learn and require access to related tools such as relevant databases. To practice an evidence-informed approach, practitioners need skills in evidence management—searching, appraisal, and storage (Gray, 2001a)—and need to have or develop the motivation to use them. Posing well-structured, answerable questions

in relation to information needs can be difficult, and there are many obstacles to the entire process. In their qualitative research, Ely and his colleagues (2002) identified 56 different obstacles to EBP. There are huge application problems, and wrestling with these is a key characteristic of EBP. There are many kinds of questions:

Effectiveness: In elderly clients who are depressed, what method is most effective in reducing depression?

Prevention: For poor, inner-city children, are Headstart programs effective in decreasing school dropout?

Risk prognosis: In children who are abused, are actuarial or consensual risk assessment measures most predictive of future abuse?

Description or assessment: In families in which there is parent-child conflict, is self-report or observation most accurate in describing interaction patterns?

Other kinds of questions concern harm, cost, and self-development. Different questions require different kinds of research methods to critically appraise proposed assumptions. These differences are reflected in the use of different "quality filters" to search for and appraise related research (Gibbs, 2003; Sackett et al., 2000). Covell, Uman, & Manning (1985) found that two questions arose for three patients physicians saw. Most questions remain unanswered. We do not know how many questions arise in the course of work by social workers or how many of these remain unanswered.

The attention of EBP to application problems has yielded an array of innovative technology. Consider the evidence cart by Sackett and Straus (1998) in which a laptop containing access to important databases was put on a cart and wheeled into a hospital ward. The authors determined the extent to which it was used by physicians to answer questions related to their information needs. The role of knowledge managers has been emphasized by Gray (e.g., Gray, 1998). Their role is to maximize knowledge flow within the agency, from outside to within and from inside to without. Workers could contact this knowledge manager with questions. There is also a rich literature on decision aids, many of which are computer based, that can maximize informed choice on the part of clients while giving clients maximal choice concerning what information they would like to have (O'Conner et al., 2002).

EBP offers practitioners and administrators a philosophy that is compatible with obligations described in professional codes of ethics and accreditation policies and standards (e.g., for informed consent and to draw on practice and policy-related research findings) and an evolving technology for integrating evidentiary, ethical, and practical issues. Related literature highlights the interconnections among these three concerns and suggests specific steps (a technology) to decrease gaps among them in all professional venues, including practice and policy (e.g., drawing on related research), research (e.g., preparing systematic reviews and clearly describing limitations of studies), and professional education (e.g., exploring the value of problem-based learning in developing lifelong learners). The key implications of this view of EBP are the following: (a) Move away from authority-based decision making in which appeals are made to tradition, consensus, popularity, and status; (b) honor ethical obligations to clients such as informed consent; (c) make practices and policies and their outcomes transparent; (d) attend to application problems, that is, encourage a systemic approach to improving services; and (e) maximize knowledge flow— encourage honest brokering of knowledge and share ignorance and uncertainty as well as knowledge. This new and evolving paradigm is systemic; for example, it has implications for educators and researchers and for administrators, line staff, and clients.

The Origins of EBP

Although its philosophical roots are old, the blooming of EBP as a process

attending to evidentiary, ethical, and application issues in all professional venues (education, practice or policy, and research) is fairly recent, facilitated by the Internet revolution. As mentioned earlier, it has not been around for decades. It is designed to break down the division among research, practice, and policy— highlighting the importance of honoring ethical obligations. Some sources (e.g., Wilson & Alexandra, 2005) cite the origin of EBP as the Institute of Medicine (2001). This is not the origin of EBP. EBP was developed by key individuals such as Sackett and his colleagues and others. A key reason for the creation of EBP was the discovery of gaps showing that professionals were not acting systematically or promptly on research findings. There were wide variations in practices (Wennberg, 2002). There was a failure to start services that work and to stop services that did not work or harmed clients (Gray, 2001a, 2001b). Economic concerns were another factor. Inventions in technology were key in the origins of EBP such as the Web revolution that allows quick access to databases. The development of the systematic review was another key innovation. Yet another origin was increased recognition of the flawed nature of traditional means of knowledge dissemination such as texts, editorials, and peer review. Gray (2001b) describes peer review as having "feet of clay" (p. 22). Also, there was increased recognition of harming in the name of helping. Gray (2001b) also notes the appeal of EBP both to clinicians and to clients. The origins of EBP suggest reasons why a narrow view of EBP may be taken (e.g., continuing to ignore limitations of practice-related research and practice, simply redubbing business as usual as evidence-based when it has none of the characteristics of the process and philosophy of EBP and policy as described by its originators).

Other Views of EBP

The most popular view is defining EBP as considering practice-related research in making decisions including using practice guidelines. For example, Rosen and Proctor (2002) state that "we use evidence-based practice here primarily to denote that practitioners will select interventions on the basis of their empirically demonstrated links to the desired outcomes" (p. 743). They define practice guidelines as "a set of systematically compiled and organized knowledge statements that are designed to enable practitioners to find, select, and use the interventions that are most effective and appropriate" (p. 1). Making decisions about individual clients is much more complex. There are many other considerations such as the need to consider the unique circumstances and characteristics of each client as suggested by the spirited critiques of practice guidelines and manualized treatments (e.g., Norcross, Beutler, & Levant, 2005). Practice guidelines are but one component of EBP, as can be seen by a review of topics in Sackett et al.'s (2000) book *Evidence-Based Medicine*; they are discussed in 1 of 9 chapters (other chapters focus on diagnosis and screening, prognosis, therapy, harm, teaching methods, and evaluation; see also later critique of imposing use of a guideline on line staff). Yet another view is that EBP consists of requiring practitioners to use empirically based treatments (Reid, 2001, p. 278; Reid, 2002). This view also omits attention to client values and their individual circumstances and resource constraints. The broad view of EBP involves searching for research related to important decisions and sharing what is found, including nothing, with clients. It involves a search not only for knowledge but also for ignorance. Such a search is required to involve clients as informed participants whether this concerns a screening test for depression or an intervention for depression (for descriptions of misrepresentations of EBP, see Gibbs & Gambrill, 2002; Straus & McAlister, 2000).

Many descriptions of EBP in the social work literature could be termed business as usual; for example, continuation of unrigorous research reviews regarding practice claims, inflated claims of effectiveness, lack of attention to ethical concerns such as involving clients as informed participants, and neglect of application barriers. A common reaction is simply relabeling the old as the new (as EBP), using the term *evidence-based* without the substance, for example, including uncritical reviews in sources labeled evidence-based). Consider the *Social Workers' Desk Reference* edited by Roberts and Greene (2002). We find descriptions of services as evidence based (e.g., Test, 2002), with no mention of critical reviews arguing otherwise (e.g., Gomory, 1999). In a book titled *Evidence-Based Practices for Social Workers* (O'Hare, 2005), there is no mention of the concerning results of key rigorous appraisals of family preservation (see Lindsey, Martin, & Doh, 2002; Schuerman, Rzepnicki, & Littell, 1994). In many sources, we find no description of the unique process of EBP. Most descriptions downplay or ignore the role of flaws in published research in the development of EBP and related enterprises such as the Cochrane and Campbell collaborations.

CHOICES

The key choice is how to view EBP—whether to draw on the broad philosophy and evolving process of EBP as described by its originators as a way to handle the uncertainty in making decisions in an informed, honest manner (sharing ignorance and knowledge) or to use one of the other approaches described earlier. The choice made has implications not only for clients, practitioners, and administrators but also for researchers and educators. I suggest that it will affect all of the following choices.

How Systemic to Be

The philosophy and process of EBP as described by its originators is a systemic approach in which the behaviors and products of researchers and educators and those of clients, practitioners, and administrators are of concern. Only via a systemic approach, including attention to application barriers in agencies, may a shift be made away from authoritarian practices. One missing link could pull down other advances. For example, poor quality professional education could compromise success by failing to help students acquire valuable skills. The wide variety of decisions related to how systemic an approach to take are reflected in the sections that follow. Related indicators include all those suggested under choices discussed.

Who Will Select the Practice and Policy Questions on Which Research Efforts Are Focused and on What Basis?

Will these questions be selected by some elite, such as a state or national board? Will administrators select them, or will clients and line staff select them? One of the characteristics of the philosophy and process of EBP as described by its originators is the importance of gathering questions from what the British call the "coal face"—line staff and clients. It is at this point that information needs regarding decisions that must be made occur. Outcomes valued by clients suggest questions to pose. To date, in the Bay Area of California, questions pursued have been posed by county social service directors. For example, Bay Area Social Services Consortium (BASSC) includes directors of county welfare agencies. Each agency pays annual dues each year to belong to this group. Reviews prepared by BASSC staff (mostly master's and doctoral degree students) focus on questions suggested by county administrators (BASSC, 2005). In the *Guide For Child Welfare Administrators On Evidence-Based Practice* (Wilson & Alexandra, 2005), it is recommended that staff in the new clearinghouse, with input from a national advisory board, select the questions to be addressed. Is it not the clients and line staff who know what questions arise most often in everyday practice? Indicators of choices here include gathering questions from line staff and clients and the percentage of research efforts focused on questions that line staff and clients identify as occurring most often (see Table 1).

What Outcomes Will Be Focused on, Who Will Select Them, and on What Basis?

What outcomes will be used as indicators of success? Who will choose them? Will clients be involved in their selection? Will line staff and administrators be involved? Or will they be determined by a governmental committee? Do indicators used (e.g., a decrease in children returning to foster care) actually indicate success? Are children really better off? These questions call for careful attention to validity and reliability of measures. Performance indicators decided on by governmental groups may not be valid. Indeed, they may have unintended negative effects if implemented. The question is what measures best reflect hoped-for performance and outcomes related to the mission and goals of a program? Indicators of choice include selection of outcomes that accurately reflect success in attaining hoped-for outcomes (they are valid) and involvement of clients in identifying outcomes.

What Kinds of Evidence Will Be Used to Select Services, and How Will These Be Weighed?

There are many kinds of evidence. Davies (2004) suggests that a broad view of evidence is needed to review policies including (a) experience and expertise, (b) judgment, (c) resources, (d) values, (e) habits and traditions, (f) lobbyists and pressure groups, and (g) pragmatics and contingencies. He suggests that we should consider all of these factors in making decisions about whether or not to implement a policy and describes six kinds of research related to evidence of policy impact: (a) implementation, (b) descriptive analytical, (c) attitudinal, (d) statistical modeling, (e) economic or econometric, and (f) ethical. Criteria relevant for appraising policy options suggested by Macintyre, Chalmers, Horton, and Smith (2001) include:

- support by systematic, empirical evidence,

- support by cogent argument,

- scale of likely health benefit,

- likelihood that the policy would bring benefits other than health benefits,

- possibility that the policy might do harm,

- ease of implementation, and

- cost of implementation.

Currently, services are usually selected based on criteria such as consensus, popularity, or what is available. EBP and policy emphasize consideration of the evidentiary status of services. Certainly other criteria and forms of evidence such as legal issues must be considered as suggested above. Yet, just as certainly, evidentiary criteria are vital to consider. Without doing so, services of unknown effectiveness will continue to be used, and perhaps service shown to be harmful as well and effective services may lie unused. Consider the continued use of programs critically tested and found to be harmful (Petrosino, Turpin-Petrosino, & Bheuler, 2003). Related indicators here include use of evidentiary status as a key criteria in selecting services.

Who Will Make Final Decisions at the Coal Face?

History suggests that organizations tend to become bureaucratic and authori-tarian and take a top-down, non-participatory approach. Will decisions made by a clearinghouse regarding the evidentiary status of services be imposed on staff? Is it unnecessary for staff to learn how to critically appraise research related to questions that arise including research

reviews? Is such an approach likely to forward integration of ethical, evidentiary, and application issues? EBP requires consideration of other sources of information such as the unique circum-stances and characteristics of clients as well as research findings. This provides other vital evidence. Indeed, such concerns are raised by critics of practice guidelines. Making decisions at the coal face requires an understanding of the differences between findings regarding a particular population and a particular client. Research regarding a population may not apply to a client. For example, many clients have multiple concerns. How can one guideline be used? (See related discussion in Norcross et al., 2005.) As Gray (2001b) notes, "The leading figures of EBP were able to demonstrate how individuals did not always fit neatly into guidelines" (p. 26). Individual chara-cteristics and circumstances of clients and unique knowledge on the part of service providers (regarding local resources and constraints) are needed. Indicators of choices here include the following: (a) Staff are given the flexibility they need to make optimal decisions in integrating external research findings with vital information regarding clients and resources; and (b) Data are collected regarding discrepancies between population data and individual clients.

What Style of EBP Will Be Used?

There are different styles of EBP (Sackett et al., 1997). For example, steps 2 and 3 of the process (see prior discus-sion) could be left to a knowledge man-ager employed by an agency (Gray, 1998). In the United Kingdom, physicians can telephone a source with a question, and within 4 hours someone will get back to the caller with an answer. We could create such a program for social workers, psy-chologists, and psychiatrists. Special training, repeated guided practice, and related tools and resources are needed to carry out the steps of EBP on the job, in

Table 1   Indicators of the Choice of a Systemic View of Evidence-Based Practice (EBP)

Researchers

Focus on questions that arise most often at the coal face.

Use rigorous tests of questions; for example, use guidelines described in the CONSORT statement. Prepare systematic reviews.

Clearly describe methodological limitations and conceptual controversies.

Clearly and accurately describe well-argued, alternative views.

Seek client input regarding valued outcomes (e.g., quality of life).

Avoid inflated claims of knowledge (methods used do not warrant them).

Practitioners

Pose well-structured answerable questions related to information needs.

Critically appraise different kinds of practice-related research.

Search effectively and efficiently for research findings related to important questions.

Decrease common errors in integrating data. Purchase services from agencies that offer practices shown to help clients.

Do not purchase services from agencies that provide ineffective or harmful programs.

Involve clients as informed participants.

Report errors made and suggest causes.

Form journal clubs to select and answer questions that arise.

Raise questions about agency practices and policies.

Be involved as informed participants; be accurately informed regarding the evidentiary status of services used.

Accurately evaluate the effects of their services.

Consider values and preferences in selecting assessment, intervention, and evaluation methods.

Supervisors

Model EBP skills.

Provide timely corrective feedback to staff.

Advocate on behalf of staff to administrators for resources needed for EBP.

Administrators

Provide needed training for staff on key EBP skills.

Provide tools required for EBP.

Arrange and maintain incentive systems that promote EBP.

Model critical appraisal (e.g., avoid propaganda strategies and welcome questions from staff).

Arrange a user-friendly way to gather errors and information about related causes and design ways to minimize avoidable errors.

Arrange a user-friendly complaint and compliment system for clients and use collected data to improve services.

Arrange an environment that provides corrective feedback allowing staff to learn how to improve services.

Professional Educators

Accurately describe biases and knowledge limitations.

Clearly describe negative findings and conceptual controversies regarding preferred views.

Clearly describe well-argued alternative views and related positive effects.

Use formats shown to be effective in helping students acquire EBP knowledge and skills.

Provide critical feedback in a supportive environment that allows students to "educate their intuition" (Hogarth, 2001).

Clients

Offer feedback regarding services.

Get access to clear, accurate descriptions of services offered and alternatives including their risks and benefits in readily available brochures and/or user-friendly computer programs.

Receive on-going feedback based on specific, relevant progress indicators.

real time. Guyatt and Rennie (2002) recommend the highest possible skill levels:

> Only if you develop advanced skills at interpreting the [practice and

policy-related] literature will you be able to determine the extent to which these attempts are consistent with the best evidence. Second, a high level of EBP skills will allow you to use the original literature effectively, regardless of whether preappraised synopses and evidence-based recommendations are available. (p. 208)

They also suggest that such skills will allow professionals to be effective leaders in introducing EBP into their agencies. Examples of skills include the following:

1. To define and identify the sources of evidence appropriate to a decision that must be made.

2. To carry out a search . . . without the help of a librarian and find at least 60% of the reviews or research studies that would have been found by the librarian.

3. To construct simple search strategies . . . using Boolean operators (*and* and *or*) . . . and to be able to do this for a variety of practice-related questions in relation to different service characteristics, including effectiveness, safety, acceptability, cost-effectiveness, quality, and appropriateness.

4. To download the [results] of a search into reference management software (Gray, 2001a, p. 329).

Sackett and his colleagues (2000) distinguish between three different styles of EBP, all of which require steps 1 and 3, but vary in how steps 2 and 4 are carried out. They suggest that for problems encountered on an everyday basis, practitioners should invest the time and energy needed to carry out both searching and critical appraisal of reports found. For level 2 (problems encountered less often), they suggest that professionals seek out critical appraisals already prepared by others who describe and use explicit criteria for deciding what research they select and how they decide whether it is valid. Here, step 3 can be omitted and step 2 restricted to sources that have already undergone critical appraisal. A third style applies to a problem encountered very infrequently in which helpers "blindly seek, accept, and apply the

recommendations we receive from authorities" (p. 5). As they note, the trouble with this mode is that it is blind to whether the advice received from the experts "is authoritative (evidence-based, resulting from their operating in the 'appraising' mode) or merely authoritarian (opinion-based, resulting from pride and prejudice)" (p. 5). One clue they suggest to distinguish which style is being used is uncritical documentation with a reluctance to describe what is in the documentation. Lack of time may result in using style 2 with most problems.

Practitioners do not have time to track down and critically appraise research related to all questions that arise. However, does this mean that they should not acquire critical appraisal skills? Should not students in bachelor's and master's degree programs acquire such skills? Indeed, is this not mandated by the Council on Social Work Education (2002) accreditation guidelines? Such skills are needed to integrate practice and research as required by the National Association of Social Workers' (1999) *Code of Ethics*. Critical thinking skills are vital to appraise the validity of assessment measures. They are needed to learn from experience (to "educate our intuition"; Hogarth, 2001) and to integrate diverse sources of information. King (1981) suggests that "for Flexner, as for us today, 'severely critically handling of experience' was an important part of scientific method, applicable to clinical practice as well as to research investigation" (pp. 303–304). He suggests that

> the [helper] who is not critical corresponds to the empiric. He does not consider alternatives, does not discriminate among their features, and does not attend to any detailed congruence with the pattern. He acts reflexively instead of reflectively. (p. 304)

He suggests that one of the characteristics that distinguishes good helpers from bad ones is that good ones "always held as an ideal the critical evaluation of the data" (p. 300). Involving all staff as critical users of practice-related research is more likely to increase their participation in needed change and to yield valuable ideas for improving the quality of services. Indicators of choice here include (a) a style of EBP being used by staff that maximizes quality of services including attention to ethical obligations such as informed consent; and (b) staff that are skilled in carrying out the steps involved in EBP.

How Transparent to Be Regarding the Evidentiary Status of Services

A key characteristic of EBP is a call for transparency; being honest about the evidentiary status of assessment, inter-vention, and evaluation methods. For example, is there evidence that genograms do more good than harm? Is there evidence that actuarial methods are superior to consensus-based methods in predicting future maltreatment of children? Has MST been clearly demonstrated to be effective? Is there evidence that following the advice of preventive medicine will do more good than harm (Sackett, 2002)? EBP calls for candid descriptions of limitations of research studies and use of research methods that critically test questions addressed. Contrary to the claim that EBP seeks for and assumes that certainty about knowledge is possible, EBP highlights the uncertainty involved in making decisions and related potential sources of bias and attempts to give helpers and clients the knowledge and skills to handle this honestly and constructively (e.g., Chalmers, 2003). Attention and resources have been devoted to helping both clients and professionals acquire critical appraisal skills they can use as quality filters to review research findings related to practice questions (e.g., the Critical Appraisal Skills Program, CASP, of the Institute of Health Sciences; Gibbs, 2003; Gray, 2001a, 2001b; Greenhalgh, 2001; Sackett et al., 2000). Transparency and rigor are intimately related. That is, rigorous tests of a claim are

more likely to reveal (to make transparent) the evidentiary status of a claim. Currently, the professional literature is awash with a lack of transparency. Consider some of the following characteristics found in a critical appraisal of content in a random selection of pages in the flagship journal *Social Work* (Gambrill & Penick, 2005): use of vague words such as *most*, claims of an association between two variables with no information regarding what it is or how it was determined, and inflated claims of effecti-veness (the research method used does not warrant the claims made).

Without transparency and rigor, clients cannot be involved as informed partici-pants; they will be uninformed or misinformed about the evidentiary status of recommended services and alternatives. Consider hiding the risks of assessment measures and diagnostic tests such as mammograms to encourage clients to take a test. A review of Web sites showed that professional advocacy groups and governmental organizations did not provide information concerning harms of mammographic screening (overdiagnosis and overtreatment). Web sites of consumer organizations provided the most balanced and comprehensive information (Jørgensen & Gøtzsche, 2004). Is it ethical to deceive clients to encourage them to undergo a test that a professional thinks is required? Is this not a form of paternalism? Indicators of choices here include the following: (a) All involved parties are accurately informed concerning the evidentiary status of services offered and of alternatives and their risks and benefits; and (b) Researchers and authors clearly describe the quality of documentation for claims including methodological limitations. They describe methodological and conceptual contro-versies in an area and accurately describe well-argued alternative views.

How and in What Ways to Involve Clients

A striking characteristic of EBP and related developments is the extent to which clients are involved in many different ways (e.g., Broclain, Hill, Oliver, & Wensing, 2002; Edwards & Elwyn, 2001; Entwistle, Renfrew, Yearley, Forrester, & Lamont, 1998). One is reflected in the attention given to individual differences in making decisions. For example, Sackett and his coauthors (1997) emphasized the importance of comparing the values and preferences of clients with recommended services and their likely consequences (p. 170). Haynes and his colleagues (2002) emphasized that "'personalizing' the evidence to fit a specific [client's] circumstances is a key area for development in evidence-based medicine" (p. 4). A second is helping clients to develop critical appraisal skills (e.g., CASP). A third is encouraging client involvement in the design and critique of practice and policy related research (e.g., Hanley, Truesdale, King, Elbourne, & Chalmers, 2001). As Chalmers (1995) suggests, "lay people can draw on kinds of knowledge and perspectives that differ from those of professional researchers" (p. 1318). A fourth is attending to outcomes clients value.

A fifth is involving clients as informed participants who share in making decisions (O'Conner et al., 2002). In their description of "evidence-informed patient choice," Entwistle and her colleagues (1998) suggest use of a form requiring professionals to inform clients about the evidentiary status of recommended services including the possibility that a method has never been rigorously tested in relation to hoped-for outcomes and that other methods have been so tested and found to be effective. This form also requires descriptions of the track record of success in using the method successfully with people such as the client in both the agency to which the client is referred and the staff member in the agency whom the client will see. The term *evidence-based patient choice* emphasizes the importance of involving clients as autonomous participants who themselves carry out the required integration of information from diverse sources in making decisions (e.g., Edwards & Elwyn, 2001).

A sixth way in which clients are involved is recognizing their unique knowledge in relation to application concerns. In their discussion of practice guidelines, Sackett and his colleagues (2000) highlight the importance of considering two distinct components of practice guidelines: (a) their evidentiary status and (b) application concerns. They emphasize that those who are the experts in deciding whether a guideline is applicable to a given client, practice, agency or community "are the clients and providers at the sharp edge of implementing the application component" (p. 181), not the researchers and academics who critically appraised research findings. The differing expertise needed to prepare reviews regarding the evidentiary status of a guideline and to identify implementation potential highlights the inappropriateness of researchers telling practitioners and clients what guidelines to use. Detailed information about unique personal characteristics and local circumstances must be considered. Indicators of choices here include the following: (a) Clients are accurately informed of the evidentiary status of recommended services and of alternatives; (b) Client characteristics are considered in applying external research findings including their values and preferences; and (c) Clients' views are sought by researchers regarding valued outcomes.

How Rigorous to Be in Reviewing the Evidentiary Status of Services

A key way in which views of EBP differ is in the degree of rigor in evaluating knowledge claims (e.g., see Schulz, Chalmers, Hayes, & Altman, 1995). Both the origins of EBP and objections to EBP reflect different views of evidence.

When do we have enough evidence to recommend a practice method? Decisions that arise here include whether to use a hierarchy of evidence, and if so, what kind, where on a hierarchy to proclaim a practice as evidence based, how rigorous and exhaustive to be in preparing reviews, and how honest to be in describing what we have and have not done (e.g., Chambless & Ollendick, 2001; Norcross et al., 2005). Experts in a content area prepare more biased reviews compared to those who, although knowledgeable concerning critical appraisal of research, are not in this area (Oxman & Guyatt, 1993). Do criteria for having enough evidence differ in relation to different kinds of decisions or different involved parties, for example, ourselves compared to our clients? Concerns about inflated claims of effectiveness based on biased research studies was a key reason for the origin of EBP and health care as discussed earlier. Inflated claims obscure uncertainties that may, if shared, influence client decisions. Different opinions about how much we know reflect use of different criteria. This is a concern in the medical field. Consider the statement of Richard Smith (2003), past editor of the *British Medical Journal*, that hardly anything is known in medicine compared to the statement by Gray (2001a) that more than 60% of methods used in medicine and psychiatry are evidence based. Who is correct? What would we find if we examined the references to psychiatry cited by Gray? How should these differences be handled?

Given the history of the helping professions (e.g., bogus claims of effectiveness and harming in the name of helping), is not the ethical road to make measured rather than inflated claims and to clearly describe related research, including its flaws, so that we are not misled and in turn mislead clients? Consider the book *What Works in Child Welfare* (Kluger, Alexander, & Curtis, 2002). [The editors] say they originally had a question mark after the title: "We decided to eliminate the question mark from the title because, despite its limitations, this book is a celebration of what works in child welfare" (p. xix). The authors do not clearly describe where they

searched, how they searched, or what criteria were used to critically appraise different kinds of research reports. We are given no information at many points as to the length of the follow-up. Contrast such a grandiose title with the statement on the back of *Clinical Evidence*, described earlier. Consider also the inflated claims made in *Evidence-Based Practice Manual* (Roberts & Yeager, 2005) described by Carlsteadt (2005). Do uncritical reviews of the literature contribute to helping clients and involving clients as informed participants?

Hierarchies of evidence. Many different hierarchies of evidence have been suggested (e.g., http://www.infopoems.com/levels.html). Some describe services in terms of their evidentiary status. For example the hierarchy used in the classic book *A Guide to Effective Care in Pregnancy and Childbirth*, by Enkin, Keirse, Renfrew, and Neilson (1995), ranges from beneficial forms of care that have been shown via rigorous tests to be effective, through services which are of unknown effectiveness, to services that have been critically tested and shown to harm clients. Gray (2001a) suggests the following hierarchy:

1. Intervention programs that have been critically tested and found to help clients.

2. Intervention programs that have not been critically tested and are not in a good experimental trial.

3. Intervention programs that have been critically tested and shown to harm clients.

4. Intervention programs of unknown effectiveness that are in a rigorous experimental trial.

Compare these with the hierarchy used in the *Guide for Child Welfare Administrators on Evidence-Based Practice* (Wilson & Alexandra, 2005):

1. Well-supported, proven efficacious practice.

2. Supported and probably efficacious practice.

3. Supported and acceptable practice.

4. Promising and acceptable practice.

5. Innovative or novel practice.

6. Experimental or concerning practice.

It would be hard to create a hierarchy more likely to hide ineffective or harmful practices. Concerns regarding this hierarchy include justificatory language that encourages confirmation biases and wishful thinking such as use of the word *proven* and repeated use of terms such as *support* and *efficacious*. The word *harm* is not mentioned at all. And, this hierarchy hides the fact that most services are of unknown effectiveness. In addition, vague terms such as *probable* are used. In Appendix A, we find that *clinical-anecdotal literature* and *generally accepted in clinical practice* are included as indicators of Level 1 evidence. This hierarchy does not bode well for a clearinghouse created to critically appraise the status of assessment, intervention, and evaluation methods.

Some hierarchies describe the kinds of tests used that differ in the rigor with which they test a question or assumption:

- *N* of 1 randomized controlled trial

- Systematic review of randomized trials

- Single randomized trial

- Systematic review of observation studies addressing [client] important outcomes

- Single observational study addressing [client] important outcomes

- Physiologic studies (e.g., blood pressure, etc.)

- Unsystematic clinical observations (Guyatt & Rennie, 2002, p. 7).

Such hierarchies are available for different kinds of questions (e.g., Guyatt & Rennie, 2002). Reliance on rankings is not a good idea, as Glasziou, Vanderbroucke, and Chalmers (2004) point out, for example because different numbers in different systems mean different things. They suggest that for important recommendations, it may be preferable to give a brief summary of key evidence together with a concise appraisal of why certain quality dimensions are important.

Another term used is *best evidence*; if there are no RCTs regarding an effectiveness question, then we may consult a hierarchy of evidence and move down the list. This is what we must do in the everyday world because most practices and policies used in fields such as psychology and social work have not been critically tested. Thus, instead of well-designed RCTs regarding an intervention, we may have to rely on findings from a pre-post test. As this example illustrates, the term *best evidence* could refer to a variety of different kinds of tests that differ greatly in their ability to critically test claims. Some guidelines claim that if there are two well-designed RCTs that show a positive outcome, this represents a well-established claim. Within a more skeptical approach to knowledge, we would say that a claim has been critically tested in two well-controlled RCTs and has passed both tests. This keeps uncertainty in view.

What kinds of reviews to prepare. There are many kinds of reviews that differ in their goal. A goal may be to combine a large, varied literature into a unifying model (Greenhalgh, Robert, Macfarlane, Bate, & Kyriakidou, 2004; see also Greenhalgh et al., 2005). Another goal is to critically appraise the evidentiary status of an intervention as in a systematic review. Thus, goals provide direction to procedures likely to maximize success. Systematic reviews differ greatly from incomplete, nonrigorous, nontransparent reviews (Higgins & Green, 2005). Compare reviews in *The Journal of Evidence-Based Practice* with Cochrane and Campbell reviews. In a systematic review, there is a search for all literature related to a question in all languages, in both published and unpublished sources, including hand searches of journals. The search process, including the databases reviewed, is clearly described. Authors describe where they searched and how they searched. Rigorous criteria are used to appraise what is found, and they are clearly described (see Cochrane and Campbell reviews and their protocols). The conclusions of systematic reviews—those that use well-defined search and retrieval procedures, explicit inclusion and exclusion criteria, and both quantitative and qualitative methods of research synthesis—differ from those of unsystematic reviews; unsystematic reviews report more positive findings. Traditional reviews do not control for as many biases and thus overestimate positive effects of services. They are misleading in their conclusions. Compare, for example, claims of effectiveness made by the developers of MST (Henggeler & Lee, 2003) and conclusions of Littell's (2005) review of reviews. Littell noted that there are more than 90 licensed MST programs in more than 30 states in the United States. Millions of dollars of research money has been given to related research, and the developers gain $400 for each youth enrolled in a program via their nonprofit company. This program has been cited as an effective, evidence-based treatment model by the U.S. National Institute of Drug Abuse (1999), National Institute on Mental Health (2003), Surgeon's General Office (U.S. Public Health Service, 2000), Center for Substance-Abuse Prevention (2000), and the Annie E. Casey Foundation (2000; see Littell, 2005, for relevant references). Thomlison (2003) states that "of particular note is the fact that MST is at Level 1 effectiveness with eight randomized, controlled trials" (p. 547). Level 1 effectiveness refers to "well-supported, efficacious treatment with positive evidence from more than two randomized

clinical trials" (p. 544). Persons (2005) describes MST as an "evidence-based protocol" (p. 114) in her presidential address to the Association for Advancement of Behavior Therapy.

Based on a critical appraisal of reviews of MST, Littell (2005) concludes that such programs have few if any significant effects on measured outcomes compared with usual services or alternative treatments (see also Henggeler, Schoenwald, Borduin, & Swenson's, 2006, response to Littell and Littell's response to Henggeler). Littell conducted a review of reviews following the guidelines developed by the Campbell and Cochrane collaborations: "Of 27 published reviews of reviews of research on effects of MST, only 7 had explicit inclusion/exclusion criteria, 5 used systematic searches of electronic databases, 8 included unpublished studies, and 6 included meta-analysis" (p. 449). Few reviews noted attrition rates, whether outcome measures were blind or included an intent to treat analysis. Using procedures developed by the Cochrane and Campbell collaborations, Littell identified eight studies that met inclusion criteria. Concerns identified in these studies were (a) inconsistent reports on the number of cases randomly assigned, (b) unyoked designs, (c) unstandardized observation periods within studies, (d) unclear randomization procedures, and (e) subjective definitions of treatment completion. Only one study met the criterion of a full intent-to-treat analysis with a well-defined follow-up. This rigorous appraisal highlights that what is proclaimed as effective or very effective, not only in the professional literature but by organizations that have the responsibility of accurately informing professionals and the public, may be in question. This review, and many other sources, show that unsystematic reviews come to different conclusions than do systematic reviews; the former report more positive effects. MST is listed as an effective therapy by the national advisory board to the newly created clearinghouse and is described as an evidence-based program by the Milbank Foundation. Which view will we accept and utilize?

At a recent leadership conference in California (July 2005), three structured reviews were presented by representatives of BASSC (2005). Such reviews were described as very similar to systematic reviews when indeed they are less exhaustive, rigorous, and transparent. There were no hand searches of journals, and criteria used to review research are not clearly described and do not appear to be rigorous. The invention of the systematic review is one of the truly great steps forward in helping practitioners gain rapid access to high-quality reviews related to specific practice questions. Do we really want to obscure differences in the rigor of reviews? Does obscuring the evidentiary status of practices and policies do more good than harm? And if so, for which involved parties? What functions does hiding the evidentiary status of services forward? Indicators of choices here include the following: (a) Research methods used are clearly described in studies of concern including their methodological and conceptual limitations; (b) Claims made match rigor of tests of assumptions; and (c) Systematic reviews are prepared.

Whether to Avoid Propaganda Strategies and Blow the Whistle on Harm, Pseudoscience, Quackery, and Fraud

During the past few years, growing attention has been given to fads, harming in the name of helping, and related fraudulent claims and pseudoscience in the helping professions (e.g., Angell, 2004; Jacobson, Foxx, & Mulick, 2005; Lilienfeld, Lynn, & Lohr, 2003; McCord, 2003; Wright & Cummings, 2005). Such efforts are clearly compatible with the call for honest brokering of knowledge and ignorance in the philosophy of EBP. Will new organizations dubbed evidence based make use of methods criticized in such sources or roundly reject them? Consider what appeared in the *Guide for Child Welfare Administrators on Evidence-Based Practice*: "The practice of child welfare has long been based on a strong professional literature" (Wilson & Alexandra, 2005, p. 5). This is highly misleading if by *strong* we mean based on high-quality research and quality of services offered.

Research suggests an absence of quality (DePanfilis & Girvin, 2005). Court challenges to child welfare practice illustrate lack of quality (Eamon & Kopels, 2004). Bogus claims are not benign. They have resulted in harming in the name of helping and interfere with further exploration. They mislead rather than inform. They stifle inquiry into needed areas. Indicators of choices here include: (a) Absence of propaganda tactics such as hiding negative findings related to favored views and inflated claims of effectiveness, (b) Accurate description of the evidentiary status of claims including complete disclosure of methodological and conceptual limitations of preferred views and negative findings, and (c) A culture that rewards staff and clients for raising questions about practices and policies.

Whether to Implement Needed Organizational Changes

A key choice is whether to implement needed organizational changes. Gray (2001a) characterizes the evidence-based organization as having "an obsession with finding, appraising, and using research-based knowledge as evidence in decision making" (p. 250). In an evidence-informed organization, questions such as the following are continually posed, and answers pursued: "(1) What was the strength of the evidence on which the decision to introduce resource management was based? (2) How good is the evidence used to justify investment in this new [procedure]?" (p. 252). What criteria should be used to select innovations? How should they be introduced? Agencies should help practitioners and their clients to deal "with inadequate information in ways that can help to identify really important uncertainties,

uncertainties that are often reflected in dramatic variations in clinical practice and which cry out for coordinated efforts to improve knowledge" (Chalmers, 2004, p. 475). Activities of an evidence-based chief administrator suggested by Gray (2001a) include modeling, searching for evidence, appraising evidence, storing important evidence in a way that allows easy retrieval, and using evidence to make decisions. Such an administrator encourages evidence-informed audit and purchasing and takes responsibility for providing tools and training needed by staff to offer clients evidence-informed services. He or she should also help those accountable to the chief administrator to acquire and use evidence-informed management skills such as arranging for feedback that contributes to learning how to improve the quality of decisions. Administrators have a responsibility to create a work environment in which behaviors that contribute to positive outcomes for clients are maximized and behaviors that diminish such outcomes are minimized.

Will services purchased be evidence informed? State agencies such as departments of children and family services contract out services to other agencies. What criteria are used to decide what services to purchase? Evidence-based purchasing refers to purchasing of services on the basis of their evidentiary status— they have been found via critical appraisal to maximize the likelihood of achieving hoped-for outcomes. Currently, eviden - tiary grounds are typically not used to purchase services from agencies. A review of parenting programs offered to child welfare clients in one urban locale showed that parents are given a list of programs and asked to select one (Gambrill & Goldman, 2005). Often these are selected based on merely practical grounds such as transportation and availability, and clients are not informed about the evidentiary status of different programs. This goes directly counter to ethical obligations to involve clients as informed participants and

maximize self-determination. And it wastes money on services likely to be ineffective (see also Barth et al., 2005). For each service purchased, we should ask: Is anything known about its effectiveness? If so, what? Do we know if a service (a) does more good than harm, (b) does more harm than good, or (c) is of unknown effect? Costs should also be considered. Ørvretveit (1995) argues that if purchasers are not able to justify their decisions, then they are "acting unethically in directly or indirectly causing avoidable suffering" (p. 99).

Will needed training and resources be provided? A key decision is whether to provide the training and resources needed for staff to carry out evidence-informed practice such as access to relevant databases and a knowledge manager. As mentioned earlier, there are different styles of EBP. A related decision is whether to take advantage of technological innovations. Use of hand-held computers on the job to guide decisions may be of value in decreasing errors and common biases (e.g., by providing reminders to check certain things). Computer-based decision aids may be used to prompt valuable behaviors, to critique a decision (e.g., purchasing services from an agency that does not use evidence-informed practices), to make a differential diagnosis, to match a client's unique circumstances and characteristics with a certain service program, to suggest unconsidered options, and to interpret different assessment pictures (Guyatt & Rennie, 2002). Knowledge and skills needed to integrate practice and research and effective self-development skills for continued learning should be acquired during professional education programs including familiarity with common pitfalls in reasoning and strategies designed to avoid them such as "fast and frugal heuristics" (e.g., Gambrill, 2006; Gigerenzer, 2002). The very notion of a professional implies use of judicious discretion. Such discretion cannot be judicious unless professionals have acquired a minimum level of effective

Instructions to the respondent were generally self-explanatory, but office staff consisting of the project director, other trained counselors, and graduate students in related fields were available to answer questions. Anonymity was assured since no unique identifiers were recorded on the questionnaire. After completing the questionnaire, students were invited to return for further consultation if they had any concerns about their own substance use. The instrument and procedures for administering it were approved by the university human subjects review committee.

Instrument

DCS-9

The 9-item DCS-9 (O'Hare, 2001), developed with a previous cohort (O'Hare, 1997a), measures three separate drinking contexts: convivial drinking, intimate drinking, and drinking to cope with negative emotions. Respondents were asked to rate each item (4 = *extremely high*, 3 = *high*, 2 = *moderate*, 1 = *low*, 0 = *extremely low*) following this question: "Based on your personal experience, how would you rate the chances that you might find yourself drinking excessively in the following circumstances?" Items include: convivial (e.g., When I am celebrating something important to me, When I am at a party, When I am at a concert), intimate (e.g., When I am on a date, Before having sex, When I am with my lover), and negative coping (When I have had a fight with someone close to me, When I am feeling sad, depressed, or discouraged, When I am angry with myself or someone else). The original 22-item version of the DCS has shown good factorial validity, very good internal consistency (Cronbach's alphas of .93, .85, .87 for 3 subscales), evidence of concurrent validity with a modified Michigan Alcoholism Screening Test, a quantity-frequency index (O'Hare, 1997a), and alcohol expectancies (O'Hare, 1998a). Confirmatory factor analysis recently supported a 9-item version of the DCS (O'Hare, 2001; three items for each subscale) with excellent fit indices and Chronbach alphas in the low-to mid-80s. The DCS-9 was demonstrated to have very good concurrent validity with the Alcohol Use Disorders Identification Test and a previous version of the College Alcohol Problem Scale (see below; O'Hare, 2001). The subscales of the DCS-9 are used as independent and interaction variables (with gender) in the logistic regression analysis in this study.

College Alcohol Problem Scale (CAPS)

The CAPS was developed and replicated with previous cohorts of the current sample (O'Hare, 1997b, 1998b). The initial item pool was derived from an array of questions used in prominent college drinking studies (O'Hare, 1990; Wechsler et al., 1994). Exploratory factor analysis with two samples replicated the same 10 of 20 original items. Chronbach alphas in both samples were comparable (socioemotional .88, .89; community .79, .76), and the CAPS demonstrated good concurrent validity with the quantity-frequency index, a version of the Michigan Alcoholism Screening Test, and a peak drinking index from the Alcohol Use Disorders Identification Test (O'Hare, 1997b, 1998b). Using the same 20 items, as in the original CAPS, Maddock, LaForge, Rossi, and O'Hare (2001) employed confirmatory factor analysis with university undergraduates to refine the original CAPS. The study resulted in an 8-item revision of the CAPS, CAPS-r, employing two subscales similar to the original, but relabeled personal problems to (a) feeling sad, blue, depressed; (b) nervousness, irritability; (c) caused to feel bad about oneself; and (d) problems with appetite or sleeping, and social problems to (a) engaged in unplanned sexual activity, (b) drove under the influence, (c) did not use protection when engaging in sex, and (d) engaged in illegal activity associated with drug use. Internal consistency reliabilities were comparable to those of the original scale (i.e., personal problems alpha = .79, social problems alpha = .75). In that study, the CAPS-r also demonstrated very good decision-making skills including critical appraisal skills. Whatever is not provided during professional education programs must be provided on the job if we are to meet our ethical obligations. Without providing effective training in EBP skills as needed, for example, in posing well-structured answerable questions, an organization cannot be evidence based. Programs offered should reflect formats and content likely to promote achievement of hoped-for outcomes and be tailored as necessary to the unique current repertoires of each staff member. Traditional continuing education programs do little to change on-the-job behavior (Thomson O'Brien et al., 2003). Such disappointing findings was one of the reasons for creating EBP and exploring problem-based learning, to encourage lifelong learning in which professionals acquire and use practice-related research on the job. A number of articles in the social work literature decry the deprofessionalization of social workers (e.g., declassification), hiring those without a master's degree in social work to offer services. Is not the idea that social workers do not have to know how to critically appraise the quality of research a dumbing down, a deprofessionalization?

Will arrangement be made to learn from errors? As Hogarth (2001) notes, many work environments are "wicked"; they do not provide corrective feedback that allows us to learn from our mistakes. Woods and Cook (1999) point out that "factors that reduce error tolerance or block error detection and recovery degrade system performance" (p. 144). The notion of a learning organization suggests an active pursuit of the flow of knowledge including errors and their causes rather than a passive stance that characterizes many (most?) social service organizations. In *Expert Group on Learning from Adverse Events in the NHS* (2000), it was estimated that as many as 850,000 serious adverse health care events might occur in the National Health Service hospital sector each year at a

cost of more than £2 billion. Half of these events are considered to be preventable. This report concluded

> that the NHS is a "passive" rather than an "active" learning organization, which has a culture of blame and of the superficial analysis of adverse events, and therefore misses many of the learning points that could have been used to improve both safety and performance, and thereby quality of care. (Gray, 2001a, p. 245)

There is extensive research regarding error and failure—how it occurs, when it occurs, why it occurs, and what could be done about it in the areas of health, aviation, nuclear energy, and environmental concerns. Related research shows that errors typically involve systemic causes, including poor training programs (Reason, 1997, 2001). There is little of this kind of research in social work, psychiatry, and psychology (for exceptions, see DePanfilis & Girvin, 2005; Munro, 1996). Options here include designing user-friendly audit systems that permit error detection and provide opportunities for corrective feedback and user-friendly complaint retrieval systems.

Will arrangements be made to learn from clients? Clients are actively involved in many ways in EBP as discussed earlier. Their preferences and expectations are actively solicited and attended to in planning services. Literature in the area of applied behavior analysis offers guidelines here (e.g., Schwartz & Baer, 1991). User-friendly client feedback systems should be in place and information collected and utilized (see also Coulter, 2002; Edwards & Elwyn, 2001).

Indicators of choices made regarding organizational factors include the following:

- Questions that arise in everyday practice are collected from line staff and clients, and high frequency ones guide research efforts on the part of interested organizations or individuals, for example systematic reviews and new studies.

- A knowledge manager is available (Gray, 1998).

- Staff have access to relevant databases.

- A user-friendly system is in place for identifying errors and related causes so avoidable ones can be minimized and staff made aware that errors are typically systemic in cause.

- Services purchased have been critically tested and found to help clients and avoid harm.

- Facilitating incentive systems are in place; for example, staff are rewarded for blowing the whistle on harmful and ineffective practices and for suggesting specific related changes.

- Administrators and supervisors model critical appraisal of claims; they raise questions regarding current practices and policies and welcome such questions from others. They avoid styles of discussion that hinder critical appraisal of different views.

Whether to Place Ethical Issues Front and Center

Choices made will in large part reflect beliefs about the ethical obligations of professionals to their clients. Ethical and evidentiary concerns are closely inter-twined. The philosophy of EBP empha-sizes the close links between evidentiary and ethical issues. Consider informed con-sent. Clients cannot take part in making decisions as informed participants if they have not been accurately appraised about the evidentiary status of recommended procedures and alternatives. Satisfying this obligation requires social workers to be accurately informed. How can social workers know that they are accurately informed if they do not know how to crit-ically appraise the evidentiary status of claims? Social work makes much of the

concept of empowerment. Here too there is a close connection between ethical and evidentiary issues. I am not empowered if I depend on doing what someone else tells me I must do and have no understanding of the basis for this requirement. Also, if I do not understand it, I am less likely to buy into it and less likely to seek and share ways to improve services.

Censoring lack of evidence for services used, wanting professionals such as physicians and dentists who we consult in our personal lives to base decisions on rigorous criteria when we do not do so for our clients, hiding methodological limitations, and presenting sloppy reviews of the literature as evidence based all fail to honor ethical obligations described in professional codes of ethics. Gray (2001a) suggests that

> when evidence is not used during clinical practice, important failures in clinical decision making occur: ineffective interventions are introduced; interventions that do more harm than good are introduced; interventions that do more good than harm are not introduced; and interventions that are ineffective or do more harm than good are not discontinued. (p. 354)

We must make a decision regarding the status of professional codes of ethics. Are these merely for window dressing, to impress interested parties that our intentions are good and therefore our outcomes are good, to convince others that we are doing the right thing? Or are these codes really meaningful? Is it ethical to agree to abide by the guidelines described in professional codes of ethics, for example, to draw on practice-related research and then simply not do so? (For a list of 20 excuses not to act ethically, see Pope & Vasquez, 1998.) Indicators of choices made here include the following: (a) Clients are involved as informed participants; (b) Services recommended have been critically tested and found to help clients attain outcomes they value; and (c) Ineffective and harmful services are not used.

OBSTACLES

There are many obstacles to enhancing integration of evidentiary, ethical, and application concerns as noted in related literature (Ely et al., 2002; Greenhalgh et al., 2004; Oxman, Thomson, Davis, & Haynes 1995). Some obstacles are practical, some ideological, some philosophical, and many ethical. Addressing application obstacles, referred to in their most intense form as "killer B's" (barriers) by Sackett et al. (2000), for example organizational barriers, is a key concern in EBP. Helping clients involves decision making in the real world. It involves naturalistic decision making in which problems are ill structured and occur in uncertain and changing environments. Goals are often ill defined and competing and they change. Time pressures, high stakes, and multiple players complicate the picture, as may lack of feedback regarding

decisions and challenges in learning from mistakes (e.g., Wu, Folkman, McPhee, & Lo, 2003; Zambok & Klein, 1997). These characteristics illustrate that imposing practice guidelines is ill advised, not only from a psychological point of view but also from political, clinical, and implementation perspectives (e.g., Beutler, 2000). External research findings are one ingredient of EBP. Individual characteristics of practitioners, including relationship skills, also influence outcome (e.g., Wampold, 2005).

A Preference for Authority-Based Practices and Policies

Perhaps of all the obstacles, a preference for authority-based practices and policies is the most challenging. Related indicators include a reluctance to be transparent, inflated claims of effectiveness, and use of the term *evidence based* to refer to business as usual such as incomplete, unrigorous research reviews (see also Table 2). Arrogance (and, I would argue, a disregard for clients' welfare) is reflected in the prevalence of pseudoscience, fads, and

Table 2   Evidence-Based in Substance or Name Only?

Evidence-Based In Substance	Evidence-Based In Name Only
Questions researchers focus on come from clients or direct line staff.	Questions focused on are selected by researchers or administrators.
The evidentiary status of services or programs is clearly described.	The evidentiary status of service programs is hidden or misrepresented.
Rigorous criteria are used to evaluate the evidentiary status of services.	Nonrigorous criteria are used to evaluate services.
Direct line staff and supervisors are provided the training and tools needed for evidence-informed decisions.	Neither line staff nor supervisors have skills or resources required to make evidence-informed decisions.
Evidentiary status is a key factor in purchasing services.	Services are purchased based on availability and popularity.
Clients are fully informed regarding the risks and benefits of recommended services and of alternatives.	Clients are involved as uninformed or misinformed participants.
Training programs offered use formats that maximize learning and focus on information needs and skills directly related to decisions made by line staff.	Training programs are selected based on entertainment value and popularity.

related propaganda tactics in the professional literature and underestimating our vulnerability to their influence. The philosophy and process of EBP as described by its originators is a deeply participatory, antiauthoritarian paradigm that encourages all involved parties to question claims about what we know. It pits Socratic questioning against those who prefer not to be questioned and who resort to a time-tested array of strategies to deflect questions. These include attitudes such as we are doing it for you, we know better, we have more experience, and this is too difficult for you to learn. Where is there a more intense clash than between those who think they have a right not to be questioned and those who question? Consider the fate of Socrates. Many prefer ideological grounds for selecting practices and policies; they are compatible with preferred views of how things should be with little concern for discovering how they indeed are. In his discussion of the irrelevance of evidence in the development of school-based drug prevention policy, Gorman (1998) suggests that ineffective

> programs thrive not because research demonstrates their efficacy and superiority over competing approaches, but because the principles upon which they are based are compatible with the prevailing wisdom that exists among policy makers and politicians. And, judging from recent government publications and the viciousness with which critics are attacked, the uncritical acceptance of school-based social skills training seems likely to continue into the near future. (p. 141)

The origins of EBP include concerns about harmful practices being continued (e.g., Chalmers, 1983). The philosophy of EBP calls for a candid recognition of the uncertainty surrounding decisions that affect clients' lives. This uncertainty is highlighted in research on judgment, decision making, and problem solving including research on clinical decision making. Biases intrude both on the part of researchers (MacCoun, 1998) and at the practitioner level when making decisions (e.g., Gambrill, 2006). Simplifying strategies based on availability (e.g., preferred practice theory) and representativeness (e.g., stereotypes) may interfere with integration of clinical expertise, external evidence, and client values and expectations. Many biases that affect the decisions professionals make occur outside of their awareness (Gilovich, Griffin, & Kahneman, 2002) including influence by advertisements and gifts from drug companies (see Wofford & Ohl, 2005). Asking questions about effectiveness raises the sensitive issue of competence, a touchy subject vital to the essence of being a professional. "To act morally in health care is to know and understand what one is doing. Competence is not a sufficient condition, but it is a necessary condition for doing morally good acts" (Bandman, 2003, p. 177). Arrogance is reflected in an unwillingness to candidly examine competence.

Appeal to Questionable Excuses

Many reasons for not using evidence-informed practices and policies reflect the paradigm shift involved and related new resources needed such as access to relevant databases. Even here, we have a choice to accept our circumstances or to work together with others to acquire needed resources. Indeed, our ethical obligations require us to do so if limitations harm clients' welfare. What about the excuse that critical appraisal and search skills are too hard for staff to learn? We should first keep in mind that Council on Social Work Education accreditation guidelines call for learning such skills in bachelor's of social work and master's of social work programs. And, learning key questions to raise regarding different kinds of research including research reviews is easy, especially with the help of user-friendly books such as *How to Read a Paper* (Greenhalgh, 2001). Data showing that 92% of social workers sampled wanted their physicians to rely on the results of RCTs when making intervention recommendations for a serious health problem of concern to them but relied on less rigorous criteria when making decisions about clients suggest that social workers understand the purpose of RCTs, that is, to control for biases (Gambrill & Gibbs, 2002). Now, in this age of the Internet and user-friendly sources that can help us learn how to critically appraise claims, we have at our disposal tools to discover the evidentiary status of claims. Len Gibbs teaches the steps of EBP to undergraduate students. For example, questions regarding research reviews include

1. Is the question addressed clear and relevant?

2. Do the authors clearly describe how they searched, where they searched, and what criteria they used to appraise studies?

3. Was a thorough search conducted using relevant databases?

4. Did the search cover unpublished as well as published work?

5. Were rigorous criteria used to review research?

Questions regarding effectiveness include

• Was the sample size adequate?

• Was there a comparison group?

• Were participants randomly distributed to different groups?

• Were ratings of outcomes blind?

• Was there a follow-up period? If so, how long?

• Was there intention to treat analysis?

Practitioners can take advantage of high-quality reviews such as those in the Cochrane and Campbell collaboration databases. They can use flowcharts to clearly describe the source of samples in complex RCTs (see Altman et al., 2001).

Yet another questionable excuse is, "We researchers and academics do not have time to prepare systematic reviews." Are not such excuses questionable, particularly when offered by staff in organizations and academics whose job is to critically appraise claims, to be honest brokers of knowledge? Some master's degree students in the evidence-based social work program at Oxford complete Cochrane reviews in one year. True, many systematic reviews will take longer to complete and require considerable resources, but others will not. Another questionable excuse is that unsystematic reviews are just as good as systematic ones. As discussed earlier, the former overestimate positive effects and thus are misleading. Flaws in the professional literature such as bogus claims of effectiveness based on incomplete, unrigorous reviews were key origins of EBP. Another excuse is that we do not need a systemic approach to improving service quality. Given that one link may bring down all the rest, it is likely that we do need a systemic approach and should identify components, implement them, and evaluate the results.

Self-Deception

Self-deception is a key obstacle, closely related to questionable excuses that lessen quality of services. The prevalence of flawed self-assessments is striking (Dunning, Heath, & Suls, 2004). Baron (2000) suggests that the essence of self-deception is that we do not know we are deceived. Thus, we may accept poor quality services and even offer them because we have fooled ourselves that these are effective. This may occur as a result of continually seeing misery in the face of a helplessness to relieve it. There is a rich literature we can draw on to reveal self-deceptions that do not match our values, for example, to offer high-quality services (e.g., Bandura, 1999).

Other Obstacles

Another obstacle is a justificatory approach to knowledge in which we search for data to confirm our views and ignore counter evidence and well-argued alternative views. This encourages confirmation biases and wishful thinking that may lead us astray. And there is a symbiotic relationship between clients' wishes for help and professionals' desire to help. Last, it takes courage to confront those who promote ineffective or harmful services from which they receive financial benefit.

In Summary

Each agency, county, and state, including the state of California in which a new clearinghouse on EBP has been established, has a choice concerning what vision of EBP to adopt. Will the broad philosophy and process of EBP as described by its originators be adopted with its implications for all involved parties including researchers, educators, administrators, supervisors, practitioners, clients, and staff in related organizations? A variety of indicators can be used to identify choices as described in this article. Choices will influence opportunities to honor ethical obligations, to help clients, to avoid harm, to involve clients as informed participants, and to maximize self-determination and autonomy. A perusal of related written material, including that from involved organizations, suggests that a narrow view of EBP will be embraced. This is a view that is antithetical to the process and philosophy of EBP as described by its originators and to ethical obligations described in professional codes of ethics (e.g., for informed consent) and

incompatible with addressing application problems and with the tentative nature of knowledge and how it advances. Paternalism is usually discussed in the helping professions as being imposed by helpers on clients, doing things for the clients' good that clients may not choose if fully informed. Paternalism is also robust on the part of administrators and researchers if we base our conclusions on descriptions of EBP that promote a top-down approach. Paternalism, from whatever source, is counter to the philosophy of EBP and social work's emphasis on participatory decision making characterized by honest brokering of knowledge and ignorance. The top-down approach ignores vital knowledge on the part of line staff and clients, for example, regarding local resources.

There is no doubt that there are many challenges to implementing EBP and policy, especially a preference for authority-based practice and related economic incentives, the "trust me" approach. Our options are limited by current circumstances that differ in their malleability. There is also no doubt that there are many exciting advances especially in options for integrating research and practice at the line staff level and honoring ethical obligations to clients. As suggested here, there are many indicators that an agency, county, or state can use to review their choices in terms of the vision of evidence-based policy and practice they implement. We can look and see how EBP is described and implemented. We can look and see whether the term EBP is used as a rubber stamp for business as usual. We can look and see whether the evidentiary status of services clients receive has improved and whether clients are involved as informed participants. We can see if there has been "a marked reduction in the use of ineffective remedies and of effective remedies used inefficiently" (Cochrane, 1972, p. 84). We can examine the extent to which services reflect a democratic, collaborative effort of all involved parties in the challenging task of improving services and making them more just and equitable.

REFERENCES

Altman, D. G., Schulz, K. F., Moher, D., Egger, M., Davidoff, F., Elbourne, D., et al. (2001). The revised CONSORT statement for reporting randomized trials: Explanation and elaboration. *Annals of Internal Medicine, 134,* 663–694.

Angell, M. (2004). *The truth about drug companies: How they deceive us and what to do about it.* New York: Random House.

Bandman, B. (2003). *The moral development of the health care professions: Rational decision making in health care ethics.* Westport, CT: Praeger.

Bandura, A. (1999). Moral disengagement in the perpetuation of inhumanities. *Personality and Social Psychology Review, 3,* 193–199.

Baron (2000). *Thinking and deciding* (3rd ed.). New York: Cambridge University Press.

Barth, R. P., Landsverk, J., Chamberlain, P., Reid, J., Rolls, J., Hurlbert, M., et al. (2005). Parent training in child welfare services: Planning for a more evidence-based approach to serving biological parents. *Research on Social Work Practice, 15,* 353–371.

Bay Area Social Services Consortium. (2005). *Evidence for practice.* Berkeley: School of Social Welfare, University of California, Berkeley.

Beutler, L. E. (2000). David and Goliath: When empirical and clinical standards of practice meet. *American Psychologist, 55,* 997–1007.

Broclain, D., Hill, S., Oliver, S., & Wensing, M. (Eds.). (2002). Cochrane consumers & communication group. *Cochrane Library, 4.*

California Child Welfare Clearinghouse for Evidence-Based Practice. (2005). Retrieved June, 2005, from http://www.chadwick.org/clearinghouse.htm.

Carlsteadt, R. A. (2005). Toward evidence-based practice: Perfunctory pursuits or potent paradigms? [Review of the book *Evidence-based practice manual: Research and outcome measures in health and human services*]. *PsychCRITIQUES.* Washington, DC: American Psychological Association.

Chalmers, I. (1983). Scientific inquiry and authoritarianism in perinatal care and education. *Birth, 10,* 151–166.

Chalmers, I. (1995). What do I want from health research and researchers when I am a patient? *British Medical Journal, 310,* 1315–1318.

Chalmers, I. (2003). Trying to do more good than harm in policy and practice: The role of rigorous, transparent, up-to-date evaluation. *The ANNALS of the American Academy of Political and Social Science, 589,* 22–40.

Chalmers, I. (2004). Well-informed uncertainties about the effects of treatment. *British Medical Journal, 328,* 475–476.

Chambless, D. L., & Ollendick, T. H. (2001). Empirically supported psychological interventions: Controversies and evidence. *Annual Review of Psychology, 52,* 685–716.

Cochrane, A. L. (1972). *Effectiveness and efficiency: Random reflections on health services.* Cambridge, UK: Cambridge University Press.

Coulter, A. (2002). *The autonomous patient: Ending paternalism in medical care.* London: Nuffield Trust.

Council on Social Work Education. (2001). *Educational policy and accreditation standards.* Retrieved November 19, 2001, from http://www.cswe.org.

Covell, D. G., Uman, G. C., & Manning, P. R. (1985). Information needs in office practice: Are they being met? *Annals of Internal Medicine, 103,* 596–599.

Davies, P. (2004, February). *Is evidence-based government possible?* Jerry Lee lecture, 4th Annual Campbell Collaboration Colloquium, Washington, DC.

DePanfilis, D., & Girvin, H. (2005). Investigating child maltreatment in out-of-home care: Barriers to effective decision making. *Children and Youth Services Review, 27,* 353–374.

Dunning, D., Heath, C., & Suls, J. M. (2004). Flawed self-assessment: Implications for health, education, and the workplace. *Psychological Science in the Public Interest, 5,* 69–106.

Eamon, M. K., & Kopels, S. (2004). For reasons of poverty: Court challenges to child welfare practices and mandated programs. *Children and Youth Services Review, 26,* 821–836.

Edwards, A., & Elwyn, G. (Eds.). (2001). *Evidence-based patient choice: Inevitable or impossible?* New York: Oxford University Press.

Ely, J. W., Osheroff, J. A., Ebell, M. H., Chambliss, M. L., Vinson, D. C., Stevermer, J. J., et al. (2002). Obstacles to answering doctors' questions about patient care with evidence: Qualitative study. *British Medial Journal, 324,* 710–718.

Enkin, M. W., Keirse, M. J., Renfrew, M. J., & Neilson, J. P. (1995). *A guide to effective care in pregnancy and childbirth* (2nd ed.). New York: Oxford University Press.

Entwistle, V. A., Renfrew, M. J., Yearley, S., Forrester, J., & Lamont, T. (1998). Lay perspectives: Advantages for health research. *British Medical Journal, 316,* 463–466.

Gambrill, E. (2003). Evidence-based practice: Sea change or the emperor's new clothes? *Journal of Social Work Education, 39,* 3–23.

Gambrill, E. (2006). *Critical thinking in clinical practice* (2nd ed.). New York: John Wiley.

Gambrill, E., & Gibbs, L. (2002). Making practice decisions: Is what's good for the goose good for the gander? *Ethical Human Services & Services, 4,* 31–46.

Gambrill, E., & Goldman, R. (2005). *Reviewing the quality of parent training programs provided by child welfare agencies.* Unpublished manuscript, University of California, Berkeley.

Gambrill, E., & Penick, A. (2005). *Critically appraising the professional literature: A propaganda index.* Unpublished manuscript, University of California, Berkeley.

Gibbs, L. (2003). *Evidence-based practice for the helping professions.* Pacific Grove, CA: Brooks/Cole.

Gibbs, L., & Gambrill, E. (2002). Arguments against evidence based practice. *Research on Social Work Practice, 14,* 452–476.

Gigerenzer, G. (2002). *Calculated risks: How to know when numbers deceive you.* New York: Simon & Schuster.

Gilovich, T., Griffin, D., & Kahneman, D. (Eds.). (2002). *Heuristics and biases: The psychology of intuitive judgment.* New York: Cambridge University Press.

Glasziou, P., Vanderbroucke, J., & Chalmers, I. (2004). Assessing the quality of research. *British Medical Journal, 328,* 39–41.

Gomory, T. (1999). Programs of assertive community treatment (PACT): A critical review. *Ethical Human Sciences and Services, 1,* 147–163.

Gorman, D. M. (1998). The irrelevance of evidence in the development of school-based drug prevention policy, 1986–1996. *Evaluation Review, 22,* 118–146.

Gray, J. A. M. (1997). *Evidence-based health care: How to make health policy and management decisions.* New York: Churchill Livingstone.

Gray, J. A. M. (1998). Where is the chief knowledge officer? *British Medical Journal, 317,* 832.

Gray, J. A. M. (2001a). *Evidence-based health care: How to make health policy and management decisions* (2nd ed.). New York: Churchill Livingstone.

Gray, J. A. M. (2001b). Evidence-based medicine for professionals. In A. Edwards & G. Elwyn (Eds.), *Evidence-based patient choice: Inevitable or impossible?* (pp. 19–33). New York: Oxford University Press.

Greenhalgh, T. (2001). *How to read a paper.* London: BMJ.

Greenhalgh, T., Robert, G., Bate, P., Kyriakidou, O., Macfarlane, F., & Peacock, R. (2005). *Diffusion of innovations for health services organizations: A systematic literature review.* Oxford, UK: Blackwell.

Greenhalgh, T., Robert, G., Macfarlane, F., Bate, P., & Kyriakidou, O. (2004). Diffusion of innovations in service organizations: Systematic review and recommendations. *The Milbank Quarterly, 82,* 581–629.

Guyatt, G., & Rennie, D. (2002). *Users' guide to the medical literature: A manual for evidence-based clinical practice.* Chicago: American Medical Association Press.

Hanley, B., Truesdale, A., King, A., Elbourne, D., & Chalmers, I. (2001). Involving consumers in designing, conducting, and interpreting randomised controlled trials: Questionnaire survey. *British Medical Journal, 322,* 519–523.

Haynes, R. B., Devereaux, P. J., & Guyatt, G. H. (2002). Clinical expertise in the era of evidence-based medicine and patient choice. *Evidence-Based Medicine, 7,* 36–38.

Henggeler, S. W., & Lee, T. (2003). Multisystemic treatment of serious clinical problems. In A. E. Kazdin & J. R. Weisz (Eds.), *Evidence-based psychotherapies for children and adolescents* (pp. 301–324). New York: Guilford.

Henggeler, S. W., Schoenwald, S. K., Borduin, C. M., & Swenson, C. C. (2006). The Littell paper: Methodological critique meta-analysis as Trojan horse. *Children and Youth Services Review, 28,* 447–457.

Higgins, J. P. T. & Green, S. (Eds.). (2005). *Cochrane handbook for systematic reviews of interventions.* 4.2.5 (Updated May 2005). In the Cochrane Library, Issue 3. Chichester, UK:Wiley

Hogarth, R. M. (2001). *Educating intuition.* Chicago: University of Chicago Press.

Institute of Medicine. (2001). *Crossing the quality chasm: A new health system for the 21st century.* Washington, DC: National Academy Press.

Jacobson, J. W., Foxx, R. M., & Mulick, J. A. (Eds.). (2005). *Controversial therapies for developmental disabilities: Fads, fashion, and science in professional practice.* Mahwah, NJ: Lawrence Erlbaum.

Jørgensen, K. J., & Gøtzsche, P. C. (2004). Presentation on websites of possible benefits and harms from screening for breast cancer: Cross sectional study. *British Medical Journal, 328,* 148–155.

King, L. S. (1981). *Medical thinking: A historical preface.* Princeton, NJ: Princeton University Press.

Kluger, M. P., Alexander, G., & Curtis, P. A. (2002). *What works in child welfare.* Washington, DC: CWLA Press.

Lehman, A. F., Goldman, H. H., Dixon, L. B., & Churchill, R. (2004). *Evidence-based mental health treatments and services: Examples to inform public policy.* New York: Millbank Memorial Fund.

Lilienfeld, S. O., Lynn, S. J., & Lohr, J. M. (Eds.). (2003). *Science and pseudoscience in clinical psychology.* New York: Guilford.

Lindsey, D., Martin, S., & Doh, J. (2002). The failure of intensive casework services to reduce foster care placements: An examination of family preservation studies. *Children and Youth Services Review, 24,* 743–775.

Littell, J. (2005). Lessons from a systematic review of effects of multisystemic therapy. *Children and Youth Services Review, 27,* 445–463.

MacCoun, R. (1998). Biases in the interpretation and use of research results. *Annual Review of Psychology, 49,* 259–287.

Macintyre, S., Chalmers, I., Horton, R., & Smith, R. (Eds.). (2001). Using evidence to inform health policy: Case study. *British Medical Journal, 322,* 222–225.

McCord, J. (2003). Cures than harm: Unanticipated outcomes of crime prevention programs. *The ANNALS of the American Academy of Political and Social Science, 587,* 16–30.

Munro, E. (1996). Avoidable and unavoidable mistakes in child protection work. *British Journal of Social Work, 26,* 793–808.

National Association of Social Workers. (1999). *Code of ethics.* Silver Spring, MD: Author.

Norcross, J. C., Beutler, L. E., & Levant, R. F. (Eds.). (2005). *Evidence-based practice in mental health: Debate and dialogue on the fundamental questions.* Washington, DC: American Psychological Association.

O'Conner, A. M., Stacey, D., Rovner, D., Holmers-Rovner, M., Tetroe, J., Llewellyn-Thomas, H., et al. (2002). Decision aids for people facing health treatment or screening decisions (Cochrane Review). *Cochrane Library, 2.*

O'Hare, T. (2005). *Evidence-based practices for social workers.* Chicago: Lyceum.

Ørvretveit, J. (1995). *Purchasing for health: A multidisciplinary introduction to the theory and practice of health purchasing.* Philadelphia: Open University Press.

Oxman, A. D., Thomson, M. A., Davis, D. A., & Haynes, R. B. (1995). No magic bullets: A systematic review of 102 trials of interventions to improve professional practice. *Canadian Medical Association Journal, 153,* 1423–1431.

Oxman, A., & Guyatt, G. H. (1993). The science of reviewing research. In K. S. Warren & F. Mosteller (Eds.), *Doing more good than harm: The evaluation of health care interventions* (pp. 125–133). New York: New York Academy of Sciences.

Paul, R. (1993). *Critical thinking: What every person needs to survive in a rapidly changing world* (3rd ed.). Sonoma, CA: Foundation for Critical Thinking.

Persons, J. B. (2005). Empiricism, mechanism, and the practice of cognitive-behavior therapy. *Behavior Therapy, 36,* 107–118.

Petrosino, A., Turpin-Petrosino, C., & Bheuler, J. (2003). Scared Straight and other juvenile awareness programs for preventing juvenile delinquency: A systematic review of the randomized experimental evidence. *ANNALS of the American Academy of Political and Social Science, 589,* 41–62.

Pope, K. S., & Vasquez, M. J. T. (1998). *Ethics in psychotherapy and counseling: A practical guide* (2nd ed.). San Francisco: Jossey-Bass.

Reason, J. (1997). *Managing the risks of organizational accidents.* Aldershot, England: Ashgate.

Reason, J. (2001). Understanding adverse events: The human factor. In C. Vincent (Ed.), *Clinical risk management: Enhancing patient safety* (2nd ed., pp. 9–30). London: BMJ.

Reid, W. J. (2001). The role of science in social work: The perennial debate. *Journal of Social Work, 1,* 273–293.

Reid, W. J. (2002). Knowledge for direct social work practice: An analysis of trends. *Social Service Review, 76,* 6–33.

Roberts, A. R., & Greene, G. J. (Eds.). (2002). *Social workers' desk reference.* New York: Oxford University Press.

Roberts, A. R., & Yeager, K. R. (2005). *Evidence-based practice manual.* New York: Oxford University Press.

Rosen, A., & Proctor, E. K. (2002). Standards for evidence-based social work practice. In A. R. Roberts & G. J. Greene (Eds.), *The social worker's desk reference* (pp. 743–747). New York: Oxford University Press.

Sackett, D. L. (2002). The arrogance of preventive medicine. *Canadian Medical Association Journal, 167,* 363–364.

Sackett, D. L., Richardson, W. S., Rosenberg, W., & Haynes, R. B. (1997). *Evidence-based medicine: How to practice and teach EBM.* New York: Churchill Livingstone.

Sackett, D. L., Rosenberg, W. M. C., Gray, J. A. M., Haynes, R. B., & Richardson, W. S. (1996). Evidence-based medicine: What it is and what it isn't. *British Medical Journal, 312,* 71–72.

Sackett, D. L., & Straus, S. E. (1998). Finding and applying evidence during clinical rounds. The "evidence cart." *Journal of the American Medical Association, 280,* 1336.

Sackett, D. L., Straus, S. E., Richardson, W. C., Rosenberg, W., & Haynes, R. M. (2000). *Evidence-based medicine: How to practice and teach EBM* (2nd ed.). New York: Churchill Livingstone.

Schuerman, J. R., Rzepnicki, T. L., & Littell, J. H. (1994). *Putting families first: An experiment in family preservation.* Hawthorne, NY: Aldine de Gruyter.

Schulz, K. F., Chalmers, I., Hayes, R. J., & Altman, D. G. (1995). Empirical evidence of bias: Dimensions of methodological quality associated with estimates of treatment effects in controlled trials. *Journal of the American Medical Association, 273,* 408–412.

Schwartz, I. S., & Baer, D. M. (1991). Social validity assessments: Is current practice state of the art? *Journal of Applied Behavior Analysis, 24,* 189–204.

Smith, R. (2003). Do patients need to read research? *British Medical Journal, 326,* 1307.

Straus, S. E., & McAlister, D. C. (2000). Evidence-based medicine: A commentary on common criticisms. *Canadian Medical Journal, 163,* 837–841.

Test, M. A. (2002). Guidelines for assertive community treatment teams. In A. R. Roberts & G. J. Greene (Eds.), *Social workers'desk reference* (pp. 511–513). New York: Oxford University Press.

Thomlison, B. (2003). Characteristics of evidence-based child maltreatment interventions. *Child Welfare, 82,* 541–569.

Thomson O'Brien, M. A., Freemantle, N., Oxman, A. D., Wolf, F., Davis, D. A., & Herrin, J. (2003). Continuing education meetings and workshops: Effects on professional practice and health care outcomes (Cochrane Review). *Cochrane Library, 1.*

U. S. Public Health Service (2000). *Youth violence: A report of the Surgeon General.* Retrieved September 1, 2004, from www.surgeongeneral.gov/library/youth/violence/youvioreport.htm.

Wampold, B. E. (2005). The psychotherapist. In J. C. Norcross, L. E. Beutler, & R. F. Levant (Eds.), *Evidence-based practices in mental health: Debate and dialogue on the fundamental questions* (pp. 202–207). Washington, DC: American Psychological Association.

Wennberg, J. E. (2002). Unwarranted variations in healthcare delivery: Implications for academic medical centers. *British Medical Journal, 325,* 961–964.

Wilson, D., & Alexandra, L. (2005). *Guide for child welfare administrators on evidence-based practice.* Washington, DC: National Association of Public Child Welfare Administrators, American Public Human Services Association.

Wofford, J. L., & Ohl, C. A. (2005). Teaching appropriate interactions with pharmaceutical company representatives: The impact of an innovative workshop on student attitudes. *BMC Medical Education, 5*(5), 1–7.

Woods, D. D., & Cook, R. I. (1999). Perspectives on human error: Hindsight biases and local rationality. In F. T. Durso, R. S. Nickerson, R. W. Schvaneveldt, S. T. Dumais, D. S. Lindsay, & M. T. Chi (Eds.), *Handbook of applied cognition* (pp. 141–171). New York: John Wiley.

Wright, R. H., & Cummings, N. A. (Eds.). (2005). *Destructive trends in mental health: The well-intended path to harm.* New York: Routledge.

Wu, A. W., Folkman, S., McPhee, S. J., & Lo, B. (2003). Do house officers learn from their mistakes? *Quality of Safety and Health Care, 12,* 221–226.

Zambok, C. E., & Klein, G. (Eds.). (1997). *Naturalistic decision making.* Mahwah, NJ: Lawrence Erlbaum.

CRITICAL THINKING QUESTIONS

Reading 1

1. Briefly describe the five steps of the evidence-based practice (EBP) process.

2. Distinguish between top-down and bottom-up efforts to track down relevant information.

3. Why is it incorrect to state that EBP tells practitioners what interventions

to use, based on the research evidence?

4. What is a more accurate statement, related to question 3 (above)?

5. Locate and read one of the systematic reviews dealing with substance abuse, to be found on the websites of either the Cochrane or Campbell Collaborations. Discuss what you found and your reactions to the comprehensiveness and transparency of this review.

Reading 2

1. Come up with one example each of the following kinds of questions: Effectiveness, Prevention, Risk Prognosis, Description or Assessment.

2. How is the ethic of 'transparency' woven into EBP?

3. How are clients involved in EBP?

4. What organizational factors can be put into place to promote EBP?

5. How can self-deception be an obstacle to EBP?

PART II

ASSESSMENT OF SUBSTANCE ABUSE

The topic of assessment in the fields of substance abuse usually relates to the clinical assessment of individuals with a presumptive or known problem with abusing alcohol or other drugs. Assessment can be seen as a metaphoric series of screenings. The initial sifting is making a clinical determination of whether or not a client meets some established diagnostic criteria needed to arrive at a formal diagnosis. The diagnostic categories found in the *Diagnostic and Statistical Manual of Mental Disorders* are among the most commonly used diagnostic system. Such a categorical system involves a seemingly binary decision-making process. A given client either does or does not meet the DSM criteria for a particular diagnosis. Some refinements might be possible (e.g., with or without physiological dependence) but the system is a relatively crude one. Later metaphorical screenings permit more detailed appraisals of the client's substance abuse, so at the end, hopefully, the clinician has a complete and useful assessment of the antecedents, concurrent circumstances, and consequences of a given client's drug involvement.

Assessment of substance abuse primarily involves three major ways to measure aspects of the client. The client's self report is perhaps the most significant and widely used approach, with information being gathered via formal and informal clinical interviews. Clients can also provide reports of their own behavior, feelings and thoughts, gathered via pencil and paper rating scales, rapid assessment instruments, and questionnaires. A second modality involves the assessment of actual client behavior, as observed by someone else. Did drinking occur or not? If so, how much, over what time period, how frequently, to what extent, and so on. The direct measure of client behavior recorded by others in real life contexts is logistically and practically much more difficult to undertake than using surrogate or indirect measures such as client self-reports, which is why most substance abuse counselors rarely directly assess client behavior. The third modality of assessment involves the assessment of some physiological measure or indicator of the client. Various tests of substance use, involving the collection of the client's urine, saliva, breath or hair can provide very reliable information relating to the client's recent (and sometimes distant) drug or alcohol use. Drug testing kits are freely available in local drug stores (how appropriate!). The results are not perfect however. One of the editors (BAT) tested positive for barbiturate use following a urine screening while he was in the Army in 1975. It was an erroneous result but caused raised eyebrows among his fellow soldiers for a while.

Each of these methods of assessment should be subjected to critical questioning related to the method's reliability and validity. The use of unreliable and invalid methods of assessment likely does more harm than good, yet substance abuse counselors often uncritically accept as legitimate methods of assessment they encounter at their agency, with little attention to credibility issues. If a client provides a urine sample, and a portion of it is tested and comes up positive for a particular drug (or negative), then another portion of that same sample should yield the same positive or negative result. If this occurs, the measure is said to have good test-retest reliability. Lacking this, it is useless for assessment purposes. If a client undergoes a structured clinical interview and a particular diagnosis is obtained, that same diagnosis should be arrived at by a second equally skilled interviewer who uses the same structured interview protocol. Without this, the method lacks inter-rater reliability and it is useless for assessment purposes. There are many different forms of reliability and validity and no effort will be made to review them here. But the take-away message of these introductory remarks is that substance abuse counselors should seek out what is known about the methods of assessment they currently employ, and also try and locate and employ those measures already established to be reliable, valid, and clinically useful.

Every method used in assessment can and should be subjected to rigorous evaluation of the approaches' reliability and validity. If it yields dichotomous results (yes abuse is present, no abuse is not present), then efforts should be made to determine the measure's extent of providing false positives (saying a particular client abuses a particular class of drug, when in reality, she does not) and false negatives (saying a particular client does not abuse a particular class of drug, when in reality she does). To the extent that a measure deviates from providing 'true positives' and 'true negatives,' it is of lesser use in evidence-based substance abuse treatment.

The two readings comprising this section of the book reflect one author's (Tom O'Hare, with the Graduate School of Social Work at Boston College) efforts to conduct validation studies on previously published assessment measures developed for use in substance abuse counseling. The *Drinking Context Scale (DSC-9)* is one such measure, intended to measure the contexts in which a student drinks alcohol; for example, convivial contexts, intimate contexts, versus drinking to escape negative emotions. Being able to tease out the reasons why someone drinks abusively is of obvious relevance to being able to provide effective treatment services. Dr. O'Hare provides us with additional information about the reliability and validity of the *DSC-9*.

Similarly, the *Alcohol Use Disorders Identification Test (AUDIT)* is a purported screening tool for use in providing a preliminary assessment of whether or not someone abuses alcohol. Dr. O'Hare's second study provides evidence that the *AUDIT* is indeed a reliable screening tool and correlates reasonably well with other indictors of alcohol abuse. We include these two studies as examples of how social work practitioner-researchers contribute to evidence-based practice through the conscientious evaluation of assessment measures intended for use in the field of substance abuse.

3

ASSESSMENT OF YOUTHFUL PROBLEM DRINKERS

Validating the Drinking Context Scale (DCS-9) With Freshman First Offenders

THOMAS O'HARE
BOSTON COLLEGE

MARGARET V. SHERRER
SOUTH SHORE MENTAL HEALTH CENTER, INC.

The current study of 389 university freshman cited by the administration for underaged drinking examines gender and three drinking contexts (i.e., convivial, intimate, and negative coping) as differential predictors of personal problems (e.g., depressed, nervous) and social problems (e.g., unplanned sex, drove under the influence) that respondents attribute to their own alcohol use. Results demonstrated that more than one third of these respondents reported at least one personal problem, which they attributed to the use of alcohol in the previous year, and about half reported at least one social problem. However, when logistic regression was employed, results showed that drinking to cope with negative emotions was the only independent predictor of personal drinking-related problems. Drinking excessively in convivial circumstances, intimate encounters, drinking to cope with negative emotions, and being male were all independently predictive of

Authors' Note: Please direct all correspondences to Thomas O'Hare, PhD, Boston College Graduate School of Social Work, 202 McGuinn Hall, Chestnut Hill, MA 02167-3807; e-mail: oharet@bc.edu.

SOURCE: "Assessment of Youthful Problem Drinkers: Validating the Drinking Context Scale (DCS-9) With Freshman First Offenders" by Thomas O'Hare and Margaret V. Sherrer. In the 2005 issue of *Research on Social Work Practice*, *15*(2), 110–117. Used with permission.

social problems related to alcohol abuse. Implications for assessment and early intervention strategies are suggested.

Keywords: college drinking; drinking context; CAPS; DCS; freshmen

Research on college drinking has demonstrated an array of problems related to youthful alcohol abuse (O'Hare, 1990; Wechsler, Davenport, Dowdall, Moeykens, & Costillow, 1994; Wechsler, Lee, Kuo, & Lee, 2000). These problems include negative psychological (e.g., depression, suicide, anxiety), interpersonal (e.g., fights, unplanned and unprotected sex) and community (e.g., driving under the influence, vandalism) problems. A recent review of five national college drinking surveys (O'Malley & Johnston, 2002) summarized the major findings and trends that have accumulated over the past 20 years: more than two thirds of college students drink alcohol, 40% are considered binge drinkers (i.e., consume five or more drinks at one sitting within the past 2 weeks), and rates of alcohol use have not changed substantially since the 1950s. In one large college sample, almost one third met the *Diagnostic and Statistical Manual of Mental Disorders* criteria for alcohol abuse (Knight et al., 2002). Although differences in alcohol consumption have narrowed between males and females over the past 10 years or so, young males are currently about one and one half times as likely as females to be binge drinkers (50% versus 34%, respectively; O'Malley & Johnston, 2002). In addition, women are known to be at greater risk than men to incur negative consequences of excessive drinking. These problems include more co-occurring depression and anxiety, higher blood alcohol levels, and greater stigma associated with drinking (O'Hare, 1997a; Wechsler, Dowdall, Davenport, & Rimm, 1995).

Freshmen in college may be among the most at risk of youthful drinkers. Although young persons between the ages of 18 and 29 account for almost half (45%) of adult drinking in the United States (Greenfield & Rogers, 1999), and college drinkers consume at least as much as their noncollege cohorts (Gfoerer, Greenblatt & Wright, 1997; O'Malley & Johnston, 2002), freshmen in college are of particular concern since they appear to have more problems related to drinking than upper classmen. Heavy drinking and associated problems only begin to decline through their senior year and beyond (O'Neill, Parra, & Sher, 2001). These changes may occur naturally through reduction in consumption, use of greater discretion regarding risky drinking situations (e.g., driving under the influence), or development of other skills that may attenuate some of the negative consequences associated with excessive alcohol use. It seems that freshman year presents a critical opportunity to reduce potential harm associated with problem drinking, but this opportunity needs to be seen in the light of cognitive, social, educational, and occupational changes and challenges they face at that age (Schulenberg & Maggs, 2002).

A Social Cognitive Framework

Social cognitive models appear to be useful in explaining youthful drinking by linking motivations for drinking, alcohol expectancies of drinking effects, stress, and social contextual factors as reciprocal determinants of problem drinking (Brown, Christiansen, & Goldman, 1987; O'Hare, 1998a; Maisto, Carey, & Bradizza, 1999). Interactions among physiological predisposition, beliefs, drinking behaviors, and preferred drinking contexts appear to operate in complex ways. Although proponents of psychiatric models, such as the self-medication hypothesis, assume a direct linkage between personal psychopathology and problem drinking, negative consequences related to alcohol abuse in young people are often associated with what are otherwise considered positive experiences, such as socializing and romantic encounters (Carey, 1993; O'Hare, 1997a). Both young men and women may cope with stress by drinking to have fun or to blow off steam—innocuous motives, perhaps, but ones that often lead to psychological and interpersonal problems, vandalism, legal consequences, strains between local residents and university administrators, and injuries or death because of driving while drunk, among other negative consequences.

Drinking is also associated with dating and sexual activity (experiences generally considered positive; Cooper, 2002; Norris, 1994; O'Hare, 1998a). Yet excessive drinking under these circumstances is too often associated with date rape and unplanned or unprotected sexual activity, accompanied by the risk of contracting sexually transmitted diseases (Abbey, 2002; Carroll & Carroll, 1995; Cooper & Orcutt, 1997). It has also been recognized that stress is especially common in college freshman (Sher, Wood & Gotham, 1996), and emotional distress and psychiatric problems are associated with college drinking (O'Hare & Sherrer, 2000; Ross & Tisdall, 1994). Drinking in young persons has been shown to be one way of coping with these negative emotions (Cooper, Russell, & George, 1988; Evans & Dunn, 1995; O'Hare, 1998a). Although substance abuse is associated with emotional and behavioral disorders in adult and adolescent males and females in the general population (Kandel et al., 1997; Kessler et al., 1996), women are more likely to experience co-occurring emotional distress (e.g., anxiety, depression), whereas substance-abusing men are more likely to engage in antisocial behaviors. In a cohort of the sample surveyed for the current study, the relationship between self-reported psychological stress and substance abuse was shown to be stronger in women than men (O'Hare & Sherrer, 2000).

Purpose of the Current Study

The current investigation serves as a test of the concurrent validity of the *Drinking Context Scale* (DCS-9) by examining the question whether youthful drinking contexts differentially predict personal and social drinking problems. It is expected that drinking excessively to cope with negative emotions will more likely be associated with personal problems (i.e., depression, anxiety, feeling bad about oneself, and somatic complaints); and convivial drinking (i.e., social groups, partying) and intimate drinking (i.e., dating and sexual situations) will more likely predict social problems (i.e., unplanned and unprotected sex, driving under the influence, and illegal drug activity). Second, given previous findings regarding gender differences based on both general population and college data, it is also expected that women will report more personal problems and men will report more social problems when, in both cases, gender by drinking-context interactions are held constant.

METHOD

Sample and Procedure

Three hundred and eighty-nine college freshmen (age: $M = 18.2$, $SD = .53$) at the University of Rhode Island responded consecutively to an anonymous questionnaire during the mid-to late 1990s as part of an adjudication process for violating university rules concerning underaged drinking or the use of illicit drugs. About one third of the respondents are female (36.8%), and two thirds are male (63.2%). Almost all of the respondents lived on campus (98.7%), and almost all respondents were White (95.6%), a proportionate reflection of university demographics. Family income was self-reported as poor (1.8%), lower middle class (5.9%), middle class (50.6%), upper middle class (36.8%) and wealthy (3.6%), with five respondents (1.3%) not reporting.

When reporting to the Office of Student Life to pay a required fine, students completed the anonymous questionnaire to provide an accurate picture of the range of experiences, relevant to substance use, among the students who were referred.

concurrent validity in that the subscales correlated significantly with the Young Adult Alcohol Problems Screening Test, three alcohol consumption measures, and self-rated pros and cons of drinking (Maddock et al., 2001). The version used in the current study uses the 8-items of the CAPS-r but retained the original scoring format used in response to the following directive: "How often have you had any of the following problems over the past year as a result of drinking too much alcohol?" Responses were scored 4 to 0 corresponding to very often, often, moderate degree, seldom, and never or almost never, respectively. Because the subscale distributions are very positively skewed, both the personal and social problem subscales were recoded into dichotomous measures. The two subscales were computed by summing the items. A report of any drinking problem was coded 1 and the absence of a drinking problem was coded 0. The two dichotomous subscales were used as dependent variables in the logistic regression models reported below.

Results

Analysis of Individual Items and Subscale Scores of the CAPS and the DCS-9

More than one third of these respondents reported at least one personal problem in the previous year, and about half reported at least one social problem, which they attributed to the use of alcohol. These problems included signs of depression, anxiety, negative feelings about themselves, problems with appetite or sleeping, unplanned and unprotected sex, driving under the influence, and engaging in illegal drug use. Since the CAPS items are dichotomous, a chi-square statistic with Cramer's V (to test the strength of the association) was employed to test for gender differences. Although there were no significant gender differences on personal problems, males were significantly more likely to engage in unplanned sexual activity (chi square

$[df, 1] = 6.50$, $p < .05$; Cramer's $V = .13$, $p < .05$) and engage in illegal activities associated with drug use (chi square $[df, 1] = 6.30$, $p < .05$; Cramer's $V = .13$, $p < .05$).

An examination of gender differences was undertaken to test whether males or females in this sample reported more total personal and social problems related to drinking, based on subscale scores of the CAPS. Results demonstrated that although there was no significant difference in the frequency of total personal problems reported between these young men and women, young males in the sample reported significantly greater number of social problems related to their alcohol use (chi square $[df, 1] = 10.24$, $p < .01$; Cramer's $V = .16$, $p < .01$). Frequency data for individual items and subscale scores of the CAPS for the total sample and by gender can be examined in Table 1.

Frequencies for individual items and subscores of the DCS-9 appear to be generally moderate for both males and females with regard to convivial drinking. That is, respondents reported being moderately likely, on average, to engage in excessive drinking under these circumstances. In romantic and sexual situations, both males and females reported a relatively low likelihood of drinking excessively. When feeling psychological distress, respondents generally reported a very low likelihood of drinking excessively to cope with negative emotions. When individual items were tested for gender differences, t tests revealed males to be significantly more likely to drink excessively at a party ($t [df, 387] = -2.45$, $p < .05$), a concert ($t [df, 387] = -2.07$, $p < .05$), before having sex ($t [df, 346.61] = -3.36$, $p < .01$), or when angry with themselves or someone else ($t [df, 380.96] = -2.66$, $p < .01$).

Gender differences in drinking context (DCS-9) subscale scores were also examined. Independent t tests showed males to be significantly more likely to drink excessively in convivial circumstances ($t [df, 387] = -2.4$, $p < .05$). There were no significant gender differences in their likelihood of drinking excessively in intimate

Table 1   Frequencies and Percentages of Drinking-Related Problems for Individual Items and Subscale Scores of the CAPS-r for Total Sample (n = 389), Women (n = 143) and Men (n = 246)

	Total		Female		Male	
	f	%	*f*	%	*f*	%
Personal problems						
Feeling sad, blue, depressed	95	24.4	33	23.1	62	25.2
Nervousness, irritability	88	22.6	28	19.6	60	24.4
Felt bad about oneself	82	21.1	24	16.8	58	23.6
Problems with appetite or sleeping	75	19.3	25	17.5	50	20.3
Subscale score	145	37.3	47	32.9	98	39.8
Social problems						
Unplanned sex	129	33.2	36	25.2	93	37.8*
Drove under the influence	101	26.0	30	21.0	71	28.9
Did not use protection during sex	62	15.9	19	13.3	43	17.5
Illegal activity or drugs	102	26.2	27	18.9	75	30.5*
Subscale score	191	49.1	55	38.5	136	55.3**

NOTE: CAPS-r = College Alcohol Problem Scale Revised

$*p < .05. **p < .01.$

circumstances or drinking to cope with negative emotions. Means and standard deviations for all individual items and subscale scores of the DCS-9 by total sample and by gender appear in Table 2.

Analysis using Spearman's rho correlations reveals significant and moderate associations between the two problem drinking scores and three drinking contexts: personal problems by convivial (.41), negative coping (.53), and intimate drinking (.41) and social problems by convivial (.52), negative coping (.47), and intimate drinking (.50). All correlations were significant at $p < .01$. problem drinking scores and three drinking contexts: personal problems by convivial (.41), negative coping (.53), and intimate drinking (.41) and social problems by convivial (.52), negative coping (.47), and intimate drinking (.50). All correlations were significant at $p < .01$.

Logistic Regression: Gender, Drinking Context, and Gender by Context Interactions

To examine the independent and collective predictive value of three different drinking contexts, gender, and gender by context interaction, two logistic regression models were designed using the three DCS subscales (i.e., convivial, intimate, and negative coping) as independent variables and the two bivariate CAPS subscales (personal and social problems) as dependent variables. Logistic regression was chosen because the dependent variables are dichotomous and the distribution on at least one of the interaction variables is highly skewed. Logistic regression provides more flexibility in handling non-normal predictor variables compared to discriminant analysis (Hosmer & Lemeshow, 1989; Tabachnick & Fidell, 2001). Logistic models were developed for both dependent variables (personal problems and social problems, respectively) in a two-step process by, first, entering the independent variables (DCS-9 subscales, gender and gender by DCS-9 subscale interaction terms) simultaneously. In the second step, only those variables that achieved a significance level of greater than .10 (in Model 1) were then entered into the new equation (i.e., Model 2). For personal problems, Model 1 produced one significant independent predictor

Table 2 Means and Standard Deviations for Individual Items and Subscale Scores of the DCS-9 for Total Sample (n = 389), Women (n = 143) and Men (n = 246)

	Total		Female		Male	
	M	*SD*	*M*	*SD*	*M*	*SD*
Convivial drinking						
When I am at a party or similar other get together	2.7	1.2	2.5	1.2	2.8	1.2*
When I am at a concert or other public event	2.1	1.4	1.9	1.3	2.2	1.4*
When I am celebrating something important to me	1.7	1.3	1.5	1.3	1.8	1.4
Subscale score	6.5	3.4	6.0	3.4	6.8	3.4*
Intimate drinking						
When I am with my lover	1.0	1.0	1.0	1.1	1.0	1.0
When I am on a date	.9	1.0	.9	1.0	.9	.9
Before having sex	.6	.9	.4	.8	.7	.9**
Subscale score	2.5	2.4	2.3	2.4	2.6	2.4
Negative coping						
When I have had a fight with someone close to me	.5	.8	.4	.8	.5	.8
When I am feeling sad, depressed, or discouraged	.5	.9	.5	.8	.5	.9
When I am angry with myself or someone else	.4	.7	.3	.6	.4	.8**
Subscale score	1.3	2.1	1.1	1.9	1.4	2.2

NOTE: DCS-9 = Drinking Context Scale

*$p < .05$. **$p < .01$.

variable, negative coping, and one interaction term that approached significance: gender by convivial drinking ($p = .09$). These two factors were reentered into the equation to form Model 2, and both were shown to be statistically significant. A nonsignificant Hosmer and Lemeshow test also demonstrated goodness of fit of the predictor variables (chi square [*df*, 6] = 10.35, p >.05). The final model identified 75.1% of cases correctly. For social problems, Model 1 revealed significant findings for all three DCS-9 subscales, and gender approached significance ($p = .08$). These four factors were entered into Model 2, and all four were shown to be statistically significant. A nonsignificant Hosmer and Lemeshow test, again, demonstrated goodness of fit (chi square [*df*, 8] = 14.23, $p > .05$). The final model identified 74.8% of cases correctly. Statistics associated with the variables in the final models can be examined in Table 3.

DISCUSSION AND APPLICATIONS TO SOCIAL WORK RESEARCH AND PRACTICE

About one fifth or more of these freshmen first offenders reported personal problems as a result of drinking. These included depression and anxiety symptoms, feeling bad about oneself, and problems with appetite or sleep as a result of their alcohol use. As for social problems, a quarter reported driving under the influence and using illegal drugs. One seventh reported engaging in unprotected sex, and about one third reported unplanned sex as a consequence of drinking. Overall, males reported experiencing more social problems related to drinking than did females and also being more likely to engage in excessive convivial drinking. Individual item analysis revealed that males were more likely to report engaging in unplanned sex and illegal drug activities and more likely than females to drink

Table 3 Logistic Regression Using Dichotomous Measures of Personal and Social Drinking
Problems as Dependent Variables (n = 389) Examining Drinking Contexts and Gender as
Predictors

Factor	β	SE	t ratio	df	Significance	95% Confidence Expanded β	Interval
Dependent Variable							
College Alcohol							
Problem Scale: personal							
problems	.54	.07	53.20	1	.000	1.72	1.49 to 1.99
Negative coping	.09	.03	10.30	30	1.00	1 1.10	1.04 to 1.16
Gender x convivial	−1.65	.20	71.60	1	.000	.19	
Constant							
Dependent Variable							
College Alcohol							
Problem Scale:							
social problems							
Convivial drinking	.20	.05	18.79	1	.000	1.22	1.12 to 1.34
Negative coping	.25	.08	10.53	1	.001	1.29	1.11 to 1.50
Intimate drinking	.23	.07	12.74	1	.000	1.26	1.11 to 1.43
Gender	.59	.26	5.36	1	.021	1.81	1.09 to 2.98
Constant	−2.59	.34	57.73	1	.000	.08	

excessively when partying at a concert, as a prelude to sex or when angry with themselves or others. Overall, correlation data show a moderate significant relationship between drinking context and problem drinking overall. Logistic regression demonstrated that those respondents who reported a higher likelihood of drinking to cope with negative emotions were more likely to report personal problems related to drinking, and males who drank excessively in convivial circumstances also reported more personal problems. Respondents who reported a greater likelihood of drinking excessively in convivial and intimate situations and when coping with negative emotions, were more likely to report greater social problems. Being male independently predicted a higher rate of social problems related to drinking. Thus, the main hypothesis of the study is confirmed: Drinking problems are likely to be differentially associated with drinking contexts. Although all situations in which young persons drink excessively appear to predict social problems, only drinking to cope with negative emotions predicted personal problems. However, gender also appears to play a significant role. Being male independently predicted more social problems related to drinking, and males who drank excessively in convivial circumstances were more likely to report personal problems, an unexpected finding in the current study. These findings generally replicate previous data on youthful drinking (O'Hare, 2001) and further support the validity of the DCS-9.

In general, these students demonstrated that most excessive youthful drinking is primarily associated with convivial, celebratory, and otherwise social events, a finding reflected in previous research with similar groups (Carey, 1993). They are less likely to drink excessively in romantic or intimate circumstances, and even less so as a way of coping with negative emotions. Nevertheless, whether drinking excessively during positive activities or when dealing with personal distress, young persons who do so incur significant risks for negative consequences. However, these data reveal quite clearly that the types of problems likely to result from heavy drinking are contextually determined: Those students who drink excessively to cope with negative emotions are more likely than those who drink in social circumstances (i.e., convivial or intimate drinking) to suffer psychological and emotional disturbances in addition to negative social consequences. This additional risk provides important data when considering differential assessment and intervention strategies.

Overall, levels of self-reported drinking problems tend to be lower than one might expect for this group of young persons. However, evidence has consistently shown that, although college students are willing to disclose prodigious amounts of alcohol consumption, they do not necessarily link their drinking with negative consequences, nor do they generally consider the consequences of heavy drinking to be serious (O'Hare & Tran, 1997; Perkins, 2002; Wechsler et al., 1994). Nevertheless, these data, in part, do reflect larger epidemiological patterns in gender differences. Males, in the current sample, are more likely to incur social and community problems as a result of problem drinking. Unplanned sex and illegal drug activities can both be considered at least moderately antisocial behaviors. Although general population data reveal greater co-occurrence between substance abuse and emotional disorders in adolescent and adult women, these differences were not evident in the current sample and may have been masked by the fact that this group is not representative of young college women. However, previous research with cohorts of this sample (O'Hare & Sherrer, 2000) and other college drinking studies (O'Hare, 1990; Wechsler et al., 1994) have revealed that, despite drinking considerably less than college males, women experience disproportionately more problems relative to consumption level, perhaps

because of inherent psychological and physiological vulnerabilities to the effects of alcohol (Wechsler et al., 1995).

Differentiating interpersonal and community consequences from psychological difficulties is more likely to lead to effective prevention efforts than relying on one-size-fits-all prevention strategies aimed at general reductions in alcohol consumption. Differential assessment can lead to more tailored interventions that emphasize psychotherapeutic or disciplinary measures, or a combination of both. Most college prevention strategies emphasize neo-prohibition models that assume a linear relationship between alcohol consumption and associated problems. However, despite massive increases in educational and environmental management prevention efforts (Clapp, Segars & Voas, 2002; Wechsler et al., 2002), there is little evidence that average rates of consumption have declined (Wechsler et al., 2002). The lack of evidence for the effectiveness of university substance prevention programs (Werch, Pappas, & Castellon-Vogel, 1996) presents a significant challenge to university administrators.

In contrast, harm reduction strategies take a more realistic view by encouraging moderation and teaching young persons skills to reduce drinking-related problems (e.g., car wrecks, HIV transmission, exacerbating emotional and psychological problems). Brief cognitive-behavioral strategies with harm-reduction goals targeting at-risk students appear to be the most promising interventions at this time (Borsari & Carey, 2000; Marlatt et al., 1998; Roberts, Neal, Kivlahan, Baer, & Marlatt, 2000). Components of these programs include some combination of motivational enhancement techniques, psycho-education about the effects of drinking, self-monitoring, drinking-moderation skills, and nutrition and exercise counseling, among other methods. Individualized assessment of contextually specific drinking and associated risks is essential for the successful implementation of these skill-based interventions. Given that college freshmen drink more than their noncollege counterparts in the community, it is reasonable to consider adapting these methods for other young men and women with substance abuse problems. Social workers who provide services for adolescent and young adult substance abusers would be well-advised to learn evidence-based cognitive-behavioral methods whether they are employed in high schools, colleges, or community treatment centers. Those who are charged with evaluating these programs should measure outcomes that include not only reduction in consumption levels and degree of personal and social problems but also a reduction in drinking in high-risk situations.

Limitations of This Study

This sample disproportionately represents students who got caught and, thus, may mask gender differences. It should also be noted that factors other than context and gender must be considered in any model of problem drinking. These factors include genetic predisposition, family history of drinking problems, and cultural background, among others. In addition, the associations between drinking contexts and problems are based on self-reported estimates of these behaviors. Future research on context-specific drinking should also employ self-monitoring methods, such as keeping personal diaries to link specific high-risk circumstances with personal or social problems related to drinking.

REFERENCES

Abbey, A. (2002) Alcohol-related sexual assault: A common problem among college students. *Journal of Studies on Alcohol, 63,* 118–128.

Borsari, B., & Carey, K. B. (2000). Effects of brief motivational intervention with college student drinkers. *Journal of Consulting and Clinical Psychology, 68,* 728–733.

Brown, S. A., Christiansen, B. A., & Goldman, M. S. (1987). The Alcohol Expectancy Questionnaire: An instrument for the assessment of adolescent and adult alcohol expectancies. *Journal of Studies on Alcohol, 48,* 483–491.

Carey, K. B. (1993). Situational determinants of heavy drinking among college students. *Journal of Counseling Psychology, 40,* 217–220.

Carroll, J. L., & Carroll, L. M. (1995). Alcohol use and risky sex among college students. *Psychological Reports, 76,* 723–726.

Clapp, J. D., Segars, L., & Voas, R. (2002). A conceptual model of the alcohol environment of colleges students. *Journal of Human Behavior in the Social Environment, 5,* 73–90.

Cooper, M. L. (2002). Alcohol use and risky sexual behavior among college students and youth: Evaluating the evidence. *Journal of Studies on Alcohol, 63,* 101–117.

Cooper, M. L., & Orcutt, H. K. (1997). Drinking and sexual experience on first dates among adolescents. *Journal of Abnormal Psychology, 106,* 191–202.

Cooper, M. L., Russell, M., & George, W. H. (1988). Coping, expectancies and alcohol abuse: A test of social learning theory formulations. *Journal of Abnormal Psychology, 97,* 218–230.

Evans, D. M., & Dunn, N. J. (1995). Alcohol expectancies, coping responses and self-efficacy judgments: A replication and extension of Cooper et al's 1988 study in a college sample. *Journal of Studies on Alcohol, 56,* 186–193.

Gfoerer, J. C., Greenblatt, J. C., & Wright, D. A. (1997). Substance use in the U.S. college-age population: Differences according to educational status and living arrangement. *American Journal of Public Health, 87,* 62–65.

Greenfield, T. K., & Rogers, J. D. (1999). Who drinks most of the alcohol in the U.S.? The policy implications. *Journal of Studies on Alcohol, 60,* 78–89.

Hosmer, D. W., & Lemeshow, S. (1989). *Applied logistic regression.* New York: Wiley.

Kandel, D. B., Johnson, J. G., Bird, H. R., Canino, G., Goodman, S. H., Lahey, B. B., et al. (1997). Psychiatric disorders associated with substance use among children and adolescents: Findings from the Methods for the Epidemiology of Child and Adolescent Mental Disorders (MECA) Study. *Journal of Abnormal Child Psychology*, *25*, 121–132.

Kessler, R. C., Nelson, C. B., McGonagle, K. A., Edlund, M. J., Frank, R. G., & Leaf, P. J. (1996). The epidemiology of co-occurring addictive and mental disorders: Implications for prevention and service utilization. *American Journal of Orthopsychiatry*, *66*, 17–31.

Knight, J. R., Wechsler, H., Kou, M., Seibering, M., Weitzman, E. R., & Schuckit, M. A. (2002). Alcohol abuse and dependence among U.S. college students. *Journal of Studies on Alcohol*, *63*, 263–270.

Maddock, J. E., LaForge, R. G., Rossi, J. S., & O'Hare, T. (2001). The College Alcohol Problems Scale. *Addictive Behaviors*, *26*, 385–398.

Maisto, S., Carey, K., & Bradizza, C. (1999). Social learning theory. In K. E. Leonard & H. T. Blane (Eds.), *Psychological theories of drinking and alcoholism* (chap. 3, pp. 106–163). New York: The Guilford Press.

Marlatt, G. A., Baer, J. S., Kivlahan, D. R., Dimeff, L. A., Larimer, M. E., Quigley, L. A., et al. (1998). Screening and brief intervention for high-risk college student drinkers: Results from a 2-year follow-up assessment. *Journal of Consulting and Clinical Psychology*, *66*, 604–615.

Norris, J. (1994). Alcohol and female sexuality: A look at expectancies and risks. *Alcohol Health and Research World*, *18*, 197–201.

O'Hare, T. (1990). Drinking in college: Consumption patterns, problems, sex differences and legal drinking age. *Journal of Studies on Alcohol*, *51*, 536–541.

O'Hare, T. (1997a). Measuring excessive alcohol use in college drinking contexts: The Drinking Context Scale. *Addictive Behaviors*, *22*, 469–477.

O'Hare, T. (1997b). Measuring problem drinking in first time offenders: Development and validation of the College Alcohol Problem Scale. *Journal of Substance Abuse Treatment*, *14*, 383–387.

O'Hare, T. (1998a). Alcohol expectancies and excessive drinking contexts in young adults. *Social Work Research*, *22*, 44–50.

O'Hare, T. (1998b). Replicating the College Alcohol Problem Scale with college first offenders. *Journal of Alcohol and Drug Education*, *43*, 75–82.

O'Hare, T. (2001). The Drinking Context Scale: A confirmatory factor analysis. *Journal of Substance Abuse Treatment*, *20*, 129–136.

O'Hare, T., & Sherrer, M. V. (2000). Co-occurring stress and substance abuse in college first offenders. *Journal of Human Behavior in the Social Environment*, *3*, 29–44.

O'Hare, T., & Tran, T. V. (1997). Predicting problem drinking in college students: Gender differences and the CAGE questionnaire. *Addictive Behaviors*, *22*, 13–21.

O'Malley, P. M., & Johnston, L. D. (2002). Epidemiology of alcohol and other drug use among American college students. *Journal of Studies on Alcohol*, *63*, 23–39.

O'Neill, S. E., Parra, G. R., & Sher, K. J. (2001). Clinical relevance of heavy drinking during the college years: Cross-sectional and prospective perspectives. *Psychology of Addictive Behaviors*, *15*, 350–359.

Perkins, W. (2002). Surveying the damage: A review of research on consequences of alcohol misuse in college populations. *Journal of Studies on Alcohol*, *63*, 91–100.

Roberts, L. J., Neal, D. J., Kivlahan, D. R., Baer, J. S., & Marlatt, G. A. (2000). Individual drinking changes following a brief intervention among college students: Clinical significance in an indicated preventive context. *Journal of Consulting and Clinical Psychology*, *68*, 500–505.

Ross, H. E., & Tisdall, G. W. (1994). Alcohol use and abuse in a university psychiatric health service: Prevalence and patterns of co-morbidity with other psychiatric problems. *Journal of Alcohol and Drug Education*, *39*, 63–74.

Schulenberg, J. E., & Maggs, J. L. (2002). A developmental perspective on alcohol use and heavy drinking during adolescence and the transition to young adulthood. *Journal of Studies on Alcohol, 63,* 54–70.

Sher, K. J., Wood, P. K., & Gotham, H. J. (1996). The course of psychological distress in college: A prospective high-risk study. *Journal of College Student Development, 37,* 42–51.

Tabachnick, B. G., & Fidell, L. S. (2001). *Using multivariate statistics* (4th ed.). Needham Heights, MA: Allyn & Bacon.

Wechsler, H., Davenport, A., Dowdall, G., Moeykens, B., & Costillow, S. (1994). Health and behavioral consequences of binge drinking in college. *Journal of the American Medical Association, 272,* 1672–1677.

Wechsler, H., Dowdall, G., Davenport, A., & Rimm, E. (1995). A gender-specific measure of binge drinking among college students. *American Journal of Public Health, 85,* 982–985.

Wechsler, H., Lee, J. E., Kuo, M., & Lee, H. (2000). College binge drinking in the 1990's: A continued problem: Results of the Harvard School of Public Health 1999 College Alcohol Study. *American Journal of College Health, 48,* 199–210.

Wechsler, H., Lee, J. E., Kuo, M., Seibring, M., Nelson, T. F., & Lee, H. (2002). Trends in college binge drinking during a period of increased prevention efforts: Findings from 4 Harvard School of Public Health College Alcohol Study Surveys: 1993-2001. *Journal of American College Health, 50,* 203–217.

Werch, C. E., Pappas, D. M., & Castellon-Vogel, E. A. (1996). Drug use prevention efforts at colleges and universities in the United States. *Substance Use and Misuse, 31,* 65–80.

4

VALIDATING THE ALCOHOL USE DISORDERS IDENTIFICATION TEST WITH PERSONS WHO HAVE A SERIOUS MENTAL ILLNESS

THOMAS O'HARE

BOSTON COLLEGE

MARGARET V. SHERRER

SOUTH SHORE MENTAL HEALTH CENTER, INC.

ANNAMARIA LaBUTTI AND KELLY EMRICK

FELLOWSHIP HEALTH RESOURCES, INC.

Objective/Method: The use of brief, reliable, valid, and practical measures of substance use is critical for conducting individual assessments and program evaluation for integrated mental health–substance abuse services for persons with serious mental illness. This investigation examines the internal consistency reliability, concurrent validity, and receiver operating characteristics of the Alcohol Use Disorders Identification Test (AUDIT) with 149 mentally ill adults in community programs. Results/Conclusions: Results suggest that the AUDIT is a reliable screening tool and shows good concurrent validity with other measures of alcohol abuse and psychosocial difficulties. In addition, receiver operating characteristics suggest that, for this population, a lower cutoff score (≥ 3) leads to more accurate detection of an alcohol use disorder (based on the Alcohol Use

Authors' Note: Please direct all correspondence to Thomas O'Hare, PhD, Boston College Graduate School of Social Work, 202 McGuinn Hall, Chestnut Hill, MA 02167-3807.

SOURCE: "Validating the Alcohol Use Disorders Identification Test With Persons Who Have a Serious Mental Illness" by Thomas O'Hare, Margaret V. Sherrer, Annamaria LaButti, and Kelly Emrick. In the 2004 issue of *Research on Social Work Practice, 14*(1), 36–42. Used with permission.

Scale) than the traditional cutoff (≥ 8). This article discusses implications for using screens routinely as part of assessment and evaluation with this population.

Keywords: *the Alcohol Use Disorders Identification Test (AUDIT); Psycho-Social Wellbeing Scale (PSWS); serious mental illness; co-occuring mental health and substance abuse; substance abuse screening*

The abuse of alcohol and other drugs has come to be seen as a major co-occurring problem for persons with serious mental illness. There is growing recognition of the need to improve detection of substance use as part of assessment and treatment evaluation efforts within integrated mental health and substance abuse services (Brems & Johnson, 1997; Drake et al., 1998; Drake & Mueser, 2000; Drake, Rosenberg, & Mueser, 1996; O'Hare, 2002). Although a number of reliable and valid instruments are available for capturing substance abuse data, few have been validated for use with persons who experience major mental illness, and practical problems make it difficult to incorporate them into routine practice. For example, the well-respected Addiction Severity Index (ASI) (McLellan, Luborsky, Woody, & O'Brien, 1980) covers the multidimensional spectrum of problems often associated with substance abuse, but it also requires considerable training and takes at least an hour to complete. Although this may be adequate for an agency exclusively focused on substance abuse, it would demand considerable effort in a broader psychosocial assessment for persons also suffering from many other difficulties. In addition, instruments such as the ASI, although they have a proven track record with primary substance abuse populations, have not been shown to be as valid with persons who suffer from severe mental illness (e.g., Zanis, McLellan, & Corse, 1997).

Other well-known screening tools such as the CAGE (Cut down, Annoyed, Guilty, Eye opener) and the Michigan Alcoholism Screening Test (MAST) are limited in their application to monitoring and evaluation instruments because they are used to query lifetime drinking and, thus, are not sensitive to detecting change in a client's behavior over time. However, one of the most effective methods for detecting substance abuse problems in health and mental health treatment populations has proven to be the simple paper-and-pencil screening tool (Babor, Kranzler, & Lauerman, 1989; Wolford et al., 1999). Evidence for the inter-rater reliability, validity, and utility of simple substance abuse indexes such as the 1-item Alcohol Use Scale (AUS) and Drug Use Scale (DUS) has been demonstrated with more extensive standardized instruments (Barry et al., 1995; Carey, Cocco, & Simons, 1996; Drake et al., 1998).

Another brief alcohol screening instrument with a growing track record of reliability and validity across different populations and clinical settings is the Alcohol Use Disorders Identification Test (AUDIT) (Babor & Grant, 1989; Bohn, Babor, & Kranzler, 1995). In an international (10 nations) study of alcohol abusers in a primary healthcare setting, the AUDIT was demonstrated to have good reliability, concurrent validity, and good to excellent sensitivity and specificity ratings for problem drinking (Saunders, Aasland, Babor et al., 1993). Barry and Fleming (1993) found the AUDIT to be internally reliable (alpha .85) and more efficient (at ≥ 8) than the Short MAST in detecting problem drinking among rural primary care patients. Other comparisons to common screening devices demonstrated that the AUDIT generally performed better (i.e., more optimal balance of sensitivity and specificity) than the CAGE and the Short MAST (Cherpitel & Clark, 1995). In a recent study of family medical practice patients, the receiver operating characteristics of the AUDIT were tested using the Alcohol Use Disorders and Associated Disabilities Interview Schedule (AUDADIS), which is derived from the *Diagnostic and Statistical Manual of Mental Disorders* (DSM), as criterion measure (Volk, Steinbauer, Cantor, & Holzer, 1997). Results indicated that the accuracy (i.e., area under the curve) of the AUDIT for detecting dependent clients ranged from .90 to .96 across male, female, White, and African American groups; sensitivity and specificity for detecting "at-risk" drinking (i.e., dependent, problem, and hazardous drinking) were good at a cutoff score of 4 (.85 and .84 for specificity and sensitivity, respectively). Recent investigations with both college studies (O'Hare & Sherrer, 1999) and outpatient mental health clients (Karno, Granholm, & Lin, 2000) demonstrated very good internal consistency reliability (.89), but factor analytic techniques did not support the hypothesized three-factor structure (consumption, dependence, consequences). The AUDIT appears to be better defined as having a two-factor structure of consumption (items 1–3 on the AUDIT) and alcohol-related problems and dependence symptoms (items 4–10). Item 9 (caused injury to self or others), however, appeared to be problematic (i.e., ambiguous factor loadings) in Karno et al. (2000) and Dawe, Seinen, and Kavanagh (2000). A recent investigation also supported a two-factor structure for the AUDIT (Maisto, Conigliaro, McNeil, Kraemer, & Kelly, 2000).

Only recently, however, have the psychometric properties of the AUDIT been analyzed with mentally ill persons. In one study, 71 persons (53 men, 18 women) with a serious mental illness (Dawe et al., 2000) were assessed with the AUDIT and the Composite International Diagnostic Interview as criteria. The AUDIT showed excellent sensitivity (.87) and specificity (.90) at a cutoff of ≥ 8 (surpassing the performance of all screens reviewed in Wolford et al., 1999), and it demonstrated very good internal consistency (.85) as a

paper-and-pencil self-report instrument. Maisto, Carey, Carey, Gordon, and Gleason (2000) interviewed psychiatric outpatients (93 men, 69 women) with serious mental illness to test the performance of the AUDIT against DSM-IV–structured interview criteria and found that an AUDIT score of ≥ 8 showed the highest sensitivity and specificity when judged against diagnostic criteria (i.e., an alcohol use disorder). When alcohol use disorder symptoms were used as criteria, an AUDIT score of ≥ 6 appeared to have the highest sensitivity. Positive predictive values appeared to be considerably higher when using lower cut scores. The authors suggested that the results be viewed with caution due to the low positive predictive value of the AUDIT in this sample, and they recommended that practitioners be concerned about any reported use of alcohol or other drugs by clients who have a serious mental illness.

Brief, reliable, valid, and practical screening methods should be incorporated into routine clinical assessment and program evaluation efforts in programs that serve mentally ill persons. Social workers, case managers, and other practitioners often collect these data, which play an increasingly essential role in coordinating community-based mental health and substance abuse services (Mueser, Bond, Drake, & Resnick, 1998; Scott & Dixon, 1995). They are in a uniquely advantageous position to assess and evaluate clients more frequently in their own environment. However, to better capitalize on this evaluative function, practitioners need valid, reliable, and practical instruments to capture basic substance abuse data. This study examines data collected by line clinicians employed by two mental health centers in Rhode Island as part of initiatives to develop outcome evaluation protocol. This study examines the reliability, validity, and receiver operating characteristics (ROC) of the AUDIT using the DSM-based Alcohol Use Scale as criterion. Receiver operating characteristics (i.e., sensitivity, specificity, positive predictor value, and area under the curve) (Griner, Mayewski, Mushlin, & Greenland, 1981; O'Hare, Cohen, & Sherrer, 1997) represent the most straightforward way of comparing a test scale against a criterion scale by combining "sensitivity and specificity in a manner that allows examination of the ability of tests to discriminate between two populations regardless of the cutoff level or weighting selected" (Wolford et al., 1999, p. 320). ROC data are more compelling than correlational analyses because those who deny substance abuse on both the AUDIT and the criterion variable (in this case, the AUS) would artificially inflate the correlation and, thus, erroneously suggest greater concurrent validity (Wolford et al., 1999).

METHOD

Sample

This investigation is based on combined samples ($N = 149$) from two community mental health centers in Rhode Island. The sample from agency #1 ($n = 100$) was derived from a systematic random sample of clients selected proportionately from several sites in the Northeast from a total of 580 clients. Clients interviewed in agency #2 ($n = 49$) were voluntary participants of a pilot investigation focused on treating mentally ill clients with substance abuse problems. Data in both samples were collected by line clinicians (bachelor's-and master's-level case managers and clinicians) in face-to-face interviews as part of routine service delivery contacts, and quality assurance officers approved the use of the instruments for this voluntary survey. These secondary data were not collected to compare the two programs in any way but were later combined to purposefully achieve a complement of clients with and without substance abuse problems. All clients received services from programs that treat persons with major mental illness, and, generally, client characteristics

from both settings are very similar. Notable differences in background client descriptors are mentioned next.

Background data from the combined sample are as follows: 89 (59.7%) were male, median age was 43 ($M = 42.7$, $SD = 10.2$). With respect to race, 130 (87.2%) were White, 11 (7.4%) Black, and 8 (5.4%) Hispanic. Mean age of onset of the clients' symptoms was 19.4 ($SD = 8.0$). Fifty-four (36.2%) were hospitalized for psychiatric reasons within the past year, and 143 (96.0%) were hospitalized at least once in their lifetimes. Ninety-one (61.1%) clients completed high school. Ninety-two (61.7%) were never married, 11 (7.4%) were married, and the remainder were either separated or divorced. One hundred and one (67.8%) were primarily dependent on supplementary security income, and only 25 (16.8%) were engaged in some paid employment. Fourteen (9.4%) were noncombat veterans. Seventy-six (51.0%) lived in private residences, and 64 (42.9%) lived in supported housing or group homes. About half (79, 53%) of the clients were diagnosed by staff psychiatrists with schizophrenia, 45 (30.2%) had major mood disorders, and 25 (16.8%) were assigned other axis I diagnoses. Agency #1 had proportionately more persons with schizophrenia (67.0% vs. 24.5%), and a greater proportion of them lived in group homes.

Instruments

AUDIT. The AUDIT is composed of 10 self-report items (scored continuously from 0–4; one item is scored 0–5; maximum score is 41). There are three items that measure alcohol use (quantity, frequency, and peak drinking: "six or more"), four items that measure dependence (unable to stop, failed responsibilities, eye opener, guilt), and three items that measure consequences (memory loss, injury to others, advised to cut down). The AUDIT is distinguished from other well-known screens in that the items are scored on a frequency continuum (rather than dichotomously), it requests measures over a limited time period (e.g., 6 months vs. lifetime), and it appears to have broader applicability by discriminating hazardous and harmful drinkers (i.e., at-risk problem drinkers) rather than those who are alcohol dependent (Saunders et al., 1993; Bohn et al., 1995).

AUS and DUS. The AUS and the DUS are single-item clinician-rated indexes of alcohol and drug abuse (Carey et al., 1996; Drake et al., 1998) measured on a 5-point scale (from *no problems* to *extremely severe*). Recent evidence suggests that the use of simple substance abuse indexes by case managers correlates well with more extensive batteries (Barry et al., 1995; Carey et al., 1996; Drake et al., 1998) and that these should be included as part of a brief, multidimensional assessment.

The Psycho-Social Wellbeing Scale. The Psycho-Social Wellbeing Scale (PSWS) is a multidimensional debriefing instrument used to summarize qualitative and quantitative clinical data collected from multiple sources. The 12 items that comprise the PSWS are rated by the practitioner on a 5-point scale (*excellent* = 4, *good* = 3, *marginal* = 2, *impaired* = 1, *poor* = 0) and cover the following problem domains: mental status–cognitive functioning, mental status–emotional functioning, impulse control, substance abuse, coping skills, health, recreational activities, living environment, immediate social network, extended social network, independent living, and work satisfaction. These items were constructed by reviewing the empirical assessment literature and related measurement research regarding psychiatric and psychosocial problems experienced by persons with severe and persistent mental illness. The initial investigation with the PSWS (O'Hare et al., 2003) was conducted with 297 community clients (55.9% female, median age 43, mostly persons with schizophrenia and major mood disorders). Two main factors emerged when exploratory factor analysis (replicated with confirmatory factor analysis) was used: psychological and social well-being. Four other items were retained as "stand-alone" indexes: global substance abuse index (GSAI), health, activities of daily living, and work satisfaction. Internal consistency was good for both brief (4-item) subscales (psychological and social) at .84 and .79, respectively. A Pearson's correlation for the psychological and social well-being subscales (r = .51, p < .001) demonstrated good discriminant validity. Testimonial evidence from many line clinicians suggests good face validity and ease of use. Although scales should be used on larger and more representative populations prior to establishing norms, conditional norms are suggested: The summary scores for the two (4-item) subscales (psychological and social) are *poor* (0–2), *impaired* (3–6), *marginal* (7–9), *good* (10–13), and *excellent* (14–16). For the two (4-item) subscales, any subscale score below 10 should be a focus of concern and any score of 2 or less (i.e., marginal, impaired, poor) should warrant clinical attention.

High-risk events. The frequency of client self-reported high risk events that occurred within the past 6 months was examined. These included events in which the client was victimized (e.g., physically or sexually abused), engaged in risky activities (e.g., self-mutilation, running away, unprotected sex, or injected street drugs), and engaged in criminal activities including misdemeanors (e.g., shoplifting) and felonies (e.g., robbery or assault). Items chosen were drawn from the literature concerning stressful events that negatively affect client well-being. For example, research on the association between traumatic events (Mueser, Trumbetta, et al., 1998) and criminal behavior by mentally ill persons (Nieves, Draine, & Solomon, 2000) is increasing. Practitioners should be aware of these relatively infrequent but critical events because they are likely to have important implications for treatment.

RESULTS

Frequency Distributions of Major Factors

Means and standard deviations for the main study factors are as follows: AUDIT, $M = 4.3$, $SD = 8.5$; psychological subscale of the PSWS, $M = 9.4$, $SD = 3.1$; social subscale of the PSWS, $M = 9.4$, $SD = 3.4$. Means and standard deviations for the four 1-item indexes of the PSWS are as follows: Global Substance Abuse Index (GSAI), $M = 2.9$, $SD = 1.4$; health, $M = 2.5$, $SD = .9$; activities of daily living, $M = 2.6$, $SD = 1.0$; work satisfaction, $M = 1.9$, $SD = 1.3$. Univariate data from the Global Assessment of Functioning is $M = 50.0$, $SD = 10.7$.

Frequency and percentages for responses to the 1-item AUS are as follows: "abstinent" = 97, 65.1%; "use without impairment" = 15, 10.1%; "abuse" = 15, 10.1%; "dependence" = 17, 11.4%; "dependence with institutionalization" = 1, .7%. The AUS was also divided into a dichotomous variable to be used as a diagnostic criterion for testing the receiver operating characteristics of the AUDIT. Frequencies and percentages for the two categories are as follows: "abstinent and use without impairment" = 112, 75.2% and "abuse, dependence and dependence with institutionalization" = 33, 22.2%, corresponding to DSM criteria for an alcohol-use disorder (four cases showed missing data).

High-Risk Events

Respondents were queried about a number of high risk events occurring over the past 6 months. Frequencies and percents of each of these occurrences are as follows: was physically abused = 9, 6.0%; was sexually abused = 6, 4.0%; attempted suicide = 12, 8.1%; engaged in self-mutilation = 13, 8.7%; ran away or was unaccounted for = 10, 6.7%; engaged in misdemeanors = 9, 6.0%; committed a felony = 5, 3.4%; threatened another person verbally or physically = 26, 17.4%; was violent toward another person = 8, 5.4%; sexually assaulted another person = 2, 1.3%; abused substances = 49, 32.9%; overdosed on prescribed medication = 9, 6.0%; injected drugs with a shared needle = 2, 1.3%; engaged in sex without protection = 28, 18.8%.

Reliability Ratings for Major Factors

Chronbach's alpha was calculated for the AUDIT (.95) and the PSWS 4-item psychological (.77) and social (.79) subscales.

Correlational Analysis of Major Variables

The AUDIT raw score correlated in the expected direction with the PSWS psychological subscale ($r = -.45$, $p < .001$) and the PSWS social subscale ($r = -.56$, $p < .001$), showing significant moderate correlations. Those clients with more serious drinking problems experience worse psychological and social well-being. The AUDIT also significantly correlated as expected with GSAI ($r = -.64$, $p < .001$), health ($r = -.21$, $p < .05$), activities of daily life ($r = -.25$, $p < .01$) and work satisfaction ($r = -.33$, $p < .001$). The AUDIT also correlated significantly with the AUS ($r = .67$, $p < .001$). The following high-risk items showed low but significant correlations with the AUDIT raw score (Spearman correlation is used due to dichotomous, nonnormal distributions on the individual high-risk items): physically abused ($rho = .18$, $p < .05$), engaged in self-mutilation ($rho = .22$, $p < .01$), ran away or was unaccounted for ($rho = .23$, $p < .01$), engaged in misdemeanors ($rho = .25$, $p < .01$), threatened another person verbally or physically ($rho = .17$, $p < .05$), was violent toward another person ($rho = .20$, $p < .05$), abused substances ($rho = .68$, $p < .001$), engaged in sex without protection ($rho = .32$, $p < .001$).

Table 1   Receiver Operating Characteristics of the AUDIT at Several Cutoff Scores With the Alcohol Use Scale as Criteria (N = 149)

Cutoff Score	Sensitivity/Specificity (%)	PPV (%)	Area Under Curve
≥ 1	100.00/77.5	55.4	.887
≥ 2	100.00/78.4	56.4	.892
≥ 3	100.00/86.5	67.4	.932
≥ 4	93.55/88.3	69.1	.909
≥ 5	87.10/92.8	77.1	.899
≥ 6	80.65/92.8	75.8	.867
≥ 7	74.19/94.6	79.3	.844
≥ 8	70.97/94.6	78.6	.828
≥ 9	50.06/94.6	75.0	.763
≥ 10	51.61/95.5	76.2	.736

NOTE: Sensitivity = probability that the test result will be positive when the condition (diagnosis) is present; specificity = probability that the test result will be negative when the condition is not present; PPV = positive predictive value, probability that the condition is present when the test is positive.

ROC Analysis With Audit and the AUS as Diagnostic Criterion Variable

Analysis with a range of cut scores can be reviewed in Table 1. In general, it appears that a cutoff score of ≥ 3 predicts the AUS (i.e., abuse/dependence) most accurately.

DISCUSSION AND APPLICATIONS TO SOCIAL WORK PRACTICE

These results suggest that the AUDIT is a reliable and valid indicator of problem drinking in persons with serious mental illness. Correlations between the AUDIT and other psychosocial indicators also suggest not only that the AUDIT detects problem drinking but that clients who abuse alcohol are experiencing more psychological and social distress including poorer health, impaired living skills, and less satisfaction with work. In addition, receiver operating characteristics in this study support a lower cut score (≥ 3) for the AUDIT than previously suggested. A recent investigation (Hulse, Saunders,

Roydhouse, Stockwell, & Basso, 2000) used the AUDIT with the standard cut (≥ 8) with 665 hospitalized psychiatric patients, and it found fewer patients consuming alcohol at hazardous, harmful, or dependent levels than is generally reported in the literature. It is possible that when the AUDIT is employed with standard cut scores it fails to detect the negative consequences of lower amounts of alcohol in persons with serious mental illness. Dawe et al. (2000) reported 87% sensitivity and 90% specificity for AUDIT at a cutoff of ≥ 8 using DSM-IV and International Classification of Disease–10 criteria derived from the Composite International Diagnostic Interview with a small sample of hospitalized psychiatric clients. The current study achieved similar sensitivity (87.1%) and specificity (92.8%) at a cutoff of ≥ 5. Maisto, Carey, et al. (2000) employed the AUDIT with 162 clients with serious mental illness with the structured interview schedule to obtain a DSM-IV diagnosis and found that a cutoff score of ≥ 8 achieved 95% sensitivity but only 65% specificity. The positive predictive value was very low (31%) with an overall correct identification of a modest 69%. However, when a less stringent criteria of alcohol-use symptoms was used, a cutoff of ≥ 5 achieved a 90% sensitivity, 72% specificity, and a positive predictive value of 72%. Cutoffs lower than 5 were not reported in the table. The authors suggested that clinical utility should be an important consideration given that "even small amounts of substance use could have negative consequences" (Maisto, Carey, et al., 2000, p. 191). As previously noted, Volk et al. (1997) used the AUDIT to detect combined "at-risk and dependent drinkers" (similar to combined abuse and dependence in the current study), and found a cut score of ≥ 4 to achieve the best balance of sensitivity (85%) and specificity (84%). However, the data implied a low positive predictive value (not reported) using the AUDADIS as the criterion variable.

Although it is difficult to compare test performances across different studies given variations in samples, training, implementation of paper-and-pencil versus structured interview methods, differences in diagnostic criteria, and, perhaps, time frames referenced for reporting, it appears that a lower cut score for the AUDIT may be in order when used with populations, such as the mentally ill, who are more at risk to suffer negative psychological and social consequences from excessive drinking. Using lower cut points for this population may make sense given the greater vulnerability of mentally ill persons to the cognitive, emotional, physiological, and behavioral effects of drugs (including alcohol). Drinking even relatively small amounts of alcohol can increase anxiety and depression and can interfere with the effectiveness of psychotropic medications.

Integrated mental health–substance abuse programs have demonstrated promising results for improved treatment engagement, better housing, and overall adjustment when compared with standard case management (Drake, Yovetich, Bebout, Harris, & McHugo, 1997; Drake et al., 1998; Bellack & DiClemente, 1999). Because common multidimensional goals are targeted by both mental health and substance abuse treatment efforts, the AUDIT could be a valid, reliable, useful, and inexpensive way for social workers who work with mentally ill persons to monitor client progress in reducing alcohol use. Evaluation methods employed in typical agency environments are best served when several ingredients are included in the design: routine integration of qualitative and quantitative judgements or measures, employing data from multiple points of view, timeliness and utility of measures, and using data at both the ideographic (individual client) and aggregated (program or agency) levels. These data can be useful in responding to private-public managed care payers, licensing reviewers, and accrediting bodies and for documenting the implementation of evidence-based practices (Bickman & Salzer, 1997; Howard & Jenson, 1999; O'Hare, 2002). The AUDIT would serve as a valuable component in such an evaluation strategy.

Limitations of this study include the lack of a more extensive diagnostic evaluation of the clients' substance abuse problems such as those that can be provided by structured interview diagnostic instruments. In addition, this study only examined a relatively small sample of clients from two agencies. More research is needed to examine the validity and generalizability of the AUDIT with persons who suffer from severe and persistent mental illnesses.

REFERENCES

Babor, T. F., & Grant, M. (1989). From clinical research to secondary prevention: International collaboration in the development of the Alcohol Use Disorders Identification Test (AUDIT). *Alcohol Health and Research World*, *13*(4), 371–374.

Babor, T. F., Kranzler, H. R., & Lauerman, R. J. (1989). Early detection of harmful alcohol consumption: Comparison of clinical, laboratory, and self-report screening procedures. *Addictive Behaviors*, *13*, 139–157.

Barry, K. L., & Fleming, M. F. (1993). The Alcohol Use Disorders Identification Test (AUDIT) and the SMAST-13: Predictive validity in a rural primary care sample. *Alcohol and Alcoholism, 28,* 33–42.

Barry, K. L., Fleming, M. F., Greenley, J., Widlak, P., Kropp, S., & McKee, D. (1995). Assessment of alcohol and other drug disorders in the seriously mentally ill. *Schizophrenia Bulletin, 21,* 313–321.

Bellack, A. S., & DiClemente, C. C. (1999). Treating substance abuse among patients with schizophrenia. *Psychiatric Services, 50,* 75–80.

Bickman, L., & Salzer, M. S. (1997). Introduction: Measuring quality in mental health services. *Evaluation Review, 21,* 285–291.

Bohn, M. J., Babor, T. F., & Kranzler, H. R. (1995). Alcohol Use Disorders Identification Test (AUDIT): Validation of a screening instrument for use in medical settings. *Journal of Studies on Alcohol, 56,* 423–432.

Brems, C., & Johnson, M. E. (1997). Clinical implications of the co-occurrence of substance use and other psychiatric disorders. *Professional Psychology Research and Practice, 28,* 437–447.

Carey, K. B., Cocco, K. M., & Simons, J. S. (1996). Concurrent validity of clinicians' ratings of substance abuse among psychiatric outpatients. *Psychiatric Services, 47,* 842–847.

Cherpitel, C. J., & Clark, W. B. (1995). Ethnic differences in performance of screening instruments for identifying harmful drinking and alcohol dependence in the emergency room. *Alcoholism: Clinical and Experimental Research, 19,* 628–634.

Dawe, S., Seinen, A., & Kavanagh, D. (2000). An examination of the utility of the AUDIT in people with schizophrenia. *Journal of Studies on Alcohol, 61,* 744–750.

Drake, R. E., McHugo, G. J., Clark, R. E., Teague, G. B., Xie, H., Miles, K., et al. (1998). Assertive community treatment for patients with co-occurring severe mental illness and substance use disorder: a clinical trial. *American Journal of Orthopsychiatry, 68,* 201–215.

Drake, R. E., & Mueser, K. T. (2000). Psychosocial approaches to dual diagnosis. *Schizophrenia Bulletin, 26,* 105–118.

Drake, R. E., Rosenberg, S. D., & Mueser, K. T. (1996). Assessing substance use disorder in persons with severe mental illness. *New Directions for Mental Health Services, 70,* 3–17.

Drake, R. E., Yovetich, N. A., Bebout, R. R., Harris, M., & McHugo, G. J. (1997). Integrated treatment for dually diagnosed homeless adults. *Journal of Nervous and Mental Disease, 180,* 298–305.

Griner, P. F., Mayewski, R. J., Mushlin, A. I., & Greenland, P. (1981). Selection and interpretation of diagnostic tests and procedures. *Annals of Internal Medicine, 94,* 553–592.

Howard, M. O., & Jenson, J. M. (1999). Clinical practice guidelines: Should social work develop them? *Research on Social Work Practice, 9,* 283–301.

Hulse, G. K., Saunders, J. B., Roydhouse, R. M., Stockwell, T. R., & Basso, M. R. (2000). Screening for hazardous alcohol use and dependence in psychiatric in-patients using the AUDIT questionnaire. *Drug and Alcohol Review, 19,* 291–298.

Karno, M., Granholm, E., & Lin, A. (2000). Factor structure of the Alcohol Use Disorders Identification Test (AUDIT) in a mental health clinic sample. *Journal of Studies on Alcohol, 61,* 751–758.

Maisto, S. A., Carey, M. P., Carey, K. B., Gordon, C. M., & Gleason, J. R. (2000). Use of the AUDIT and the DAST-10 to identify alcohol and drug use disorders among adults with severe and persistent mental illness. *Psychological Assessment, 12,* 186–192.

Maisto, S. A., Conigliaro, J., McNeil, M., Kraemer, K., & Kelley, M. E. (2000). An empirical investigation of the factor structure of the AUDIT. *Psychological Assessment, 12,* 346–353.

McLellan, A. T., Luborsky, L., Woody, G. E., & O'Brien, C. P. (1980). An improved diagnostic evaluation instrument for substance abuse patients: the addition severity index. *Journal of Nervous and Mental Disorders, 168,* 26–33.

Mueser, K. T., Bond, G. R., Drake, R. E., & Resnick, S. G. (1998). Models of community care for severe mental illness: a review of research on case management. *Schizophrenia Bulletin, 24*, 37–74.

Mueser, K. T., Trumbetta, S. L., Rosenberg, S. D., Vidaver, R., Goodman, L.B., Osher, F. C., et al. (1998). Trauma and post-traumatic stress disorder in severe mental illness. *Journal of Consulting and Clinical Psychology, 66*, 493–499.

Nieves, K., Draine, J, & Solomon, P. (2000). The validity of self-reported criminal arrest history among clients of a psychiatric probation and parole service. *Journal of Offender Rehabilitation, 30*, 133–151.

O'Hare, T. (2002). Evidence-based social work practice with mentally ill persons who abuse alcohol and other drugs. *Social Work in Mental Health, 1*(2), 43–62.

O'Hare, T., Cohen, F. C., & Sherrer, M. V. (1997). Comparing the QFI, the retrospective diary and binge drinking in college first offenders. *Journal of Alcohol and Drug Education, 42*, 40–53.

O'Hare, T., & Sherrer, M. V. (1999). Validating the Alcohol Use Disorders Identification Test in college first offenders. *Journal of Substance Abuse Treatment, 17*, 113–119.

O'Hare, T., Sherrer, M. V., Cutler, J., McCall, T. M., Dominique, K. N., & Garlick, K. (2003). Validating the Psycho-Social Wellbeing Scale with community clients. *Social Work in Mental Health, 1*(2), 15–30.

Saunders, J. B., Aasland, O. G., Babor, T. F., de la Fuente, J. R., & Grant, M. (1993). Development of the Alcohol Use Disorders Identification test (AUDIT): WHO Collaborative Project on Early detection of Persons with Harmful alcohol Consumption-II. *Addiction, 88*, 791–804.

Scott, J. E., & Dixon, L. B. (1995). Assertive community treatment and case management for schizophrenia. *Schizophrenia Bulletin, 21*, 657–668.

Volk, R. J., Steinbauer, J. R., Cantor, S. B., & Holzer, C. E. (1997). The Alcohol Use Disorders Identification Test (AUDIT) as a screen for at-risk drinking in primary care patients of different racial/ethnic backgrounds. *Addiction, 92*, 197–206.

Wolford, G. L., Rosenberg, S. D., Drake, R. E., Mueser, K. T., Oxman, T. E., Hoffman, D., et al. (1999). Evaluation of methods for detecting substance use disorder in persons with severe mental illness. *Psychology of Addictive Behaviors, 13*, 313–326.

Zanis, D. A., McLellan, T. A., & Corse, S. (1997). Is the Addiction Severity Index a reliable and valid assessment instrument among clients with severe and persistent mental illness and substance abuse disorders? *Community Mental Health Journal, 33*, 213–227.

CRITICAL THINKING QUESTIONS

Reading 3

1. Why did the authors undertake this study?

2. What is the purpose of the DCS-9?

3. In what ways is the sample of students used in this study limited?

4. What factor seems most closely associated with having personal drinking-related problems?

5. How could further research on this assessment instrument improve upon the current study?

Reading 4

1. Why did the authors undertake this study?

2. What were the characteristics of the sample of respondents used in this study?

3. What may a score of 3 or higher on the AUDIT indicate?

4. How could further research on the AUDIT improve upon the current study?

PART III

Gender- and Culturally Based Interventions

Several themes transcend the readings in this section. The first of these is the impact of traumatic victimization on individual coping skills. The second is that the significance of gender in the experience of trauma and in pathways that lead to substance abuse and addiction generally. The importance of shaping treatment interventions to the special needs of clients, needs based on gender and cultural differences, is emphasized throughout the selections in Part III.

The first of the readings by Kubiak explores the relationship between posttraumatic stress disorder and substance abuse in men and women on parole. The findings, which are disturbing, have important implications for policy. This contribution deserves a close reading, not only because of what is shown about the link between trauma and substance abuse which is significant, but also because of what it says about the source of the trauma in men.

Johansson and Kempf-Leonard track official records of juveniles to empirically test feminist theory on pathways to delinquency. The methodology deserves special attention due to the difficulty in drawing qualitative data from official sources. An excellent review of the literature is contained in this offering. Tapia, Schwartz, et al. use a different form of evidence to describe an empirically-supported intervention with Latino families of adolescents at risk for substance abuse problems. *Familias Unidas* is a culturally specific program of demonstrated effectiveness.

As an introduction to issues pertaining to treatment effectiveness for women with alcohol problems, we have chosen to include a review of the research literature as provided by Karoll. The connection between traumatic experiences and drinking as self-medication is explored in this reading. A grasping of the significance of this fact is essential for an appreciation for the empirically-based findings presented by Bennett and O'Brien. Their research is of major significance to the fields of substance abuse treatment and domestic violence services. As background for the reading of this research you need to know that the feminist models that dominate in women's shelters are very different from the models that inform substance abuse treatment.

Substance abuse issues tend to be minimized in the former, and the reality of domestic violence tend to be overlooked in the latter. Having this awareness, you can appreciate the significance in this study in offering a systematic program evaluation of a unique pilot study that integrates services so that the dual problems can be handled simultaneously to enhance the protection of women who live in situations characterized by both substance abuse and family violence.

5

THE EFFECTS OF PTSD ON TREATMENT ADHERENCE, DRUG RELAPSE, AND CRIMINAL RECIDIVISM IN A SAMPLE OF INCARCERATED MEN AND WOMEN

SHERYL PIMLOTT KUBIAK

WAYNE STATE UNIVERSITY

Objective/Method: Given the relationship between posttraumatic stress disorder (PTSD) and substance use disorders (SUD), and the prevalence of SUD among offenders, the inattention to trauma before, during, and after incarceration is troubling. This exploratory study compared those with and without co-occurring PTSD among men (n = 139) and women (n = 60) involved in prison-based substance abuse treatment. Results: More than one half the sample met criteria for lifetime PTSD with women experiencing a greater number of events and men experiencing more recent events. Women with PTSD were significantly more likely to relapse than women without. Men with PTSD were more likely to enter community aftercare treatment and recidivate than those without. Conclusion: The findings suggest that trauma-related disorders, among those with SUD,

Author's Note: This work was supported through a National Institute of Mental Health Fellowship (T32 MH 19996-5). Thanks to Carol Boyd and Isabel Rose for their comments on earlier drafts. All correspondence should be directed to Sheryl Pimlott Kubiak, Assistant Professor, Wayne State University School of Social Work, 4756 Cass Ave, Detroit, MI 48202; e-mail: spk@wayne.edu.

SOURCE: "The Effects of PTSD on Treatment Adherence, Drug Relapse, and Criminal Recidivism in a Sample of Incarcerated Men and Women" by Sheryl Pimlott Kubiak. In the 2004 issue of *Research on Social Work Practice*, *14*(6), 424–443. Used with permission.

affect postincarceration outcomes. Therefore, from a practice and policy perspective, interventions addressing this co-occurring disorder should be available to men and women within the criminal justice system.

Keywords: *substance abuse; trauma; gender; treatment; prison*

Rarely is trauma discussed in relation to incarceration— either the effect of incarceration on those with trauma histories, prison as a site of new trauma, or the effect of trauma-related disorders on recidivism. This is particularly troublesome given the relationship between posttraumatic stress disorder (PTSD) and substance use disorders (SUD), and the high prevalence of SUD among those involved in the criminal justice system. Men and women entering prisons and jails have considerable histories of psychological trauma prior to incarceration (Gibson et al., 1999; Jordan, Schlenger, Fairbank, & Cadell, 1996; Kupers, 1996; Teplin, Abram, & McClelland, 1996), and certainly the incidence of violence within the institution has been well documented (Kupers, 1996; Toch, 1998; Websdale & Chesney-Lind, 1998). Although there is a dearth of information on the prevalence of offenders with both disorders, as many as 50% of those entering community-based substance abuse treatment are thought to have a co-occurring PTSD and generally demonstrate poorer long-term outcomes compared to those without (Ouimette, Finney, & Moos, 1999). Although prison-based treatment has generally been successful in reducing recidivism and relapse (Inciardi, Martin, Butzin, Hooper, & Harrison, 1997; Pelissier, Wallace, & O'Neil, 2001; Wexler, De Leon, Thomas, Kressel, & Peters, 1999), only 10% of those who need substance abuse treatment actually receive it (Lo & Stephens, 2000).

The purpose of the current study was to examine the prevalence of both disorders among men and women involved in prison-based substance abuse treatment and to compare treatment adherence, drug relapse, and criminal recidivism among those with and without symptoms of PTSD.

BACKGROUND

The incidence of co-occurring mental health and substance abuse disorders has been estimated to affect almost one half of those with serious and chronic mental health disorders (Kessler et al., 1997; Rogier et al., 1990). Those individuals with these dual disorders absorb a large proportion of the human and fiscal resources in the mental health and substance abuse service systems because they are among the most challenging to treat, often requiring repeated hospitalizations or intensive residential treatment (Drake, Yovetich, Bebout, Harris, & McHugo, 1997; Dumaine, 2003). A recent report to Congress by the Substance Abuse and Mental Health Services Administration (SAMHSA, 2002) outlined a multitude of factors (i.e., lack of cross-screening, dearth of programming, funding regulations, etc.) that result in comorbid substance abuse/mental health clients entering one system or the other, or volleying between systems, with inadequate services and support systems. However, there has been little attention to the issue of co-occurring disorders among incarcerated men and women.

The U.S. Department of Justice estimated that in 1999 approximately 16% of inmates in state prisons and local jails were mentally ill (Ditton, 1999). Furthermore, approximately 13% received mental health therapy or counseling from a "trained professional" while incarcerated and 10% receive psychotropic medications (Beck & Maruschak, 2001). In addition, estimates of drug or alcohol dependence among incarcerated men and women are considerably higher than epidemiological estimates (Kessler et al., 1997; Warner, Kessler, Hughes, Anthony, & Nelson, 1995), ranging from 51% (Lo & Stephens, 2000) to 70% (Pimlott Kubiak, Boyd, Young, & Slayden, 2005). In fact, 80% of federal and state inmates were either convicted of a drug-related crime, were using at the time of the offense, or committed their crime to support their drug use (Center for Substance Abuse Treatment, 1998).

Of late, there has been an increased awareness of PTSD co-occurring with SUD. PTSD can occur after exposure to a life-threatening event where the individual experiences a sense of horror and believed his or her life was in danger. Symptoms of the disorder involve psychologically re-experiencing the event and wanting to avoid people and places that might trigger memories of the trauma (American Psychiatric Association, 2000). Although research studies have been mixed on support of the "self-medication" hypothesis of drug use, research indicates that trauma exposure usually precedes the development of an SUD (Chilcoat & Breslau, 1998; Stewart, Pihl, Conrod, & Dongier, 1998). In other words, drugs and alcohol are initially used to alleviate the painful symptoms associated with PTSD but then become problems in their own right that can exacerbate PTSD symptoms and increase the risk of subsequent trauma.

Exposure to a traumatic event is common, however, most people recover psychologically in a relatively brief period of time. For example, the National Comorbidity Study found that 61% of men and 51% of women in the United States experience a trauma over the course of their lifetime; however, of those who experience an event, only 8% of men and 20% women manifest symptoms of PTSD (Kessler, Sonnega, Bromet, Hughes, & Nelson, 1995).

However, among those with PTSD, nearly 52% of men and 28% of women experienced an alcohol dependency while 35% of men and 28% of women reported

a co-occurring drug dependency (Kessler, Crum, et al., 1997). These results suggest that 2.9% of women, and 2.5% of men, experience co-occurring PTSD and an alcohol abuse disorder. Similarly, 2.9% of women and 1.7% of men would be expected to experience PTSD and a cooccurring drug abuse disorder.

While examining the prevalence of PTSD among those with a serious SUD we find a similar pattern. National epidemiological studies estimate that 9% of men and 6% of women experience a drug dependency over the life course (Warner et al., 1995). Among those with an SUD, 8.3% meet criteria for PTSD (Cottler, Compton, Mager, Spitznagel, & Janca, 1992). Of individuals seeking treatment for substance use, lifetime prevalence rates of PTSD have been estimated as high as 50%, with approximately one fourth to one third meeting criteria for current PTSD (Brown, Recupero, & Stout, 1995; Jacobsen, Southwick, & Kosten, 2001; Najavits, Gastfriend, & Barber, 1998).

Although there is little data on the intersection of SUD and PTSD among offenders, we can only assume that the high prevalence of SUDs translates into an enhanced prevalence of this particular co-occurring disorder. Certainly exposure to psychological trauma is higher among the incarcerated than those in the general population (Ehlers, Maercker, & Boos, 2000; Gibson et al., 1999; Jordan et al., 1996; O'Keefe, 1998). One study documented a lifetime prevalence rate for PTSD among incarcerated men at 33% (Ehlers et al., 2000), more than 4 times higher than the rate for men in the general population. Similarly, Jordan and colleagues (1996) compared the rates of several mental health disorders among women in prison and women from the surrounding geographic area, finding that incarcerated women had twice the rate of depression and had been exposed to a far greater number of traumatic incidents.

Estimates of PTSD may be higher among those incarcerated for several reasons. First, involvement in illegal behavior such as drug seeking (Forney, Inciardi, & Lockwood, 1992) and residing in areas of extreme poverty (Pimlott Kubiak, 2002) may increase exposure. Second, in addition to stress, prison may be a production site of new traumatic experiences, as well as triggering traumatic memories. Toch (1998) illustrated the threat of violence within male prisons for physical and sexual assault, as well as the codes of silence maintained by inmates and guards. Similarly, women's prisons have come under greater scrutiny because of the incidence of sexual assault by male corrections staff (General Accounting Office, 1999; Websdale & Chesney-Lind, 1998).

Substance abuse treatment outcomes for those with PTSD have generally been less favorable when compared to those without. In a study comparing outcomes for women with and without PTSD at 3 months posttreatment, those with PTSD were more likely to relapse sooner than those without (Brown, Stout, & Mueller, 1996). In a sample of 1,630 male veterans attending substance abuse treatment, 1-year outcomes for those with co-occurring PTSD, were less favorable; those with the dual disorder were more likely to be readmitted for treatment and less likely to be employed than those in the SUD-only group (Ouimette, Ahrens, & Moos, 1997). At 2 years posttreatment, clients with co-occurring SUD and PTSD were more likely to report problems related to substance use and more likely to consume alcohol than either the SUD-only group or the group with SUD and other psychiatric disorders (Ouimette et al., 1999).

Initial assessments of an integrated approach to the treatment of trauma and substance-related disorders have been positive (Najavits, Weiss, & Shaw, 1998). In addition to community-based intervention studies, this same cognitive behavioral treatment approach was conducted in a correctional setting with a sample of 17 women. At the end of the 3-month treatment period, 53% no longer met criteria for PTSD, and at 6 weeks postrelease 70% did not meet criteria for an SUD (Najavits, 2002). Certainly treatment for women seems especially salient because women have higher epidemiological rates of PTSD, usually enter prison with more severe SUD, and represent a small proportion of the criminal justice population. However, in general, prison programs have not explicitly attended to this co-occurrence and have only recently been involved in the systematic screening and assessment of substance abuse disorders (see Pimlott Kubiak et al., 2005).

CURRENT STUDY

Although the use of substance abuse treatment within criminal justice settings is gaining federal and state support (Farabee, Prendergast, Cartier, & Wexler, 1999), attention to the need for integrated approaches to treatment of co-occurring SUD and psychiatric disorders has been lagging. The focus of the current study was to examine treatment adherence, relapse, and recidivism among those who voluntarily entered a prison-based substance abuse treatment program, comparing those with co-occurring PTSD and those without. Based on prior research we expected to find that treatment outcomes for those in the co-occurring group would be poorer than those without PTSD. Specifically we expected that treatment failure, recidivism, and relapse would be higher in those with co-occurring disorders.

METHOD

Participants

One hundred ninety-nine state prisoners (60 women and 139 men) voluntarily entered a residential substance abuse treatment (RSAT) program on the grounds of their respective institutions between November 1999 and May 2000 and completed treatment between May 2000 and February 2001. Participants resided in specially designated living units within the prison where they engaged in more than 40 hours of therapeutic activities each week including group and individual therapy as well as didactic lectures and community meetings. The units were staffed by a combination of treatment staff, contracted from community-based substance abuse treatment agencies, and corrections officers (see Pimlott Kubiak, 2003). Eligibility for the treatment program was based on assessment of substance dependency, as determined by the Substance Abuse Subtle Screening Inventory (Miller, Roberts, Brooks, & Lazowski, 1997), free from psychotropic medications, minimum-security status, and within 12 to 18 months from prison release. All program participants signed consent to treatment forms and agreed to participate in the evaluation process.

The program was widely advertised throughout minimum-security facilities across the state. Treatment participants were selected from the population of inmates who applied and were determined to be eligible. When accepted prisoners were transferred to the institution where the treatment program was housed, assessment instruments were self-administered prior to a clinical interview.

Although the cognitive behavioral models of treatment for men and women were similar, there were some differences between programs. First, the male program was 9 months in duration and the women's was 6 months. Men could meet criteria for Level II security status (a higher form of minimum security) while women had to be Level I. In addition, the women's program staff received some specialized training in treating trauma exposure.

Measures

Independent Variable

PTSD. Traumatic events were assessed using the Life Events subscale contained in the National Comorbidity Survey (NCS; Kessler, McGonagle & Zhao, 1994). In the NCS a modified version of the Composite International Diagnostic Interview (CIDI) was utilized which was developed collaboratively by the World Health Organization (WHO, 1990) and the U.S. Alcohol, Drug and Mental Health Administration. The CIDI is a comprehensive diagnostic interview designed for assessing mental health disorders. Within the NCS, a small validation study of the CIDI Trauma scale was conducted with 29 respondents of the larger sample who reported the occurrence of lifetime trauma. Approximately one half of the validation sample had a diagnosis of PTSD using the CIDI. These individuals were reassessed by trained interviewers using other validated instruments. Agreement between the CIDI and these two instruments was .75. Furthermore, the CIDI was found to somewhat underdiagnose PTSD (Kessler, Sonnega, et al., 1995).

The CIDI measure contained 11 closed-ended questions pertaining to specific traumatic events asking respondents to indicate if they have ever experienced the event. In addition, there was one open-ended question that queries the possibility of other traumatic experiences not included in the closed-ended questions. The CIDI evaluates life-threatening accident; natural disaster; witness of severe injury or death; death of loved one as a result of homicide, suicide, or accident; rape; molestation; serious attack; threatened with weapon or held captive; direct combat; and experience of a terrible event most people never do. In an effort to reduce the possibility of triggering psychological discomfort related to the trauma during incarceration, we gave participants the option of marking the individual event or simply tallying the number of event categories that had occurred over their lifetime and how many occurred within the past 12 months.

Measurement of the disorder was based on the definitions and criteria specified in the American Psychiatric Association's *Diagnostic and Statistical Manual of Mental Disorders* (2000). Diagnosis of PTSD requires that two criteria are met. The first is experiencing or witnessing an event that involved actual or threatened death, or serious injury in which the individual response involved fear, helplessness, or horror. The second is that the person is experiencing a specific constellation of symptoms. The first criterion was met if the offender marked any of the previously noted events. Those who did not mark any events or did not write in a total number of events were eliminated from further scoring. The second criterion was determined by asking if symptoms were currently present using a 5-point scale from 0 (*absent*), 1 (*don't know*), 2 (*few times*), 3 (*a lot*), and 4 (*all the time*). An individual symptom was counted as present if the participant assessed it as 2 or higher (a *few times* to *all the time*).

Symptom segues are situated with three categories: triggers (re-experiencing), avoidance, and arousal. Those with at least one re-experiencing symptom proceed to avoidance symptoms where at least three are required for diagnosis. Finally, those with two or more arousal symptoms have met symptom criteria for PTSD. Each respondent ends with a categorical variable on PTSD diagnosis as well as total number of symptoms in each segue and mean level of intensity.

Dependent Variables

There are three major treatment outcomes measured in this study—treatment adherence, drug relapse, and criminal recidivism. Each outcome and their sources are explained below.

Treatment adherence. Adherence to treatment was measured using two indicators, the first measured completing the initial treatment program and the second entrance into aftercare, which measured adherence to the continuum of care.

- Program Completion: Successful completion of the program is defined using three criteria: (a) completion of all four program phases, (b) active participation and no major rule violations, and (c) no positive drug screens during treatment. Because treatment admission is considered a privilege, with usually a waiting list for admission, those noncompliant with program or institutional rules are terminated and sent back into general prison population.

- Aftercare: One of the treatment objectives is to create a continuum of care so that the offenders are supported in their transition to the community. In the first 7 months after prison release the offender is required to enter an outpatient treatment program. Participation in aftercare was documented in one of three ways: by the program staff that monitored aftercare, parole reports, and through Corrections Management Information System (CMIS) records because the community treatment was financially supported by the state. We were interested in whether the individual followed through with community treatment and the length of time it took to enter treatment after their release from prison.

Relapse. Relapse was considered if there was a positive drug screen documented in the CMIS. Drug screening is conducted in the prison, as well as in the community, allowing us to track treatment participants from institution to community parole. However, the database does not account for all testing, and testing is not systematically conducted. The unavailable screens primarily pertain to the "instant" testing devices utilized by parole agents. This is a strip that can be dipped into a urine sample to determine the offenders' recent drug use. If this preliminary test is positive, the sample is sent to the lab for confirmation. The positive urine screen would then be documented on CMIS; however, the instant test may not. In addition, urine samples are collected randomly and for "cause" so that the rate of sampling may change from offender to offender.

Recidivism. Recidivism is defined in two ways, new arrest and parole revocation. Because the same person can have a new arrest and a parole revocation, a third variable—legal problems—is used to represent unique cases of recidivism.

- New Arrest: Arrest data is obtained by accessing the Law Enforcement Information Network (LEIN) database maintained by the state police. LEIN data provide information on three types of violations: ordinance, misdemeanor, and felony. If a felony arrest occurred, postprison release, then the arrest is recorded and considered as recidivism.

- Parole Revocation: A parole revocation is when offenders have received a sustained violation of parole, lose their current community status, and are returned to the prison on the same sentence. Although some offenders may be in violation of their parole for not maintaining specific conditions (e.g., employment, treatment, etc.), rarely is parole revoked for such behavior. Some may be sent to a Technical Rule Violation Center; however, this is not considered a revocation. Parole revocation is obtained from the CMIS data.

Analysis

Descriptive statistics were used to describe the population and document differences between program participants as well as PTSD status. Inferential statistics, such as t tests and chi-squares, were used to ascertain differences between those with SUD only and those with co-occurring PTSD. The sample is also assessed for possible program/gender differences. Finally, we used linear and logistic regression to obtain the percentage of variance in outcomes associated with PTSD status (i.e. adjusted R^2 or Nagelkerke pseudo-R^2).

RESULTS

There were few demographic differences between program participants (see Table 1) except that Program 1 was all women and Program 2 all men. Women were slightly older, and men were incarcerated more frequently. Overall, men and women did not differ on type of offense, although there was some variation. Although most were sentenced for property offenses (41%), women were more likely to have been convicted of a drug offense (24% vs. 19%), $\chi^2(1) = .56$, $p = .46$, and 7% of men, compared to no women, were convicted of criminal sexual misconduct $\chi^2(1) = 4.07$, $p = .04$. Men were more likely than women to have been incarcerated previously; however, for one half the women and nearly one third of the men this was their first prison experience. The majority, 80% of men and 70% of women, had previous substance abuse treatment. In addition, women were significantly more likely to have received previous mental health counseling and psychiatric hospitalization than men.

Table 2 demonstrates that the primary drug of choice was cocaine or crack (34% of the men and 40% of the women), $\chi^2(1) = .88$, $p = .35$. Nearly one third of the men, as compared to 18% of women, claimed alcohol as their primary drug of choice, $\chi^2(1) = 2.40$, $p = .12$; however, women were more likely than men to use heroin (28% vs. 17%), $\chi^2(1) = 3.63$, $p = .06$. Although the majority of men claim use of multiple drugs, women appeared to be the heavier users prior to incarceration. In the 30 days before being locked up, women averaged using 23 of those days. In fact, 75% of the women claimed daily use (30 of 30 days) in the month before incarceration. In addition, an examination of the combined sample by PTSD status yielded no statistically significant differences for any of the characteristics included in either Tables 1 or 2.

Table 1 Demographics of Participants Overall and by Program

Variable	Overall (N = 196) M (SD) / %	Program 1 (Male) (n = 139) M (SD) / %	Program 2 (Female) (n = 60) M (SD) / %	t Test or χ^2
Gender				
Male	69.8	100%		
Female	30.2		100%	
Age	36.1 (8.1)	35.2 (8.2)	38.1 (7.5)	2.34*
Race				2.81
Minority	59.3	63%	50%	
White	40.7	37%	50%	
Partner	21.4	20%	25%	.60
Children	70.9	69%	75%	.64
Criminal history offense				5.42
Property	41.3	42%	41%	
Drug	20.4	19%	24%	
Assaultive	33.7	31%	36%	
Sex offense	5.6	7%	0%	
Prior incarcerations		2.5 (1.5)	2.0 (1.4)	2.38*
Prior treatment experiences				
Substance abuse	77.6	81%	70%	2.83
Mental health counseling	23.0	17.6	35.0	7.09**
Psychiatric hospitalization	10.7	7%	18%	5.25*

NOTE: Partner defined as being married, engaged, or living with a committed partner.

*p<.05

**p<.01.

Table 2 Comparison of Substance Abuse Variables Overall and by Program (Sex)

Variable	Overall (N = 196) % or M (SD)	Program 1 (Male) (n = 139) % or M (SD)	Program 2 (Female) (n = 60) % or M (SD)	t Test or χ^2
Drug of choice				7.34
Alcohol	26.0	29.4	18.3	
Heroin	20.4	16.9	28.3	
Marijuana	15.8	17.6	11.7	
Crack/Cocaine	35.7	33.8	40.0	
Other	1.0	2.0	2.0	
Poly drug user	74.0	89%	40%	51.87***
No. of family/friend use	2.6 (5.3)	3.15	1.27	3.20**
No. of days using / 30	16.0 (14.1)	13.1	22.7	4.60***
Daily use before prison	44.7	31.7	75.0	31.85***

NOTE: Number of days using/30 =number of days using in the 30 days before incarceration.

**p< .01. ***p< .001.

Determining who met event and symptom criteria for PTSD began by assessing the number of traumatic events over the life course and within the past 12 months. Overall, there was an average of 2.9 (SD 2.6) traumatic events experienced over the life course, with women experiencing significantly more events than men (3.70 vs. 2.57), $t(191) = 2.83$, $p = .005$. In contrast, men were more likely to report having experienced trauma within the past 12 months. In fact, only one woman claimed exposure in the past 12 months as compared to 75% of the men. Men averaged 2.7 events during the past 12 months compared to .02 for women (one woman reported), resulting in a highly significant difference, $t(184) = 12.05$, $p < .001$.

Men were more likely to report exposure of traumatic events during incarceration than women, who primarily reported exposure prior to incarceration. Although this assumption cannot be definitively tested, further analysis comparing treatment start dates (when the trauma assessment was administered) and prison entrance revealed that more than one half the men (52%), as compared to 33% of women, had been in prison longer than 1 year before they entered the program, $\chi^2(1) = 5.75$, $p = .02$. Of the 72 men incarcerated longer than 1 year before treatment began, 79% ($n = 57$) experienced at least one trauma during that time, in other words, during the course of confinement. Although there were no statistical differences between men and women in the length of time incarcerated prior to treatment, men averaged nearly 6 months longer (719 days vs. 533 days), $t(197) = 1.24$, $p = .22$.

Overall one half the population (55%) of those entering treatment met criteria for lifetime PTSD. The rates did not differ between male and female populations; 53% of men and 60% of women report event and symptom criteria for PTSD diagnosis, $\chi^2(1) = .78$, $p = .38$. Comparing the number of symptoms and symptom intensity levels (across all symptoms clusters as well as overall) of those who met PTSD criteria with those who did not, we found significant differences ($p < .001$) on all measures across both programs. These consistently significant differences suggest that symptoms are associated with trauma exposure and not the prison or institutional environment per se. Comparisons between men and women meeting criteria for PTSD found that women experience more events (4.57 compared with 3.27), $t(107) = 2.55$, $p = .01$, and average more re-experiencing symptoms (3.71 compared to 3.19), $t(107) = 1.82$, $p = .07$. Furthermore, the intensity level of re-experiencing symptoms is greater for women than men (1.10 vs. 0.88), $t = 1.99$, $p = .05$.

A comparison of the dependent variables between programs by PTSD status (Table 3)

Table 3   Comparison of Outcomes by Program and PTSD Status

Variable	Program 1:Male				Program 2:Female			
	Non-PTSD ($n = 65$)	PTSD ($n = 74$)			Non-PTSD ($n = 24$)	PTSD ($n = 36$)		
	$M(SD)$ or %	$M(SD)$ or %	t Test or X^2 p Value	R^2	$M(SD)$ or %	$M(SD)$ or %	t Test or c^2 p Value	R^2
Successful completion	73.8	81.1	.307	.01	100	97.2	.410	.11
Drug relapse	13.8	17.6	.549	.00	0	16.7	.035	.22
If paroled	($n = 35$)	($n = 41$)	($n = 18$)	($n = 29$)				
Aftercare admission	25.7	51.2	.023	.09	50.0	48.3	.908	.00
Recidivism	5.7	17.1	.127	.06	22.2	13.8	.455	.02

NOTE: Positive drug screens either during incarceration or on parole.

found that men with PTSD were more likely to complete the program and have a positive drug screen, although neither were statistically significant. Similarly, recidivism did not significantly differ by PTSD diagnosis, however 17% ($n = 7$) of the PTSD group, compared to 6% ($n = 2$) on the non-PTSD group, experienced some legal problem postprison release. For men, the only significant outcome was aftercare—one half of those with PTSD (51.2%) compared to one fourth of those with SUD only were admitted to community-based aftercare.

For women (Table 3), completion rates and entrance into aftercare were nearly identical between groups, however relapse was significantly higher among women with PTSD. In fact, although there was no evidence of relapse among the 24 women in the non-PTSD group, 16.7% ($n = 6$) of the women with PTSD recorded at least one positive drug screen. In fact, a probable diagnosis of PTSD accounted for 22% of the variation in whether a woman has a positive drug screen. Although equal numbers of women from both groups ($n = 4$) have encountered legal problems, it is a higher percentage of women in the non-PTSD group (22% vs. 14%).

DISCUSSION AND APPLICATIONS TO SOCIAL WORK PRACTICE

This exploratory study examined differences in treatment adherence, drug relapse and criminal recidivism between those with a co-occurring PTSD and SUD and those with only SUD in two prison-based substance abuse treatment programs. Both programs used similar models, and we expected that those with a dual disorder would experience treatment failure, relapse, and recidivism more frequently than those with an SUD only. Our results, although somewhat mixed, support the original hypothesis and provide useful information to social work practitioners, researchers, teachers, and policy makers.

The strongest evidence to support our hypothesis is that women with SUD and PTSD are significantly more likely to relapse than women with only an SUD. In fact, PTSD diagnosis accounts for 22% of the variance in whether a woman tests positive for drug use posttreatment. Although there are no other statistical differences among women based on PTSD status, those with SUD only were more likely to recidivate. Men with PTSD were significantly more likely to enter community-based aftercare than those with SUD only. Although a greater proportion of men with both disorders were more likely to relapse (18% vs. 14%) and recidivate (17% vs. 6%), neither outcome reached statistical significance.

Certainly women's heavy drug use and prior victimization history may explain relapse posttreatment. However, there were no significant differences between those with and without PTSD in the proportion of women who used daily prior to incarceration (77% of those with PTSD compared to 71% for those without), χ^2 (1) = .30, p = .60. Similarly, trauma history may be related to women's higher utilization of mental health treatment and psychiatric hospitalization; however, we found no statistical differences even though women with PTSD symptoms were more likely to have received prior mental health counseling (39% vs. 29%), χ^2 (1) = .60, p = .44, and psychiatric hospitalization (22% vs. 13%), χ^2 (1) = .17, p = .68. Therefore, the higher relapse rate of those with symptoms of PTSD supports previous findings (Brown et al., 1996) and theory that inattention to PTSD may negate the success of substance abuse treatment (Najavits et al., 1998; Najavits, Weiss, & Shaw, 1997; Ouimette, Brown & Najavits, 1998). Attention to trauma-related disorders among incarcerated women may be pivotal in preventing relapse and as a consequence, recidivism.

More interesting, there were no statistical differences between treatment-seeking incarcerated men and women in meeting diagnostic criteria for PTSD. Certainly this differs from epidemiological data in which women are twice as likely to be diagnosed with PTSD as men (Kessler et. al., 1995) and from other studies of treatment studies seeking men and women. In the National Institute of Drug Abuse Cocaine Study, Najavits, Gastfriend, and Barber (1998) found that twice the number of women (30%) had a co-occurring PTSD when compared to men (15%). Certainly some of this variation may be attributed to how PTSD was assessed. Stewart and colleagues (1998) found a higher incidence of PTSD when conducting clinical assessments versus chart reviews. Therefore, higher rates of PTSD among this treatment-seeking population may be the self-report of symptoms and events at treatment onset. However, the measure used here (CIDI) has also been found to underdiagnose (Kessler et al., 1995).

Of importance to social workers involved in assisting prisoners with re-entry are differences between men and women in their experiences during incarceration and in the community. Women, in contrast to men, may experience returning to their community as re-entering a traumatic environment. Women not only experienced more episodes of trauma but experienced them in the community. This may result in women feeling vulnerable and perhaps "re-experiencing" their trauma when returning to that environment. Thus substance use may be attributed to their desire to minimize symptoms that trigger memories of the original event. Although we are not suggesting that women feel safe in prison, especially in light of recent investigations and settlements on behalf of women victimized during incarceration (see Geer, 2000), the women in the current study entered prison with significantly more trauma than did men. In addition, the current study suggests that men may experience the majority of their trauma as a result of the incarceration. Therefore, men leaving the facility may take some comfort in departing from their source of trauma, whereas women may be more hypervigilant in the community. Alternately, and perhaps as a result of the aforementioned investigations in women's prisons, women may be victimized during incarceration and reluctant and/or ashamed to discuss or name these events.

Prison exit could also explain why men experiencing PTSD symptoms, and perhaps abuse during incarceration, may seek aftercare treatment more than men without PTSD. This difference between groups may be a desire to confront the trauma and alleviate symptoms by acknowledging their need for ongoing services that address their experiences of trauma during incarceration. However, it is questionable if men receive such services addressing the trauma-related sequelae during reintegration or at any other time. Although male victimization, particularly sexual assault, may be glibly referred to as part of the sentence (see Human Rights Watch, 2001), it is rarely attended to by clinical professionals during incarceration, or in planning reintegration services. Part of this inattention may be the reluctance of male offenders, as well as service providers, to acknowledge such victimization. Certainly masculine social norms may obstruct such candor. However, social worker practitioners and educators must understand the rules of masculine help seeking (Addis & Mahalik, 2003), as well as prison norms (Toch, 1998), creatively seeking solutions that confront such obstruction to meeting men's treatment needs.

These findings emphasize our earlier call for attention to trauma exposure among men and women in the criminal justice system. Certainly social workers recognize that victimization during incarceration requires a safe therapeutic space, for those who have experienced trauma (Herman, 1992). Although this study suggests that prison may be "unsafe," there is some evidence that prison-based treatment programs can, in fact, provide a safe therapeutic space (Pimlott Kubiak, 2003). Therefore, it seems plausible that social workers could strive for the creation of an organizational climate in prison in which the inmate/client feels safe.

However, the presence of social workers employed by corrections, or working inside prisons, is extremely low, generating some speculation that social work has abandoned the field of corrections (Gibelman, 1995). Because funding for such opportunities may be increasing, it is crucial that social work professionals have greater visibility within the criminal justice system, as well as advocates for reform. Thus, social work educators need to include curricula that inform social workers about the system and the challenges for those entering and exiting the system.

Certainly the current study has many limitations, and we encourage other investigators to replicate this study. Although some of these limitations may be more easily remedied (e.g., the use of self-report measures, more systematic collection of drug screens), others are site dependent and more difficult to remedy. For example, there was little control over adherence to the treatment model. Although release into the community was planned subsequent to treatment discharge, frequently this did not occur. In fact, at the time data were collected nearly 40% of the men and women who participated in treatment remained in prison. Similarly, our comparison of outcomes by program for those with co-occurring PTSD found one significant difference; women were more likely to complete treatment than their male counterparts (97% compared with 81%), $\chi^2 = 5.36$, $p = .02$. However, this difference could be attributed to programmatic or facility differences and not gender per se.

The final limitation is in our analyses. In Table 3 we found two significant differences between PTSD and non-PTSD groups, whereas by chance alone we would have expected less than one (0.4). However, using the conservative Bonferroni correction to reduce the likelihood of chance findings (Type I errors), the new cut point for significance would be 0.0125, and neither of our findings would remain significant. This is another reason why our findings should be replicated in more rigorous studies.

CONCLUSION

The U.S. Surgeon General estimates that between 41% and 65% of individuals with an SUD also have a history of another mental health disorder. Similarly, about one half of those with a lifetime history of a mental health disorder also have a lifetime history of an SUD (U.S. Department of Health and Human Services, 1999). Despite the high prevalence of co-occurring mental health and SUD, there are many barriers to the effective assessment and treatment of individuals experiencing these dual disorders (SAMHSA, 2002). Perhaps nowhere are these barriers more acutely felt than in the nation's prisons and jails.

Although the lack of appropriate treatment within the criminal justice system may mirror the lack of treatment in the community, in many respects the justice system has become the default provider for many with co-occurring mental health disorder and SUD. The myriad of issues surrounding victimization, trauma, and substance abuse are of particular salience to men and women who are, or have been, incarcerated—and may be exacerbated as a result of incarceration. Therefore appropriate treatment of these particular co-occurring conditions may be important psychologically for the offender, fiscally in reducing recidivism and institutional confinement costs and socially in reducing family disintegration and financial dependency.

Finally, as the United States continues to lead the world in incarceration rates, greater numbers of men and women—especially minority men and women—are experiencing incarceration. Social workers and other mental health professionals should assess incarceration as a possible site trauma. We must not only assess the trauma they enter the prison with but also that which they leave with.

REFERENCES

Addis, M. E., & Mahalik, J. R. (2003). Men, masculinity, and the context of help seeking. *American Psychologist, 58*, 5–14.

American Psychiatric Association. (2000). *Diagnostic and statistical manual of mental disorders* (4th ed., text rev.). Washington, DC: Author.

Beck, A. J., & Maruschak, L. M. (2001). *Mental health treatment in state prisons* (NCJ188215). Washington, DC: U.S. Department of Justice, Office of Justice Programs.

Brown, P. J., Recupero, P. R., & Stout, R. (1995). Substance abuse comorbidity and treatment utilization. *Addictive Behavior, 20,* 251–254.

Brown, P. J., Stout, R. L., & Mueller, T. (1996). Posttraumatic stress disorder and substance abuse relapse among women. *Psychology of Addictive Behavior, 10,* 124–128.

Center for Substance Abuse Treatment. (1998). *Planning for alcohol and other drug abuse treatment for adults in the criminal justice system* (CSAT TIP #17). Washington, DC: U.S. Department of Health and Human Services, Substance Abuse and Mental Health Services Administration.

Chilcoat, H. D., & Breslau, N. (1998). Investigations of causal pathways between PTSD and drug use disorders. *Addictive Behavior, 23,* 827–840.

Cottler, L. B., Compton, W., Mager, D., Spitznagel, E., & Janca, A. (1992). Posttraumatic stress disorder among substance users from the general population. *American Journal of Psychiatry, 149,* 664–670.

Ditton, P. M. (1999). *Mental health and treatment of inmates and probationers* (Bureau of Justice Special Report #174463). Washington, DC: U.S. Department of Justice.

Drake, R. E., Yovetich, N. A., Bebout, R. R., Harris, M., & McHugo, G. (1997). Integrated treatment for dually diagnosed homeless adults. *Journal of Nervous and Mental Disorders, 185,* 298–305.

Dumaine, M. L. (2003). Meta-analysis of interventions with co-occurring disorders of severe mental illness and substance abuse: Implications for social work practice. *Research on Social Work Practice, 13,* 142–165.

Ehlers, A., Maercker, A., & Boos, A. (2000). Posttraumatic stress disorder following political imprisonment: The role of mental defeat, alienation, and perceived permanent change. *Journal of Abnormal Psychology, 109,* 45–55.

Farabee, D., Prendergast, M., Cartier, J., & Wexler, H. (1999). Barriers to implementing effective correctional drug treatment programs. *Prison Journal, 79,* 150–162.

Forney, M., Inciardi, J., & Lockwood, D. (1992). Exchanging sex for crack-cocaine: A comparison of women from rural and urban communities. *Journal of Community Health, 17,* 73–85.

Geer, M. (2000). Human rights and wrongs in our own backyard: Incorporating international human rights protections under domestic civil rights law—A case study of women in United States prisons. *Harvard Human Rights Journal, 13,* 71–140.

General Accounting Office. (1999). *Women in prison: Sexual misconduct by correctional staff* (Report to the Honorable Eleanor Holmes Norton, House of Representatives). Washington, DC: Author.

Gibelman, M. (1995). *What social workers do.* Washington, DC: NASW Press.

Gibson, L. E., Holt, J. C., Fondacaro, K. M., Tang, T. S., Powell, T. A., & Turbitt, E. L. (1999). An examination of antecedent trauma and psychiatric comorbidity among male inmates with PTSD. *Journal of Traumatic Stress, 12,* 473–484.

Herman, J. (1992). *Trauma and recovery.* New York: Basic Books.

Human Rights Watch. (2001). *No escape: Male rape in U.S. prisons.* New York: Author.

Inciardi, J., Martin, S., Butzin, C., Hooper, R., & Harrison, L. (1997). An effective model of prison-based treatment for drug-involved offenders. *Journal of Drug Issues, 27,* 261–278.

Jacobsen, L. K., Southwick, S. M., & Kosten, T. R. (2001). Substance use disorders in patients with posttraumatic stress disorder: A review of the literature. *American Journal of Psychiatry, 158,* 1184–1190.

Jordan, K., Schlenger, W., Fairbank, J., & Cadell, J. (1996). Prevalence of psychiatric disorders among incarcerated women. *Archives of General Psychiatry, 53*, 513–519.

Kessler, R., Crum, R., Warner, L., Nelson, C., Schulenberg, K., & Anthony, J. (1997). Lifetime co-occurrence of DSM-III-R alcohol abuse and dependence with other psychiatric disorders in the national comorbidity survey. *Archives of General Psychiatry, 54*, 313–321.

Kessler, R., McGonagle, K., & Zhao, S. (1994). Lifetime and 12 month prevalence of DSM-III-R psychiatric disorders in the United States. *Archives of General Psychiatry, 51*, 8–19.

Kessler, R., Sonnega, A., Bromet, E., Hughes, M., & Nelson, C. (1995). Posttraumatic stress disorder in the National Comorbidity Survey. *Archives of General Psychiatry, 52*, 1048–1060.

Kupers, T. (1996). Trauma and its sequelae in male prisoners: Effects of confinement, overcrowding, and diminished services. *American Journal of Orthopsychiatry, 66*, 190–196.

Lo, C., & Stephens, R. (2000). Drugs and prisoners: Treatment needs on entering prison. *American Journal of Drug and Alcohol Abuse, 28*, 229–245.

Miller, F. A., Roberts, J., Brooks, M. K. & Lazowski, L. (1997). *Substance Abuse Subtle Screening Inventory (SASSI-3): A quick reference for administration and scoring.* Bloomington, IN: Bargh Enterprises.

Najavits, L. M. (2002). Seeking safety: Therapy for trauma and substance abuse. *Corrections Today, 64*, 136–139.

Najavits, L., Gastfriend, D., & Barber, J. (1998). Cocaine dependence with and without PTSD among subjects in the National Institute on Drug Abuse Collaborative Cocaine Treatment Study. *American Journal of Psychiatry, 155*, 214–219.

Najavits, L., Weiss, R., & Shaw, S. (1997). The link between substance abuse and posttraumatic stress disorder in women. *American Journal on Addictions, 6*, 273–283.

Najavits, L., Weiss, R., & Shaw, S. (1998). "Seeking safety": Outcome of a new

cognitive-behavioral psychotherapy for women with posttraumatic stress disorder and substance dependence. *Journal of Traumatic Stress, 11*, 437–456.

O'Keefe, M. (1998). Posttraumatic stress disorder among incarcerated battered women: A comparison of battered women who killed their abusers and those incarcerated for other offenses. *Journal of Traumatic Stress, 11*, 71–85.

Ouimette, P., Ahrens, C., & Moos, R. (1997). Posttraumatic stress disorder in substance abuse patients: Relationship to 1-year posttreatment outcomes. *Psychology of Addictive Behaviors, 11*, 34–47.

Ouimette, P. C., Brown, P. J., & Najavits, L. M. (1998). Course and treatment of patients with both substance use and posttraumatic stress disorders. *Addictive Behaviors, 23*, 785–796.

Ouimette, P. C., Finney, J. W., & Moos, R. H. (1999). Two-year posttreatment functioning and coping of substance abuse patients with posttraumatic stress disorder. *Psychology of Addictive Behaviors, 13*, 105–114.

Pelissier, B., Wallace, S., & O'Neil, J. (2001). Federal prison residential drug treatment reduces substance use and arrests after release. *American Journal of Drug and Alcohol Abuse, 27*, 315–337.

Pimlott Kubiak, S. (2002). *Social location and cumulative adversity in multiply traumatized women.* Unpublished doctoral dissertation, University of Michigan, Ann Arbor.

Pimlott Kubiak, S. (2003). *Is treatment in prison an oxymoron? A comparison of prisoner perceptions in therapeutic and non-therapeutic units.* Manuscript submitted for publication.

Pimlott Kubiak, S., Boyd, C., Young, A.Slayden, J., & 2005). Assessment of the substance abuse treatment needs of prisoners: Implementation of integrated statewide approach. *Journal of Offender Rehabilitation, 41*, 1–19.

Rogier, D., Farmer, M., Rae, D., Locke, B., Keith, S., Judd, L., et al. (1990). Comordidity of mental disorders with alcohol and other drug abuse: results from the Epidemiologic Catchment Area (ECA) study. *Journal of the American Medical Association, 264,* 2511–2518.

Stewart, S. H., Pihl, R. O., Conrod, P. J., & Dongier, M. (1998). Functional associations among trauma, PTSD, and substance-related disorders. *Addictive Behaviors, 23,* 797–812.

Substance Abuse and Mental Health Services Administration. (2002). *Report to Congress on the prevention and treatment of co-occurring substance abuse disorders and mental disorders.* Washington, DC: U.S. Department of Health and Human Services.

Teplin, L., Abram, K., & McClelland, G. (1996). Prevalence of psychiatric disorders among incarcerated women. *Archives of General Psychiatry, 53,* 505–512.

Toch, H. (1998). Hypermasculinity and prison violence. In L. H. Bowker (Ed.), *Masculinities and violence* (pp. 168–178). Thousand Oaks, CA: Sage.

U.S. Department of Health and Human Services. (1999). *Mental health: A report of the surgeon general.* Washington, DC: U.S. Department of Health and Human Services, Office of the Surgeon General, Substance Abuse and Mental Health Services Administration.

Warner, L., Kessler, R., Hughes, M., Anthony, J., & Nelson, C. (1995). Prevalence and correlates of drug use and dependence in the United States: Results from the national comorbidity survey. *Archives of General Psychiatry, 52,* 219–229.

Websdale, N., & Chesney-Lind, M. (1998). Doing violence to women: Research synthesis on the victimization of women. In L. H. Bowker (Ed.), *Masculinities and violence* (pp. 55–81). Thousand Oaks, CA.: Sage.

Wexler, H., De Leon, G., Thomas, G., Kressel, D., & Peters, J. (1999). The Amity Prison TC evaluation: Reincarceration outcomes. *Criminal Justice and Behavior, 26,* 147–167.

World Health Organization. (1990). *Composit diagnosit review (CIDI), Version 1.0.* Geneva, Switzerland: Author.

6

A GENDER-SPECIFIC PATHWAY TO SERIOUS, VIOLENT, AND CHRONIC OFFENDING?

Exploring Howell's Risk Factors for Serious Delinquency

PERNILLA JOHANSSON

UNIVERSITY OF TEXAS AT DALLAS

KIMBERLY KEMPF-LEONARD

SOUTHERN ILLINOIS UNIVERSITY, CARBONDALE

In Preventing and Reducing Juvenile Delinquency, Howell proposes a female-specific pathway to serious, violent, and chronic offending. Incorporating ideas from feminist research about risk factors for female delinquency, he proposes five distinct and interrelated risk factors—child abuse victimization, mental health problems, running away, gang involvement, and juvenile justice involvement—as those that lead to serious, violent, and chronic offending for girls. This study is an exploration of Howell's hypothesis, assessing the independent effect of the suggested risk factors on girls' and boys' involvement in serious, violent, and chronic offending. The sample consists of 10,405 youths, one third of whom are females, who were referred to a metropolitan juvenile court in Texas and tracked in official records from 1997 to 2003. This large sample allows for robust statistical

Authors' Note: Address correspondence to Kimberly Kempf-Leonard, 1000 Faner Drive, Carbondale, IL 62901; e-mail: kleonard@siu.edu.

SOURCE: "A Gender-Specific Pathway to Serious, Violent, and Chronic Offending? Exploring Howell's Risk Factors for Serious Delinquency" by Pernilla Johansson and Kimberly Kempf-Leonard. In the 2009 issue of *Crime and Delinquency*, 55(2), 216–240. Used with permission.

analysis of the independent effect of the risk factors on serious, violent, and chronic offending by gender.

Keywords: abuse; runaway; mental health problems; gang involvement; juvenile justice; gender and female-specific delinquency

Research on the risk factors for serious, violent, and chronic juvenile offenders has important policy implications, given these offender groups' increased risk for adult offending (Kempf-Leonard, Tracy, & Howell, 2001; Tracy & Kempf-Leonard, 1996); consequently, identifying risk factors associated with serious, violent, and chronic offending among youth of both genders also has important theoretical implications. Yet, the research about female risk factors for general delinquency, as well as research addressing girls' serious, violent, and chronic offending, has been insufficient. As such, this study addresses the relationship between gender and serious, violent, and chronic delinquency by analyzing the impact of risk factors found to be important for females' path into delinquency. Specifically, we explore the proposition about a female-specific pathway to serious, violent, and chronic offending suggested by James Howell (2003), who proposes five risk factors as potentially being more important than others for this subgroup of girls involved in serious, violent, and chronic offending: child abuse and victimization, mental health problems, running away (being thrown away), gang involvement, and juvenile justice involvement. Howell asserts,

My central proposition is that the "gendered" nature of these risk factors and environments may well have a greater impact on girls than on boys for the most severe delinquency outcomes—that is, serious, violent and chronic juvenile offending careers. (p. 68)

Howell further argues,

Except for child abuse, boys and girls suffer these experiences about equally; however, the combination of all these experiences may have greater negative effects on girls than on boys, propelling a subgroup of girls toward serious, violent and chronic juvenile offender careers. (p. 68)

The present study conducts a partial test of Howell's proposition by assessing the five stepping-stones (see Farrington, 1986) as possible female-specific risk factors for serious, violent, and chronic behavior. As such, we do not evaluate the time ordering of the risk factors but rather analyze their independent and cumulative effects on serious, violent, and chronic offending. We further focus on the first important step in the evaluation of Howell's female-specific pathway, to see whether these risk factors differ in importance between female and male youth who are referred to juvenile court.

FEMALE JUVENILE CRIMINALITY

Serious, violent, and chronic offending are highly gendered, with significantly more males than females being involved in these types of offending (Feld, 2006; Steffensmeier, Schwartz, Zhong, & Ackerman, 2005). The small number of females observed in the most serious categories of delinquency in the past has posed a substantial problem for studies of this topic (Tracy & Kempf-Leonard, 1996; Wolfgang, Thornberry, & Figlio, 1987). Despite reports of and a focus on the increase of female violence in the last two decades, delinquent girls still make up small proportions of serious, violent, and chronic offenders, and researchers have repeatedly emphasized the less serious character of female delinquency (Chesney-Lind, 1997; Feld, 2006; Lanctot & Le Blanc, 2002; Steffensmeier et al., 2005).

A central debate in the research literature addressing gender and crime focuses on the applicability of traditional criminological theories to females— mainly, those developed from studies of males. Generalizability research rests on the assumption that the theoretical propositions and research based on male samples are applicable to female offenders (Daly & Chesney-Lind, 1988). Although feminist researchers have criticized this assumption, empirical research examining mainstream criminological theories and variables has found support that the same explanatory variables and processes explain deviant behavior and general delinquency for both males and females (Canter, 1982; Lanctot & Le Blanc, 2002; Rowe, Vazsonyi, & Flannery, 1995; D. A. Smith & Paternoster, 1987; Steffensmeier & Allan, 1996). Steffensmeier and Allan (1996) clarify that "both traditional and more recent theoretical perspective can help explain both female offending patterns and gender differences for less serious crime [but that] the explanation of serious female crime and of gender differences in serious crime is more problematic" (p. 465). As such, to broaden the knowledge of female criminality, they suggest that future research examine to what extent criminogenic factors vary by gender in magnitude or directions of effect and that analysis focus on risk factors "seen as uniquely relevant to the explanation of females crime (e.g. childhood abuse, personal maladjustment, victimization)" (p. 483).

Similarly, in a review of the literature about adolescent females' deviance, Lanctot and Le Blanc (2002) assert that research about female youth's offending can use mainstream theories but that they should be adjusted to integrate concepts relevant to gender difference found in research. They also suggest that a key component involve "adjusting the dependent variable to make it more representative of behaviors specific to girls"; this adjustment means that "the dependent variable would then refer to a myriad of deviant activities" (p. 169).

A central criticism of mainstream criminological theories has been that theories of delinquency explain crime among lower-class males and therefore fail to capture "the full nature of delinquency in America" (Chesney-Lind, 1995, p. 72). Feminist criminologists emphasize the need to incorporate and represent gendered risk factors, experiences, and processes, to better understand females' pathways into deviance. A major contribution of the feminist pathway approach has been to identify the connection between victimization and abuse, mental health problems (including substance abuse), running away, and later delinquency as being central in females' pathway to offending (Acoca & Dedel, 1998; Belknap & Holsinger, 1998, 2006; Chesney-Lind, 1995, 1997; Daly, 1992, 1994; Gilfus, 1992). Feminist research has also called attention to how the reactions from the juvenile justice system to troubled runaway girls function to criminalize their survival strategies (Belknap & Holsinger, 1998; Chesney-Lind, 1997; Gilfus, 1992). In sum, to better understand gendered paths into offending for boys and girls, analysis should include independent variables found to be important for female offending and should incorporate dependent variables that capture differences in offending patterns between boys and girls, especially for more chronic offenders involved in serious and violent offending.

HOWELL'S FEMALE-SPECIFIC PROPOSITION

The model that Howell offers includes five risk factors that may coalesce to explain a unique female-specific pathway to serious, violent, and chronic delinquency. As a theoretical approach, Howell's model builds on Farrington's stepping-stones model (1986). Sampson and Laub (1993) summarize the stepping-stones approach as a model in which factors are time ordered by age and assessed with respect to outcome variables and "causality is 'represented by a developmental network of causal factors' in which dependent variables become independent over time" (p. 303).

One of Howell's risk factors is that of victimization or child abuse. He describes research that has established that girls are significantly more likely to be victims of child abuse up to age 4 and twice as likely to be victims of sexual abuse throughout childhood. Similarly, researchers have found that girls who have been victims of neglect and abuse are more likely to have been arrested for violence both as juveniles and as adults.

Howell identifies mental health problems as another stepping-stone. He summarizes that teenage girls have a higher prevalence of psychiatric disorders and depression and that depression has been linked to aggressive behavior. Thus, an analysis of female offending should include an examination of the role of mental health problems as a possible pathway into delinquency.

Third, Howell identifies running away or being thrown away. Although research has indicated that boys and girls run away in similar proportions, Howell points to the links between early victimization in the home, running away, and later homelessness. Howell argues that the cumulative effects of these risk factors—which may include substance abuse, risky sexual behavior, violent victimization, sexual exploitation, and juvenile justice involvement—may have significantly more impact on girls, serious, violent, and chronic offending.

A fourth proposition in Howell's theory is that of gang involvement. Howell concludes that for girls, gang involvement may serve as a way to avoid a chaotic family life (including victimization and conflict) and as a replacement for family. Howell also cites recent research by Thornberry, Krohn, Lizotte, Smith, and Tobin (2003), who found that "girls who are actively involved in gangs become the most serious, violent, and chronic juvenile offenders of all girls." Research on gang involvement also indicates that gang membership tends to lead to "increased criminal embeddedness" with lifelong consequences.

A fifth risk factor is that of juvenile justice involvement. Howell asserts that girls often come into contact with the juvenile justice system as a result of status offenses—in particular, running away. Their juvenile justice involvement then often continues with probation violations and new offenses. Whereas early intervention in criminal careers is beneficial, incarceration in detention centers is not. Instead, there are indications that girls' victimization continues in detention centers in the form of emotional and physical abuse, isolation, and staff intimidation. Thus, the consequences of juvenile justice involvement may be different for girls than for boys.

In summary, Howell suggests five risk factors as potential antecedents to serious, violent, and chronic delinquency—specifically for females. He labels these factors *stepping-stones*, thereby suggesting a chronological order among them and the increased seriousness in delinquency behavior over time. However, Howell does not bring complete analytical and conceptual clarity to this ordering, including (a) whether the stepping-stones in the female pathway are age-graded risk factors that initiate and reinforce a serious, violent, and chronic delinquency pathway and (b) whether the stepping-stones model represents a causal chain of dependent variables that become independent variables over time and may therefore have only an indirect effect on serious, violent, and chronic offending as an outcome variable. As such, the focus in this study is the independent effect of the five stepping-stone risk factors on serious, violent, and chronic offending. Although Howell, like many others, does not differentiate between serious, violent, and chronic delinquency, we observe not only this overall group but also subgroups separating the most serious offenders from chronic but less serious recidivists.

RESEARCH QUESTIONS AND APPROACH

We explore the viability of Howell's suggested female-specific pathway to serious, violent, and chronic offending among females and males in a sample of juveniles offenders. We use data from more than 10,000 juveniles referred to juvenile court during 2002–2003 in a large metropolitan area to explore the extent to which five risk factors (childhood victimization, mental health problems, running away, gang involvement, and juvenile justice involvement) make up a pathway to serious, violent, and chronic offending for females and males—thus, our first research question:

> Are the five risk factors presented in Howell's pathway specific to a subgroup of girls involved in serious, violent, and chronic offending? Specifically, do the included risk factors differ in direction or magnitude between males and females?

Second, to incorporate the suggestion to adapt the dependent variable to a broader set of delinquent behavior (Lanctot & Le Blanc, 2002), we analyze whether the five risk factors are differently related to three offender groups across gender: chronic-only offenders, chronic offenders involved in serious and violent offending, and occasional offenders. The rationale for a comparison between offender groups is to adjust or use a dependent variable that may better reflect a female offending pattern of less serious but still repeat offending—thus, our second research question:

> Which of the five risk factors are related to chronic-only offending versus serious, violent, and chronic offending? And do these risk factors differ in direction and magnitude between females and males?

Finally, because Howell emphasizes that it may be the cumulative effects of these risk factors that propel girls into serious, violent, and chronic offending, we assess the additive negative effects of the risk factors by estimating the predicted probabilities for involvement in chronic-only and serious, violent, and chronic offending for girls and boys with and without these risk factors present.

DATA AND METHODS

This study is a secondary analysis of data including youth aged 12 to 16 who were referred during 2002 and 2003 to one juvenile court jurisdiction in a four-county metropolitan area in Texas of more than 5 million people. This area is among the 10 most populous in the United States, and it is among the most diverse. This jurisdiction aptly represents the demographic representation of the area. The 2-year period was chosen to increase the sample size and to allow for more robust statistical analyses of gender differences, which pose difficulty because of the smaller number of girls with serious, violent, or chronic offending.[1] From the 13,940 total children who had at least one referral to the department, we excluded 221 because race and ethnicity were ambiguously identified as other, 2,222 were missing information about mental health problems, and 734 were without information about family. The analysis was based on almost 10,000 youth.[2]

Most individual history information and offense data were recorded at intake by juvenile department staff, from self-reported information from youth, parents, and police reports. Additional information, primarily on official decisions and dispositions, accrued at later processing stages. The data system is computer based, which ensures more uniform entry of data than that of the handwritten case files commonly used in juvenile justice systems. To the extent possible, the independent variables were measured on the basis of data entered from 1997 to 2001, and the dependent variables were measured in the 2002–2003 period, to maintain proper time order. Accurate dates were recorded for several variables. However—and, again, like most official criminal justice information systems—when subsequent referrals occur and situations change, data fields on abuse, gang involvement, and residential family structure are overwritten. Accordingly, the exact time ordering of these variables in relation to the dependent variables is less certain. This is not likely a problem for child abuse because the period covers the lifetime and thereby back to infancy. Similarly, whom the youth currently reside with is the issue of importance, and the measure reflects the time of the latest referral. The mental health measure reflects test scores obtained in 2002–2003, because the court had not fully implemented the Massachusetts Youth Screening Instrument–Second Version (MA-SI-2; an instrument for mental health screening) as a regular part of the intake process until 2002. As such, no reliable and widely used mental health indicators were available before 2002. Although this is not ideal, we are fortunate that the system routinely records mental health measures at all, given how rare the practice is among juvenile justice systems in the United States. The analysis avoids the dilemma of many cross-sectional self-report studies in which past year's delinquent behavior is explained by current values of explanatory variables. In sum, the independent variables were defined as follows.

Child abuse. The child abuse database includes four variable fields tapping known or suspected victimization of the youth at anytime in his or her life: suspected sexual abuse ever in the youth's life, suspected physical abuse, suspected emotional abuse, and any involvement between the family and Child Protective Services. These four categories were combined into one dichotomous variable, which reflects whether any kind of abuse was indicated.[3]

Mental health problems. The MAYSI-2[4] is administered to identify youth who may need immediate intervention or treatment for mental health problems at the entry point of the juvenile justice system. The five scales reflect mental health needs in the following areas: alcohol/drug use, angry/irritability, depressed/anxious, somatic complaints, and suicide ideation. Herein, youth were defined as having mental health problems if they scored above the *warning* cutoff point on at least one scale on the MAYSI-2 during 2002 or 2003.

Runaway. This dichotomous indicator captures whether the youth had a referral for the status offense *runaway* between 1997 and 2001.

Gang involvement. Youth were identified as being involved with gangs if there was affirmative information for one or more of the following categories: former gang member, gang member, hard core gang member, and wannabe gang member. Gang involvement was operationalized as a dichotomous indicator (*yes/no*) to ensure adequate prevalence for analysis.

Juvenile justice involvement. This dichotomous measure distinguishes youth with secure detention of 2 or more days from those with short or no detention, anytime between 1997 and 2001. Secure detention reflects the most intrusive response, short of disposition from the system, and so taps the aspects of juvenile justice involvement that are hypothesized by Howell to affect future offending. The cutoff was set to 2 days to exclude youth held in detention while waiting to be picked up by guardians.

In addition to race/ethnicity, four other measures that may affect the hypothesized relationship were included as control variables. First, *family* structure has five categories: two parents (biological, adoptive, stepparents), single mother, single father, extended family–other (grandparents, other relatives and friends, or living with spouse), and institution–foster care (foster care, group home, institution). Second, *age* was calculated on the basis of date of birth and calendar years. For youth with referrals in both 2002 and 2003, the 2-year average age was used. Third, *prior disposition* refers to the most restrictive disposition between 1997 and 2001, and it has three categories: no prior disposition (coded 0), at least one informal disposition but no formal court-ordered disposition (coded 1), and at least one formal court-ordered disposition (coded 2). Fourth, *substance abuse* measures reported levels of no abuse or mild substance abuse (coded 0) and moderate or severe substance abuse (coded 1). Standard tests for multicollinearity showed that it is not problematic in these data.

There were three dichotomous offense measures: serious and violent offending, chronic-only offending, and chronic offending that involves serious offending and/or violent offending. Violence includes homicide, kidnapping, sexual assaults, aggravated assaults, and robbery during 2002–2003. Serious offending includes all felonies during 2002–2003 that are not in the violent category (arson, burglary, assault, theft, vehicle theft, drug possession, weapon offenses, and forgery/fraud). Following the work of Wolfgang, Figlio, and Sellin (1972) in which the concept was established, chronic offending was defined as five or more court referrals between 1997 and 2003. Chronic-only offending includes five or more referrals, among which none were serious or violent. The overall measure includes youth with five or more referrals and at least one serious or violent offense during 2002–2003.

ANALYSES

First we explored the predictive power of Howell's five risk factors: abuse, mental health problems, running away, gang activities, and juvenile justice involvement. The dependent variables were dichotomous, and the statistical models were estimated using binary logistic regression. These models estimate the log odds of involvement in serious offending, violent offending, serious and violent offending, chronic-only offending, and serious, violent, and chronic offending. We examined the independent effect of the five main risk factor variables on offending, and we controlled for race/ethnicity, age, family structure, prior record, and substance abuse. The primary goal was to see if the risk factors were better predictors of serious, violent, and chronic offending as compared to occasional offending among females. Accordingly, separate models were estimated for males and females. Finally, an important aspect of Howell's suggested model is the cumulative effects of the five independent variables on the dependent variables. To assess the cumulative or additive effects for each of the logit regression models of all females and males, we present predicted probabilities for two extreme combinations of the risk factors, with the other variables held constant at their means.

Any test of a developmental network of stepping-stones would be able to address the time ordering of the variables and their impact on each of the following variables as well as serious, violent, and chronic offending. Although our data are valuable and unique in many regards, they allow such time ordering of some, but not all, independent variables. Thus, the direction of the steps between abuse, family structure, mental health problems, and gang involvement cannot be determined here. In the case of abuse/maltreatment and gang involvement, this is less problematic because the likely assumption is that abuse and gang involvement affect offending, rather than the other way around. Less clear, however, is whether mental health problems precede or follow offending. Accordingly, the interpretation of the predictive power of these variables is based solely on theory. The next section presents the findings, including some that were unexpected.

FINDINGS

The initial descriptive statistics for the risk factors, control variables, and dependent variables are shown for the total sample and separately by gender in Table 1 (see p. 94). First, nearly 25% of females but only 7% of males had been subject to suspected abuse or maltreatment. An analysis of the gender distribution of each variable—sexual abuse, physical abuse, emotional abuse, and Child Protective Services involvement—showed a distinct gender difference. Second, 30% of the females and 15% of the males had some form of mental health problems. The examination of each MAYSI-2 scale generally supports the overall results. Third, charges of running away were more common among females: 4% had at least one runaway charge, but the same was true of only 2% of the males; multiple runaway charges were noted for 3% of females and 1% of males. Fourth, although gang involvement was not high, it was more common among males (8%) than females (4%). Fifth, 4% of females but 11% of males were held in secure detention before 2002. The mean number of days in secure detention from 1997 through 2001 was 4 days for males and 2 days for females.

The mean age for females was 15.8 years and for males 15.9 years. Among the females, 37% were Hispanic, 35% were African American, and 29% were White. For males, the order was the same, but minorities had greater representation (39%, 37%, 23%, respectively).

In this sample, 42% of the children lived with a single mother. This was somewhat more common among females than males. Almost 37% of the youth lived with two parents, which was slightly more common among males than females. Living with a single father was also more common for males (8%) than females (6%). Furthermore, a higher proportion of males (8%) lived in an institutional setting or in foster care, as compared to females (5%). However, a higher proportion of

females (7%) than males (6%) lived with extended family. For all family structure categories, the general patterns were similar for males and females.

More males (21%) had substance abuse problems classified as *moderate* or *severe* as compared to females (13%). Most of the substance abuse referred to alcohol and marijuana, with a smaller percentage referring to cocaine, "other substances," and inhalants.

Prior dispositions were included primarily to control for prior offending and prior juvenile justice experience other than detention. Most youth referred in the 2002–2003 period did not have a prior disposition. A higher proportion of males (12%) had at least one prior formal disposition as compared to females (5%). A slightly higher proportion of males than females also had at least one prior informal disposition. However, the gender difference for informal disposition was smaller than that for formal disposition.

Table 1 also shows the distributions for offending outcomes during 2002 and 2003. The results show marked gender differences. Although almost 30% of the males were serious offenders, the same was true of only about 10% of females. Females made up a slightly higher proportion of chronic-only offenders without recorded serious or violent offending. The most encompassing dependent variable was the intersection of chronic offenders who were also referred for serious or violent offenses. This includes 8% overall, but males had twice the level of females (about 10% to 5%).

Next we tested Howell's risk factors on three offending outcomes. Specifically, Table 2 (see p. 96) shows the models for three types of delinquency: serious and violent offending; chronic-only offending; and serious, violent, and chronic offending.

First, for serious or violent offending, two variables were significant for females, but four were significant for males. Contrary to expectations, the coefficients for abuse and maltreatment were negative, thereby indicating that experience of abuse decreases the probability of serious or violent offending for females and males. Gang involvement, however, had positive and statistically significant coefficients for females and males. Being involved with a gang increases the odds of serious and/or violent offending 2.3 times for females and 1.5 for males, holding other variables constant. Mental health problems appeared to only be positively related to males' serious and/or violent offending, increasing the odds of such offending 22%. For males, the coefficient for secure detention was negative; that is, experience of secure detention decreases the odds of serious and violent offending by 24%, holding other variables constant. Experience of secure detention had no statistically significant effect for females. However, the serious and/or violent offending variable includes youth who may have been referred to the juvenile department on a single occasion for a serious or violent offense rather than for repeated offending, which is a central assumption in Howell's proposition.

Second, for chronic offending, defined as five or more referrals between 1997 and 2003 but without reported serious or violent offending, two of the five risk factors were significant for males and females: Mental health problems and runaway violations were directly related to chronic offending. For girls with at least one prior runaway, the risk of chronic offending (as compared to occasional offending) was 5.0 times higher than the risk for females without a prior runaway, holding other variables constant. Similarly for males, at least one prior running-away referral increases the odds of chronic offending 4.5 times.

Although the chronic-offending category could include a nontrivial number of frequent runaways, the correlation coefficient between chronic offending and prior runaway was only moderate ($r = .37$). Thus, the runaway–chronic offending

relationship should refer to chronic offending other than running away. Having mental health problems increased the odds of chronic offending, as compared to occasional offending, with 67% for females and 72% for males, holding other variables constant. Abuse and maltreatment, gang involvement, and prior secure detention were not significantly related to chronic-only offending for either gender.

The final models[5] attempt to distinguish youth involved in chronic as well as serious or violent offending from those involved in occasional nonserious offending and are thus shown in the last columns of Table 2. Although females were less involved in both serious and violent offending, they were more likely than males to be involved in chronic offending, which this all-inclusive variable reflects. For females and males, four of the five risk factors—mental health problems, running away, gang involvement, and secure detention—increased the risk of serious, violent, and chronic offending, as compared to less frequent nonserious offending.[6] The coefficients for abuse and maltreatment were not statistically significant. For mental health problems, the odds of serious, violent, and chronic offending were 2.2 times higher for females and 2.0 times higher for males.

Gang involvement increased the odds of serious, violent, and chronic offending 2.4 times for females and 1.8 times for males. The impact of running away was even larger: For females with at least one prior runaway, the odds of serious, violent, and chronic offending were 4.8 times higher than for those without prior runaway referrals and for males, 5.0 times higher. Finally, the results suggest that prior secure detention experience increased the risk of serious, violent, and chronic offending, as compared to less frequent nonserious offending, for females (4.0 times) and for males (3.0 times). Contrary to expectations, abuse was not significantly related to serious, violent, and chronic delinquency. For the final models, we also calculated a likelihood ratio test[7] to assess the joint effect of the five risk variables: For the female model, $\chi^2 = 95.98$, $p = .000$; for the male model, $\chi^2 = 241.90$, $p = .000$. These results indicate that the risk variables as a group contribute to the predictive power of the model.

Table 3 (see p. 97) shows the change in predicted probabilities of offending based on the model results from (a) youth without any of the risk factors to (b) youth with

Table 1 Summary Statistics (in Percentages)

	Total (n =10,405)	Females (n =3,422)	Males (n =6,983)
Abuse/maltreatment	12.4	23.1	7.1
Suspected sexual	5.8	13.7	1.9
Suspected physical	6.5	11.7	4.0
Suspected emotional	3.9	7.8	2.0
Child Protective Services involvement	7.7	14.6	4.4
Mental health problems	19.7	29.5	14.9
Alcohol/drug	1.9	2.1	1.9
Depression/anxiety	6.6	10.5	4.7
Anger/irritability	7.3	11.1	5.6
Somatic complaints	4.7	7.9	3.1
Suicide ideation	11.4	19.6	7.4
Runaway charge (1997–2001)	4.4	6.9	3.1
Gang involvement	6.8	3.7	8.4
Secure detention (2 or more days, 1997–2001)	8.7	4.2	10.9
Family structure			
Extended family/other	6.3	7.4	5.8
Single mother	42.9	45.9	41.5
Single father	7.4	6.3	7.9
Parents	36.7	35.7	37.2
Institution/foster home	6.7	4.7	7.6
Age	15.9	15.8	15.9
Race			
White	25.2	28.9	23.4
African American	36.4	34.7	37.2
Hispanic	38.4	36.4	39.4
Substance abuse			
Moderate/severe	18.7	13.3	21.3
Most serious prior disposition, 1997–2001			
No prior involvement	76.8	83.1	73.7
Informal	13.5	12.3	14.0
Formal	9.7	4.5	12.3
Current offending			
Serious offending	23.6	10.2	30.2
Violent offending	8.1	4.3	10.0
Serious or violent offending	31.7	14.5	40.2
Chronic-only offending	2.1	2.5	1.9
Chronic and serious or violent offending	8.1	4.7	9.8

NOTE: All differences are statistically significant given the large number of cases.

all five risk factors present, holding other variables constant at their means. For serious and/or violent offending, the changes in the predicted probabilities were fairly small. For females, a partial change from 0 to 1 on the stepping-stone risk factors changed the predicted probability of serious and violent offending from .146 to .163. For males, the equivalent change was from .395 to .407. Accordingly, the cumulative effect of the five risk factors on serious and/or violent offending was quite small for males and females. One of two statistically significant stepping-stone variables in the female model had a negative impact on serious and violent offending. Two of four statistically significant risk variables in the male model had a negative impact on serious and violent offending. This finding explains the small change in the predicted probabilities because the negatively related variables will reduce the predicted probability of serious and violent offending.

The predicted probability for chronic-only offending, based on a partial change from 0 to 1 on the risk variables, was more noticeable for both genders: For females, the predicted probability of chronic offending changed from .004 to .066; for males, the change in the predicted probability of chronic-only offending changed from .007 to .108. Clearly, the statistically significant effects of mental health problems and running away increased the probability of chronic offending.

The predicted probabilities changed dramatically between the two cases for serious, violent, and chronic offending. For females with experience of all five risk factors, the predicted probability of serious, violent, and chronic offending was .471, which can be compared to a predicted probability of serious, violent, and chronic offending of .007 for females without any of the risk factors. For males, the predicted probability of serious, violent, and chronic offending changed from .030 to .576. Accordingly, the cumulative or additive impact of the five risk factors on serious, violent, and chronic offending for females and males was noteworthy.

SUMMARY AND DISCUSSION

This study examined whether or not Howell's proposed risk factors represented a female-specific pathway to serious, violent, and chronic offending, and it revealed that they do not. Except for abuse and maltreatment, which was insignificant in the female model and the male model, Howell's risk factors predict serious, violent, and chronic offending for females and males. The general conclusion was that mental health problems, running away, gang involvement, and secure detention predict serious, violent, and chronic offending among males and females. The analysis of predicted probabilities for the different offending categories further indicated that the cumulative effect of mental health problems, running away, gang involvement, and experience of secure detention was striking and so clearly increased the risk of serious, violent, and chronic offending.

Substance abuse problems and foster care or institutional group home settings also made serious, violent, and chronic delinquency more likely for girls and boys. Race was a factor only among boys, with heightened offending more apt to occur among African American and Hispanic boys.

In the models of chronic offending without serious or violent charges, females and males were also similar in that only two variables—mental health problems and runaway charges—plus substance abuse made chronic offending more likely. Girls in foster care or group home settings were also more apt to become chronic offenders, but this relationship did not appear among boys. Gang involvement was directly related to serious and/or violent offending for girls and boys. In contrast to the expected direction, abuse and maltreatment was negatively related to serious and/or violent offending, and it was gender neutral. Boys with secure detention experiences were less likely to subsequently commit serious or violent offenses. Substance

Table 2 Three Offending Outcomes Regressed on Risk Factors and Controls

	Serious or Violent Offending				Chronic-Only Offending				Serious and/or Violent Offending and Chronic Offending			
	Females		Males		Females		Males		Females		Males	
	B	Exp (B)	B	Exp (B)	B	Exp (B)	B	Exp (B)	B	Exp (B)	B	Exp (B)
Constant	0.622		0.186		-4.329*		-4.521**		-2.563		-4.315**	
Abuse/maltreatment	-0.364**	0.69	-0.222*	0.80	0.352	1.42	0.407	1.50	0.161	1.17	-0.185	0.83
Mental health problems	-0.006	0.99	0.195**	1.22	0.511*	1.67	0.542**	1.72	0.801**	2.23	0.718**	2.05
Runaway	-0.186	0.83	-0.056	0.95	1.636**	5.13	1.500**	4.48	1.576**	4.84	1.608**	4.99
Gang involvement	0.849**	2.34	0.408**	1.50	0.161	1.17	0.367	1.44	0.862*	2.37	0.603**	1.83
Secure detention	-0.165	0.85	-0.277*	0.76	0.166	1.18	0.005	1.00	1.389**	4.01	1.113**	3.04
Extended family–other[a]	0.114	1.12	0.132	1.14	-0.163	0.84	0.009	1.10	0.163	1.18	-0.108	0.90
Single father	-0.311	0.73	-0.100	0.90	0.114	1.12	-0.357	0.70	0.134	1.14	-0.196	0.82
Parents	0.015	1.02	0.166**	1.18	0.151	1.16	-0.046	0.95	-0.029	0.97	-0.108	0.90
Institution–foster care	0.740**	2.10	0.883**	2.42	0.757*	2.13	0.095	1.10	1.185**	3.27	0.924**	2.52
Age	-0.165*	0.85	-0.056**	0.95	-0.094	0.91	-0.075	0.93	-0.183	0.83	-0.019	0.98
African American[b]	0.299*	1.35	0.226**	1.25	-0.174	0.84	0.233	1.26	0.409	1.50	0.618**	1.85
Hispanic	-0.056	0.95	0.001	1.00	-0.515	0.60	0.234	1.26	-0.325	0.72	0.376*	1.46
Substance abuse (mod/sev)[c]	0.640**	1.90	0.475**	1.61	0.886**	2.42	0.626**	1.87	0.804**	2.23	0.555**	1.74
Informal disposition[d]	0.194	1.21	0.065	1.07	2.190**	8.93	1.903**	6.71	1.904**	6.72	1.959**	7.09
Formal disposition	0.031	1.03	-0.401**	0.67	2.993**	19.90	1.906**	6.73	2.699**	14.87	2.320**	10.20
Log likelihood	-1,371.96		-4,579.10		-254.42		-529.33		-358.21		-1,408.10	
Pseudo R^2	.031		.027		.367		.186		.446		.372	
n	3,422		6,983		3,422		6,983		3,422		6,983	

[a] Reference category: single mother.

[b] Reference category: White.

[c] Reference category: no/mild substance abuse.

[d] Reference category: no prior disposition.

* $p <.05$. ** $p <.01$.

abuse problems contribute to all offending models.

LIMITATIONS

The data used in this exploratory study of Howell's theory comprise official juvenile court records for a large jurisdiction serving a diverse population of White, African American, and Hispanic youth. These data are unique in that the jurisdiction processes an unusually large number of cases (indeed, the equivalent processed by some states); however, as in all official databases, not all measures are ideal for specific research purposes. First, although the single jurisdiction controls for jurisdictional differences in processing, the findings herein may reflect idiosyncrasies of one jurisdiction. Second, our data did not allow us to determine the time ordering of the independent variables to one another or to the dependent offending variables. Although this would have been desirable, given that Howell (2003) offered the risk factors as part of a developmental network (Sampson & Laub, 1993) via steppingstones (Farrington, 1986), the causal chain was not explicitly identified and thus not requisite to the theory. Third, related to the source of data is the possibility of measurement error in the demographic variables—for example, underreporting of suspected abuse and maltreatment. The main concern is that of potential systematic bias. Reporting abuse is a sensitive matter, especially by someone who knows or is close to the victim.

It is likely that youth referred to the juvenile court are most likely to report abuse in a situation where they are one-on-one with staff—during psychological or psychiatric evaluation, for instance. A higher proportion of females generally scored above the warning cutoff points on the MAYSI-2 screening instrument and thus were more likely to receive further psychological or psychiatric evaluation; so, this in itself may contribute to better reporting of abuse for females, in addition to any officials' gendered assumptions of victimization. As such, a systematic measurement error in the suspected abuse variables is not unlikely, which is not unique to our data but a problem inherent to all official data reporting systems. Fourth, there is a potential for omitted-variable bias. For example, effective control for socioeconomic status at the neighborhood level has proved to reduce the effect of race on offending, thus indicating that race effects may, to a large degree, be omitted-variable bias (Kempf-Leonard et al., 2001). The fixed-effects models that we examined of school context effects may also capture community and neighborhood effects, including those associated with socioeconomic status and poverty. However, the absence of satisfactory controls for socioeconomic status is potentially a source of bias in the present results. Finally, although these data provided sufficient numbers of cases to allow us to examine by gender and, controlling for race and other personal traits, subgroups of chronic offenders from those with serious and violent court referrals, still more cases would be required to further disaggregate offending. The official nature of these data also preclude examination of non-delinquents involved in a myriad of deviant activities

Table 3 Change in Predicted Probabilities of Offending Outcome Based on Models

Youth With . . .	Serious or Violent Offending		Chronic-Only Offending		Chronic Offending and Serious or Violent	
	Females	Males	Females	Males	Females	Males
No stepping-stone risks	.146	.395	.004	.007	.007	.030
All risks present	.163	.407	.066	.108	.471	.576

(Lanctot & Le Blanc, 2002), those that may disproportionately involve females.

IMPLICATIONS FOR RESEARCH AND THEORY

Despite limitations, the results of this study help to inform delinquency research on gender and so provide considerably more detail on risk factors and personal traits of youth than what is available in other large-scale studies of officially recorded serious, violent, and chronic delinquency (Kempf-Leonard et al., 2001; Tracy & Kempf-Leonard, 1996). In particular, the findings provide insights on the five risk factors that Howell put forward as being potentially female specific for serious, violent, and chronic delinquency. First, in this sample of youth referred to juvenile court, experience of abuse and maltreatment was significantly higher among girls than boys, which has been found in other research (Chesney-Lind, 1995; Chesney-Lind & Shelden, 1992; Dembo, Williams, & Schmeidler, 1993; Walrath et al., 2003). However, the findings did not support a direct relationship between abuse and more serious, violent, and chronic offending, as compared to less serious or occasional offending. In the model for serious and/or violent offending, abuse was negatively related to offending for females and males. In the models with chronic-only offending and serious, violent, and chronic offending, abuse was not significant. Although the chronic-only criterion reflects repeated but nonserious offending and thus could capture a relationship between abuse and status offending among females (Acoca & Dedel, 1998; Chesney-Lind & Shelden, 1992; Dembo et al., 1993), the findings failed to show empirical support for such a relationship.

One possible explanation is that abuse is heavily underreported and so may be captured in the other significant risk factors, such as running away, mental health

problems, or the control variable of family structure, particularly in the categories of living with extended family and being in an institution or in foster care. Another possible explanation is that abuse affects the likelihood of deviant behavior, delinquency, and initial referral to the juvenile justice system but that abuse/maltreatment is not a predictor of serious, violent, or chronic offending in a group of youth referred to juvenile court (Swanston et al., 2003; Zingraff, Leiter, & Myers, 1993). With respect to gender differences, girls were considerably more likely than boys to have experienced abuse or maltreatment, a finding that illustrates that abuse/maltreatment is a gendered risk factor for referral to juvenile court. The findings clearly point to the need for further research into the victimization– delinquency relationship. The validity of a relationship between abuse/maltreatment and offending has been questioned (Schwartz & Rendon, 1994; Widom, 1989), and the findings in this study do not provide conclusive evidence of the effect of abuse. Future research would ideally be able to disentangle the potentially differential effect of abuse versus neglect and to what extent the timing and persistence of abuse and neglect affect later offending (Ireland, Smith, & Thornberry, 2002).

Second, our indicator of mental health problems reflects youths' self-report of symptoms of distress in five areas: drugs and alcohol use, depression and anxiety, anger and irritability, somatic complaints, and suicide ideation. The findings in the multivariate analysis show that having mental health problems was positively related to chronic offending and serious, violent, and chronic offending for females and males. These results provide support for the existing literature about a general relationship between mental health problems and offending (Elliott, Huizinga, & Menard, 1989; Hodgins & Janson, 2002; Loeber, Farrington, Stouthamer-Loeber, & Van Kammen, 1998; Sullivan, Veysey, & Dorangrichia, 2003).

Third, we found that running away was statistically insignificant in the models predicting serious and/or violent offending but that running away was a strong predictor of chronic offending and serious, violent, and chronic offending for boys and girls. Accordingly, these findings confirm that running away was related to other types of delinquency and especially to repeat offending (Lessen, Doreleijers, Van Dijk, & Hartman, 2000; Loeber et al., 1998; Rohr, 1996; Walrath et al., 2003). However, we did not find firm empirical support that running away increases the likelihood of serious and/or violent offending (Brennan, Huizinga, & Elliott, 1978). Although running away was significant in the model for serious, violent, and chronic offending, this relationship was most likely driven by the chronic offending.

Fourth, the descriptive statistics showed gender differences in gang involvement, with a significantly higher proportion of males involved in gangs. In the multivariate analyses, however, gang involvement was found to be related to serious and/or violent offending, as well as serious, violent, and chronic offending, for females and males. Gang involvement was not a predictor of chronic-only offending. These results provide additional empirical support that gang involvement, as suggested by Thornberry and colleagues (2003), is qualitatively related to different and more severe offending among juveniles, as found in other research. Although girls may join gangs for reasons different than those of boys (Bloom, Owen, Rosenbaum, & Deschenes, 2003; Joe & Chesney-Lind, 1995; Miller, 2001), the results in this study lend support to other research findings showing that the facilitating effect of gang membership on serious and violent offending applies to girls (Thornberry et al., 2003).

Fifth, the analyses showed that experience of secure detention was negatively related to serious and/or violent offending for males but insignificant in the same models for females. The negative coefficients on secure detention in the male models were unexpected in that secure detention was hypothesized to have a positive coefficient, thereby reflecting a criminogenic effect. However, the model for serious and violent offending did not separate chronic offenders with prior referrals from first-time or low-incidence offenders. In the model for serious, violent, and chronic offending, the coefficient for secure detention was positive for females and males after controlling for other relevant variables, including prior dispositions. In the regression models with chronic-only offending as the dependent variable, secure detention was not significant for either females or males. Given that chronic offending included only status offenses and misdemeanor offenses for all years (1997–2003), the lack of effect for prior secure detention was not surprising and so likely related to federal mandates restricting the use of secure detention in the juvenile justice system.

These results lend support to findings from prior research that system involvement in general (Fagan, Slaughter, & Hartstone, 1987; Johnson, Simons, & Conger, 2004) and detention in particular (Krisberg & Howell, 1998; Lederman, Dakof, Larrea, & Li, 2004) result in subsequent delinquency and continued juvenile justice involvement. Future research should ideally include measures that capture the timing of different juvenile justice interventions. For example, Tracy and Kempf-Leonard (1996) found that early probation decreased recidivism among three-time delinquents. Incarceration, however, was found to be ineffective. The incarceration effect for females could not be examined in this study with a general population of 14,000 females, which underscores the continuing small-number problem and the need for future research on female offending to have substantial numbers of cases. Other research has found that commitment to residential placement may have a suppression effect for serious juvenile offenders (Krisberg & Howell, 1998).

Our findings should also have value to theoretical explanations of delinquency for females and males. Feminist researchers have emphasized the importance of extending the knowledge of female offending, an area that has been widely neglected within criminology. Feminist researchers have hypothesized correlates of victimization and abuse, running away, and status offending with more serious offending among females (Belknap & Holsinger, 1998; Chesney-Lind, 1997). These findings clearly show that several of these proposed female-specific risk factors, as suggested by Howell, appear to be equally applicable to males. Our purpose was to observe serious, violent, and chronic offending. These factors could produce gender differences if the outcomes include other types of misconduct that are not within the purview of juvenile justice treatment and sanctions (including harm of self) but may be more representative of deviance by females (Lanctot & Le Blanc, 2002).

These findings highlight the need for mainstream criminology to incorporate theoretical aspects and empirical findings from feminist research to further an understanding of female and male offending. Future research needs to extend the analysis of potentially female-specific risk factors to samples including large numbers of males and females, to better determine what are gender-specific causes and correlates in offending pathways. Although the experiences of abuse may well differ in gendered ways for boys and girls and although gender may influence youth's motivations and situational contexts for progression to offending, the findings herein indicate that these risk factors appear to have similar effects for boys' and girls' seriousness and chronicity of offending.

Our data set did not allow for an analysis of the sequencing of the risk factors and their indirect effect on serious, violent, and chronic offending. Although the risk factors correlated with offending for girls and boys, it is possible that gender-specific differences in strength of effects could be observed if temporal ordering could be fully distinguished. This is a recommendation for future research. However, to the extent that chronic juvenile offending (especially, chronic offending that includes serious and violent offending) is significantly related to adult offending, the results from this study have implications for the developmental perspective. The analyses identified a set of risk factors that appear to be equally important for serious, violent, and chronic offending among males and females and that can differentiate between chronic offenders and serious, violent, and chronic offenders.

NOTES

1. The focus of the analysis is to explore gender differences in the direction and magnitude of the five suggested risk factors across offending patterns in multivariate logistic regressions. Because the dependent variable of serious, violent, or chronic offending is a rare event—even among offending youth and especially for females—the 2-year period is chosen to increase the sample size in the multivariate statistical analysis.

2. Excluded youth may belong to more than one excluded category; so, the numbers exceed the difference between the original sample size and the final sample size. The study sample is significantly different (in the statistical sense) from the omitted subsample on some key independent variables. The study sample has a higher proportion of youth with child abuse and gang involvement but less secure detentions and prior formal dispositions. The two groups do not differ statistically for mental health problems or runaway charges. Overall, the omitted subsample may be a source of bias, therefore making the results less likely to represent the larger population of youth referred to the juvenile department.

3. Because the literature generally refers to abuse and neglect to capture maltreatment, we use a more global measure of the experience of maltreatment. Additional research indicates that there is considerable overlap in the types of maltreatment, which justifies this more

inclusive measure (e.g., Smith & Ireland, 2005). Consequently, independent multivariate analysis using each measure of maltreatment in the regressions yielded similar results.

4. The Massachusetts Youth Screening Instrument–Second Version is designed to be administered within 48 hrs of intake, and it is available as a computer-based test and a pen-and-paper test, in English and Spanish. Each of the five scales includes between five and nine items with *yes/no* response alternatives. The test has two defined cutoff points, *caution* and *warning*, based on the additive scores for each scale: *Caution* indicates that close monitoring is necessary for signs of psychological distress, and *warning* indicates the immediate need for further evaluation and possible treatment.

5. A fixed-effects regression model replicating these final models for females and males was also calculated to control for unmeasured variables within schools or school locations that might be correlated with the stepping-stone risk factors and that might therefore bias the coefficients in the model (table not shown). The results showed that school context does not affect the statistical significance of the stepping-stone variables in either the female model or the male model.

6. To test whether the risk factor coefficients are significantly different for males and females, we ran a model predicting serious, violent, and chronic offending including both genders and with interaction terms for female gender and the five theoretical risk factors. None of the coefficients for the interaction terms were statistically significant, thereby indicating that the coefficients for males and females are not significantly different from each other.

7. The likelihood ratio (LR) test was a test of the null hypothesis that the five stepping-stone coefficients are jointly equal to zero. The LR test involved a comparison of the log-likelihood of the restricted model ($\ln L_{res}$), that is, with the coefficients set equal to zero, and the log-likelihood of the unrestricted model ($\ln L_{unres}$). As such,

$$\text{LR test} = -2(\ln L_{res} - \ln L_{unres}).$$

The test statistic is distributed asymptotically as a chi-square with degrees of freedom equal to the number of restrictions (Kennedy, 1998, p. 60; also see Long, 1997, p. 94).

REFERENCES

Acoca, L., & Dedel, K. (1998). *No place to hide: Understanding and meeting the needs of girls in the California juvenile justice system*. Oakland, CA: National Council on Crime and Delinquency.

Belknap, J., & Holsinger, K. (1998). An overview of delinquent girls: How theory and practice have failed and the need for innovative change. In R. T. Zaplin (Ed.), *Female offenders: Critical perspectives and effective interventions* (pp. 31–64). Gaithersburg, MD: Aspen.

Belknap, J., & Holsinger, K. (2006). The gendered nature of risk factors for delinquency. *Feminist Criminology, 1,* 48–70.

Bloom, B., Owen, B., Rosenbaum, J., & Deschenes, E. P. (2003). Focusing on girls and young women: A gendered perspective on female delinquency. *Women and Criminal Justice, 14,* 117–136.

Brennan, T., Huizinga, D., & Elliott, D. S. (1978). *The social psychology of runaways*. Lexington, MA: Lexington Books.

Canter, R. J. (1982). Family correlates of male and female delinquency. *Criminology, 20,* 149–167.

Chesney-Lind, M. (1995). Girls, delinquency, and juvenile justice: Toward a feminist theory of young women's crime. In B. R. Price & N. J. Sokoloff (Eds.), *The criminal justice system and women: Offenders, victims, and workers* (pp. 71–88). New York: McGraw-Hill.

Chesney-Lind, M. (1997). *The female offender: Girls, women, and crime*. Thousand Oaks, CA: Sage.

Chesney-Lind, M., & Shelden, R. G. (1992). *Girls, delinquency, and juvenile justice*. Pacific Grove, CA: Brooks/Cole.

Daly, K. (1992). A woman's pathway to felony court. *Review of Law and Women's Studies, 2,* 11–52.

Daly, K. (1994). *Gender, crime and punishment*. New Haven, CT: Yale University Press.

Daly, K., & Chesney-Lind, M. (1988). Feminism and criminology. *Justice Quarterly, 5,* 497–535.

Dembo, R., Williams, L., & Schmeidler, J. (1993). Gender differences in mental health service needs among youths entering a juvenile detention center. *Journal of Prison and Jail Health, 12*, 73–101.

Elliott, D. S., Huizinga, D., & Menard, S. (1989). *Multiple problem youth: Delinquency, substance use, and mental health problems.* New York: Springer Verlag.

Fagan, J., Slaughter, E., & Hartstone, E. (1987). Blind justice? The impact of race on the juvenile justice process. *Crime and Delinquency, 33*, 224–258.

Farrington, D. (1986). Stepping stones to adult criminal behavior. In D. Olweus, J. Block, & M. Radke-Yarrow (Eds.), *Development of antisocial and prosocial behavior: Research, theories, and issues* (pp. 359–383). London: Academic Press.

Feld, B. (2006). *Final report of the Girl's Study Group.* Washington, DC: Office of Juvenile Justice and Delinquency Prevention.

Gilfus, Mary E. (1992). From victims to survivors to offenders: Women's routes of entry and immersion into street crime. *Women and Criminal Justice, 4*, 63–90.

Hodgins, S., & Janson, C.G. (2002). *Criminality and violence among the mentally disordered. The Stockholm Project Metropolitan.* Cambridge, UK: Cambridge University Press.

Howell, J. C. (2003). *Preventing and reducing juvenile delinquency: A comprehensive framework.* Thousand Oaks, CA: Sage.

Ireland, T. O., Smith, C. A., & Thornberry, T. P. (2002). Developmental issues in the impact of child maltreatment on later delinquency and drug use. *Criminology, 40*, 359–400.

Joe, K. A., & Chesney-Lind, M. (1995). Just every mother's angel: An analysis of gender and ethnic variations in youth gang membership. In K. Daly & L. Maher (Eds.), *Criminology at the crossroads: Feminist readings in crime and justice* (pp. 87–109). Oxford, UK: Oxford University Press.

Johnson, L. M., Simons, R. L., & Conger, R. D. (2004). Criminal justice system involvement and continuity of youth crime: A longitudinal analysis. *Youth and Society, 36*, 3–29.

Kempf-Leonard, K., Tracy, P., & Howell, J. C. (2001). Serious, violent, and chronic juvenile offenders: The relationship of delinquency career types to adult criminality. *Justice Quarterly, 18*, 449–478.

Kennedy, Peter. (1998). *A guide to econometrics.* Cambridge, MA: MIT Press.

Krisberg, B., & Howell, J. C. (1998). The impact of the juvenile justice system and prospects for graduated sanctions in a comprehensive strategy. In R. Loeber & D. P. Farrington (Eds.), *Serious and violent juvenile offenders: Risk factors and successful interventions* (pp. 346–366). Thousand Oaks, CA: Sage.

Lanctot, N., & Le Blanc, M. (2002). Explaining deviance by adolescent females. In M. Tonry (Ed.), *Crime and justice: A review of research* (Vol. 29, pp. 113–202). Chicago: University of Chicago Press.

Lederman, C. S., Dakof, G. A., Larrea, M. A., & Li, H. (2004). Characteristics of adolescent females in juvenile detention. *International Journal of Law and Psychiatry, 27*, 321–337.

Lessen, S. A. M., Doreleijers, T. A. H., Van Dijk, M. E., & Hartman, C. A. (2000). Girls in detention: What are their characteristics? *Journal of Adolescence, 23*, 287–303.

Loeber, R., Farrington, D., Stouthamer-Loeber, M., & Van Kammen, W. B. (1998). *Antisocial behavior and mental health problems: Explanatory factors in childhood and adolescence.* London: Lawrence Erlbaum.

Long, J. S. (1997). *Regression models for categorical and limited dependent variables.* Thousand Oaks, CA: Sage.

Miller, J. (2001). *One of the guys: Girls, gangs, and gender.* Oxford, UK: Oxford University Press.

Rohr, M. E. (1996). Identifying adolescent runaways: The predictive utility of the personality inventory for children. *Adolescence, 31,* 605–624.

Rowe, D. C., Vazsonyi, A. T., & Flannery, D. J. (1995). Sex differences in crime: Do means and within-sex variation have similar causes? *Journal of Research in Crime and Delinquency, 32,* 84–100.

Sampson, R. J., & Laub, J. H. (1993). *Crime in the making: Pathways and turning points trough life.* Cambridge, MA: Harvard University Press.

Schwartz, I. M., & Rendon, J. A. (1994). Is child maltreatment a leading cause of delinquency? *Child Welfare, 73,* 639–655.

Smith, C. A., & Ireland, T. O. (2005). Les consequences developpementales de la maltraitance des filles [Developmental consequences of maltreatment among young women]. *Criminologie, 38,* 67–102.

Smith, D. A., & Paternoster, R. (1987). The gender gap in theories of deviance: Issues and evidence. *Journal of Research in Crime and Delinquency, 24,* 140–173.

Steffensmeier, D., & Allan, E. (1996). Gender and crime: Toward a gendered theory of female offending. *Annual Review of Sociology, 22,* 459–487.

Steffensmeier, D., Schwartz, J., Zhong, H., & Ackerman, J. (2005). An assessment of recent trends in girls' violence using diverse longitudinal sources: Is the gender gap closing? *Criminology, 43,* 355–405.

Sullivan, C. J., Veysey, B. M., & Dorangrichia, L. (2003). Examining the relationship between problem history and violent offending in high-risk youth. *Journal of Offender Rehabilitation, 38,* 17–39.

Swanston, H. Y., Parkinson, P. N., O'Toole, B. I., Plunkett, A. M., Shrimpton, S., & Oates, K. R. (2003). Juvenile crime, aggression and delinquency after sexual abuse. *British Journal of Criminology, 43,* 729–749.

Thornberry, T. P., Krohn, M. D., Lizotte, A. J., Smith, C. A., & Tobin, K. (2003). *Gangs and delinquency in developmental perspective.* Cambridge, UK: Cambridge University Press.

Tracy, P., & Kempf-Leonard, K. (1996). *Continuity and discontinuity in criminal careers.* New York: Plenum Press.

Walrath, C., Ybarra, M., Holden, W. E., Manteuffel, B., Santiago, R., & Leaf, P. (2003). Female offenders referred for community-based mental health service as compared to other service-referred youth: Correlates of conviction. *Journal of Adolescence, 23,* 45–61.

Widom, C. (1989). Child abuse, neglect, and adult behavior: Research design and findings on criminality, violence, and child abuse. *American Journal of Orthopsychiatry, 59,* 355–367.

Wolfgang, M., Figlio, R., & Sellin, T. (1972). *Delinquency in a birth cohort.* Chicago: University of Chicago Press.

Wolfgang, M., Thornberry, T., & Figlio, R. (Eds.). (1987). *From boy to man, from delinquency to crime.* Chicago: University of Chicago Press.

Zingraff, M. T., Leiter, J., & Myers, K. A. (1993). Child maltreatment and youthful problem behavior. *Criminology, 31,* 173–202.

Pernilla Johansson recently completed her doctorate in public policy and political economy at the University of Texas at Dallas, where she also lectures in criminal justice. Her research interests include gender, race and crime, juvenile and criminal justice policy, criminological theory, and comparative criminal justice.

Kimberly Kempf-Leonard is professor of administration of justice and chair of the Center for Study of Crime, Delinquency, and Corrections at the Southern Illinois University. Her research examines the development of criminal careers, gender, race, and criminal justice processing. Recent publications include *Our Children, Their Children* (with D. F. Hawkins, 2005) and *The Encyclopedia of Social Measurement* (2005).

7

PARENT-CENTERED INTERVENTION

A Practical Approach for Preventing Drug Abuse in Hispanic Adolescents

MARIA I. TAPIA AND SETH J. SCHWARTZ
UNIVERSITY OF MIAMI

GUILLERMO PRADO
FLORIDA INTERNATIONAL UNIVERSITY

BARBARA LOPEZ AND HILDA PANTIN
UNIVERSITY OF MIAMI

Objective: The objective of the present article is to review and discuss Familias Unidas, an empirically supported, family-based, culturally specific drug abuse and HIV prevention intervention for Hispanic immigrant adolescents and their families. Method: The authors focus on engagement and retention as well as on intervention delivery. Conclusions: The present article serves as a guide for social workers and

Authors' Note: Special gratitude is extended to all the schools, counselors, and families that participated in this project. Preparation of this article was supported by National Institute on Mental Health Grant MH63402 awarded to Dr. José Szapocznik and National Institute on Drug Abuse Grants DA17462 and DA19101 awarded to Drs. Hilda Pantin and Guillermo Prado, respectively. Correspondence and reprint requests should be sent to Maria Tapia, L.C.S.W., Center for Family Studies, Department of Psychiatry and Behavioral Sciences, Leonard M. Miller School of Medicine, University of Miami, 1425 N.W. 10th Avenue, Miami, FL 33136 (e-mail MTapia@med.miami.edu).

SOURCE: "Parent-Centered Intervention: A Practical Approach for Preventing Drug Abuse in Hispanic Adolescents" by Maria I. Tapia, Seth J. Schwartz, Guillermo Prado, Barbara Lopez, and Hilda Pantin. In the 2006 issue of *Research on Social Work Practice, 16*(2), 146–165. Used with permission.

mental health practitioners in carrying out effective family-based adolescent substance use and HIV preventive interventions. Recommendations for and challenges to implementing the intervention in practice-based settings are discussed.

Keywords: drug use; prevention; parent-centered intervention; Hispanic; adolescent; immigrant

Although extensive drug abuse and HIV prevention efforts have been developed, evaluated, and implemented (e.g., DiClemente et al., 2004; Dishion & Kavanagh, 2000; Hanish & Tolan, 2001; Hawkins, Guo, Hill, Battin-Pearson, & Abbott, 2001; Pantin, Coatsworth, et al., 2003), a fairly large number of American youth are still using alcohol and other drugs and engaging in unsafe sex. Substance use, especially when it begins in childhood or early adolescence, is often associated with future substance abuse and dependence (Kalant, 2004), involvement in delinquent activities (Flory, Lynam, Milich, Leukefeld, & Clayton, 2004), school dropout (McCluskey, Krohn, Lizotte, & Rodriguez, 2002), and sexual risk-taking behaviors that can lead to teen pregnancy, sexually transmitted diseases, and HIV infection (Brook et al., 2004). As a result, preventing substance use, unsafe sex, and HIV infection in children and adolescents is an important public health concern.

Although early and persistent substance use represents a significant problem for adolescents from many different ethnic groups, Hispanics are at particularly high risk. Johnston, O'Malley, Bachman, and Schulenberg (2004) found that among 8th- and 10th-grade adolescents, Hispanics reported higher rates of use than non-Hispanic Whites or African Americans for most classes of drugs, including alcohol. However, Johnston et al. found that for most substances, Hispanic 12th graders tended to fall between African Americans and non-Hispanic Whites in terms of percentage of adolescents currently using, with the exception of crack and ecstasy (for which Hispanics ranked highest). Johnston et al. concluded that the discordant positioning of Hispanics at 8th and 10th grade versus 12th grade may be because of the fact that many Hispanic students drop out of high school and are therefore not included in the 12th-grade statistics. Recent statistics indicate that as many as 40% of Hispanic students do not finish high school (Greene & Forster, 2003). It is therefore critical that interventions designed to prevent substance use in Hispanic adolescents, especially those programs that recruit through or are delivered in the school system, be designed to reach students before they drop out of school. Once students drop out of school, they become much more difficult to reach and are much more likely to use substances (Guagliardo, Huang, Hicks, & D'Angelo, 1998).

Although Hispanics as a group are at high risk for drug use, there are important differences among Hispanic nationalities in risks for drug use. For example, data from the Monitoring the Future study suggest that Cuban American adolescents are more likely to use illicit drugs than are Mexican American or Puerto Rican adolescents (Wallace & Muroff, 2002). Moreover, U.S.-born Hispanics are more likely to use drugs than are immigrant Hispanic adolescents (Vega et al., 2002). However, despite these differences, specific processes inherent in the Hispanic immigrant experience may increase Hispanic adolescents' vulnerability to drug use and related risks such as sexual risk taking (Pantin, Schwartz, Sullivan, Coatsworth, & Szapocznik, 2003; Pantin, Schwartz, Sullivan, Prado, & Szapocznik, 2004). These specific processes are discussed in the next section. It should be noted that these processes, rather than nationality or nativity per se, are the targets of intervention (Pantin, Prado, Schwartz, & Sullivan, 2005).

The purpose of this article is to discuss some possible reasons for the heightened substance use rates among Hispanic adolescents as well as to outline potential ways to prevent substance use, sexual risk taking, and HIV in this population. Our approach centers on countering the difficulties that Hispanic immigrant families face in raising healthy, drug-free adolescents. Consistent with such an approach, we outline a family-based preventive intervention that we have designed and are currently testing to reduce Hispanic adolescents' risk for conduct problems, involvement with antisocial peers, drug use, and unsafe sexual behavior. We include specific coverage of engagement and retention, which are often difficult issues in prevention and treatment interventions (e.g., Perrino, Coatsworth, Briones, Pantin, & Szapocznik, 2001; Prado, Pantin, Schwartz, Lupei, & Szapocznik, 2006; Szapocznik, Hervis, & Schwartz, 2003). We then discuss our methods and some implications of our work for social work practice. Where appropriate, case studies are presented to illustrate some of the challenges for social workers and mental health practitioners in working with Hispanic families.

The Hispanic Immigrant Family: Acculturation Issues

Migration from Latin America represents more than 50% of the foreign-born population in the United States today (Larsen, 2004). Hispanics represent the largest minority group, especially in urban areas, in the United States (Marotta & Garcia, 2003). Hispanics also tend to be overrepresented among poor Americans; nearly 22% of Hispanics, as compared to 8% of non-Hispanic Whites, lived below the poverty line in 2002 (Procter & Dalaker, 2003). Moreover, more than 23% of adult Spanish speakers in the United States reported not speaking English well or at all (Shin & Bruno, 2003). These demographic statistics suggest the presence of multiple barriers facing Hispanic immigrant parents. A review of relevant literature, as described next, supports and extends such a conclusion.

When Hispanic immigrant parents with limited English proficiency first arrive in the United States, they are faced with the daunting task of raising children in an unfamiliar and foreign culture. These parents are often faced with numerous obstacles that can potentially place their children at risk for drug abuse and other antisocial behaviors (Pantin, Schwartz, et al., 2003; Pantin et al., 2004). Such obstacles include cultural incompatibilities between the receiving culture and the immigrant's culture of origin, social isolation, and marginalization from sources of support. These challenges may pose the greatest difficulties for low-income parents, who often do not have access to supportive resources that can assist them in the transition to a new homeland. In Latin American countries, the family is generally prioritized above the individual. Values such as respect for adults, conformity, and a sense of duty to parents are regarded as important aspects of parent-child relationships in Latin American countries (Santisteban, Muir-Malcolm, Mitrani, & Szapocznik, 2002). These cultural values sometimes conflict with those commonly endorsed in American society, where the individual is generally prioritized over the family. There is a robust social-psychological literature demonstrating that individuals perceived as foreigners because of linguistic, cultural, or ethnic differences may be ostracized and marginalized from the mainstream cultural group (e.g., Mummendey, Klink, & Brown, 2001). Therefore, as a result of linguistic and cultural incompatibilities between Hispanic and American culture, Hispanic immigrants often find themselves isolated from sources of support in the United States, even in predominantly Hispanic neighborhoods (Leon & Dziegielewski, 2000; Pantin, Schwartz, et al., 2003; Pantin et al., 2004). Social isolation, coupled with the stresses of daily living, long work hours, and lack of support from family and community may increase the likelihood that parents will become frustrated and overwhelmed and will disinvest from their adolescents' lives. Parental disinvestment, in turn, can place adolescents at even greater risk for drug involvement and other problem behaviors (Gray & Steinberg, 1999).

When they leave their homelands, many immigrant families leave behind extended family members and neighbors that provided parents with sources of support in raising children. After arriving in the United States, parents in these families often lack the sources of support on which they relied in their countries of origin (Garcia-Coll, Meyer, & Brillon, 1995). Moreover, poor English skills force parents to rely on their adolescents, who learn English in school and from peers, to help them with everyday transactions such as banking and grocery shopping (e.g., Weisskirch & Alva, 2002). Such language brokering places adolescents in a leadership position within the family. This inverted family hierarchy is at odds with traditional values endorsed by Hispanic culture, where adolescents are expected to obey and respect parental authority without much questioning (Santisteban et al., 2002). This inverted family hierarchy may be associated with problematic adolescent outcomes resulting from a lack of parental guidance (Kurtines & Szapocznik, 1996).

Language brokering may be associated with differential acculturation (Pantin, Schwartz, et al., 2003; Pantin et al., 2004), in which adolescents endorse American cultural values and practices to a much greater extent and endorse Hispanic cultural values and practices to a much lesser extent than their parents do. Proficiency in English allows adolescents to immerse themselves in American culture and its practices (e.g., television shows, social fads). Hispanic-oriented parents, on the other hand, often not only lack English language proficiency but also may be opposed to many American cultural practices (e.g., diet, styles of dress, music preferences).

Differential acculturation may then be associated with compromised family functioning, which in turn may be positively related to adolescent behavior problems (Pantin, Prado, Schwartz, Sullivan, & Szapocznik, 2005). Parents may perceive their adolescents' Americanized behaviors as disrespectful to the family and may try to reassert their authority in hopes of regaining control of their adolescents. In turn, the adolescent may perceive the parent's behavior as overly controlling and may withdraw and rebel further. At this juncture, parents tend to follow one of two courses of action: (a) give up supervising their adolescents or (b) employ restrictive tactics, such as not allowing the adolescent go out with friends and searching the adolescent's personal belongings such as drawers and backpacks. In the first case, parental disengagement is likely to lead to increased affiliation with deviant peers and to problematic outcomes (Dishion, Nelson, & Bullock, 2004). In the latter case, an overly restrictive and mistrustful parenting style is likely to produce rebellion in the adolescent (Mason, Cauce, Gonzales, & Hiraga, 1996). Such downward spirals in the parent-child relationship leave adolescents vulnerable to deviant peer associations and subsequently to substance use (Dishion et al., 2004).

In the United States, adolescents are expected to spend time with peers and to learn to make choices on their own with proper parental support and guidance. However, in traditional Hispanic families, such behavior can be interpreted as a clear indication of disrespect and disengagement from the family of origin. This cultural disparity interferes with family boundaries and compounds intercultural conflicts onto normative intergenerational conflicts (Felix-Ortiz, Fernandez, & Newcomb, 1998; Szapocznik & Kurtines, 1993). Parents can become increasingly discouraged and may give up their attempts to control and monitor their youth (Kurtines & Szapocznik, 1996). During adolescence, positive and caring parent-child relationships are crucial for adolescent well-being and development (Masten & Coatsworth, 1998; Steinberg, 2001). When intercultural conflicts are compounded onto normative parent-adolescent disagreements, adolescents may be less likely to reach out to their parents for support and guidance (De la Rosa, Vega, & Radisch, 2000). Adolescents may then turn to their peers for support instead. As a result, risks for adolescent drug abuse and problem behaviors are further increased (Pabon, 1998; Vakalahi, 2002).

It should be noted that the patterns discussed here may apply across Hispanic nationalities. For example, prioritizing the family over the individual has been found to be a pan-Hispanic cultural orientation (Sabogal, Marin, Otero-Sabogal, Marin, & Perez-Stable, 1987). Moreover, issues of acculturation, language barriers, and unfamiliarity are applicable to nearly all Hispanics, regardless of their country of origin. As a result, it is possible that a single set of prevention strategies may be applicable across Hispanic nationalities.

WORLDS OF THE ADOLESCENT: FAMILY, SCHOOL, AND PEERS

In light of all of these risks for substance abuse and other behavior problems in Hispanic adolescents, what can immigrant parents do to protect their adolescents from these negative outcomes? To address these important issues, we will examine the influence of adolescents' family, peer and school worlds on these negative outcomes. We will note ways in which parents can involve themselves in the peer and school worlds to help protect their adolescents from risks in these worlds.

Family

Extensive research has established the crucial role that families play in healthy child and adolescent development (Resnick et al., 1997), including behavior problems (Patterson & Dishion, 1985; Tolan, Guerra, & Kendall, 1995) and drug use or abuse (Dishion & McMahon, 1998; Tolan & Gorman-Smith, 1997). Research has also identified a number of

risk and protective factors (e.g., parental investment, parent-adolescent communication, parental monitoring of peers) that predispose adolescents in general, and Hispanic adolescents in particular, to behavior problems and drug abuse (Hawkins, Catalano, & Miller, 1992). The family is the most important social system influencing human development and, when effectively mobilized, can provide a context for lasting behavioral change (Bronfenbrenner, 1979, 1986; Szapocznik & Coatsworth, 1999). Family support for the adolescent (Crosby et al., 2001; Rodgers, 1999), parent-adolescent communication (Brody & Ge, 2001; O'Sullivan, Jaramillo, Moreau, & Meyer-Bahlburg, 1999), parent-adolescent connectedness (Miller, 2002; van den Bree & Pickworth, 2005), and parental monitoring of adolescent activities (Getz & Bray, 2005; Huebner & Howell, 2003) are powerful protective factors against both substance use and unsafe sexual contact. Parent-adolescent communication about sex is an additional protective factor against unsafe sex (Whitaker & Miller, 2000). Therefore, in our intervention, we work closely with the family to implement long-lasting changes (e.g., increases in parental investment, parent-adolescent communication, parental monitoring of peers) to prevent or reduce drug use and behavior problems.

Peers

Peers are the primary vehicle through which immigrant adolescents learn to navigate through and adjust to their new host culture. Often, immigrant adolescents quickly learn and adapt to the host culture's values, beliefs, and behaviors (e.g., individualism in American culture). However, these new cultural ideals tend to pull them away from traditional Hispanic values such as respect and obedience to parents (Gil, Wagner, & Vega, 2000).

What, then, can Hispanic parents do to counteract the effect of the influences of Americanized peers on their children and on the traditional Hispanic family hierarchy?

First, parents can (and should) supervise and actively monitor adolescents' peer relationships (Mounts, 2001). This means knowing the adolescent's peers and their peers' parents as well as participating in planning adolescent social activities. When an adolescent's parents meet with other parents, they can plan and supervise adolescents' outings together, thus creating a social network that not only can decrease exposure to antisocial activities and potential drug use but also can build a social network through which parents support one another. Mancilla et al. (2005) reported that involving youth in parent-organized peer activities decreased adolescent behavior problems and that these relationships tended to relieve parents' sense of isolation. When working with Hispanic immigrant parents, the importance of monitoring adolescents' peer relationships should be emphasized, and creating collaborative relationships with peers' parents should be advocated as a way of ensuring that monitoring indeed occurs. Research suggests that Hispanic immigrant parents' connection to their adolescents' peer networks may help to reduce adolescents' behavior problems (Coatsworth, Pantin, McBride, et al., 2002).

School

Schools play a vital role in the lives of children and adolescents. Children and adolescents spend much of their waking time in school, and in school, they come into contact with potentially positive role models such as counselors, teachers, and coaches. Adolescents who are not bonded to (or lack interest in) school, however, may be at risk for substance abuse and problem behaviors (Simons-Morton et al., 1999; Vazsonyi & Flannery, 1997). Moreover, once adolescents drop out of school, their risk for substance use increases dramatically (Ellickson, Bui, Bell, & McGuigan, 1998; Guagliardo et al., 1998). School is an especially important domain for Hispanic adolescents, given that almost 40% of Hispanics fail to complete high school (Greene & Forster, 2003).

For immigrant parents, and especially for those who do not understand English, the school system can be intimidating. Even for parents who do understand enough English to communicate with school officials, lack of knowledge about the American school system may prevent them from becoming involved in their children's school. Whereas many Hispanic immigrants come from villages and small towns where teachers are friends or neighbors who can be found at the local post office or church (Coatsworth, Pantin, & Szapocznik, 2002), the American school system is large and impersonal. Some Hispanic immigrant parents may not even know that direct contact with the school is possible. They may not understand the grading system well enough to read and understand report cards (Rodriguez-Brown & Meehan, 1998). Moreover, many Hispanic immigrant parents are employed in the service industry (e.g., hotels, restaurants). Such businesses often have inflexible schedules and place strict limitations on personal time (e.g., days off). These limitations serve to further restrict parents' access to the school system during times when most teachers are able to meet with parents. In turn, when parents are uninvolved in their children's schooling, regardless of the reason, children's academic performance may suffer (Hill & Craft, 2003).

ECODEVELOPMENTAL THEORY AND THE FAMILIAS UNIDAS INTERVENTION

We (Pantin, Schwartz, et al., 2003; Pantin et al., 2004) have designed a parent-centered, culturally specific preventive intervention for Hispanic adolescents and their families. This intervention is designed for Hispanic families with immigrant parents. The program can be (and has been) implemented with families of both immigrant and U.S.-born adolescents. We refer to this intervention as *Familias Unidas*, which means "United Families" in

Spanish. Familias Unidas has been tested in two randomized clinical trials. In the first trial (Pantin, Coatsworth, et al., 2003), Familias Unidas was found to be significantly more efficacious than a no-contact control condition in improving family functioning and decreasing adolescent behavior problems—both of which may protect against substance use. The second trial examined the efficacy of Familias Unidas combined with Parent-Preadolescent Training for HIV Prevention (PATH; Krauss et al., 2000), a parent-adolescent HIV prevention module, in preventing substance use and unsafe sexual behavior. Familias Unidas plus PATH was found to be significantly more efficacious than two attention control conditions in preventing drug and alcohol use and unsafe sexual behavior at 2 years postintervention. Results of this second trial are currently being prepared for publication.

Ecodevelopmental theory (Szapocznik & Coatsworth, 1999) serves as a framework for the Familias Unidas intervention (Pantin, Schwartz, et al., 2003; Pantin et al., 2004). This theory outlines ways in which risk and protective factors are interrelated in adolescents' lives and interact to produce positive or negative developmental outcomes. For instance, when parents are emotionally close to their adolescents, they tend to be involved in their lives and to provide supervision and guidance, and the effects of peer deviance on adolescent behavior are decreased (Frauenglass, Routh, Pantin, & Mason, 1997). In this case, a strength within the family carries over into the other adolescent worlds and offers protection against association with deviant peers and possibly against behavior problems and substance use.

Ecodevelopmental theory is composed of three components: social ecological theory, developmental theory, and a focus on social interactions. The first component, social ecological theory, is rooted in Bronfenbrenner's (1979, 1986) conceptualization of four overlapping levels of social context. The macrosystem is the outermost layer of an individual's environment that encompasses the social and philosophical ideals that define the dominant culture. The macrosystem that defines a given cultural context cascades, or trickles down, into the other contextual levels (Pantin et al., 2004). For example, on January 8, 2002, the No Child Left Behind Act of 2001 was enacted (U.S. Department of Education, 2002) and has influenced the composition of academic curricula, which, in turn, influences both the teachers' and adolescents' classroom experiences. This shows how the macrosystem can have an impact in the lives of individuals and how public policies have a trickle-down effect.

The exosystem refers to experiences that directly involve the parent but that do not directly involve the adolescent. Although the adolescent is not an active or direct participant, events occurring in the exosystem still affect the adolescent's life. For example, parental work stress decreases the amount and quality of time that parents spend with their children (Kelloway & Barling, 1994).

The mesosystem is composed of interactions between or among important members of different contexts in which the adolescent participates directly. For example, increasing parental involvement in the adolescent's school world protects adolescents against school disinterest and dropout and consequently against substance use and other problem behaviors (Hong & Ho, 2005). The stronger the connections between an adolescent's worlds, especially between the family and peers and school, the lower the risk for problem behaviors (Coatsworth, Pantin, McBride, et al., 2002).

The innermost layer is the microsystem. The microsystem refers to the immediate settings in which the child is a direct participant (e.g., family, peers, school). Within each microsystem, the adolescent maintains relationships with a network of people. The quality and integrity of these relationships has the potential to influence an adolescent's course of development.

For example, within the context of school, administrative personnel, teachers, and classmates shape an adolescent's academic performance through encouragement, criticism, and other forms of feedback. If this feedback is delivered in a constructive and supportive way, the adolescent's developmental course may benefit as a result; in contrast, criticism that is perceived as harsh or unsupportive may undermine students' motivation to achieve (see Harter, 1996).

The second component of ecodevelopmental theory is a developmental perspective that emphasizes the changing nature of youth across time as a function of the adolescent's current social context as well as the changing conditions in the social context throughout the adolescent's life. Thus, a developmental perspective is applied to the youth and her or his social context, where both person and context are viewed as evolving and changing across the life span. For example, adolescent substance abuse is influenced not only by the youth's current social context, as manifested in family cohesion and parental monitoring (Bogenschneider, Wu, Raffaelli, & Tsay, 1998) during adolescence but also possibly by previous levels of parental investment (Barnes, Farrell, & Banerjee, 1994), by school bonding and academic achievement (Ellickson et al., 1998), and in the child's self-regulation and behavior control (Vitaro, Brendgen, LaDouceur, & Tremblay, 2001).

The final component of ecodevelopmental theory is a focus on social interactions. Whereas Bronfenbrenner's (1979) social ecology theory places an emphasis on an individual's development as guided by the four levels of social context, the social interactional component refers to specific sequences of interpersonal transactions that affect risk and protection. For example, parental monitoring of peer activities serves to counteract the deleterious effects of deviant peer exposure on adolescents' risk for substance use (Fletcher, Darling, & Steinberg, 1995).

ENGAGEMENT AND RETENTION: IMPORTANT CHALLENGES FOR PRACTITIONERS

An important problem in implementing parent-centered interventions, however, is that engagement and participation rates are often less than optimal (DeMarsh & Kumpfer, 1986; Kazdin, 1993; Perrino et al., 2001). In this section, we discuss successful strategies to engage and retain Hispanic parents and adolescents in parent-centered preventive interventions. Practitioners face two related challenges when working with families— engagement and retention. Engagement refers to bringing clients into the intervention, whereas retention refers to keeping them enrolled through the entire program. Family-based prevention programs often fail to engage and retain more than half of all families who are initially recruited (Brody et al., 2004; Fox & Gottfredson, 2003; Hawkins et al., 2001).

Engagement

Engaging clients into treatment represents a major obstacle in providing services for many mental health professionals (Kazdin, 1993, 1994). Many families identified as in need of services fail to see a therapist even once (Costello, Burns, Angold, & Leaf, 1993; Staghezza-Jaramillo, Bird, Gould, & Canino, 1995). There are a number of reasons that may account for these engagement failures, but whatever the reasons, when families fail to engage into treatment services, they lose the opportunity to receive a valuable service. Moreover, although Hispanics are at higher risk for drug use (Johnston et al., 2004) and suicidality (O'Donnell, O'Donnell, Yardlaw, & Stueve, 2004) than are non-Hispanic Whites or African Americans, Hispanic immigrants tend to receive fewer health services than do non-Hispanic Whites (Miranda, Azocar, Organista, Muñoz, & Lieberman, 1996). As a result, to help ensure that this growing and often vulnerable population receives services as needed, it is imperative that facilitators and therapists use multiple effective strategies to engage Hispanic families.

Research has begun to explore how families might best be engaged. Work conducted at our center has shown that both the initial contact (i.e., first phone call; Szapocznik et al., 2003) and the first intervention session (Prado et al., 2006) are critical for engaging families into the intervention. Concerning the initial contact, the quality of the relationship between the therapist and the caller, the caller's perceptions of the therapist's interest and genuineness, and the caller's belief that the intervention can meet the family's needs are important in determining whether the family will attend sessions (see Muir, Schwartz, & Szapocznik, 2004; Szapocznik & Williams, 2000, for reviews). It is therefore vitally important that a facilitator or therapist—not a receptionist or clerical person—make the first contact with the family (Prado et al., 2006). In most social services agencies, the first contact the family or the individual has is with a receptionist, clerical person, or intake worker. Such individuals generally do not have the clinical skills required to join with the entire family, to identify the family's specific areas of need, and to assure the family that the intervention has the potential to address these needs. Without these important joining functions, it may be difficult to maintain the family's interest and desire to receive services—especially if the family must endure a long delay between the first contact with the service agency and the first counseling or intervention session. Systemic family work begins with the first contact with a family member, and care must be taken to ensure that this first contact is handled by someone with the necessary skills and experience to do systemic work.

The facilitators who have conducted the Familias Unidas intervention in our studies have all been of Hispanic origin, but it may also be possible for non-Hispanic facilitators to implement the intervention provided that they are fluent in Spanish and intimately familiar with Hispanic cultures. For example, a White American or African American who has been immersed in Hispanic culture and understands the hierarchical and family-based emphasis underlying parent-child relationships in Hispanic cultural contexts could successfully implement the Familias Unidas intervention. It is important, however, that the issue of the facilitator's non-Hispanic ethnicity be addressed with participating families as soon as possible. A non-Hispanic facilitator may have to convince families, both in the engagement phase and during group sessions, that she or he understands their cultural background, issues, and challenges.

The first face-to-face interaction between the facilitator and the family, usually in the form of a family visit, should occur soon after the initial phone contact. In our experience in working with Hispanic immigrant families, the likelihood of engagement tends to be higher when we conduct the initial family visit as close as possible to the initial telephone call rather than when we allow more time to elapse. This extra effort in joining and accommodating to the family is essential to achieving treatment outcomes later on. This may seem like an intensive engagement effort from the therapist's perspective, but by joining with the family and beginning to address the family's areas of need, along with capitalizing on momentum and progress, the therapist maximizes the chances of engaging the family.

Moreover, the first family visit, which focuses on joining and engagement, is also extremely important in engaging the family. One of the studies conducted at our center (Prado et al., 2006) found that the facilitator-family relationship quality in the first family visit strongly predicted whether the family successfully engaged into the intervention. Some of the specific techniques used in the joining family visits included actively listening to the parent and validating some of his or her concerns and highlighting the parent's legitimate concerns for herself or himself or the adolescent. Likely because of these intensive engagement efforts, we were able to engage 90% of families into one of our recent preventive interventions. This is consistent with our prior research showing that intensive engagement strategies that (a) form alliances with family members and (b) identify and target sources of family resistance are most likely to engage families into intervention programs (Coatsworth, Santisteban, McBride, & Szapocznik, 2001; Santisteban et al., 1996; Szapocznik et al., 1988). Although family members' characteristics, such as income and stress level, have been found to predict engagement into parent-centered interventions (Spoth, Goldberg, & Redmond, 1999; Spoth & Redmond, 1995), in our work (Coatsworth et al., 2001; Prado et al., 2006; Santisteban et al., 1996; Szapocznik et al., 1988), we have found that interventionist behaviors also facilitate or inhibit engagement. In some cases (e.g., Prado et al., 2006), interventionist behaviors and the interventionist-family relationship have been better predictors of engagement than have the characteristics of families or their members.

When joining a family, it is essential to validate the parents' concerns. Many parents in the study sample reported feeling validated by a professional in a way that they had never experienced before. Even in cases where the parent does not seem to be "getting it," validation and encouragement may help to motivate parents to engage in the intervention. Such motivation may help parents to catch on once group sessions begin.

It is also important to raise parents' awareness about the realities that their adolescents face. Raising awareness is often accomplished by introducing content areas such as drug use, sexual risk taking, and school dropout. Facilitators may mention some of these issues to parents and give prevalence statistics. Parents often respond with examples of these problems from their own lives, families, or communities. In turn, these examples and the content areas from which they are drawn can be used to raise parents' awareness regarding the need for preventive intervention. The specific content areas mentioned (e.g., types of drugs discussed) are tailored to match the specific problems of the family and community in which the parents reside. For example, in Miami, marijuana and ecstasy are among the most commonly used drugs. As a result, our engagement efforts in Miami often focus on preventing the use of these drugs.

Some of the qualities that help facilitators to engage families are genuineness, unconditional positive regard, and empathy. Families are often sensitive to the fact that something is wrong and that they may be criticized for it (Szapocznik et al., 2003), and family members often do not know what to expect from a mental health professional. Accordingly, the joining family visit often involves a delicate balancing act on the part of the facilitator. During the process of exploring the family's problem areas and offering information about the intervention, therapists need to be careful not to take sides regarding any of the family's issues. Each family member may have a different perspective on the family's issues, and taking sides may alienate some family members. This is a delicate initial step where some inexperienced therapists may have trouble understanding and implementing the engagement procedures. The facilitator should listen actively to, empathize with, and offer unconditional positive regard to each family member without alienating anyone else in the family. Active listening does not mean that the therapist sides with or agrees with the family member who is speaking. It simply indicates that the facilitator is listening to and in tune with the family.

It is important, however, that the facilitator should avoid excessive lecturing and should not act as a switchboard for the family. If something that one family member says is unclear to another family member, or if a family member reacts angrily in response to something that another family member says, the facilitator should not attempt to solve the issue. Rather, the facilitator should encourage family members to clarify and discuss the issue among themselves, and she or he should intervene only to redirect and summarize the discussion. In our own work (Prado et al., 2006), facilitator switchboard behaviors have been associated with lowered likelihood of engaging families.

Families need to be informed about the project, and the project description should be framed in terms of the family's specific needs. Each family member should be reassured that the program will help to meet her or his needs. This involves starting where the family is and figuring out how the intervention can help meet the family's needs. The intervention should be described in detail, focusing on its applicability to the problems of the family. For example, a father may complain that his wife bothers him too much. In such a case, the facilitator might reassure him by saying that she or he would work with the family to find ways for the mother to complain less. At the same time, the therapist might tell the mother she or he will work with the family to help the mother to get the help and support she needs from the other family members (including the adolescent). By creating optimism, enthusiasm, and motivation, the therapist increases the chances of bringing the family in for the first group session.

In cases where parents express concerns about their adolescents, these concerns can be used to engage the family into the intervention. For example, if a mother tells the facilitator that she is concerned about her adolescent's school grades, the facilitator immediately validates the mother's concern, highlighting the parent's interests and the legitimacy of the concern. The facilitator attempts to instill hope in the parent and to reassure her that the intervention will address her concern and will help to improve the adolescent's school performance. For another example, many parents are concerned that their adolescents will use drugs. Therefore, the majority of parents are willing to learn ways to help their children avoid substance use. Substance use is an appropriate topic to address in efforts to engage a parent in a prevention project, especially given the prevalence of substance use and related problems in news reports and other media outlets. It is important to emphasize that Familias Unidas provides skills that parents can use in communicating drug prevention messages to their adolescents.

It is also important to note that, in engaging families into Familias Unidas, we often encounter families in crisis. Examples of such crises include parental divorce or separation, adolescents being arrested, or adolescents running away. We draw on crisis intervention theory and practice in these cases. Previous work on engagement into intervention programs has shown that family crises provide a vehicle to mobilize family members for change (Szapocznik et al., 2003). When crises occur during the engagement phase, the facilitator assesses the situation and determines whether the crisis can be handled as part of the Familias Unidas intervention. For example, if the adolescent is placed on probation, the family may be especially motivated to ensure that she or he does not recidivate. In cases where the adolescent is incarcerated or otherwise unavailable to participate, the facilitator provides appropriate referrals to services in the community.

Handling Hard-to-Engage Families

Some families may not respond to the standard engagement procedures described above. It is important to recognize that families often fail to engage into therapeutic interventions for systemic reasons (Coatsworth et al., 2001; Santisteban et al., 1996; Szapocznik et al., 1988). Specifically, in most families who fail to engage, not everyone is on the same page in terms of the need and desire to seek clinical services. The goal is not to blame the family for failing to engage but rather to explore and address the systemic issues that prevent the family from engaging. If we place the blame on the family for not engaging, then we perpetuate the cycle of losing families who are most in need of support and guidance. In working with hard-to-engage families, it is often necessary to go the extra mile to engage the family. "Going the extra mile" indicates spending extra time with parents, explaining the program in different ways to appeal to the family's various needs, and answering family members' questions in a way that helps them to feel at ease with the therapist. Other techniques include using humor when talking about the adolescent. For example, it may be useful to normalize the adolescent experience and to highlight some humorous aspects (e.g., musical preferences and dress styles) of adolescents' behavior.

When working with hard-to-engage families, the process of engagement requires that the therapist or facilitator listen to everyone in the family and particularly to the most powerful member of the family (see Szapocznik et al., 2003, for an extended discussion). We have identified at least two general types of hard-to-engage families in our preventive intervention work. In the first family type, the adolescent has the majority of power in the family, and the parents inadvertently rely on the adolescent to make decisions (such as translating for them and seeking services). Facing the prospect of losing her or his position of power, the adolescent will likely resist enrolling in clinical services with the parent. In this type of family, the facilitator must make especially sure not to ignore the adolescent's resistance to engage. Rather, the facilitator should acknowledge some of the issues that are salient for the adolescent,

such as helping her or his parents understand what she or he is going through. For example, in one of our families, the adolescent girl had so much power in the family that the facilitator had to talk to her in the school to explain the program and the possible benefits of participation. Rather than having her mother bring her, which proved unsuccessful after two missed appointments, we instructed the adolescent to be in charge of bringing her mother. We told the adolescent that the intervention could help her by improving her relationships with the family members in the house. Once the adolescent is engaged in the intervention, however, the parents are encouraged and helped to assume their role as the leader of the family. Szapocznik et al. (2003) have found this engagement strategy to be successful with families in which parents have ceded power to the adolescent, and we have used it successfully with many families.

The second type of family identified is the family in which the parent is a very guarded authoritarian figure (usually a father, but sometimes a mother). Just as is the case with powerful adolescents, it is necessary to first engage the most powerful member of the family. In one of our cases, we encountered a Honduran father whose beliefs about how his daughter should behave with peers were extremely rigid and inflexible. This father treated his daughter like a much younger child; he made the rules, and no negotiation was allowed. Such authoritarian parents often do not recognize or adapt to the developmental milestones of adolescence, such as increased autonomy and the desire to participate in family decision-making processes (Steinberg, 2001). Our tendency as therapists is to remind the parent that adolescence in the United States is quite different from the ways of rural villages in Latin America. For example, talking to friends on the telephone, wanting to go to dances, and having friends over are normative adolescent activities in the United States. However, during the initial contact with a family, where the goal is to engage them into the intervention, we need to be careful not to challenge the father's authority. Instead, we might reframe his iron-fisted style by (a) acknowledging how much he cares about his daughter and (b) explaining that he will benefit significantly from learning about how he can still protect her without constantly fighting with her over minor issues. Once he is engaged into the intervention and becomes a member of the group, this father will likely realize that he is not alone and that other parents have faced the same concerns. In another family, the therapist initially believed that the stepfather was preventing the family from engaging. The mother had labeled the stepfather as an alcoholic and was blaming him for the family's resistance. It was not until the facilitator met with the stepfather and validated his concerns that the facilitator discovered that the mother was making a scapegoat of the stepfather for the family's problems. This pattern of blaming protected the status quo of this particular family system and prevented the family's pattern of interactions from changing.

Other skills that are important in joining families are reflection, mimesis (i.e., following the family's ways of behaving), and accommodation (setting up the first appointment so that it is most convenient to the family). The technique of reflection is widely used by mental health professionals. Most therapists are well instructed in reflecting back parents' comments without challenging them. For example, in the Perez family (all names used in this article are fictitious, and details have been changed to conceal the identities of participants and families described here), both parents seemed very suspicious about participating in a program that would accommodate their schedules and in which they could participate for free. The facilitator acknowledged and validated their concern and provided additional details about the program (e.g., that it was being implemented as part of a research study). The detailed explanation helped to allay the

parents' suspicions, and they subsequently enrolled. In this case, rather than focusing on family problems and how the intervention could address these problems, the facilitator reflected their concerns and acknowledged the intelligence and thoughtfulness behind the concerns. Because the parents expressed an interest in the research study of which the intervention was a part, the facilitator emphasized the research study and the parents' opportunity to help other families and to contribute to science.

Mimesis

To successfully join the family, the counselor needs to blend with the family and become a temporary family member. By mimicking the family's style, the counselor makes the family feel comfortable and encourages the family to accept her or him. If the father likes jokes, for example, the facilitator can be playful while taking care not to say anything that could offend the family. Other ways to join a family include following traditional customs and enjoying their food. Family visits offer a unique opportunity to join the family, much more so than in office-based modalities. Hispanic families from modest backgrounds often take pride in offering and sharing whatever they have, despite their lack of material possessions. Such offerings can take the form of a cup of their favorite beverage or a hand-made gift. It is important to be grateful and accept their offerings during home visits. Such interactions provide opportunities to join and establish relationships with the family.

Availability and Flexibility

When facilitators make themselves available based on the family's schedule, they increase the chances of engaging the family. By arranging their schedules to match families' availability, facilitators communicate a sense of care and concern for the family as well as maximizing opportunities for joining. Later on, once a solid bond has been formed between the facilitator and the family, it may be more feasible to ask the family to adapt to the therapist's schedule. At that point, family members may already be invested in the intervention and may be more willing to rearrange their schedules.

Retention

We have explained the different skills and processes that facilitators could use in engaging families into a preventive intervention. However, it is equally important to ensure that families engaged into the intervention complete an adequate dose of intervention activities. Familias Unidas activities center on weekly parent support groups that begin shortly after the first home visit. In an empirical study evaluating predictors of engagement into and retention in Familias Unidas (Prado et al., 2006), we found that facilitator reports of within-group processes during the first group session—such as positive relationships with other group members, working on one's own problems, and contributing to group discussions (MacGowan, 1997; MacGowan & Levenson, 2003)—were significantly associated with retention in the project. In other words, facilitators reported that those parents who contributed the most during the first group session, who bonded the most with other parents, and who worked on their problems were most likely to attend the greatest number of group sessions.

Given our findings, it is important to explore what strategies facilitators can employ to retain families once they have been engaged into the intervention. In preparing for the first group session, the facilitator should take into account each participating parent's personality and how she or he is likely to respond to the intervention strategies that the facilitator is planning to use. The first session is crucial because most people have never participated in a group intervention and are not sure what to expect. It is important for the facilitator to convey empathy and understanding to the group participants, as this will likely help the participants to work well together as a group, to work on one another's problems, and to make progress on their own issues. The facilitator should highlight similarities between group members, encourage the group to operate on their own, and intervene only to start, redirect, or interpret the conversation. Our findings showed clearly that the internal workings of the group— not the group members' relationship with the facilitator— was what predicted retention in the program.

Some preparation on the part of the facilitator may be important in promoting group process. Proper seating positions, appropriate supplies, and refreshments can also contribute to members' feelings about the group. A semicircle is often the best way to conduct a group, when each member and the facilitator face each other and can interact and make eye contact. The facilitator should be prepared with name tags, pencils, and paper, and she or he should be well versed in the topics that will be discussed at the upcoming group session. Refreshments are important as well, because they create opportunities for group members to get to know one another in a more informal way. In turn, as participants become comfortable with one another, they may begin to discuss personal issues with each other and to collaborate in working on one another's issues.

It is important to take certain aspects of Hispanic culture into consideration when attempting to engage and retain Hispanic families. Hispanics tend to view authority figures with respect, but at the same time "may need a cup of coffee together" before the real work begins. The proper combination of humor and respect is often the best recipe to attract and retain these types of families. For example, by addressing parents formally and with proper titles (e.g., Mr. or Mrs.) and shaking hands, one can earn the respect of Hispanic families. At the same time, humor is important. For example, if the group becomes so loud and enthusiastic that conducting an organized group session is difficult, the facilitator might say that the group is so invested and ready to go that it wants to walk before it is able to crawl. For another example, suppose that group members are so passionate about the subject matter and eager to speak that they repeatedly interrupt one another. In this case, the facilitator might announce that she is bringing a ball to the next session, and that only the person holding the ball is permitted to speak.

Cultural diversity among Hispanic families may also be important to address. One group was so diverse in terms of nationalities—including participants from the Caribbean, Central America, and South America—that the facilitator had to explore commonalities among the participants and their countries of origin before any substantial intervention work could begin. Stereotypes and prejudices that some Hispanic nationalities hold about other Hispanic nationalities might have prevented empathy and support among group members had it not been addressed (Huddy & Virtanen, 1995). In this instance, the facilitator emphasized the contribution that each member and nationality could bring to the group and that the variation in customs and perceptions could serve as a source of knowledge for the group as a whole. The facilitator suggested that for the next session, each member would bring an ethnic dish to share with the rest of the group. To our satisfaction, the group developed an identity based on pride, and in the process, they discovered that they had one important attribute in common—the challenges of raising adolescents in the United States—and that the most important task of the group was to support each parent in meeting this challenge. Group cohesion was achieved by drawing from group differences and using them as a strength, rather than by allowing competition among nationalities to weaken the group. Cohesion was created by creating a common bond among group members (i.e., We are all Hispanics, no matter what our nationality is) and by stating the group's mission simply and powerfully (i.e., We are all here to work to prevent problems with our children).

In another Familias Unidas group that consisted of one father and several mothers, the facilitator used the gender issue to retain families in the intervention. The father was authoritarian and was initially skeptical as to how the group could help him. However, the mothers in the group, with some reframing from the facilitator, created an opportunity to help this father to feel supported by the group. During the first group session, the group is divided into pairs, and each person is asked to become acquainted with her or his partner by asking questions such as number of children and length of time in the United States. At the end of this exercise, each person introduces his or her partner and identifies at least one or two things that they have in common. After the father was introduced as a single father who had raised his teenage daughter almost since birth, the facilitator was careful to recognize and commend the father for his actions and to acknowledge how difficult this situation must have been for him. In turn, all of the mothers in the group praised this father for raising his teenage daughter alone. The mothers told him that they were impressed because, although many of them had husbands who offered them support, they still were having difficulties with their children. They expressed, with the help of the facilitator, a sense of respect and admiration toward this father. The father reported that this attention and recognition gave him a sense of pride and helped to convince him to participate in the intervention. Moreover, during the course of the intervention, he began to soften his parenting style. The experience of sharing his achievements and challenges with the mothers in the group, as well as obtaining information from a female perspective, helped him to understand and appreciate his daughter more. Furthermore, some of the mothers in the group brought their husbands to some of the sessions to provide this single father with additional support and validation. At the end of the intervention, during a farewell party, the mothers gave him a book about raising teenage daughters. Retention in this group may have been, in part, a function of the father's working on his own issues and the mothers helping him to work on his issues. This success story was, in part, created through the facilitator's carefully crafting the conditions necessary to use the father's gender as a source of strength, rather than as a problem, in raising a daughter alone. This case illustrates the principle that facilitators should use difficult challenges and problems as ways to engage, retain, and instill motivation in families.

It is important to acknowledge that most of the parents who participate in Familias Unidas are mothers. Although our engagement strategies are equally appropriate for engaging both mothers and fathers, in many Hispanic cultures women are primarily responsible for child-rearing functions (Gomez & Marin, 1996). As a result, Hispanic mothers may be more likely than Hispanic fathers to volunteer for and enroll in parenting programs.

Description of the Intervention

Engagement and retention are critical to ensuring that participants receive the ingredients that are included in the Familias Unidas intervention. Once participants have been engaged and retained, the focus turns to targeting the three important adolescent worlds (family, peers, and school). Familias Unidas is delivered through parent support groups that meet weekly to discuss and role-play key parenting skills critical to protecting adolescents from behavior problems and substance use in the United States. Familias Unidas is designed to increase protection against risks for drug abuse and other problem behaviors in the three primary adolescent worlds: family, peers,

and school. The program also works to decrease the effect of differential acculturation while empowering parents to increase their involvement in their adolescents' lives. Familias Unidas also helps to establish bonds between parents and the adolescent's peer network and school system.

One of the major goals of Familias Unidas is to empower parents with the necessary skills to manage the various microsystems in which youth are embedded. Primarily, successful parental management of the youth's microsystems involves reaching out to the youth and the members of her or his microsystems and thereby becoming more positively involved in the adolescent's life (Mounts, 2001). Familias Unidas consists of nine 90-min parent support group sessions, four 1-hr family visits, and four 1-hr parent-adolescent discussion circles.

Parent Support Group and Skill Development

Joining and engagement efforts do not stop after the first phone call or family visit; joining and engagement continue throughout the intervention. Once the intervention has begun, joining is accomplished through building parent-support networks during parent-group sessions. Parents meet weekly with a group facilitator to discuss and practice parenting skills and ways to become involved in their adolescents' lives. One of the roles of the group facilitator is to promote group cohesion by (a) identifying and drawing on commonalities among members and (b) creating a unified mission statement for the group. In the participatory learning format that characterizes the group sessions, parents learn how to give and receive feedback from others and to counsel each other with the guidance of the facilitator (Freire, 1970/1983). For example, three parents might role-play an interaction in which one parent assumes the role of an adolescent while another plays the parent and the third serves as a coach. The three parents also receive feedback from the other group members, and during the course of the group session, each parent is provided with an opportunity to play each of the three roles. In our experience, these types of activities are likely to be effective in identifying ways to best meet the needs of parents of adolescents from Hispanic immigrant families. Such activities may help both (a) to relieve parents' feelings of inadequacy and isolation and (b) to increase their competence in using new strategies to involve themselves with their adolescents.

Family Visits

As described previously, Familias Unidas consists of family visits as well as group sessions. Once a new skill has been introduced to the group, parents are provided with an opportunity to practice the skill at home with their families as part of a family visit conducted by the facilitator. Similar to the group sessions, family visits target parental involvement in the three primary adolescent worlds—family, peers, and school. Parental involvement in the family world centers around relationships between parents and adolescents, with a specific focus on communication skills and behavior management. With the exception of the first family visit, which focuses on joining and engaging the family, the family visits follow a standard format. The facilitator leads and guides a parent-adolescent discussion exercise using the skills and knowledge covered in the parent-group sessions. For example, the facilitator can ask the parent and the adolescent to talk about a recent issue regarding schoolwork, family communication, or supervision of peers.

After each successful parent-adolescent transaction, the facilitator praises the parent for effectively using the target skills. In cases where the parent experiences difficulty implementing the target skills, the facilitator intervenes by identifying the parent's strengths and gently reminds the parent to continue practicing the target skills so that her or his proficiency increases.

Parent-Adolescent Discussion Circles

The third type of activity in Familias Unidas is the parent-adolescent discussion circle. In this exercise, the parents sit on one side of the room and the adolescents on the other, and the parents ask the adolescents questions (and adolescents provide information) about life as a teenager in the United States. In these discussions, parents take the lead with minimal input from the facilitator. For example, in one of the sessions adolescents are asked to tell their parents about their experiences and the risks they perceive in their own environments, plans they have for their future, and how parents can help them to achieve their dreams. Parents are encouraged to respond to the adolescents' concerns with empathy and interest in a way that helps adolescents to feel at ease when disclosing personal and sensitive issues. In the same way, adolescents are encouraged to be open and honest with their parents. This discussion process is useful because many Hispanic parents are not accustomed to talking to adolescents in an open and nonjudgmental manner. Parents are cautioned that the adolescents may not share much information during the first discussion exercise (i.e., because of the hierarchical interactions in which they normally engage with their parents), and they are encouraged to support and nurture the adolescents as they begin to disclose sensitive information. At the end of each discussion circle, parents meet as a group and process their reactions to the activity. During this meeting, parents discuss what they learned and comment on the effectiveness of the conversations. Many parents often report feeling quite surprised to hear some of their children's statements—almost as if they were discovering a new child.

Sequence of Topics and Session Contents

At this point, we will outline the sequence of content areas addressed in the parent support groups, parent-adolescent discussion circles, and family visits (see Table 1). Broadly, the intervention begins with coverage of the adolescent's worlds and the ways in which parents can intervene in each world to promote positive adolescent development and to prevent substance use and problem behavior. The facilitator gives a presentation, including descriptions, statistics, and graphical summaries, about processes that can increase or decrease risk for substance use and problem behaviors in the family, peer, and school worlds. She or he stresses the fact that parental involvement is crucial in all three worlds. Specific examples and prevalence rates are used to introduce each topic. For example, rates of drug use or sexual risk taking in the communities where the parents live are often used to lead off the discussion. Parents usually respond with specific examples and concerns from their own communities. These personalized examples and concerns often help to raise awareness and increase the sense of urgency to work on preventing problematic outcomes among the parents' adolescents.

The facilitator then asks parents what specific roles they can play in protecting their adolescents from risks in the family, peer, and school worlds. Parents often mention techniques such as communicating with and supporting their adolescents, managing behavior problems, involving themselves in the adolescent's school, and supervising adolescents' social activities. The facilitator validates relevant parental suggestions and informs parents that the remainder of the intervention will focus on fostering and enhancing parenting skills in each of the three primary adolescent worlds.

The intervention then focuses on the family world. Parents discuss and practice skills such as nonjudgmental communication, support, and behavior management. Role-playing is used in the group sessions to reinforce the target skills, and family visits are used to provide opportunities for parents to enact these skills at home with their adolescents.

The intervention then shifts to the school world. The most noteworthy activity in the school world is a group session in which the adolescents' school counselor visits the parent support group, explains how the American school system works, and fields questions from parents. Because the adolescents are about to enter high school, the school counselor explains the workings of the high school system, including necessary credits, extracurricular activities, and college or vocational preparation. Parents are encouraged to participate in the school system and to set individualized appointments with the school counselor if they wish.

The peer world is covered next. In the peer world, facilitators help parents to arrange supervised outings with their adolescents, one of the adolescent's friends, and the friend's mother or father. This activity gives parents an opportunity to involve themselves in the adolescent's peer world and to become acquainted with their adolescent's peers and their parents. The activity also helps parents to form supervisory networks with the parents of their adolescent's peers, and in turn, these networks can help the parents to supervise the friendship.

Finally, the intervention addresses substance use directly. In group sessions, parents practice discussing substance use with their adolescents in a supportive and nonjudgmental way. In family visits, the facilitator supports the parent in communicating important messages to her or his adolescent about dangers of and abstaining from substance use. Parents are

Table 1   Familias Unidas Session Content

Session Name	Session Description
Engagement Home Visit	Explain the intervention, join with the family, frame potential benefits in terms of parents' concerns, address barriers to engagement, and secure parents' participation.
Parental Investment Group Session	Introduce participatory learning format, build group cohesion, review risks of adolescence, and establish objectives for the intervention.
Youth Worlds Group Session	Present the various contexts in which youth are embedded, enumerate parental protective mechanisms in each context, and provide ways in which parents can foster these protective mechanisms.
Family Communication Group Session	List characteristics of effective communication and role-play parent-adolescent communication skills.
Parent-Child Discussion Circle, Communication	Enact parent-adolescent conversations in group, encourage adolescents to be open and honest with their parents, and discuss effective and ineffective communication techniques.
Family Communication Home Visit	Parents explain communication skills to adolescents, family enacts conversation about important topic, and facilitator provides feedback.
Family World Group Session	Enumerate components and significance of parental support for adolescents, and parents devise and implement a collaborative support activity with their adolescents.
Behavior Management Group Session	Cover significance of behavior management, and role-play use of communication, support, and effective discipline to manage adolescent behavior problems.
Behavior Management Home Visit	Enact a behavior management conversation in the family's home, and address hypothetical future conduct issues.
School Bonding Group Session	Address the role of school in the adolescent's life, and enumerate how parental connections to school can serve as protective mechanisms.
School Counselor Meeting Group Session	Parents meet with their adolescents' guidance counselor, counselor informs parents about adolescents' academic needs and services available in school, and parents role-play interactions with the school system.
School Bonding Home Visit	Discuss the school counselor meeting and ways to implement the suggestions and information gained from that meeting.
Peer Management/Monitoring Group Session	Highlight the role of peers in youth development, discuss the protective functions of parental management and monitoring of adolescents' peer relationships, and address how parents can implement strategies to invoke these protective factors.

(Continued)

Table 1 (Continued)

Session Name	Session Description
Peer-Supervised Activity	Plan and carry out a leisure activity with parents, adolescents, adolescents' peers, and peers' parents and encourage parents and peers' parents to build supervisory networks.
Parental Monitoring/Management Home Visit	Troubleshoot interactions between parents and the adolescent's peer world and assign second peer-supervised activity to be conducted outside of group.
General Investment Home Visit	Troubleshoot parents' connections to youth's family, school, and peer worlds.
Drug Use Group Session	List risks for and effects of adolescent substance use, discuss parents' own attitudes toward drugs and alcohol, and role-play parent-adolescent discussions about drugs and alcohol.
Drug Use Home Visit	Parents initiate conversation with adolescents about drugs and alcohol and families form a collaborative plan to institute and practice refusal skills.
Summary Group Session/Home Visit	Solidify commitment to continue using the Familias Unidas skills.

also encouraged to communicate their own expectations and values about substance use to their adolescents. Visual materials and hands-on exercises are provided to parents to help them practice drug use prevention communication skills in group sessions. Additionally, parents are coached to discuss sexuality, an especially sensitive topic in Hispanic cultures (Gomez & Marin, 1996), with their adolescents using general communication skills facilitated earlier in the intervention. In group sessions (as practice exercises) and in family visits (directly with the adolescent), parents are asked to discuss specific contents and issues (e.g., drug use, HIV prevention) with their adolescents. Facilitators use these sensitive topics as a vehicle to help to shape the parents' communication style and to promote open parent-adolescent discussions about important risk prevention issues.

OUTCOME ASSESSMENT ISSUES

As mentioned earlier, the Familias Unidas intervention has now been evaluated twice in randomized, carefully controlled outcome studies, and a third outcome study is under way. In the first study (Pantin, Coatsworth, et al., 2003), in a sample of 167 6th and 7th grade Hispanic adolescents and their families, Familias Unidas was found to be significantly more efficacious than a community control condition in increasing parental investment and decreasing adolescent behavior problems (both of which have been conceptualized as risks for later drug use; Hawkins et al., 1992). In the second study, 266 eighth-grade adolescents and their families were randomized to one of three conditions: (a) Familias Unidas plus PATH (Krauss et al., 2000), a parent-adolescent HIV communication module; (b) English for Speakers of Other Languages (ESOL) plus PATH; or (c) ESOL plus HeartPower! for Hispanics, a cardiovascular health intervention. Thus far, we have completed data collection and analysis for the first of two cohorts, but outcome data for the second cohort were collected very recently and have not yet been analyzed. In preliminary analyses using only the first cohort, Familias Unidas plus PATH was found to be significantly more efficacious than either ESOL plus PATH or ESOL plus HeartPower! for Hispanics in increasing parent-adolescent involvement, general communication, and communication about sexuality. Familias Unidas plus PATH was also found to be associated with the lowest levels of drug use and unsafe sexual behavior at the 2-year follow-up assessment (Pantin, Prado, Schwartz, Feaster, et al., 2005).

When conducting outcome assessments with Hispanics, it is important to select appropriate measures and to provide Spanish translations that capture the meaning and valence of the English versions. Measures selected should possess adequate internal consistency and construct validity (i.e., they relate to comparison variables in theoretically consistent ways). At the very least, the outcomes (e.g., drug use, unsafe sexual behavior) and the mechanisms targeted in the intervention (e.g., parental involvement, parent-adolescent communication, parental monitoring of adolescent peers) should be assessed before, during, and after the intervention. At least one follow-up assessment should be conducted after the end of intervention to examine the extent to which intervention effects are maintained over time.

Other specific methodological issues also warrant discussion. Because different Hispanic nationalities often use different words and expressions, a Spanish translation that has been used with one Hispanic group (e.g., Mexican Americans) may not necessarily be appropriate for another Hispanic group (e.g., Cuban Americans). Where existing Spanish translations of research measures are available, a small number of individuals from the target population should be recruited and asked to evaluate the measures. In cases such as Miami and New York, where individuals from many different Hispanic nationalities reside in the same communities, it may be necessary to recruit at least one person from each nationality to evaluate the measures. A measure should be approved for use in the study only after all of the community evaluators have agreed that it is appropriate. If evaluators from different nationalities cannot agree on the appropriateness of idioms, dictionary or textbook language should be used.

In cases where an existing Spanish translation is not available, the research team will need to conduct the translation themselves. Kurtines and Szapocznik (1995) recommend that one bilingual individual should translate the English version into Spanish, a second bilingual individual should translate the Spanish version back into English, and a committee of bilingual individuals should resolve discrepancies between the original and back-translated English versions and translate the final version back into Spanish. The reading level of the target population should also be considered when translating a research measure; in some cases, the wording may have to be simplified for individuals with low reading ability.

Finally, the method of assessment is important to consider. In cases such as Familias Unidas, where the ultimate outcome is a sensitive or illegal adolescent behavior such as drug use or unsafe sexual behavior, using computer-assisted assessment methods may help to increase the accuracy and honesty of adolescents' reports (Turner et al., 1998). For example, in our first outcome study, where adolescent assessments were conducted using face-to-face interviews, less than 4% of adolescents reported any lifetime alcohol or marijuana use at the 1 year postbaseline assessment (when the adolescents were 12 to 13 years old). At the baseline assessment for our second outcome study (when most of the adolescents were 13 years old), where adolescent assessments were conducted using computer-assisted technology, 24% of adolescents reported having used marijuana or alcohol during their lifetimes.

In our studies evaluating Familias Unidas, we have used three measures to index general family functioning, the process that is targeted in the intervention and that is hypothesized to produce reductions in risk for drug use and sexual risk taking: the Parenting Practices scale (Gorman-Smith, Tolan, Zelli, & Huesmann, 1996), which assesses parental involvement, positive parenting, and parental monitoring and supervision; the Family Relations scale (Tolan, Gorman-Smith, Zelli, & Huesmann, 1997), which assesses family cohesion, communication, support, and developmentally appropriate parenting; and the Parent-Adolescent Communication scale (Barnes & Olson, 1985), which assesses open and problematic parent-adolescent communication. We obtain both parent and adolescent reports of each of these processes. We assess adolescent behavior problems, an important prerequisite to drug use and sexual risk taking, using the Revised Behavior Problem Checklist (Quay & Peterson, 1987), which assesses parent reports of adolescent conduct problems, attention problems, and delinquency in the company of peers. In our most recent tests of Familias Unidas, we have used the Youth Self-Report (Achenbach, Dumenci, & Rescorla, 2002) to index adolescent aggressive behavior, law-breaking behavior, and attention problems. Drug use is measured using the instrument used to gather the Monitoring the Future data set (Johnston et al., 2004), and sexual risk taking is measured using an instrument that has been used in a number of HIV prevention outcome studies (e.g., Hutchinson, Jemmott, Jemmott, Braverman, & Fong, 2003; Jemmott, Jemmott, & Fong, 1998; Jemmott, Jemmott, Fong, & McCaffree, 1999). All of these measures have been translated into Spanish using the procedures recommended by Kurtines and Szapocznik (1995), as described above.

Conclusion

The purpose of this article was to describe a family-based preventive intervention designed to prevent substance use, sexual risk taking, and HIV contraction in Hispanic adolescents. In the context of the isolation and frustration that Hispanic immigrant parents often face in raising their adolescents, the therapist's job is to give them hope, to help reduce their feelings of isolation, to connect them with the social systems (e.g., peers, school) in which their adolescents function, and ultimately to help them to increase the efficacy (both actual and perceived) of their parenting. In Familias Unidas, parental isolation is addressed by embedding intervention activities within a parent support group format, where parents meet weekly with other parents facing the same circumstances. Facilitators capitalize on commonalities between and among parents by encouraging parents to work together on issues that they have in common. Specific intervention activities are delivered to connect parents to their adolescents' school and peer worlds. All of these activities, along with specific family strengthening and parent empowering activities conducted within the family (e.g., behavior management techniques, exercises to improve parent-adolescent communication), are designed to increase parenting efficacy. This article may have important implications for social work practice because we place special emphasis on the different techniques and skills that can be used to engage and retain Hispanic families. This is an important practical strategy given the difficulties involved in engaging and retaining families in family-based prevention programs. It is hoped that the present article will serve to improve service delivery practices by increasing engagement and retention of Hispanic families as well as offering specific skills and techniques that parents can use to promote positive development and prevent substance use and problem behavior in their adolescents. Improved service delivery, in turn, may help to decrease the elevated rates of substance use and problem behavior in this vulnerable and often underserved population.

REFERENCES

Achenbach, T. M., Dumenci, L., & Rescorla, L. A. (2002). Ten-year comparisons of problems and competencies for national samples of youth: Self, parent, and teacher reports. *Journal of Emotional and Behavioral Disorders, 10,* 194–203.

Barnes, G., Farrell, M., & Banerjee, S. (1994). Family influences on alcohol abuse and other problem behaviors among Black and White adolescents in a general population sample. *Journal of Research on Adolescence, 4,* 183–201.

Barnes, H. L., & Olson, D. H. (1985). Parent-adolescent communication and the circumplex model. *Child Development, 56,* 438–447.

Bogenschneider, K., Wu, M., Raffaelli, M., & Tsay, J. (1998). "Other teens drink, but not my kid": Does parental awareness of adolescent alcohol use protect adolescents from risky consequences? *Journal of Marriage and the Family, 60,* 356–373.

Brody, G. H., & Ge, X. (2001). Linking parenting processes and self-regulation to psychological functioning and alcohol use during early adolescence. *Journal of Family Psychology, 15,* 82–94.

Brody, G. H., Murry, V. M., Gerrard, M., Gibbons, F. X., Molgaard, V., McNair, L., et al. (2004). The Strong African American Families Program: Translating research into prevention programming. *Child Development, 75,* 900–917.

Bronfenbrenner, U. (1979). *The ecology of human development: Experiments by nature and design.* Cambridge, MA: Harvard University Press.

Bronfenbrenner, U. (1986). Ecology of the family as a context for human development. *American Psychologist, 32,* 513–531.

Brook, J. S., Adams, R. E., Balka, E. B., Whiteman, M., Zhang, C., & Sugerman, R. (2004). Illicit drug use and risky sexual behavior among African American and Puerto Rican urban adolescents: The longitudinal links. *Journal of Genetic Psychology, 165,* 203–220.

Coatsworth, J. D., Pantin, H., McBride, C., Briones, E., Kurtines, W., & Szapocznik, J. (2002). Ecodevelopmental correlates of problem behavior in young Hispanic females. *Applied Developmental Science, 6,* 126–143.

Coatsworth, J. D., Pantin, H., & Szapocznik, J. (2002). Familias Unidas: a family-centered ecodevelopmental intervention to reduce risk for problem behavior among Hispanic adolescents. *Clinical Child and Family Psychology Review, 5,* 113–132.

Coatsworth, J. D., Santisteban, D. A., McBride, C. K., & Szapocznik, J. (2001). Brief strategic family therapy versus community control: Engagement, retention, and an exploration of the moderating role of adolescent symptom severity. *Family Process, 40,* 313–332.

Costello, E. J., Burns, B. J., Angold, A., & Leaf, P. J. (1993). How can epidemiology improve mental health services for children and adolescents? *Journal of the American Academy of Child and Adolescent Psychiatry, 32,* 1106–1114.

Crosby, R., DiClemente, R., Wingood, G., Cobb, B., Harrington, K., Davies, S., et al. (2001). HIV/STD-protective benefits of living with mothers in perceived supportive families: A study of high-risk African American female teens. *Preventive Medicine, 33,* 175–178.

De la Rosa, M., Vega, R., & Radisch, M. (2000). The role of acculturation in the substance abuse behavior of African-American and Latino adolescents: Advances, issues, and recommendations. *Journal of Psychoactive Drugs, 32*(1), 33–42.

DeMarsh, J., & Kumpfer, K. (1986). Family-oriented interventions for the prevention of chemical dependency in children and adolescents. In S. Griswold-Ezekoye, K. L. Kumpfer, & W. Bukoski (Eds.), *Childhood and chemical abuse: Prevention and intervention* (pp. 117–152). New York: Haworth.

DiClemente, R. J., Wingwood, G. M., Harrington, K. F., Lang, D. L., Davies,

S. L., Hook, E. W., et al. (2004). Efficacy of an HIV prevention intervention for African American adolescent girls a randomized controlled trial. *Journal of the American Medical Association, 292,* 171–179.

Dishion, T. J., & Kavanagh, K. (2000). A multilevel approach to family-centered prevention in schools: Process and outcome. *Addictive Behaviors, 25,* 899–911.

Dishion, T. J., & McMahon, R. J. (1998). Parental monitoring and the prevention of problem behavior: A conceptual and empirical reformulation. *Clinical Child and Family Psychology Review, 1*(1), 61–75.

Dishion, T. J., Nelson, S. E., & Bullock, B. M. (2004). Premature adolescent autonomy: Parent disengagement and deviant peer process in the amplification of problem behaviour. *Journal of Adolescence, 27,* 515–530.

Ellickson, P., Bui, K., Bell, R., & McGuigan, K. A. (1998). Does early drug use increase the risk of dropping out of high school? *Journal of Drug Issues, 28,* 357–380.

Felix-Ortiz, M., Fernandez, A., & Newcomb, M. D. (1998). The role of intergenerational discrepancy of cultural orientation in drug use among Latina adolescents. *Substance Use and Misuse, 33,* 967–994.

Fletcher, A. C., Darling, N. E., & Steinberg, L. (1995). Parental monitoring and peer influences on adolescent substance use. In J. McCord (Ed.), *Coercion and punishment in long-term perspectives* (pp. 259–271). New York: Cambridge University Press.

Flory, K., Lynam, D., Milich, R., Leukefeld, C., & Clayton, R. (2004). Early adolescent through young adult alcohol and marijuana use trajectories: Early predictors, young adult outcomes, and predictive utility. *Development and Psychopathology, 16,* 193–213.

Fox, D. P., & Gottfredson, D. C. (2003). Differentiating completers from non-completers of a family-based prevention program. *Journal of Primary Prevention, 24,* 111–124.

Frauenglass, S., Routh, D. K., Pantin, H. M., & Mason, C. A. (1997). Family support decreases influence of deviant peers on Hispanic adolescents' substance use. *Journal of Clinical and Child Psychology, 26,* 15–23.

Freire, P. (1983). *Pedagogy of the oppressed.* New York: Herder and Herder. (Original work published 1970)

Garcia-Coll, C. T., Meyer, E. C., & Brillon, L. (1995). Ethnic and minority parenting. In M. H. Bornstein (Ed.), *Handbook of parenting, Vol. 2: Biology and ecology of parenting* (pp. 189–209). Hillsdale, NJ: Lawrence Erlbaum.

Getz, J. G., & Bray, J. H. (2005). Predicting heavy alcohol use among adolescents. *American Journal of Orthopsychiatry, 75,* 102–116.

Gil, A., Wagner, E., & Vega, W. (2000). Acculturation, familism and alcohol use among Latino adolescent males: Longitudinal relations. *Journal of Community Psychology, 28,* 443–458.

Gomez, C. A., & Marin, B. V. (1996). Gender, culture and power: Barriers to HIV prevention strategies for women. *Journal of Sex Research, 33,* 355–362.

Gorman-Smith, D., Tolan, P. H., Zelli, A., & Huesmann, L. R. (1996). The relation of family functioning to violence among inner-city minority youth. *Journal of Family Psychology, 10,* 115–129.

Gray, M. R., & Steinberg, L. (1999). Unpacking authoritative parenting: Reassessing a multidimensional construct. *Journal of Marriage and the Family, 61,* 574–587.

Greene, J. P., & Forster, G. (2003). *Public high school graduation rates and college readiness rates in the United States* (Education Working Paper No. 3). New York: Manhattan Institute for Policy Research.

Guagliardo, M. F., Huang, Z., Hicks, J., & D'Angelo, L. (1998). Increased drug use among old-for-grade and dropout urban adolescents. *American Journal of Preventive Medicine, 15,* 42–48.

Hanish, L. D., & Tolan, P. H. (2001). Patterns of change in family-based aggression prevention. *Journal of Marital and Family Therapy, 27,* 213–226.

Harter, S. (1996). The perceived directionality of the link between approval and self-worth: The liabilities of a looking glass self-orientation among young adolescents. *Journal of Research on Adolescence, 6,* 285–308.

Hawkins, J. D., Catalano, R. F., & Miller, J. Y. (1992). Risk and protective factors for alcohol and other drug problems in adolescence and early childhood: Implications for substance abuse prevention. *Psychological Bulletin, 112,* 64–105.

Hawkins, J. D., Guo, J., Hill, K. G., Battin-Pearson, S., & Abbott, R. D. (2001). Long-term effects of the Seattle Social Development Intervention on school bonding trajectories. *Applied Developmental Science, 5,* 225–236.

Hill, N. E., & Craft, S. A. (2003). Parent-school involvement and school performance: Mediated pathways among socioeconomically comparable African American and Euro-American families. *Journal of Educational Psychology, 95,* 74–83.

Hong, S., & Ho, H.-Z. (2005). Direct and indirect longitudinal effects of parental involvement on student achievement: Second-order latent growth modeling across ethnic groups. *Journal of Educational Psychology, 97,* 32–42.

Huddy, L., & Virtanen, S. (1995). Subgroup differentiation and subgroup bias among Latinos as a function of familiarity and positive distinctiveness. *Journal of Personality and Social Psychology, 68,* 97–108.

Huebner, A. J., & Howell, L. W. (2003). Examining the relationship between adolescent sexual risk-taking and perceptions of monitoring, communication, and parenting skills. *Journal of Adolescent Health, 33,* 71–78.

Hutchinson, M. K., Jemmott, J. B., III, Jemmott, L. S., Braverman, P., & Fong, G. T. (2003). The role of mother-daughter sexual risk communication in reducing sexual risk behaviors among urban adolescent females: A prospective study. *Journal of Adolescent Health, 33,* 98–107.

Jemmott, J. B. III, Jemmott, L. S., & Fong, G. T. (1998). Abstinence and safer sex HIV risk reduction interventions for African American adolescents: A randomized controlled trial. *Journal of the American Medical Association, 279,* 1529–1536.

Jemmott, J. B. III, Jemmott, L. S., Fong, G. T., & McCaffree, K. (1999). Reducing HIV risk-associated sexual behavior among African American adolescents: Testing the generality of intervention effects. *American Journal of Community Psychology, 27,* 161–187.

Johnston, L. D., O'Malley, P. M., Bachman, J. G., & Schulenberg, J. E. (2004). *Monitoring the future national results on adolescent drug use: Overview of key findings, 2003* (NIH Publication 04–5506). Bethesda, MD: National Institute on Drug Abuse.

Kalant, H. (2004). Adverse effects of cannabis on health: An update of the literature since 1996. *Progress in Neuro-Psychopharmacology and Biogical Psychiatry, 28,* 849–863.

Kazdin, A. E. (1993). Treatment of conduct disorder: Progress and directions in psychotherapy research. *Development and Psychopathology, 5,* 277–310.

Kazdin, A. E. (1994). Psychotherapy for children and adolescents. In A. E. Bergin & S. L. Garfield (Eds.), *Handbook of psychotherapy and behavior change* (pp. 543–594). New York: John Wiley.

Kelloway, E. K., & Barling, J. (1994). Stress, control, well-being, and marital functioning: A causal correlational analysis. In J. Hurrell & G. Keita (Eds.), *Job stress in a changing workforce: Investigating gender, diversity, and family issues* (pp. 241–251). Washington, DC: American Psychological Association.

Krauss, B. J., Godfrey, C., Yee, D., Goldsamt, L., Tiffany, J., Almeyda, L., et al. (2000). Saving our children from a silent epidemic: The PATH program for parents and preadolescents. In W. Pequegnat & J. Szapocznik (Eds.), *Working with families in the era of HIV/AIDS* (pp. 89–112). Thousand Oaks, CA: Sage.

Kurtines, W. M., & Szapocznik, J. (1995). Cultural competence in assessing Hispanic youths and families: Challenges in the assessment of treatment needs and treatment evaluation for Hispanic drug abusing adolescents. In E. Rahdert & D. Czechowicz (Eds.), *Adolescent drug abuse: Clinical assessment and therapeutic interventions* (NIDA Monograph No. 156, pp. 172–189). Rockville, MD: National Institute on Drug Abuse.

Kurtines, W. M., & Szapocznik, J. (1996). Structural family therapy in contexts of cultural diversity. In E. D. Hibbs & P. S. Jensen (Eds.), *Psychosocial treatment research with children and adolescents*. Washington, DC: American Psychological Association.

Larsen, L. J. (2004). *The foreign-born population in the United States: 2003* (Current Population Report P50–551). Washington, DC: U.S. Census Bureau.

Leon, A. M., & Dziegielewski, S. F. (2000). Engaging Hispanic immigrant mothers: Revisiting the time-limited psycho-educational group model. *Crisis Intervention, 6*, 13–27.

MacGowan, M. J. (1997). Evaluation of a measure of engagement for group work. *Research on Social Work Practice, 10*, 348–361.

MacGowan, M. J., & Levenson, J. S. (2003). Psychometrics of the Group Engagement Measure with male sex offenders. *Small Group Research, 34*, 155–169.

Mancilla, Y. E., Newman, F. L., Tejeda, M. J., Zarate, M., Schwartz, S. J., & Szapocznik, J. (2005). *Padres lideres de la familia hispana: A structural ecosystemic community intervention to strengthen Hispanic immigrant families of adolescents with problem behaviors*. Manuscript submitted for publication.

Marotta, S. A., & Garcia, J. G. (2003). Latinos in the United States in 2000. *Hispanic Journal of Behavioral Sciences, 25*, 13–34.

Mason, C. A., Cauce, A. M., Gonzalesz, N., & Hiraga, Y. (1996). Neither too sweet nor too sour: Problem peers, maternal control and problem behavior in African American adolescents. *Child Development, 67*, 2115–2130.

Masten, A. S., & Coatsworth, J. D. (1998). The development of competence in favorable and unfavorable environments: Lessons from research on successful children. *American Psychologist, 53*, 205–220.

McCluskey, C., Krohn, M. D., Lizotte, A. J., & Rodriguez, M. L. (2002). Early substance abuse and school achievement: An examination of Latino, White, and African American youth. *Journal of Drug Issues, 32*, 921–943.

Miller, B. (2002). Family influences on adolescent sexual and contraceptive behavior. *Journal of Sex Research, 39*, 22–26.

Miranda, J., Azocar, F., Organista, K. C., Muñoz, R. F., & Lieberman, A. (1996). Recruiting and retaining low-income Latinos in psychotherapy research. *Journal of Consulting and Clinical Psychology, 64*, 868–874.

Mounts, N. S. (2001). Young adolescents' perceptions of parental management of peer relationships. *Journal of Early Adolescence, 21*, 92–122.

Muir, J. A., Schwartz, S. J., & Szapocznik, J. (2004). A program of research with Hispanic and African American families: Three decades of intervention development and testing influenced by the changing cultural context of Miami. *Journal of Marital and Family Therapy, 30*, 285–303.

Mummendey, A., Klink, A., & Brown, R. (2001). Nationalism and patriotism: National identification and out-group rejection. *British Journal of Social Psychology, 40*, 159–172.

O'Donnell, L., O'Donnell, C., Yardlaw, D. M., & Stueve, A. (2004). Risk and resiliency factors influencing suicidality among urban African American and Latino youth. *American Journal of Community Psychology, 33*, 37–49.

O'Sullivan, L., Jaramillo, B., Moreau, D., & Meyer-Bahlburg, H. (1999). Mother-daughter communication about sexuality in a clinical sample of Hispanic adolescent girls. *Hispanic Journal of Behavioral Sciences, 21*, 447–469.

Pabon, E. (1998). Hispanic adolescent delinquency and the family: A discussion of sociocultural influences. *Adolescence, 33,* 941–955.

Pantin, H., Coatsworth, J. D., Feaster, D. J., Newman, F. L., Briones, E., Prado, G., et al. (2003). Familias Unidas: The efficacy of an intervention to promote parental investment in Hispanic immigrant families. *Prevention Science, 4,* 189–201.

Pantin, H., Prado, G., Schwartz, S. J., & Sullivan, S. (2005). Methodological challenges in designing efficacious drug abuse and HIV preventive interventions for Hispanic adolescent subgroups. *Journal of Urban Health, 82,* 92–102.

Pantin, H., Prado, G., Schwartz, S. J., Feaster, D. J., Sullivan, S., & Szapocznik, J. (2005). *Efficacy of a family-based, ecodevelopmental intervention in preventing substance use and unsafe sexual behavior in Hispanic adolescents.* Manuscript in preparation.

Pantin, H., Prado, G., Schwartz, S. J., Sullivan, S., & Szapocznik, J. (2005). *An ecodevelopmental understanding of family functioning in Hispanic immigrant families.* Unpublished manuscript, University of Miami, Coral Gables, FL.

Pantin, H., Schwartz, S. J., Sullivan, S., Coatsworth, J., & Szapocznik, J. (2003). Preventing substance abuse in Hispanic immigrant adolescents: An ecodevelopmental, parent-centered approach. *Hispanic Journal of Behavioral Sciences, 25,* 469–500.

Pantin, H., Schwartz, S. J., Sullivan, S., Prado, G., & Szapocznik, J. (2004). Ecodevelopmental HIV prevention programs for Hispanic adolescents. *American Journal of Orthopsychiatry, 74,* 545–558.

Patterson, G. R., & Dishion, T. J. (1985). Contributions of families and peers to delinquency. *Criminology, 23,* 63–79.

Perrino, T., Coatsworth, J. D., Briones, E., Pantin, H., & Szapocznik, J. (2001). Initial engagement in parent-centered interventions: A family systems perspective. *Journal of Primary Prevention, 22,* 21–44.

Prado, G., Pantin, H., Schwartz, S., Lupei, N., & Szapocznik, J. (2006). Predictors of engagement and retention into a parent-centered, ecodevelopmental HIV preventive intervention for hispanic adolescents and their families. *Journal of Pediatric Psychology, 31,* 874–890.

Procter, B. D., & Dalaker, J. (2003). *Poverty in the United States: 2002* (Current Population Report P60–222). Washington, DC: U.S. Census Bureau.

Quay, H. C., & Peterson, D. R. (1987). *Manual for the Revised Behavior Problem Checklist.* Unpublished manuscript, University of Miami, Coral Gables, FL.

Resnick, M., Bearman, P. S., Blum, R. W., Bauman, K. E., Harris, K. M., Jones, J., et al. (1997). Protecting adolescents from harm. *Journal of the American Medical Association, 278,* 823–832.

Rodgers, K. B. (1999). Parenting processes related to sexual risk taking among adolescent males and females. *Journal of Marriage and the Family, 61,* 99–110.

Rodriguez-Brown, F. V., & Meehan, M. A. (1998). Family literacy and adult education: Project FLAME. In M. C. Smith (Ed.), *Literacy for the twenty-first century: Research, policy, practices, and the National Adult Literacy Survey* (pp. 175–193). Westport, CT: Praeger.

Sabogal, F., Marin, G., Otero-Sabogal, R., Marin, B. V., & Perez-Stable, E. (1987). Hispanic familism and acculturation: What changes and what doesn't? *Hispanic Journal of Behavioral Sciences, 9,* 397–412.

Santisteban, D. A., Muir-Malcolm, J., Mitrani, V., & Szapocznik, J. (2002). Integrating the study of ethnic culture and family psychology intervention science. In H. A. Liddle, D. A. Santisteban, R. F. Levant, & J. H. Bray (Eds.), *Family psychology: Science based interventions* (pp. 331–352). Washington, DC: American Psychological Association.

Santisteban, D. A., Szapocznik, J., Perez-Vidal., A, Kurtines, W. M., Murray, E. J., & LaPerriere, A. (1996). Efficacy of intervention for engaging youth families into treatment and some variables that may contribute to differential effectiveness. *Journal of Family Psychology, 10*, 35–44.

Shin, H. B., & Bruno, R. (2003). *Language use and English-speaking ability: 2000* (Census 2000 brief). Washington, DC: U.S. Census Bureau.

Simons-Morton, B., Haynie, D. L., Crump, A. D., Saylor, K. E., Eitel, P., & Yu, K. (1999). Expectancies and other psychosocial factors associated with alcohol use among early adolescent boys and girls. *Addictive Behaviors, 24*, 229–238.

Spoth, C. L., Goldberg, C., & Redmond, C. (1999). Engaging families in longitudinal preventive intervention research: Discrete-time survival analysis of socioeconomic and social-emotional risk factors. *Journal of Consulting and Clinical Psychology, 67*, 157–163.

Spoth, R. L., & Redmond, C. (1995). Parent motivation to enroll in parenting skills programs: A model of family context and health belief predictors. *Journal of Family Psychology, 9*, 294–310.

Staghezza-Jaramillo, B., Bird, H. R., Gould, M. S., & Canino, G. (1995). Mental health service utilization among Puerto Rican children ages 4 through 16. *Journal of Child and Family Studies, 4*, 399–418.

Steinberg, L. (2001). We know some things: Parent-adolescent relationships in retrospect and prospect. *Journal of Research on Adolescence, 11*, 1–19.

Szapocznik, J., & Coatsworth, J. D. (1999). An ecodevelopmental framework for organizing the influences on drug abuse: A developmental model for risk and prevention. In M. Glantz & C. R. Hartel (Eds.), *Drug abuse: Origins and interventions* (pp. 331–366). Washington, DC: American Psychological Association.

Szapocznik, J., Hervis, O. E., & Schwartz, S. J. (2003). *Brief strategic family therapy for adolescent drug abuse* (NIDA Therapy Manuals Series, NIH Publication 03–4751). Rockville, MD: National Institute on Drug Abuse.

Szapocznik, J., & Kurtines, W. M. (1993). Family psychology and cultural diversity: Opportunities for theory, research and application. *American Psychologist, 48*, 400–407.

Szapocznik, J., Perez-Vidal, A., Brickman, A., Foote, F. H., Santisteban, D., Hervis, O. E., et al. (1988). Engaging adolescent drug abusers and their families into treatment: A strategic structural systems approach. *Journal of Consulting and Clinical Psychology, 56*, 552–557.

Szapocznik, J., & Williams, R. A. (2000). Brief strategic family therapy: Twenty-five years of interplay among theory, research and practice in adolescent behavior problems and drug abuse. *Clinical Child and Family Psychology Review, 3*(2), 117–135.

Tolan, P. H., & Gorman-Smith, D. (1997). Families and development of urban children. In H. J. Walburg, O. Reyes, & R. P. Weissberg (Eds.), *Urban children and youth: Interdisciplinary perspective on policies and programs* (Vol. 1, pp. 67–91). Thousand Oaks, CA: Sage.

Tolan, P. H., Gorman-Smith, D., Zelli, A., & Huesmann, L. R. (1997). Assessment of family relationship characteristics: A measure to explain risk for antisocial behavior and depression in youth. *Psychological Assessment, 9*, 212–223.

Tolan, P. H., Guerra, N., & Kendall, P. C. (1995). Introduction to special section on prediction and prevention of antisocial behavior in children and adolescents. *Journal of Consulting and Clinical Psychology, 63*, 515–517.

Turner, C. F., Ku, L., Rogers, S. M., Lindberg, L. B., Pleck, J. H., & Sonsenstein, L. H. (1998). Adolescent sexual behavior, drug use, and violence: Increased reporting with computer survey technology. *Science, 280*, 867–873.

U.S. Department of Education. (2002). *No child left behind.* Retrieved on April 14, 2005, from http://www.ed.gov/nclb/landing.jhtml.

Vakalahi, H. F. (2002). Family-based predictors of adolescent substance use. *Journal of Child and Adolescent Substance Use, 11*(3), 1–15.

van den Bree, M. B. M., & Pickworth, W. B. (2005). Risk factors predicting changes in marijuana involvement in teenagers. *Archives of General Psychiatry, 62,* 311–319.

Vazsonyi, A. T., & Flannery, D. J. (1997). Early adolescent delinquent behaviors: Associations with family and school domains. *Journal of Early Adolescence, 17,* 271–293.

Vega, W. A., Aguilar-Gaxiola, S., Andrade, L., Bijl, R., Borges, G., Caraveo-Anduaga, J. J., et al. (2002). Prevalence and age of onset for drug use in seven international sites: Results from the International Consortium of Psychiatric Epidemiology. *Drug and Alcohol Dependence, 68,* 285–297.

Vitaro, F., Brengden, M., LaDouceur, R., & Tremblay, R. E. (2001). Gambling, delinquency, and drug use during adolescence: Mutual influences and common risk factors. *Journal of Gambling Studies, 17,* 171–190.

Wallace, J. M., & Muroff, J. R. (2002). Preventing substance abuse among African American children and youth: Race differences in risk factor exposure and vulnerability. *Journal of Primary Prevention, 22,* 235–261.

Weisskirch, R. S., & Alva, S. A. (2002). Language brokering and the acculturation of Latino children. *Hispanic Journal of Behavioral Sciences, 24,* 369–378.

Whitaker, D., & Miller, K. (2000). Parent-adolescent discussions about sex and condoms: Impact on peer influences of sexual risk behavior. *Journal of Adolescent Research, 15,* 251–273.

8

WOMEN AND ALCOHOL-USE DISORDERS

A Review of Important Knowledge and Its Implications for Social Work Practitioners[1]

BRAD R. KAROLL

UNIVERSITY OF ILLINOIS AT URBANA-CHAMPAIGN

Abstract

- *Summary*: This article reviews the extent of current knowledge, particularly with reference to US sources about gender-specific alcohol-related life experience consequences, and explores the implications of these differences for practice.

- *Findings*: Alcohol affects women in significantly different ways from men. Women's consumption of alcohol is capable of inflicting more severe problems over shorter periods of time with less alcohol consumed. The sequence of alcohol-related life experience consequences also differs significantly between genders. Women with alcohol-use disorders experience gender-specific medical impairments as well as other significant differences and are more likely to be exposed to victimization.

- *Applications*: The purpose of this article is to provide social work practitioners with relevant information about the effects of alcohol on women. It also provides important interviewing strategies for workers who will encounter women with alcohol-related problems. These strategies are intended to enhance the practitioner's ability to broach the subject and initially screen for alcohol-related problems among female clients.

Keywords: alcohol abuse; alcohol and women; alcohol-use disorders; screening substance misuse

SOURCE: "Women and Alcohol-Use Disorders: A Review of Important Knowledge and Its Implications for Social Work Practitioners" by Brad R. Karoll. In the 2002 issue of *Journal of Social Work, 2*(3), 337–356. Used with permission.

Social work practitioners encounter clients with alcohol-use disorders in all areas of professional practice (van Wormer, 1995). Considering the extent of the problem, practitioners often lack suffcient knowledge of alcohol-related problems, particularly among women. Most baccalaureate[2] and master's-level social work curricula include little extensive training on substance-use disorders. For example, although alcohol and drugs were not differentiated, social workers in New England substance-use disorders treatment centers reported significantly lower knowledge and skill levels in the area of assessment than their non-social work counterparts (Hall et al., 2000).

Alcohol-use disorders represent one of the greatest health and mental health care issues in both the US and other industrialized countries, affecting millions of people and costing billions of dollars annually (Maxmen and Ward, 1995; van Wormer, 1995). These disorders have been referred to as 'America's most serious drug problem' (Maxmen and Ward, 1995: 144). Alcohol is the most commonly used drug among America's youth and is the first drug of choice among both adolescents and adults (Schneider Institute for Health Policy, 2001). As a drug, it is the one most commonly causing problems for women (Center for Substance Abuse Treatment, CSAT, 1994).

A projected 7.4–10.5 percent of the US adult population meets diagnostic criteria for alcohol-use disorders (Grant et al., 1994; Royce and Scratchley, 1996). Roughly 1.3–6 million of this group are women (Roth, 1991; US Department of Health and Human Services, USDHHS, 1991). Others suggested the figure meeting criteria for an alcohol-use disorder could be as high as 10.7 million women (CSAT, 1994). The estimated economic cost of alcohol-use disorders in the US in 1998 was $184.6 billion (Harwood, 2000). This included the economic impact associated with crime, lost work productivity, foster care, medical and mental health care, death, and other social problems (French et al., 1998; National Center for Addiction and Substance Abuse, 1998; National Institute of Alcohol Abuse and Alcoholism, NIAAA, 1997, 2000; Schneider Institute for Health Policy, 2001).

As evidenced in the field of child welfare, the majority of social work practitioners' clients are women and children. These practitioners are increasingly involved with women with alcohol- and drug-use disorders (US General Accounting Office, USGAO, 1994, 1998). The purpose of this article is to expose practitioners to some of the pertinent information on gender-related differences in the use and effects of alcohol. Of greater significance, it is also the intention of this author to provide interviewing strategies for social workers who will encounter women with alcohol-related problems. These strategies are intended to enhance the practitioner's ability to broach the topic and initially screen for alcohol-use disorders among women.

Background Information

Alcohol-use disorders are commonly framed in terms of abuse and dependence. They are traditionally defined by frequency of use, amount consumed at any given time, and the inherent negative consequences that result; that is, employment, legal, financial, social and psychological problems, and physical and medical impairments. The ratios of alcohol-dependent men to women have been estimated to range in the US from 2.3:1 to 8:1 (Maxmen and Ward, 1995; Wilsnack et al., 1994). Recently, this gap appears to be narrowing. For example, Grant (1997) reported that men born in the Vietnam War period were only 1.4 times as likely as women to be given a lifetime diagnosis of alcohol dependence. Data from the National Comorbidity Study revealed a similar trend in the converging ratio of women to men meeting the diagnostic criteria for alcohol dependence (Nelson et al., 1998).

alcohol-use disorders. From a treatment perspective, women who are affected invariably have an exaggerated sense of guilt and shame (Morell, 1997). Their defense mechanisms, or what this author refers to as care strategies (as termed by D'Angelo, 1982), are sharply honed. Clients are amazingly quick to pick up on any negative feelings directed towards them by practitioners, whether intentional or not.

Practitioners' ownership and acceptance of their negative emotions and beliefs is crucial to increase their self-awareness. These unresolved negative attitudes and feelings may often be unintentionally displaced on to the client, intensifying the latter's guilt. Workers and agencies may also perpetuate the stigma to which women with alcohol-use disorders are subjected. Self-awareness and self-change are key to eradicating the stigma sustained by both agency and practitioner as well as clients' mistrust and ill-feelings.

Screening Skills

Social work practitioners are well positioned to effectively screen women for alcohol-use disorders due to their person-in-environment and holistic training (Nelson-Zlupko et al., 1995) and unique biopsychosocial viewpoint (Straussner, 2001). In assisting women who are affected to seek help and develop the desire for change, practitioners can employ approaches that help disarm denial and resistance; that is, motivational interviewing and interventions (CSAT, 1999; Hohman, 1998; Miller and Rollnick, 1991). Offering hope and compassion throughout the process characterizes other significant strategies.

Denial Denial is commonly characterized as the hallmark of alcohol-use disorders. It is generally considered to be 'rationalization, emotional blindness, kidding ourselves, [or] honest self-deception' (Royce and Scratchley, 1996, p. 96). Conventional screening and assessment protocols for alcohol problems often call for strong confrontation of denial to bring individuals to a point of surrender and willingness to seek healthy changes. This often literally evokes outright denial and glaring resistance (Taleff, 1997). This strategy is perpetuated in the treatment process in mixed-gender group therapy sessions where this confrontation may be seriously detrimental to women with depression or PTSD resulting from physical and sexual assault or abuse (Hanke and Faupel, 1993; Wallen, 1992; Young, 1990).

Social work practitioners need to realize that the development of denial or resistance is a logical, adaptive consequence of problematic alcohol use. They also need to understand that denial is more than simply being resistant to change. Amodeo and Liftik (1990, p. 135) wrote, 'practitioners must accept the client's view of reality. Discounting or demeaning the client's views is counterproductive'. Denial needs to be viewed as an unconscious self-protective care strategy rather than a conscious effort to thwart and rebel against change.

From a clinical viewpoint, the presence of denial or resistance is not the client's problem; rather, it is the practitioner's responsibility. Motivational interviewing suggests, 'resistance is observable behavior . . . It signals the therapist that the client is not keeping up' (Miller and Rollnick, 1991, p. 101). This viewpoint is based on the stages of change proposed in the transtheoretical model of change (Prochaska and DiClemente, 1982; Prochaska et al., 1992). Specifically, those who are precontemplative are either completely unaware or underaware of any existing problem. They may either be uninformed of the extent of the consequences of their choices, lack any motivation to think about the issue, be discouraged about their capacity to make positive changes, or be defensive against the social pressures being exerted on them for change. Those who are contemplative are fully aware of an existing problem but are unwilling or not prepared to make any commitment to change. However, they intend to make positive changes within the next six months.

Practitioners must suspend all judgment while interviewing women for the presence of an alcohol-use disorder (Copeland, 1997; Russell et al., 1997). Women who are affected often suffer a lack of ego strength, diminished or deflated self-esteem, and exaggerated guilt and shame (Finkelstein, 1993). Any sign of judgment by the practitioner will only result in greater harm and cause her to shut down emotionally. This will manifest itself in signs of resistance or denial.

Motivational interviewing Social work practitioners need to avoid asking why a client drank or engaged in socially unacceptable behaviors. Approaching denial or resistance in a 'care-frontational' rather than 'con-frontational manner' gains client participation and her needed support for change to begin. 'Care-frontation' is the fundamental style of intervention in motivational interviewing (Miller and Rollnick, 1991). Using the elements of client-centered therapy (Rogers, 1951), the practitioner can assess alcohol use in a non-judgmental matter-of-fact manner while avoiding terms that may trigger defensiveness. Listening intently to a client's responses to direct questions about her alcohol use is essential.

Motivational interviewing was developed to identify alcohol-use disorders (Miller and Rollnick, 1991). Theoretically based on the transtheoretical model of change, this technique primarily focuses on the stages of change. Moreover, it integrates Rogers' (1951) concept of client-centered interpersonal relationships. Essential to this strategy is using Rogers' four basic therapeutic elements of unconditional positive regard, empathy, genuineness and concreteness. Remarkably, these components are useful when interviewing any client, not just those suspected of having an alcohol-use disorder.

Motivational interviewing has been expanded to include a greater variety of interventions applicable for working with this population (CSAT, 1999). These strategies are evidence-based practice in the field of substance-use disorders. Emergency departments (Bernstein et al., 1997), obstetric clinics (Handmaker et al., 1999), and medical settings (Ockene et al., 1997), have demonstrated their effectiveness in motivating clients towards positive changes in their alcohol and drug use and other behaviors. They have also proven successful with populations of African Americans, adolescents, women, clients in short-term residential treatment and group therapy settings (CSAT, 1999).

Avoiding labeling or declaring any problem exists, the practitioner simply reports what the data obtained through the interview seem to indicate. The worker summarizes the findings by reviewing the impairments and consequences experienced by the client, such as any withdrawal symptoms, obstetric and gynecological medical problems, alcohol-related motor vehicle issues, assault and abuse history, and diagnosis of co-occurring psychiatric disorders. Next, the woman is asked whether she sees alcohol contributing to her current situation. It is then suggested she express her perception of what significant others might say based on the current findings of the interview. This is generally effective in helping individuals recognize alcohol problems on their own without harsh confrontation.

Offering hope and compassion Hope and compassion are powerfully effective tools that practitioners can use with women with alcohol-use disorders (Akin and Gregoire, 1997; Copeland, 1997). The absence of confrontation allows someone the dignity to reassess her lifestyle in a safe, supportive environment, based solely on factual gender-specific information on alcohol use. For many, this will be the first time they have considered alcohol as being the essence of their problems. Others have probably contemplated it for some time, but feared frank discussion of this possibility. The ability to discuss such an emotionally charged subject with compassion in a nonjudgmental, nonconfrontational manner provides the preliminary groundwork for hope in potential recovery. It dispels any expectations of anticipated stigma attached to women's alcohol use. Maintaining poise and compassion positions the worker as a powerful ally when the client is feeling at her most vulnerable.

Offering hope is a diverse undertaking. The practitioner needs to let the client know that she is capable of recovery even if she does not believe it is possible. To this end, the worker can utilize a core value that is embedded within social work, which emphasizes that all people are capable of change. Next, the worker will need to continually reiterate that recovery is possible. Having recovering women available as references and guides through the recovery process should she desire assistance will help overcome this hurdle.

As a social work practitioner, help the client know you will support her throughout the recovery process. Make yourself available as a safe supportive ally in whom she can confide at any time. Coordinating services and facilitating change help the client realize you are there for her and are prepared to advocate on her behalf. The early recovery from alcohol-use disorder requires having such safe, supportive people being available.

Topic introduction The initiation of questions about alcohol use is difficult for many practitioners. Hesitating because of not knowing how to intervene when a problem is identified, finding it safer not to ask in the first place, or wishing to avoid embarrassment for the client may be the cause of this (Maxmen, 1986). Alternatively, holding negative biases and feelings may provide a plausible explanation for this phenomenon. Either will lead to failed screening efforts. Women with alcohol-use disorders sensing any judgment or negativism concerning their lifestyle will not honestly participate in the screening interview process.

To elicit the most honest responses, directness and specificity of the questions asked in a nonchalant fashion are recommended. A matter-of-fact introductory statement indicating a need to enquire about the client's lifestyle that includes alcohol and drug use is the preferred approach. This reduces the client's shock and possible defensiveness. An uncomfortable practitioner may defer the responsibility for following this line of questioning to supervisors or agency policy requiring the exploration of alcohol and drug use.

It is best to assume clients consume alcohol from time to time. However, cultural aspects need to be considered, such as large segments of Christian and Muslim populations. An opening of 'When you drink' or 'After a drinking episode' will elicit more honest responses than 'Do you drink?'. Using closed-ended questions about alcohol use provides clients with the opportunity to sabotage screening efforts from the onset with negative responses. If negative responses to initial alcohol-related questions are nondefensive, the practitioner may accept them as probably true.

Practitioners need to avoid emotionally charged terms during the interview. Avoid asking if she abuses alcohol or has a problem with it. Never refer to her as an alcoholic. Labeling of any kind during the interview will only cause her to immediately shut down. Once this shutting down occurs, it is most difficult to re-engage her in the interview process.

If defensiveness arises, a practitioner's skills at overcoming it are challenged. Reassure her that the concern is only with possible impairments and consequences and not about frequency or quantity. Remain calm and draw on your knowledge of women's gender-specific alcohol-related issues, then continue with a nonjudgmental probe into her response to 'never' drinking. It is highly important to go beyond an initial negative response for several reasons. Some may not consider certain drinks to be alcoholic beverages, such as wine, wine coolers, beer, malt liquor or liqueurs. Others may not consider past use problematic. Finally, individuals presenting with a drug problem often may not consider drinking alcohol to be problematic. Practitioners easing a client's tension this way will most likely gain an admission of occasional alcohol use. This retraction of non-use is the first positive step towards getting a thorough screening with someone who is unaware, under-aware, or knowingly attempting to conceal alcohol-related problems.

Screening Indicators

Klee et al. wrote, 'An indicator is evidence that a woman has or is developing a drinking problem, and it may be apparent to the woman herself or to others' (1991, p. 881). Screening for alcohol-use disorders requires knowledge of significant gender differences. Elevated peak BAC levels with less consumed and the influence of hormonal variation caused by menstrual cycles are prime examples. Obstetric and gynecological impairments associated with women's alcohol use are others. Their help-seeking patterns and a higher prevalence of physical abuse or sexual assault or abuse and co-occurring psychiatric disorders among affected women must also be considered in an interviewing protocol. Thus, frequency and quantity formulae are less important than enquiries concerning impairments and consequences.

Significant problem indicators include withdrawal symptoms and medical problems related to obstetric and gynecological difficulties. Telescoping of withdrawal symptoms among women is noteworthy, so it is logical to explore possible alcohol-related obstetric and gynecological impairments. Richmond (1917/1944) and Blume (1985) proposed the need for a separate set of questions related to the menstrual cycle for investigating problematic alcohol use. Past psychological problems are also worthy of investigation. Women's

help-seeking behaviors are indicative of this phenomenon.

Exploration of alcohol-related motor vehicle difficulties will also serve to detect problematic alcohol use. While this may be a function of age, all women with alcohol-use disorders are at risk of being involved in alcohol-related motor vehicle accidents or being arrested for driving under the influence. Admittedly, younger women drink more heavily in public settings, thus exposing them to legal intervention. Conversely, because older women were found to experience these problems later in their drinking career than men (Karoll and Memmott, 2001), exploration of alcohol-related motor vehicle consequences is justified.

Finally, a sensitive enquiry into a woman's history of past or current physical or sexual assault or abuse and domestic violence is indicated. This must be conducted in a fact-finding, non-judgmental fashion. It is important to screen for alcohol-use disorders, childhood trauma, adult trauma, or both, and domestic violence whenever either has been identified. This will aid in determining appropriate interventions and effective relapse prevention strategies for the client with this constellation of problems (Bennett, 1995).

It is accepted practice that many of these areas are explored in other sections of intake screening and assessment protocols. By connecting them to one's alcohol use, a client may draw conclusions for herself about her alcohol-related problems based on their relationship to her past and current situation. Once a connection is made, positive change and growth may earnestly begin.

CONCLUSION

Alcohol-use disorders continue to be serious health and mental health issues in the US. Society is only beginning to acknowledge that alcohol and other drugs affect women in almost equal numbers compared with men, though stigma persists.

Key research indicates that there is substantial evidence of the existence of several significant gender-specific differences in relation to alcohol-use disorders and that all social work practitioners need to recognize these differences. The existing barriers to screening, assessment and treatment and the improper diagnosis of women with alcohol-use disorders need to be overcome.

More importantly, lack of adequate training for practitioners in problematic alcohol use in general, and women's issues in particular, must be addressed. This author suggests using classrooms as working laboratories for social work practitioners where the students may explore their personal negative biases and feelings towards those with alcohol-use disorders. In addition, baccalaureate and master's-level curricula in schools of social work are encouraged to integrate substantive gender-specific information on women and alcohol use. Role-playing the various stages of change in groups will aid students to better understand each one through personal engagement and observation. *Enhancing Motivation for Change in Substance Abuse Treatment* (CSAT, 1999) and the work of Patricia Dunn (2000) both serve as excellent educational resources for understanding the stages of change and motivational interviewing. This process may also be integrated into agency in-service programs.

Social work practitioners are called upon daily to conduct psychosocial screening and assessments. They are the front-line workers who provide the bulk of direct services. As such, it is essential that they have sufficient knowledge of alcohol-use disorders so that they may perform their duties effectively.

NOTES

1. The author wishes to thank Dr. John Poertner, Dr. Jay Memmott and Dr. Edward Taylor for all their help and support in preparing this article for publication.

2. Outside the US this is known as 'undergraduate' or 'bachelors' level.

3. The 'quantity plus frequency formulae' is a measure of how much alcohol is consumed over what period of time.

REFERENCES

Akin, B. A. and Gregoire, T. K. (1997) 'Parents' Views on Child Welfare's Response to Addiction', *Families in Society: The Journal of Contemporary Human Services* 78(4): 393–404.

Allen, D. (1996). 'Are Alcoholic Women More Likely to Drink Premenstrually?', *Alcohol and Alcoholism* 31(2): 145–7.

Allen, K. (1995) 'Barriers for Treatment for Addicted African American Women', *Journal of the National Medical Association* 87(10): 751–65.

Allen, L. M., Nelson, C. J., Rouhbakhsh. P., Scifres, S. L., Greene, R. L., Kordinal, S. T., Davis, L. J. Jr and Morse, R. M. (1998) 'Gender Differences in Factor Structure of the Self-Administered Alcoholism Screening Test', *Journal of Clinical Psychology* 54(4): 439–45.

American Psychiatric Association (2000) *Diagnostic and Statistical Manual of Mental Disorders*, 4th edn (Text Revision; DSM-IV-TR). Washington, DC: APA.

Ames, G., Schmidt, C., Klee, L. and Saltz, R. (1996) 'Combining Methods to Identify New Measures of Women's Drinking Problems Part I: The Ethnographic Stage', *Addiction* 91(6): 829–44.

Amodeo, M. and Liftik, J. (1990) 'Working Through Denial in Alcoholism', *Families in Society: The Journal of Contemporary Human Services* 71(3): 131–5.

Beckman, L. J. (1994) 'Treatment Needs of Women with Alcohol Problems', *Alcohol Health and Research World* 18(3): 206–11.

Bennett, L. W. (1995) 'Substance Abuse and the Domestic Assault of Women', *Social Work* 40(6): 760–71.

Bernstein, E., Bernstein, J. and Levenson, S. (1997) 'Project ASSERT: An ED-based Intervention to Increase Access to Primary Care, Preventive Services, and the Substance Abuse Treatment System', *Annals of Emergency Medicine* 30(2): 181–97.

Blow, F. C. (2000) 'Treatment of Older Women with Alcohol Problems: Meeting the Challenge for a Special Population', *Alcoholism: Clinical and Experimental Research* 24(8): 1257–66.

Blume, S. B. (1985) 'Women and Alcohol', in T. E. Bratter and G. G. Forrest (eds) *Alcoholism and Substance Abuse: Strategies for Clinical Intervention*, pp. 623–38. New York: The Free Press.

Blume, S. B. (1986) 'Women and Alcohol', *Journal of the American Medical Association (JAMA)* 256(11): 1467–70.

Blume, S. B. (1997) Women and Alcohol: Issues in Social Policy', in R. W. Wilsnack and S. C. Wilsnack (eds) *Gender and Alcohol. Individual and Social Perspectives*, pp. 462–89. New Brunswick, NJ: Rutgers Center of Alcohol Studies.

Bongers, I. M. B., van de Goor, L. A. M., van Oers, J. A. M. and Garretsen, H. F. L. (1998) 'Gender Differences in Alcohol-Related Problems: Controlling for Drinking Behavior', *Addiction* 93(3): 411–21.

Bradley, K. A., Boyd-Wickizer, J., Powell, S. H. and Burman, M. L. (1998) 'Alcohol Screening Questionnaires in Women', *JAMA* 280(2): 166–71.

Brady, K. T., Grice, D. E., Dustan, L. and Randall, C. (1993) 'Gender Differences in Substance Use Disorders', *American Journal of Psychiatry* 150(11): 1707–11.

Center for Substance Abuse Treatment (CSAT) (1994) *Practical Approaches in the Treatment of Women Who Abuse Alcohol and Other Drugs*, DHHS Publication No. (SMA) 94–3006. Rockville, MD: Department of Health and Human Services, Public Health Service.

Center for Substance Abuse Treatment (CSAT) (1997) *Substance Abuse Treatment and Domestic Violence*, Treatment Improvement Protocol (TIP) Series, No.25, DHHS Publication No. (SMA) 97–3163. Washington, DC: US Government Printing Office.

Center for Substance Abuse Treatment (CSAT) (1999) *Enhancing Motivation for Change in Substance Abuse Treatment*, Treatment Improvement Protocol (TIP) Series, No.35, DHHS Publication No. (SMA) 01–3519. Washington, DC: US Government Printing Office.

Chermack, S. T., Stoltenberg, S. F., Fuller, B. E. and Blow, F. C. (2000) 'Gender Differences in the Development of Substance-Related Problems: The Impact of Family History of Alcoholism, Family History of Violence and Childhood Conduct Problems', *Journal of Studies on Alcohol* 61: 845–52.

Cochrane, J. J., Goering, P. and Lancee, W. (1992) 'Gender Differences in the Manifestations of Problem Drinking in a Community Sample', *Journal of Substance Abuse* 4: 247–54.

Copeland, J. (1997) 'A Qualitative Study of Barriers to Formal Treatment Among Women Who Self-Managed Change in Addictive Behaviours', *Journal of Substance Abuse Treatment* 14(2): 183–90.

D'Angelo, R. (1982) 'Theory of Gestalt Therapy', training lecture presented at the Gestalt Association of New York, New York City.

Deal, S. R. and Gavalier, J. S. (1994) 'Are Women More Susceptible Than Men to Alcohol-Induced Cirrhosis?', *Alcohol Health and Research World* 18(3): 189–91.

Dunn, P. C. (2000) 'The Stages and Process of Change Model: Implications for Social Work ATOD Practice', in A. A. Abbott (ed.) *Alcohol, Tobacco, and Other Drugs. Challenging Myths, Assessing Theories, Inividualizing Interventions*, pp. 111–143. Washington, DC: NASW Press.

Finkelstein, N. (1993) 'Treatment Programming for Alcohol and Drug-Dependent Pregnant Women', *International Journal of the Addictions* 28(13): 1275–1309.

French, M. T., Rachal, J. V., Harwood, H. J. and Hubbard, R. L. (1998) 'Does Drug Abuse Treatment Affect Employment and Earnings of Clients?', *Benefits Quarterly* 6: 58–67.

Frezza, M., di Padova, C., Pozzato, G., Terpin, M., Baraona, E. and Lieber, C. S.

(1990) 'High Blood Alcohol Levels in Women. The Role of Decreased Gastric Alcohol Dehydrogenase Activity and First-pass Metabolism', *New England Journal of Medicine* 322(2): 95–9.

Fuchs, C. S., Stampfer, M. J., Colditz, M. B., Giovannucci, E. L., Manson, J. A., Kawachi, I., Hunter, D. J., Hankinson, S. E., Hennekens, C. H., Rosner, B., Speizer, F. E. and Willett, W. C. (1995) 'Alcohol Consumption and Mortality Among Women', *New England Journal of Medicine* 332(19): 1245–50.

Fullilove, M. T., Fullilove, R. E., Smith, M., Winkler, K., Michael, C., Panzer, G. and Wallace, R. (1993) 'Violence, Trauma, Post-Traumatic Stress Disorder Among Women Drug Users', *Journal of Traumatic Stress* 6(4): 533–43.

Goldbloom, D. S., Naranjo, C. A., Bremner, K. E. and Hicks, L. K. (1992) 'Eating Disorders and Alcohol Abuse in Women', *British Journal of Addiction* 87: 913–20.

Gomberg, E. S. L. (1993) 'Women and Alcohol: Use and Abuse', *Journal of Nervous and Mental Disease* 181(4): 211–19.

Gomberg, E. S. L. (1996) 'Women's Drinking Practices and Problems from a Lifespan Perspective', in J. M. Howard, S. E. Martin, D. Mail, M. E. Hilton and E. D. Taylor (eds) *Women and Alcohol: Issues for Prevention Research*, pp. 185–214. NIAAA Research Monograph No. 32, National Institute of Health (NIH) Publication No. 96–3817. Bethesda, MD: NIH.

Gomberg, E. S. L. (1997) 'Alcohol Abuse: Age and Gender Differences', in R. W. Wilsnack and S. C. Wilsnack (eds) *Gender and Alcohol. Individual and Social Perspectives*, pp. 225–44. New Brunswick, NJ: Rutgers Center of Alcohol Studies.

Grant, B. F. (1997) 'Prevalence and Correlates of Alcohol Use and DSM-IV Alcohol Dependence in the United States: Results of the National Longitudinal Alcohol Epidemiological Survey', *Journal of Studies on Alcohol* 58(5): 464–73.

Grant, B. F., Harford, T. C., Dawson, D. A., Chou, P., Dufour, M. and Pickering, R.

(1994) 'Prevalence of DSM-IV Alcohol Abuse and Dependence: United States, 1992', *Epidemiological Bulletin No. 35, Alcohol Health and Research World* 18(3): 243–8.

Hall, M. N., Amodeo, M., Shaffer, H. J. and Vander Bilt, J. (2000) 'Social Workers Employed in Substance Abuse Treatment Agencies: A Training Needs Assessment', *Social Work* 45(2): 141–55.

Handmaker, N. S., Miller, W. R. and Manicke, M. (1999) 'Findings of a Pilot Study of Motivational Interviewing with Pregnant Drinkers', *Journal of Studies on Alcohol* 60(2): 285–7.

Hanke, J. and Faupel, C. E. (1993) 'Women Opiate Users' Perceptions of Treatment Services in New York City', *Journal of Substance Abuse Treatment* 10: 513–22.

Harwood, H. (2000) 'Updating Estimates of the Economic Costs of Alcohol Abuse in the United States: Estimates, Update Methods, and Data', Report prepared by the Lewin Group for the NIAAA.

Helzer, J. F. and Pryzbeck, T. R. (1988) 'The Co-occurrence of Alcoholism with Other Psychiatric Disorders in the General Population and Its Impact on Treatment', *Journal of Studies on Alcohol* 49: 219–24.

Hesselbrock, M. N. and Hesselbrock, V. M. (1997) 'Gender, Alcoholism, and Psychiatric Comorbidity', in R. W. Wilsnack and S. C. Wilsnack (eds) *Gender and Alcohol. Individual and Social Perspectives*, pp. 49–71. New Brunswick, NJ: Rutgers Center of Alcohol Studies.

Hohman, M. M. (1998) 'Motivational Interviewing: An Intervention Tool for Child Welfare Case Workers Working with Substance-Abusing Parents', *Child Welfare* LXXVII(3): 275–89.

Jones, B. M. and Jones, M. K. (1976) 'Women and Alcohol: Intoxication, Metabolism, and the Menstrual Cycle', in M. Greenblatt and M. A. Schuckit (eds) *Alcoholism Problems in Women and Children*, pp. 103–36. New York: Grune and Stratton.

Karoll, B. R. (2002) 'A Review of Alcoholism Screening Instruments and Their Appropriateness for Women', *Social Work in Mental Health* 1: 115–39.

Karoll, B. R. and Memmott, J. (2001) 'The
Order of Alcohol-Related Life
Experiences: Gender Differences',
*Journal of Social Work Practice in the
Addictions* 1(2): 45–60.

Kessler, R. C., Nelson, C. B., McGonagle, K.
A., Edlund, M. J., Frank, R. G. and Leaf,
J. (1996) 'The Epidemiology of Co-
occurring Addictive and Mental
Disorders: Implications for Prevention
and Service Utilization', *American
Journal of Orthopsychiatry* 66(1): 17–31.

Kessler, R. C., Crum, R. M., Warner, L. A.,
Nelson, C. B., Schulenberg, J. and
Anthony, J. C. (1997) 'Lifetime Co-
occurrence of DSM-III-R Alcohol
Abuse and Dependencewith Other
Psychiatric Disorders in the National
Comorbidity Survey', *Archives of
General Psychiatry* 54: 313–21.

Kinney, J. (1996) 'Impaired Health Care
Professionals', in J. Kinney (ed.)
Clinical Manual of Substance Abuse,
2nd edn, pp. 349–61. St. Louis, MO:
Mosby Year Book.

Klee, L., Schmidt, A. and Ames, G. (1991)
'Indicators of Women's Alcohol
Problems: What Women Themselves
Report', *International Journal of the
Addictions* 26(8): 879–95.

Leonard, K. E. and Quigley, B. M. (1999)
'Drinking and Marital Aggression in
Newlyweds: An Event-Based Analysis
of Drinking and the Occurrence of
Husband Marital Aggression', *Journal of
Studies on Alcohol* 60(4): 537–45.

Lewis, C. E., Bucholz, K. K., Spitznagel, E.
and Shayka, J. J. (1996) 'Effects of
Gender and Comorbidity on Problem
Drinking in a Community Sample',
*Alcoholism: Clinical and Experimental
Research* 20(3): 466–76.

Lex, B. W. (1991) 'Some Gender Differences
in Alcohol and Polysubstance Abusers',
Health Psychology 10(2): 121–32.

Lex, B. W. (1994) 'Alcohol and Other Drug
Abuse Among Women', *Alcohol Health
and Research World* 18(3): 212–19.

Lieber, C. S. (1997) 'Gender Differences in
Alcohol Metabolism and Susceptibility',
in R. W. Wilsnack and S. C. Wilsnack
(eds) *Gender and Alcohol. Individual
and Social Perspectives*, pp. 77–89. New

Brunswick, NJ: Rutgers Center of
Alcohol Studies.

Loneck, B., Garrett, J. and Banks, S. M.
(1997) 'Engaging and Retaining
Women in Outpatient Alcohol and
Other Drug Treatment: The Effect of
Referral Intensity', *Health and Social
Work* 22(1): 38–46.

Maxmen, J. S. (1986) *Essential
Psychopathology*. New York: W. W.
Norton.

Maxmen, J. S. and Ward, N. G. (1995)
*Essential Psychopathology and Its
Treatment*, 2nd edn (rev. for DSM-IV).
New York: W. W. Norton.

McGrath Morgan, S. and Kinney, J. (1996)
'Women', in J. Kinney (ed.) *Clinical
Manual of Substance Abuse*, 2nd edn,
pp. 318–32. St Louis, MO: Mosby Year
Book.

Miller, B. A. (1996) 'Women's Alcohol Use
and Their Violent Victimization', in J.
M. Howard, S. E. Martin, D. Mail,
M. E. Hilton and E. D. Taylor (eds)
*Women and Alcohol: Issues for
Prevention Research*, pp. 239–60.
NIAAA Research Monograph No. 32,
NIH Publication No. 96–3817.
Bethesda, MD: NIH.

Miller, B. A. and Downs, W. R. (1993)
'The Impact of Family Violence on the
Use of Alcohol by Women', *Alcohol
Health and Research World* 17(2):
137–43.

Miller, B. A., Downs, W. R. and Gondoli, D.
M. (1989) 'Spousal Violence Among
Alcoholic Women as Compared to a
Random Household Sample of
Women', *Journal of Studies on Alcohol*
50: 533–40.

Miller, B. A., Downs, W. R. and Testa, M.
(1993) 'Interrelationships Between
Victimization Experiences and
Women's Alcohol Use', *Journal of
Studies on Alcohol*, Supplement No. 11:
109–17.

Miller, W. R. and Rollnick, S. (1991)
*Motivational Interviewing. Preparing
People to Change Addictive Behavior*.
New York: The Guilford Press.

Monroe, A. D., Levy, S. and McQuade, W.
(1997) 'Effects of Gender on
Documentation of Alcohol Use in

Patients with Psychiatric Symptoms', *Substance Abuse* 18(2): 79–87.

Morell, C. (1997) 'Women with Depression and Substance Abuse Problems', in S. L. A. Straussner (ed.) *Gender and Addictions. Men and Women in Treatment*, pp. 223–42. Northvale, NJ: Jason Aronson.

Morse, R. M. and Flavin, D. K. (1992) 'The Definition of Alcoholism', *JAMA* 268(8): 1012–14.

National Center for Addiction and Substance Abuse (1998) *Behind Bars: Substance Abuse and America's Prison Population.* New York: National Center for Addiction and Substance Abuse at Columbia University.

National Institute of Alcohol Abuse and Alcoholism (NIAAA) (1997) *Ninth Special Report to the US Congress on Alcohol and Health.* NIH Publication No. 97–4017. Bethesda, MD: Author.

National Institute of Alcohol Abuse and Alcoholism (NIAAA) (2000) *Tenth Special Report to the US Congress on Alcohol and Health. NIH Publication No. 00–1583.* Bethesda, MD: Author.

Nelson, C. B., Heath, A. C. and Kessler, R. C. (1998) 'Temporal Progression of Alcohol Dependence Symptoms in the US Household Population: Results from the National Comorbidity Survey', *Journal of Consulting and Clinical Psychology* 66(3): 474–83.

Nelson-Zlupko, L., Kauffman, E. and Dore, M. M. (1995) 'Gender Differences in Drug Addiction and Treatment: Implications for Social Worker Intervention with Substance-Abusing Women', *Social Work* 40(1): 45–54.

Ockene, J. K., Wheeler, E. V., Adams, A., Hurley, T. G. and Hebert, J. (1997) 'Provider Training for Patient-Centered Alcohol Counseling in a Primary Care Setting', *Archives of Internal Medicine* 157(20): 2334–41.

Pape, P. A. (1993) 'Issues in Assessment and Intervention with Alcohol and Drug Abusing Women', in S. L. Straussner (ed.) *Clinical Work with Substance-Abusing Clients*, pp. 251–69. NewYork: The Guilford Press.

Prochaska, J. O. and DiClemente, C. C. (1982) 'Transtheoretical Therapy: Toward a More Integrative Model of Change', *Psychotherapy: Theory, Research, and Practice* 19(3): 276–88.

Prochaska, J. O., DiClemente, C. C. and Norcross, J. C. (1992) 'In Search of How People Change. Applications to Addictive Behaviors', *American Psychologist* 47(9): 1102–14.

Ramlow, B. E., White, A. L., Watson, D. D. and Leukefeld, C. G. (1997) 'The Needs of Women with Substance Abuse Problems: An Extended Vision for Treatment', *Substance Use and Misuse* 32(10): 1395–1404.

Randall, C. L., Roberts, J. S., Del Boca, F. K., Carroll, K. M., Connors, G. J. and Mattison, M. E. (1999) 'Telescoping of Landmark Events Associated with Drinking: A Gender Comparison', *Journal of Studies on Alcoholism* 60: 252–60.

Reichman, M. E. (1994) 'Alcohol and Breast Cancer', *Alcohol Health and Research World* 18(3): 182–4.

Rice, C., Mohr, C. D., Del Boca, F. K., Mattison, M. E., Young, L., Brady, K. and Nickless, C. (2001) 'Self-reports of Physical, Sexual and Emotional Abuse in an Alcoholism Treatment Sample', *Journal of Studies on Alcohol* 62: 114–23.

Richmond, M. E. (1917/1944) *Social Diagnosis.* New York: The Free Press.

Robbins, C. (1989) 'Sex Differences in Psychosocial Consequences of Alcohol and Drug Abuse', *Journal of Health and Social Behavior* 30(1): 117–30.

Rogers, C. R. (1951) *Client-centered Therapy. Its Current Practice, Implications, and Theory.* Boston, MA: Houghton Miffiin.

Ross, H., Rehm, J. and Walsh, G. (1997) 'Patterns of Alcohol Consumption and Psychiatric Disorders Among Ontario Adults', *Contemporary Drug Problems* 24(3): 533–6.

Ross, R. R., Fortney, J., Lancaster, B. and Booth, B. M. (1998) 'Age, Ethnicity, and Comorbidity in a National Sample of Hospitalized Alcohol-Dependent Women Veterans', *Psychiatric Services* 49(5): 663–8.

Roth, P., ed. (1991) *Alcohol and Drugs Are Women's Issues*, Volume 2, *The Model Program Guide*. Metuchen, NJ: Women's Action Alliance and Scarecrow Press.

Royce, J. E. and Scratchley, D. (1996) *Alcoholism and Other Drug Problems*. New York: The Free Press.

Russell, M., Chan, A. W. K. and Mudar, P. (1997) 'Gender and Screening for Alcohol-Related Problems', in R. W. Wilsnack and S. C. Wilsnack (eds) *Gender and Alcohol. Individual and Social Perspectives*, pp. 417–44. New Brunswick, NJ: Rutgers Center of Alcohol Studies.

Schneider Institute for Health Policy (2001) *Substance Abuse. The Nation's Number One Health Problem. Key Indicators for Policy* (update). Princeton, NJ: Robert Wood Johnson Foundation.

Schober, R. and Annis, H. M. (1996) 'Barriers to Help-Seeking for Change in Drinking: A Gender Focused Review of the Literature', *Addictive Behaviors* 21(1): 81–92.

Sinha, R. (2000) 'Women', in G. Zernig, A. Saria, M. Kurz and S. S. O'Malley (eds) *Handbook of alcoholism*, pp. 151–64. Boca Raton, FL: CRC Press.

Straussner, S. L. A. (1997) *Gender and Addictions. Men and Women in Treatment*. Northvale, NJ: Jason Aronson.

Straussner, S. L. A. (2001) 'The Role of Social Workers in the Treatment of Addictions, A Brief History', *Journal of Social Work Practice in the Addictions* 1(1): 3–9.

Taleff, M. J. (1997) *A Handbook to Assess and Treat Resistance in Chemical Dependence*. Dubuque, IA: Kendall/Hunt.

US Department of Health and Human Services (USDHHS) (1991) 'Facts and Figures on Pregnant/Postpartum Women and Their Infants', in *Prevention Resource Guide: Pregnant/Postpartum Women and Their Infants*. Washington, DC: US Government Printing Office.

US General Accounting Office (USGAO) (1994) 'Foster Care: Parental Drug Abuse Has Alarming Impact on Young Children'. Report to the Chairman, Subcommittee on Human Resources, Committee on Ways and Means, House of Representatives. Washington, DC: US Government Printing Office.

US General Accounting Office (USGAO) (1998) 'Foster Care. Agencies Face Challenges Securing Stable Homes for Children of Substance Abusers'. Report to the Chairman, Committee on Finance, US Senate, GAO/HEHS-98–182. Washington, DC: Author.

Walitzer, K. S. and Connors, G. J. (1997) 'Gender and Treatment of Alcohol-Related Problems', in R. W. Wilsnack and S. C. Wilsnack (eds) *Gender and Alcohol. Individual and Social Perspectives*, pp. 445–61. New Brunswick, NJ: Rutgers Center of Alcohol Studies.

Wallen, J. (1992) 'A Comparison of Male and Female Clients in Substance Abuse Treatment', *Journal of Substance Abuse Treatment* 9: 243–8.

Wegscheider-Cruse, S. (1989) *Another Chance. Hope and Health for the Alcoholic Family*, 2nd edn. Palo Alto, CA: Science and Behavior Books.

Weisner, C. and Schmidt, L. (1992) 'Gender Disparities in Treatment for Alcoholic Women', *JAMA* 268(14): 1872–6.

Wells-Parker, E., Popkin, C. L. and Ashley, M. (1996) 'Drinking and Driving Among Women: Gender Trends, Gender Differences', in J. M. Howard, S. E. Martin, D. Mail, M. E. Hilton and E. D. Taylor (eds) *Women and Alcohol: Issues for Prevention Research*, pp. 215–38. NIAAA Research Monograph No. 32, NIH Publication No. 96–3817. Bethesda, MD: NIH.

Wilke, D. (1994) 'Women and Alcoholism. How a Male-as-norm Bias Affects Research, Assessment, and Treatment', *Health and Social Work* 19(1): 29–35.

Wilsnack, S. C., Vogeltanz, N. D., Klassen, A. D. and Harris, R. (1997) 'Childhood Sexual Abuse and Women's Substance

Abuse: National Survey Findings',
Journal of Studies on Alcohol 58:
264–71.

Wilsnack, S. C., Wilsnack, R. W. and Hiller-Strumhofel, S. (1994) 'How Women
Drink. Epidemiology of Women's
Drinking and Problem Drinking',
Alcohol Health and Research World
18(3): 173–81.

Windle, M., Windle, R. C., Scheidt, D. M.
and Miller, G. B. (1995) 'Physical and
Sexual Abuse and Associated Mental
Disorders Among Alcoholic Inpatients',
American Journal of Psychiatry 152(9):
1322–8.

World Health Organization (WHO) (1992)
The ICD-10 *Classification of Mental
and Behavioral Disorders: Clinical
Descriptions and Diagnostic Guidelines.*
Geneva, Switzerland: WHO.

Wormer, K. van (1995) *Alcoholism
Treatment. A Social Work Perspective.*
Chicago: Nelson-Hall.

Young, E. B. (1990) 'The Role of Incest
Issues in Relapse', *Journal of
Psychoactive Drugs* 22(2): 249–58.

Brad R. Karoll, MSW, LCSW, is associated
with the University of Illinois at Urbana-Champaign as both a doctoral candidate
working on his dissertation and as a research
assistant. He is also Regional Case Manager for
the Missouri Physicians' Health Program, a
therapist for the Assisted Recovery Centers of
America, LLC in St Louis, MO, and in private
practice working with those with substance-use disorders. Address: University of Illinois at
Urbana-Champaign, School of Social Work,
1207 West Oregon Street, Urbana, IL 61801,
USA. (e-mail: karoll@uiuc.edu)

9

EFFECTS OF COORDINATED SERVICES FOR DRUG-ABUSING WOMEN WHO ARE VICTIMS OF INTIMATE PARTNER VIOLENCE

LARRY BENNETT AND PATRICIA O'BRIEN

UNIVERSITY OF ILLINOIS AT CHICAGO

This article summarizes outcomes from a demonstration project on collaboration between substance abuse and domestic violence agencies. Researchers recruited women seeking services for substance abuse or intimate partner violence at 1 of 6 participating agencies. Admitted women were both victims of domestic violence and abusing alcohol or drugs. Following an initial screening, participants were interviewed at program entry (n =255) and again 4 to 6 months later (n =128, 50%). Key outcomes were the number of days substances were used in the past 30 days, women's perceptions of harm from battering, and domestic violence self-efficacy. Results suggest participants used substances less frequently and experienced themselves as more efficacious following services, but they were also more fearful of the consequences of domestic violence. Repeated-measures MANOVA found that substance abuse days and domestic violence self-efficacy significantly contributed to the multivariate function. Implications for services for women with co-occurring substance abuse and domestic violence victimization are discussed.

Keywords: domestic violence services; interagency collaboration; substance abuse services

Authors' Note: This research was supported by a contract from the Illinois Department of Human Services to Dr. O'Brien.

SOURCE: "Effects of Coordinated Services for Drug-Abusing Women Who Are Victims of Intimate Partner Violence" by Larry Bennett and Patricia O'Brien. In the 2007 issue of *Violence Against Women*, *13*(4), 395–411. Used with permission.

Based on estimates from the National Violence Against Women Survey, 1.9 million women are assaulted in the United States each year (Tjaden & Thoennes, 1998). Among women in community samples, the lifetime prevalence of substance abuse and domestic violence is on the order of 18% and 34%, respectively (Miller & Downs, 1993), but the history of violence and trauma for women in substance abuse treatment samples is even more prevalent than for women in the general population, with lifetime abuse histories ranging from 55% to 99% (Najavits, Weiss, & Shaw, 1997). Likewise, battered women have a much higher prevalence of substance abuse. In a study of 222 women receiving domestic violence services in Iowa, Downs (2001) found that 26.2% had a CIDI-based lifetime diagnosis of alcohol or drug abuse more than 5 times the rate in the general population.

The relationship between substance abuse and victimization by partners appears to be bidirectional. Substance use may increase their risk of victimization through numerous paths, such as impairing both their judgment and the perpetrator's judgment alike, increasing financial dependency, and exposing women to violent men who also abuse substances (El-Bassel, Gilbert, Schilling, & Wada, 2000). Women's risk for alcohol and drug abuse is also increased by their victimization (Harris & Fallot, 2001; Stark & Flitcraft, 1996). Other factors may also moderate or mediate the relationship between current drug use and victimization, such as childhood abuse (Dunnegun, 1997) and marital conflict (Hotaling & Sugarman, 1990). At present, all available evidence suggests that substance abuse by women and domestic violence toward women have a reciprocal relationship; either problem increases the risk for the other. In a longitudinal study using a national probability sample of 3,006 women followed for 2 years, Kilpatrick, Acierno, Resnick, Saunders, and Best (1997) identified a cyclic relationship where drug use increased the risk of domestic violence and domestic violence increased the risk of both drug and alcohol use. In particular, active drug use (but not alcohol use) was predictive of future victimization for women who had a history of being battered, and both lifetime and recent battering were predictive of future alcohol and drug use.

Women with co-occurring substance abuse and interpersonal victimization present a dilemma to social service and treatment providers. The complex needs of these women, coupled with constraints on providers to link and coordinate services, increase the likelihood of service failure, future injury, and relapse. Improvements in well-being most likely occur when systems coordination results in improved access to high-quality and effective services that appropriately address the need for both safety and sobriety (Collins, Kroutil, Roland, & Moore-Gurrera, 1997; Moses, Huntington, D'Ambrosio, Mazelis, & Reed, 2004). However, examples and evaluations of such coordination have been slow to appear.

Background

Given the issues outlined above, it is not surprising that substance abuse professionals and domestic violence professionals do not agree about best practices when these problems co-occur. By the 1980s, observers were noting barriers to cooperation between substance abuse and domestic violence programs (Harner, 1987–1988; Levy & Brekke, 1990; Rogan, 1985–1986; Wright & Popham, 1982). Such barriers arose not only from a lack of knowledge and experience with the other problem focus but also from differing worldviews by the professionals and volunteers involved. One study of 388 substance abuse and domestic violence staff in 74 programs found little awareness of the co-occurring condition coupled with professional prejudice, misinformation, paradigmatic conflicts, and weak or nonexistent linkages between agencies (Bennett & Lawson, 1994). Despite these barriers, the researchers found that more than 70% of staff had a strong desire for cross-collaboration between substance abuse agencies and domestic violence agencies, regardless of their setting or discipline.

In 1997, the Center for Substance Abuse Treatment (CSAT) published a protocol (TIP 25) for improving treatment when domestic violence and substance abuse co-occur (CSAT, 1997). This protocol suggested that domestic violence and substance abuse are separate problems requiring distinct interventions. TIP 25 did not endorse the dominant practice wisdom of the day in the substance abuse field that women needed to be abstinent before receiving help with other problems in their life, in this case domestic violence. Neither did TIP 25 endorse a widespread belief among domestic violence advocates that battered women's substance abuse was caused primarily by their victimization. TIP 25 recognized domestic violence and substance abuse as serious primary problems and designated safety of the person experiencing domestic violence as the primary consideration in intervention planning in these situations.

To date, there has been little empirical documentation of collaboration between substance abuse agencies and domestic violence agencies. In an organizational study, Reed and her colleagues (2002) identified 6 distinct organizational arrangements in 17 domestic violence–substance abuse collaborations. Six of 17 (35%) organizational modifications were characterized as either adding domestic violence services to an existing substance abuse agency or adding substance abuse services to an existing domestic violence agency. Another 6 (35%) organizational modifications involved independent substance abuse and domestic violence agencies cooperating to provide services. The remaining agencies were either combined agencies, multiservice agencies, or

third-party brokerage of services. The authors presented no data indicating the processes involved in forming and maintaining these various collaborations or the outcomes of the services provided by the collaborations.

In 1998, the Substance Abuse and Mental Health Services Administration (SAMHSA) launched the Women Co-occurring Disorders and Violence Study to examine the development of comprehensive, integrated service model approaches for women with mental health or substance abuse issues and a history of physical or sexual abuse (McHugo et al., 2005). Fourteen U.S. treatment program sites and 2,000 women participated in the intervention development phase of this study, and 9 sites were continued into the evaluation phase. This study included a range of organizations including residential and outpatient mental health and substance abuse service providers, hospitals, jails, public health agencies, universities, and other community groups. A process evaluation of each of the 5 years of the study has been completed (Moses et al., 2004), and empirical findings of outcomes of program participants are just now emerging (e.g., Cocozza et al., 2005).

In the first randomized clinical trial of an integrated relapse prevention and relationship safety program for women in a methadone maintenance program, researchers found marginally significant changes in physical and psychological abuse, illicit drug use, risky sexual behavior, and psychological distress compared to controls (Gilbert et al., 2005). Although only 34 women participated in this small study, the findings suggest that a group-based, relatively short-term intervention (12 sessions during 6 weeks) with an integrated format targeting both safety and relapse may be effective for substance-abusing women who are victims of domestic abuse.

Our article will add additional findings to the emerging research on substance abusing battered women and the services designed to help them by summarizing the substance use and IPV outcomes for a sample of women receiving services in an Illinois demonstration project. The Illinois Department of Human Services (IDHS, 2000) supported a pilot study to explore how substance abuse and domestic violence collaboration and integration would work at the community level. In 2000, domestic violence and substance abuse treatment programs in four communities were selected by IDHS to develop and implement service models. The purpose of the outcome evaluation was to describe the impact of the services provided using goals of reduced substance use or increased sobriety, resolution of personal and family safety issues, and satisfaction with services.

Conceptual Framework

Central to this article and to the demonstration project is the view that violence against women is located and maintained by the use and threat of power and control (Schechter, 1982). This analysis, which still grounds practice in the shelter and walk-in programs where women in this study received services, recognizes that abuse in relationships may be physical or nonphysical. Rather than simply enumerated events, a partner's abuse establishes a context where fear maintains women in situations in which it is difficult if not impossible to see other, nonabusive options available to them. Substance use and abuse and intimate partner violence overlap in multiple ways, and there are not discrete categories where the woman's use is associated with her experience of violence. Active substance abuse by the perpetrator of domestic violence or active substance abuse by the victim of domestic violence threatens the safety of the victim. Domestic violence impairs the opportunity for addiction recovery and threatens sobriety. Although there are multiple causes for both substance abuse and domestic violence, there is little evidence that one causes the other. Regardless of

setting, helpers will be more able to support women healing from both violence and substance abuse if they are responsive to women's multiple and interconnected needs, recognizing that no one treatment is appropriate for all individuals and should be assessed and modified as necessary, the importance of treatment or services being readily available.

Method

Sample and Design

A nonrandom sample of 255 women seeking services from pilot agencies was admitted to the evaluation study. The typical woman in this sample was a 36-year-old African American (45%) mother of one child who did not work either full- or part-time (54%). Of the women, 58% were required to attend treatment, and 33% were on probation or parole. Participants had been treated an average of 2.42 times for substance use problems, and nearly half (42%) were living with someone with a substance abuse problem.

All women entering service at 1 of the 6 agencies were screened for the co-problem. A substance abuse screen was administered to women entering through domestic violence programs consisting of nine yes-no questions and a substance use history. Questions included family history, DUI, arrest, concern expressed by others, attendance at support group meetings, treatment history, using more than intended, and guilt. Substance use history was organized by eight classes of substances by age started, how much used, effect, and last date used. The domestic violence screen was administered to women entering substance abuse treatment and consisted of 16 yes-no questions and an observational guide. The questions covered stress in the family, eight items modified from the revised Conflict Tactics Scale (Straus, Hamby, Boney-McCoy, & Sugarman, 1996), police response, fear of the partner, and concerns about harm.

Observations recorded appearance, bruises, affect, anger, and anxiety at questioning. There was no "cutting score" or minimum response, but admission was based on at least one positive response and the screener's opinion that the woman met the criteria for the study. Women who screened positive were invited to participate in the program and in the research. Following screening and securing their informed consent to participate in the research, staff members interviewed participants at the onset of service delivery (baseline) and research assistants interviewed them again 4 to 6 months after baseline (follow-up).

Service and Program Characteristics

All of the pilot agencies had a similar mix of treatment and services for the women who had been identified as eligible for the pilot through their agency-wide screening process. Two pilot sites used integrated service models, providing both substance abuse services and domestic violence services within their single agency. The other two settings were collaborations of local domestic violence and substance abuse agencies. In all four settings, the services provided were typical services provided by substance abuse agencies (assessment, referral for detoxification, intensive outpatient treatment, toxicology, 12-step groups, individual and group counseling, linkage to methadone maintenance, relapse prevention, and recreation) and domestic violence agencies (24-hour crisis, shelter, case management, psychoeducation, advocacy or protection orders, transportation, children's program, and individual, group, or mother-child counseling).

Measures

Women's Experience of Battering (WEB). The WEB is a 10-item scale created by asking about chronic experiences of battering and the psychological terror associated with intimate partner violence (Smith, & Earp, 1999). The WEB quantifies the experience of battering rather than the frequency of battering events. Possible scores on the WEB are between 10 and 60. A lower score on the WEB indicates more perceived vulnerability to the effects of domestic violence. Sample items in the WEB are, "I feel like he keeps me prisoner." and "He can scare me without laying a hand on me." Scores on the WEB in this sample range from 10 to 60 ($M =29.9$, $SD =15.9$). Cronbach's alpha for the WEB was .99 in the original study and .95 in this sample.

Domestic Violence Self-Efficacy (DVSE). An 8-item index of self-confidence in managing abuse-related difficulties, solving problems, and helping oneself was developed by Riger and her colleagues (2002) for use in a statewide evaluation of domestic violence programs. Although not named as such by Riger et al., we have labeled this measure an index of DVSE. Possible scores on the DVSE are between 8 and 40. A higher score on the DVSE indicates the woman experiences herself as more capable of handling the effects of domestic violence. Sample items on the DVSE are, "I trust my ability to solve difficult problems." and "I have ways to help myself when I feel troubled." DVSE scores in this sample ranged between 9 and 40 ($M =27.3$, $SD =6.8$). Cronbach's alpha for the DVSE was .86 in a sample of 575 domestic violence service consumers (Riger et al., 2002) and .84 for the 255 women in the current sample.

Substance Use Days (SUD). SUD is the woman's report of the total number of days in the past month (30 days) when she used any psychoactive drugs and/or alcohol. A higher SUD score indicates more drinking and drugging. As is usually the case, the SUD is not normally distributed ($M =6.1$, $SD =10.0$, $MD =1.0$, range =0 to 30); 49% of this sample had zero drinks in the previous 30 days at baseline. For some analyses, we transformed the SUD score using a natural logarithm function, LN (1 +SUD). This transformation results in an approximately normal distribution (M =1.9, SD =1.2, MD =1.8, range =0 to 3.4). For other analyses, we dichotomized SUD into an abstinence measure (1:SUD =0, 0:SUD >0).

The DVSE and WEB were positively correlated at baseline (r =.35, n =248, p <.001), suggesting the WEB and the DVSE measure different but related constructs.

This is consistent with our definition that a positive DVSE score indicates perceived competence of the participant and a positive WEB score indicates perceived resistance to the actions of the abuser. The frequency of alcohol and drug use (SUD) inversely varies with both perception of self-efficacy (r =–.23, n =255, p <.01) and perception of battering (r =–.13, n =248, p >.05).

Participants also provided demographic and historical information. In this study, we report on age, ethnicity, education in years, employment level, living situation, psychiatric treatment history, substance use and substance abuse treatment history, arrest history, number of children living with them, probation or parole status, and child protection service status. All these variables were self-reported and quantified in a traditional way.

Procedure

Institutional review boards of both the Illinois Office of Alcoholism and Substance Abuse and the researchers' university approved the research protocol. From July 2000 to June 2001, all women who requested domestic violence or substance abuse services from the six pilot agencies were screened on the cross-issues. Consent to participate in the study was not obtained until after the woman was referred to the integrated program. Because this was a pilot project, providers requested that the evaluation not include a specific instrument to measure discrete acts of violence. As this was a collaborative project that depended on the buy-in of the on-site agency staff to administer the measures, the request was accommodated. If the woman screened positive for both substance abuse and intimate partner violence, self-disclosed within a week of starting services, or, in conversation with a staff member, indicated a need for cross-services, she was admitted to the specialized services and invited to participate in the evaluation, which, depending on the agency, could be in the same building, down the street, or several miles away. Trained staff members administered the baseline interview to eligible, consenting clients. Clients who consented to participate generated a code name to later link responses given at admission to information gleaned during follow-up interviews, without linking any of the data to the study participants by name. Trained interviewers working under the supervision of the second author administered telephone follow-up interviews.

Although there might have been criminal justice consequences for women's drug use, the study was approved under a university protocol that ensured that what the participants told us about drug use at the follow-up was confidential and, in fact, was not associated with their name or agency once the information was included in the database.

Analysis

Following a description of the entire sample, we explore differences in characteristics between the 128 participants for whom follow-up data are available and the 127 individuals who were evaluated only at baseline. The three outcomes were then evaluated using repeated-measure multivariate analysis of variance (MANOVA). We used MANOVA rather than three ANOVAs to account for the correlation among WEB, DVSE, and SUD and to reduce the possibility of Type I error. If the multivariate function was significant for MANOVA, Roy-Bargmann stepdown analysis evaluated the relative contribution of WEB, DVSE, and SUD to the multivariate function. In the stepdown analysis, SUD was entered as the first covariate because of the unusual distribution of abstinent participants at baseline. The final step was to enter DVSE as a covariate in a repeated-measure ANCOVA of WEB. Results were then explored with bivariate statistics.

RESULTS

Participant Characteristics

A total of 255 women met the study screening criteria of both substance abuse and domestic violence victimization. Key demographic, substance use, and violence characteristics of these women are in Table 1. To illuminate the subsequent analysis of follow-up interviews, descriptors in Table 1 are separately listed for two groups of participants: 128 women who completed follow-up interviews and 127 women who did not complete follow-up interviews. Women participating in follow-up interviews did not differ from nonparticipating women by race, current living arrangement, education, full-time employment in the past 30 days, age, residential days, overnight psychiatric days, arrests, or number of children living with them. Likewise, there were no differences between followed and not-followed women in number of prior substance abuse treatments or outpatient treatment days. There were, however, baseline differences between the two groups on all three outcomes. Women who were followed, at baseline, were less vulnerable to the effects of violence, were more efficacious with domestic violence coping skills, and used substances less often than did women who were not followed.

Overall Outcomes

The average participant received a mean of 22.2 counseling sessions (MD =25, SD =6.1). Baseline and follow-up values for the three outcome measures are arrayed in Table 2. The multivariate function was significant (Pillai's trace =.41),

$F(3, 116)$ =26.7, p <.001. SUD was then entered as a covariate in a within-subjects MANOVA model of DVSE and WEB scores. The multivariate function in this first stage model remained significant (Pillai's trace =.21), $F(2, 117)$ =15.3, p <.001. In the final stage of the stepdown, we entered both SUD and DVSE as covariates in an ANCOVA model of WEB. In this model, the multivariate F was no longer significant (Pillai's trace =.03), $F(1, 118)$ =3.15, p >.07. This analysis suggests that both substance use frequency and DVSE are significant contributors to overall change during the program. Although WEB also changed significantly during the program, when considered together with the other two outcome variables, WEB did not significantly contribute to our understanding of the effects of these coordinated programs.

For SUD and DVSE, pre-post differences are in the intuitive direction. Participants report significantly reduced substance use and significantly higher levels of self-efficacy at follow-up compared to the baseline period. However, because a lower score on the WEB indicates increased vulnerability to the effects of domestic violence, participants reported increased vulnerability at follow-up compared to baseline, although this increase was not significant after considering DVSE and SUD changes. To better understand these results, we will explore each individual outcome in greater detail.

As we see in Table 2, participants report higher levels of DVSE at follow-up compared to baseline, and this change remains significant when we also consider its relationship with WEB and SUD. Change in self-efficacy is unrelated (p >.10) to baseline age, ethnicity, education, employment, independent living, residential treatment during the previous 6 months, psychiatric treatment history, substance abuse treatment history, arrest history, number of children, probation or parole status, or child protection service status.

Table 1   Means and Standard Deviations or Percentages of Key Demographic, Substance Use, and Violence Characteristics by Follow-Up Status

| | Follow-Up Status | | | | |
| | Followed Up | | Not Followed Up | | |
	M	SD	M	SD	Difference
n	128		127		
Age	35.2	(8.1)	35.2	(8.0)	ns
Race					ns
African American, not Hispanic (%)	38		52		
Hispanic (%)	13		6		
European, not Hispanic (%)	42		33		
Other (%)	4		7		
Education (years)	11.9	(1.7)	11.7	(2.3)	ns
Full-time employment (%)	15		17		ns
Living arrangement past 30 days					ns
Independent or with someone else (%)	71		74		
Hospital, treatment, or incarceration (%)	13		20		
Shelter (%)	9		10		
Other (%)	7		6		
Residential days past 6 months	56.4	(59.9)	48.9	(46.4)	ns
Overnight psych hospital days past 6 months	1.4	(6.6)	1.6	(13.5)	ns
Times arrested past 6 months	0.5	(0.9)	0.5	(1.1)	ns
Children younger than 18 living with participant	1.1	(1.3)	0.9	(1.3)	ns
Times treated for alcohol or drug abuse	2.2	(2.3)	2.5	(3.5)	ns
Outpatient treatment days past month	3.9	(5.6)	3.0	(4.4)	ns
On probation or parole (%)	31		35		ns
Child protection services involved (%)	37		46		ns
Outcome variables					
Substance Use Days (SUD)[a]	6.4	(15.3)	8.4	(10.7)	$t = 6.2^{***}$
Women's Experience of Battering (WEB)	28.6	(16.9)	23.3	(14.6)	$t = 2.7^{**}$
Domestic Violence Self-Efficacy (DVSE)	28.6	(6.8)	26.1	(6.7)	$t = 2.9^{**}$

[a] Values in table are in drinks per month, but SUD was transformed for paired t test using natural logarithm function, $\ln(1 + \text{SUD})$.

Table 2   Repeated-Measure MANOVA of WEB, DVSE, and SUD at Baseline and Follow-Up With Roy-Bargmann Stepdown and Univariate F at Each Step

| | Baseline | | Follow-Up | | | | |
	M	SD	M	SD	Step 0 F	Step 1 F	Step 2 F
WEB	28.64	16.75	25.18	15.71	7.20**	5.20*	3.15
DVSE	28.55	6.93	32.20	6.01	31.80***	22.35***	—
SUD	5.90	13.19	0.92	3.93	40.18***	—	—

NOTE: WEB =Women's Experience of Battering; DVSE =Domestic Violence Self-Efficacy; SUD = Substance Use Days past month. Step 0 =univariate F in repeated-measure MANOVA of SUD, WEB, and DVSE; Step 1 =univariate F in repeated-measure MANOVA of DVSE and WEB, with SUD covariate; Step 2 = univariate F of DVSE in repeated-measure ANCOVA with SUD and DVSE covariates. $^*p < .01$. $^{**}p < .001$.

Although changes in the DVSE from baseline to follow-up were statistically significant, it is reasonable to wonder whether this is a clinically significant change. One way to address this is to compare the follow-up scores to a benchmark. In a study of counseling for domestic violence victims using the DVSE, Bennett, Riger, Schewe, Howard, and Wasco (2004) reported that the before-service mean was 29.51 (SD =6.09) and the after-service mean was 31.08 (SD =5.96), reflecting a change of approximately one fourth standard deviation unit for a before-after sample of 549 battered women. In our study, using the same outcome measure and a similar elapsed time, we documented a baseline mean of 28.55 (SD =6.93) and a follow-up mean of 32.20 (SD =6.01), a change of approximately two thirds of a standard deviation unit for a sample of 127 women. Both studies represent modest effect sizes compared to those reported in controlled studies of treatment of mental health disorders where other disorders have been screened out (Lipsey & Wilson, 1993) but are substantial when compared to studies of domestic violence intervention (e.g., Babcock, Green, & Robie, 2004). An alternative perspective on clinical significance is that 67% of the 127 participants improved during the course of the program.

The average number of SUD declined among program participants from about 6 days per month to 1 day per month (Table 2). Changes in SUD were not related to baseline age, ethnicity, employment, independent living, residential treatment days, psychiatric treatment history, arrest history, number of children, probation or parole status, or child protection service status. Reduction in SUD score was weakly related to years of education (r =.20, n =127, p <.05) and the number of times the woman had been treated for substance abuse (r =.23, n =127, p <.01). Reduction in substance use was also moderated by

probation or parole status. In part because of the conditions of their supervision, 39 women on probation or parole reduced their 30-day consumption from a mean 2.3 days (SD =6.1) to a mean of 1.4 days (SD =5.8), whereas 88 women not on probation or parole reduced their consumption days from a mean of 8.2 days (SD =17.7) to a mean of 0.8 days (SD =2.7).

Reporting SUD as a mean can be misleading because one goal of substance abuse treatment may be not only reduction in consumption but also abstinence. Abstinence is taken to mean zero use of all drugs, not just the drug of choice. This sample has an observable "basement effect": Of the 128 individuals who were in the follow-up sample, 73 (57.0%) reported no substance use in the 30 days prior to the baseline interview. At follow-up, 111 (87.0%) did not use drugs or alcohol in the previous month. Of the follow-up sample, 63.0% maintained their condition of either use (9.4%) or abstinence (53.5%) during the course of the program, whereas 43 (33.9%) became abstinent at least for a month during the course of the program. In Table 3, we describe substance use at baseline and follow-up in greater detail, including abstinence. As we see in Table 3, there is considerable variation in SUD and abstinence at baseline by drug of choice, but far less at follow-up.

In part, the results of this study are compromised by the fact that a number of initial assessments were done after the participants had been in the treatment program for a substantial period, evidenced by the fact that 42% of the nonfollowed participants and 57% of the follow-up participants were abstinent for the 30 days prior to the baseline interview. In fact, 9% of the nonfollowed group and 13% of the followed group had been in substance abuse treatment during the 30-day baseline period, and 15% of the nonfollowed group and 16% of the

Table 3   Rate of Problem Use by Drug of Choice (DOC), Primary DOC, 30-Day Substance Use, and
Rate of Abstinence at Baseline and at Follow-Up

| Substance | Problem Use (%) | Primary DOC (%) | Baseline | | | Follow-Up | | |
| | | | SUD | | | SUD | | |
			M	SD	Abstinent (%)	M	SD	Abstinent (%)
Alcohol	71	38	3.1	8.4	71	1.0	4.4	87
Cocaine or crack	51	31	5.2	9.9	54	1.8	5.0	77
Marijuana	38	12	11.7	25.6	31	0.3	1.0	94
Heroin	16	14	14.1	24.6	50	0		100
Other[a]	5	5	2.6	5.1	57	0		100
Any	—	—	6.4	15.3	57	0.9	3.9	87

NOTE: SUD = Substance Use Days. Rate of abstinence at baseline is for the 127 women in the follow-up sample.

[a] Methamphetamine ($n = 2$), PCP ($n = 3$), hallucinogens ($n = 1$), and over the counter ($n = 1$).

followed group had been in some form of residential program during the previous 30 days (jail, prison, medical, or psychiatric). A typical scenario creating this situation is that of a woman who has been in substance abuse treatment and attending support groups for a few months and then discloses in treatment that she is the victim of domestic violence, triggering a referral to the demonstration project. This situation also accounts for the low rate of SUD among women in substance abuse treatment compared to women in domestic violence programs, a result that may initially seem counterintuitive.

The finding that women's perceived vulnerability to battering increased nearly 20% of a standard score from baseline to follow-up was unexpected. The researchers initially suspected this increase represented a coding error, but review of the raw data revealed no errors. WEB at follow-up was unrelated to age, ethnicity, education, employment, independent living, residential treatment during the previous 6 months, psychiatric treatment history, substance abuse treatment history, arrest history, number of children, probation or parole status, or child protection service status.

DISCUSSION

In this report, we have documented that coordinated or integrated services for women with the co-occurring conditions of substance abuse and domestic violence are associated with significant changes in self-efficacy and substance use. Perception of harm from battering may also change, but these results require additional study. All outcomes are independent of demographic factors. Pre-post differences in substance use frequency and DVSE are in the intuitive direction: Substance use declines during the period of service reception, whereas self-efficacy increases. Multivariate analysis supports a hypothesis that women with co-occurring substance abuse and domestic violence issues benefit from coordinated or integrated programs of intervention. However, the finding that they may see themselves as more vulnerable following the program, if replicated, suggests we may not fully understand the changes. Women in these programs significantly reduced substance use behavior and, independently, significantly increased their perceived effectiveness in coping with domestic violence. However, as a group, women perceived that they were more adversely affected by battering at the end of these programs than at the beginning of these programs.

At least three explanations, two substantive and one methodological, fit the data reflecting a greater vulnerability to battering. One explanation is that newfound sobriety and competence have opened the women's eyes to the seriousness of their situation. Alcohol and drug use may have numbed their fear and made their life palatable. Lack of self-efficacy may have reduced their expectations for a safer life. Now, the veil cast asunder, they are more fearful of the abuser—or abuse—than they used to be. A second explanation involves a batterer's response to a woman's newfound sobriety. A woman who is successful in her recovery from substance abuse may face increasing levels of physical and nonphysical abuse from a partner in response to her abstinence or reduction in substance use, particularly if drinking and drugging were a shared activity prior to treatment. At baseline, almost one third of the follow-up sample lived with someone who was a substance abuser, and a substantial (but unknown) proportion of these roommates were probably romantic partners. A third methodological explanation fitting these data is that experiences of battering and self-efficacy are different outcroppings of an underlying construct. The MANOVA stepdown analysis is consistent with this explanation. After removing the effects of both substance use frequency and domestic violence self-efficacy, women's experience of battering no longer changed significantly from baseline to follow-up. Disentangling these effects is beyond the scope of this evaluation project, however.

Limitations

The current research is hampered by the usual conditions of field evaluations, most notably the lack of a comparison group. Consequently, we are unable to establish beyond speculation the factors responsible for the changes in substance use, experience of battering, and self-efficacy that we observed. A second methodological problem is the rate of follow-up of research participants. Battered women and substance abusers are notoriously difficult populations to relocate and, if relocated, to reengage. This limitation certainly affects any conclusions we might draw from this research. In particular, the fact that unfollowed women differed at baseline on all three outcome variables suggests that the outcomes may have been different had these missing women participated in the study at follow-up.

Finally, we would have preferred to measure both the events of battering and the experience of battering. Although we concur with Smith, Tessaro, and Earp (1993) that capturing women's experience of battering is an important addition to simply counting its occurrence, in a situation where battering experience changes in an unexpected direction, the lack of event data hampers our ability to shed light on a potentially important phenomenon beyond mere speculation. In addition to a context of fear, battering is also a series of discrete events (Dutton, 1999), and research on battering, to be informative, is enhanced by more, rather than less, information. In the current evaluation, the situation beyond the initial screening did not permit using event-based measures in addition to a contextual measure, but future research should do so.

Suggestions for Further Research

In addition to addressing the problems discussed above, practice and policy with this population would be greatly enhanced by more information addressing key questions. First of all, how does the acuity of violence affect the effectiveness of services? In our sample, only 26% of the participants reported that violence was still occurring, and 19% reported that there had been no violence in the past year. This is not an unusual situation. In the Riger et al. (2002) sample of 5,260 women seeking counseling services from domestic violence programs in Illinois, only 30% of the women reported that violence was still occurring at the time of admission, and 24% reported no physical abuse in the past 12 months. The effects of domestic violence last longer than the index aggression—one of the reasons we used the WEB in this study—but we still lack information on how remote and recent violence differentially affect the measurable outcomes of services.

A second area of future work would be examining the relative effects of coordinated and integrated programs. Our four research settings featured two coordinated systems (separate agencies for domestic violence and substance abuse) and two integrated systems (the same agency provides both programs). There is much to learn about the differential effects of coordination versus integration, particularly in light of the current push toward "one stop shopping," which encourages agencies to offer more comprehensive services. Related to this issue, future research should explore whether the path of participants into a program has a bearing on outcomes. Coordinated settings can be further divided into whether the participant entered through the "domestic violence door" or the "substance abuse door." Are there differences in program effects depending on the path to services? More specifically, are there personal or situational characteristics that favor entry through one or another door? The current practice would suggest that door is not an important construct, to wit, "no wrong door" (Whitten, 2004). "No wrong door" is an assumption, not an empirical statement, and data would make that assumption more convincing.

Implications for Practice

Empirical findings, satisfaction with services, and qualitative findings from focus groups with participants in this pilot project indicate that women with substance abuse disorders and experiences of partner abuse can improve when provided with counseling and support services that address their range of service needs. Building on TIP 25 (CSAT, 1997), more effective treatment and support services for women must include recognition that the effects of past and present violence are central concerns in women's lives.

This research supports current efforts to increase screening and assessment for co-occurring conditions. All domestic violence agencies should screen and refer for substance use problems, and all substance abuse agencies should screen and refer for domestic violence. Before this happens, however, these agencies need to build bridges of collaboration, made all the more difficult by important issues such as confidentiality, philosophical differences, power differentials, and competition for funding. SAMHSA's efforts to coordinate domestic violence and substance abuse services appear to be the right policy at the right time. However, the disquieting increase in perception of the adverse effects of battering that we have identified in this study suggest that there is no free lunch, even in seemingly no-brainer policies such as coordinated services and "no wrong door." We are particularly concerned that the architects of public awareness and programs for the victims of violence—the women's movement, feminists, and community-based violence against women programs—are increasingly marginalized in our "ownership society," which emphasizes both personal responsibility and personal dysfunction. We wonder how community-based domestic violence programs grounded in a social understanding of violence against women will do when they begin to coordinate services with corporate behavioral health care entities traded on Wall Street. Obviously, such concerns are beyond the sights of our little program evaluation, perhaps even beyond the pale of science.

References

Babcock, J. C., Green, C. E., & Robie, C. (2004). Does batterers' treatment work?: A meta-analytic review of domestic violence treatment outcome research. *Clinical Psychology Review, 23,* 1023–1053.

Bennett, L., & Lawson, M. (1994). Barriers to cooperation between domestic-violence and substance-abuse programs. *Families in Society: The Journal of Contemporary Human Services, 75,* 277–286.

Bennett, L. W., Riger, S., Schewe, P., Howard, A., & Wasco, S. (2004). Effectiveness of hotline, advocacy, counseling, and shelter services for victims of domestic violence: A statewide evaluation. *Journal of Interpersonal Violence, 19,* 815–829.

Center for Substance Abuse Treatment. (1997). *Substance abuse treatment and domestic violence* (SMA 97–3163). Retrieved September 25, 2005, from http://www.health.org/govpubs/BKD239/index.htm.

Cocozza, J. J., Jackson, E. W., Hennigan, K., Morrissey, J. P., Reed, B. G., Fallot, R., et al. (2005). Outcomes for women with co-occurring disorders and trauma: Program-level effects. *Journal of Substance Abuse Treatment, 28,* 109–119.

Collins, J. J., Kroutil, L. A., Roland, E. J., & Moore-Gurrera, M. (1997). Issues in the linkages of alcohol and domestic violence services. In M. Galanter (Ed.), *Recent developments in alcoholism, Vol. 13: Alcohol and violence: Epidemiology, neurobiology, psychology, family issues* (pp. 387–405). New York: Plenum.

Downs, W. R. (2001). *Alcohol problems and violence against women: Report of summary findings.* Washington, DC: U.S. Department of Justice.

Dunnegun, S. (1997). Violence, trauma, and substance abuse. *Journal of Psychoactive Drugs, 29,* 345–351.

Dutton, M. A. (1999). Multidimensional assessment of woman battering: Commentary on Smith, Smith, and Earp. *Psychology of Women Quarterly, 23,* 195–198.

El-Bassel, N., Gilbert, L., Schilling, R., & Wada, T. (2000). Drug abuse and partner violence among women in methadone treatment. *Journal of Family Violence, 15,* 209–228.

Gilbert, L., El-Bassel, N., Manuel, J., Wu, E., Hyun, G., Golder, S., et al. (2005). *An integrated relapse prevention and personal safety intervention for women on methadone: Testing effects of intimate partner violence and substance abuse.* Manuscript submitted for publication.

Harner, I. C. (1987–1988). The alcoholism treatment client and domestic violence. *Alcohol Health and Research World, 12,* 150–152, 160.

Harris, M., & Fallot, R. D. (2001). Envisioning a trauma-informed service system: A vital paradigm shift. In M. Harris & R. D. Fallot (Eds.), *Using trauma theory to design service systems* (pp. 3–22). San Francisco: Jossey-Bass.

Hotaling, G. T., & Sugarman, D. B. (1990). A risk marker analysis of assaulted wives. *Journal of Family Violence, 5,* 1–25.

Illinois Department of Human Services. (2000). *Best practices for domestic violence and substance abuse services.* Springfield: Author.

Kilpatrick, D., Acierno, R., Resnick, H., Saunders, B., & Best, C. (1997). A 2-year longitudinal analysis of the relationships between violent assault and substance abuse in women. *Journal of Consulting and Clinical Psychology, 65,* 834–847.

Levy, A. J., & Brekke, J. S. (1990). Spouse battering and chemical dependency: Dynamics, treatment, and service delivery. In R. T. Potter-Efron & P. S. Potter-Efron (Eds.), *Aggression, family violence and chemical dependency* (pp. 81–97). New York: Haworth.

Lipsey, M. W., & Wilson, D. B. (1993). The efficacy of psychological, behavioral, and educational treatment: Confirmation from meta-analysis. *American Psychologist, 48,* 1181–1209.

McHugo, G. J., Kammerer, N., Jackson, E. W., Markoff, L. S., Gatz, M., Larson, M. J., et al. (2005). Women, co-occurring disorders, and violence study: Evaluation design and study population. *Journal of Substance Abuse Treatment, 28*, 91–107.

Miller, B. A., & Downs, W. R. (1993). The impact of family violence on the use of alcohol by women. *Alcohol Health & Research World, 17*, 137–143.

Moses, D. J., Huntington, N., D'Ambrosio, B., Mazelis, R., & Reed, B. G. (2004). *Developing integrated services for women with co-occurring disorders and trauma histories: Lessons from the SAMHSA women with alcohol, drug abuse and mental health disorders who have histories of violence study.* Washington, DC: U.S. Department of Health and Human Services.

Najavits, L. M., Weiss, R. D., & Shaw, S. R. (1997). The link between substance abuse and posttraumatic stress disorder in women: A research review. *American Journal on Addictions, 6*, 273–283.

Reed, B. G., Shires, D., Rao, M., Barr, E. K., Bernard, M., & Fehr, T. (2002, November). *Working with domestic violence (DV) and alcohol and other drugs (AOD): Best practices, barriers, and incentives.* Ann Arbor: University of Michigan, School of Social Work.

Riger, S., Bennett, L., Schewe, P., Campbell, R., Frohmann, L., Camacho, J., et al. (2002). *Evaluation of services for survivors of domestic violence and sexual assault.* Thousand Oaks, CA: Sage.

Rogan, A. (1985–1986). Domestic violence and alcohol: Barriers to cooperation. *Alcohol Health and Research World, 9*, 22–27.

Schechter, S. (1982). *Women and male violence: The visions and struggles of the battered women's movement.* Boston: South End.

Smith, P. H., Smith, J. B., & Earp, J. L. (1999). Beyond the measurement trap: A reconstructed conceptualization and measurement of woman battering. *Psychology of Women Quarterly, 23*, 177–193.

Smith, P. H., Tessaro, I., & Earp, J. E. (1993). Women's experience with battering: A conceptualization from qualitative research. *Women's Health Issues, 5*, 173–182.

Stark, E., & Flitcraft, A. (1996). *Women at risk: Domestic violence and women's health.* Thousand Oaks, CA: Sage.

Straus, M. A., Hamby, S. L., Boney-McCoy, S., & Sugarman, D. B. (1996). The revised Conflict Tactics Scales (CTS2): Development and preliminary psychometric data. *Journal of Family Issues, 17*, 283–316.

Tjaden, P., & Thoennes, N. (1998). *Prevalence, incidence and consequences of violence against women: Findings from the National Violence Against Women Survey.* Washington, DC: U.S. Department of Justice.

Whitten, L. (2004). "No wrong door" for people with co-occurring disorders. *NIDA Notes, 19*(4). Retrieved October 1, 2005, from http://www .nida.nih .gov/NIDA_notes/NNvol19N4/No.html.

Wright, J., & Popham, J. (1982). Alcohol and battering: The double bind. *Aegis, 36*, 53–59.

Larry Bennett, PhD, is associate professor, Jane Adams College of Social Work, University of Illinois at Chicago. His research interests focus on co-occurring substance abuse and intimate partner violence and evaluation of community and correctional interventions for men who batter.

Patricia O'Brien, PhD, is associate professor, Jane Adams College of Social Work, University of Illinois at Chicago. Her research interests are holistic assessment and reintegration of formerly incarcerated women and the application of qualitative/feminist research methods.

CRITICAL THINKING QUESTIONS

Reading 5

1. As Kubiak suggests, there is a high rate of PTSD in the histories of men and women who are incarcerated; the prevalence of substance use disorders is high as well. Account for how these factors are interrelated.

2. Discuss the differences between men and women in terms of past trauma. How was the original hypothesis relevant to re-offending in aftercare supported by the findings?

3. Discuss the significance of the finding that a significant number of men are emerging from prison suffering from PTSD directly related to their prison experience.

4. How does the author explain the finding that PTSD in women with substance abuse problems apparently is more closely associated with a return to prison in women than in men? Are there possible other explanations for these women's recidivism rates.

Reading 6

1. Do you agree or disagree with Howell's theory on gendered pathways to crime?

2. Discuss each one of Johansson and Kempf-Leonard's interrelated risk factors for violence in the girls.

3. How would the pathway to delinquency be different for boys?

4. Critique the methodology used in this study. Is the information in the records complete?

5. What role does substance abuse play in the pathway to delinquency? How did the results fail to support Howell's theory on one of the items tested? What is the best explanation for the unexpected result?

Reading 7

1. What was the purpose of this study?

2. For what clientele is this program intended?

3. Describe this study's independent and dependent variables?

4. What seem to be the outcomes of the Familias Unidas program, thus far?

5. What other evidence or considerations may you wish to take into account prior to advocating for this program?

Reading 8

1. On what basis does Karoll conclude that women have a different physiological response to heavy drinking compared to me?

2. What role does victimization play in the development of drinking problems in women? Do you think the effect could be the same in men as well, for example, men who have engaged in war combat?

3. What can social workers and other practitioners learn from the facts presented in this literature review that would enhance their work with women?

4. Discuss how the principles of motivational interviewing which are scientifically validated might be especially helpful in work with women.

5. What do you think are some of the negative biases concerning women alcoholics to which the author refers? Consider whether or not the discussion provided here helps counter such a bias.

Reading 9

1. Do you detect in reading the discussion by Bennett and O'Brien that there is a theoretical difference in the way treatment services explain domestic violence and substance abuse?

2. What are some of the difficulties in bringing programming together when the professional training and orientation is in contradiction?

3. How do the findings in this reading validate some of the claims

and facts presented in the preceding readings (especially readings 5 and 8)?

4. Describe the methodology used and results of the study concerning treatment effectiveness. Consider how if funding were adequate, the researcher could redesign this study to include a control group for comparison.

PART IV

TREATMENT ISSUES AND INNOVATIONS

Because most people who recover from alcohol and drug use do so outside of the treatment arena, we start this section on treatment with an article that reviews the research literature on recovery across the life course. Hser, Longshore, and Anglin ask questions that are not usually asked about key events in one's life that serve as turning points, and the significance of the timing of these key events. Often natural recovery doesn't take place soon enough, however, to prevent an alcoholic or drug dependent individual from sinking deeper and deeper into the throes of addiction.

For clients who are resistant to the treatment process, motivational interviewing is the treatment of choice. Counselors trained in this approach direct particular responses to the client's readiness to change. Because this approach is of proven effectiveness, we have chosen two readings on motivational interviewing, the first to describe the process, and the second to discuss its application to meet the needs of a special population—older adults.

The National Institute of Drug Abuse (NIDA) recommends motivational interviewing, behavioral-cognitive, and pharmacological approaches to prevent relapse and help people overcome their cravings for drugs. In the reading chosen for this section NIDA summarizes some of the new medications that are being prescribed by doctors to suppress withdrawal symptoms, and to prevent drug cravings. The section ends with a detailed account of the use of the illicit drug **methamphetamine** (meth). In this reading, Shrem and Halkitis provide a synthesis of findings from the empirical research regarding the prevalence of meth use within certain populations and the role of this drug in sexual risk-taking. Treatment implications are discussed.

10

THE LIFE COURSE PERSPECTIVE ON DRUG USE

A Conceptual Framework for Understanding Drug Use Trajectories

YIH-ING HSER

DOUGLAS LONGSHORE

M. DOUGLAS ANGLIN

UNIVERSITY OF CALIFORNIA, LOS ANGELES

This article discusses the life course perspective on drug use, including conceptual and analytic issues involved in developing the life course framework to explain how drug use trajectories develop during an individual's lifetime and how this knowledge can guide new research and approaches to management of drug dependence. Central concepts include trajectories marked by transitions and social capital and turning points influencing changes. The life course perspective offers an organizing framework for classifying varying drug use trajectories,

Authors' Note: The project described was supported in part by Grant P30 DA016383 from the National Institute on Drug Abuse. The content is solely the responsibility of the authors and does not necessarily represent the official views of the National Institute on Drug Abuse or the National Institute of Health. The authors are grateful to Alison Hamilton for helpful editing and to several reviewers for providing helpful comments and suggestions on earlier versions of this article. Special thanks are due to staff at the UCLA Integrated Substance Abuse Programs for manuscript preparation.

Our co-author, colleague, and friend, Douglas Longshore, died December 30, 2005, of metastatic melanoma. We dedicate this article to him and his pursuit of excellence in researching, preventing, and treating substance abuse.

SOURCE: "The Life Course Perspective on Drug Use: A Conceptual Framework for Understanding Drug Use Trajectories" by Yih-Ing Hser, Douglas Longshore and M. Douglas Anglin. In the 2007 issue of *Evaluation Review, 31*(6), 515–547. Used with permission.

identifying critical events and factors contributing to the persistence or change in drug use, analytically ordering events that occur during the life span, and determining contributory relationships.

Keywords: life course; drug use trajectory; chronic disorder; turning points; long-term care; disease management

Drug use persists as a major national problem that severely affects individual and public health and many social institutions, such as the health, mental health, criminal justice, and welfare systems. Research findings have generally shown that patterns of lifetime drug use and related problems are extremely heterogeneous. Many people experiment with drug use and then desist, whereas a subset become frequent users, and some of these become problematic or dependent users (Chen, Kandel, and Davies, 1997; Kandel, 2000; Warner et al., 1995). Severe or dependent users tend to persist in their drug use, often for substantial periods of their life span. Adverse consequences of drug dependence (i.e., addiction) have been well documented and include mortality, morbidity, criminality, and lost productivity. The social and health costs associated with drug dependence in the United States have been estimated to be approximately $180.9 billion annually (Office of National Drug Control Policy, 2004). Therefore, the importance of understanding and addressing the full spectrum of drug use patterns cannot be overstated. This article focuses on the life course drug use trajectories of dependent users, who place the heaviest burden on social services.

Previously, we have examined the longitudinal patterns of drug use and related issues within a drug addiction and treatment "career" framework (Hser et al., 1997). *Career* is defined as a process in which drug use "often escalates to more severe levels, with repeated cycles of cessation and relapse occurring over an extended period," and which we have argued needs to be studied through a "longitudinal, dynamic approach" (Hser et al., 1997, p. 543). We suggested that short-term intervention strategies are not optimal for curtailing drug dependence because it tends to persist over a long period for the majority of dependent users. Most drug abuse research has approached drug abuse as an acute disorder, however, and longitudinal studies have typically focused on general population samples and have concentrated on onset patterns of drug use. Studies of dependent users with extended follow-ups are scarce, resulting in limited empirical examinations of addiction careers.

Within the past decade, studies with extended follow-up periods have begun to appear in the literature, and both the scientific and medical communities increasingly acknowledge that drug dependence can be a chronic disorder that requires long-term care or management (Anglin, Hser, and Grella, 1997; McLellan et al., 2000; Hser, Hoffman et al., 2001). In addition, evidence continues to demonstrate that drug users often come in contact with multiple service systems (e.g., drug treatment, criminal justice, mental health, welfare, primary health care), necessitating an integrated and comprehensive approach to addressing drug dependence and its optimal management.

Unfortunately, theoretical development has not kept pace with recent empirical developments within the field of drug abuse research. In this article, we endeavor to expand our drug and treatment career framework by incorporating theoretical and empirical perspectives from several disciplines (sociology, psychology, criminology, health) that similarly address phenomena often characterized as chronic in nature such as criminality and illness. Our expansion of the drug use and treatment career to the life course drug use framework is based on the following:

- The terminology of drug use or treatment *career* has an unwanted connotation (e.g., *career* typically is something to be sought or encouraged, as in employment), and by shifting to a neutral term we avoid potential misinterpretation.

- The empirical findings of the heterogeneity of life course drug use patterns and frequent interplays with multiple service systems require a more comprehensive account that takes into consideration historical contexts, social structure and environments, and intra- and interindividual differences.

- Theoretical developments in other disciplines may be informative for studying drug addiction and its management; concepts and methods applied in different disciplines are useful and applicable for consideration in developing the life course drug use framework. The cross-fertilization of concepts and methods from these research traditions can enrich a life course drug use perspective uncovering the dynamics of drug use trajectories during the life span and transitions (including service system contacts) that occur within these trajectories.

By focusing on the patterns or trajectories across individuals' lives and the ways in which those patterns are shaped by the broader historical context and social structures, the life course perspective offers a broadened organizing framework that potentially allows for characterizing distinctive patterns of drug use trajectories, identifying critical events and factors contributing to the persistence or change during the life span and analytically ordering the events that occur during that course. The article is organized as follows. We first briefly describe and summarize theory and research in life course studies, developmental criminal careers, and illness careers that are relevant to the study of drug dependence and to our life course perspective of drug use. Second, we apply key concepts within the life course perspective to examine existing data

applicable to drug addiction. By doing so, we identify areas requiring further research as suggested by the expanded concepts within this framework. We conclude by identifying future research directions within this expanded framework.

LIFE COURSE, DEVELOPMENTAL CRIMINOLOGY, AND CHRONIC ILLNESS

A life course approach to the study of human behavior and experience explicitly recognizes the importance of time, timing, and temporal processes during an individual's lifetime. The life course perspective has a long history in the health and public health fields, particularly in the social sciences (Lynch and Smith, 2005; Elder, 1985). Here, we briefly describe three areas of application that are most relevant for consideration in the life course framework applied to drug use research.

Life Course

The life course has been defined as "pathways through the age-differentiated life span" (Elder, 1985, p. 17), in particular the "sequence of culturally defined age-graded roles and social transitions that are enacted over time" (Caspi, Elder, and Herbener, 1990, p. 15). Trajectories, transitions, and turning points are key concepts in life course research (Elder, 1985; Hagestad, 1990). A trajectory is a pathway or line of development during the life span, such as work life, parenthood, or criminal behavior. Trajectories refer to long-term patterns of behavior and are marked by a sequence of transitions. Transitions are marked by life events that are embedded in trajectories and that evolve during shorter time spans (Elder, 1985, p. 31–32). Transitions refer to changes in status that are discrete and bounded in duration (e.g., starting or leaving school, entering or leaving the first job, giving birth, committing the first crime), although their consequences may be long term (George, 1993). Trajectories are long-term patterns of stability and change, often including multiple transitions that can be reliably differentiated from alternate patterns. Transitions and trajectories are interrelated. As Elder (1985) notes, "Transitions are always embedded in trajectories that give them distinctive form and meaning" (p. 32).

The interlocking nature of trajectories and transitions may generate turning points or a change in the life course (Elder, 1985, p. 32). Adaptation to life events is crucial because the same event or transition followed by different adaptations can lead to different trajectories (Elder, 1985, p. 35). Most studies on life course transitions focus on normative changes in developmental or social roles (e.g., education, work, marriage, military, or retirement). Life transitions, such as starting school or entering or leaving the workforce, impose stress on adaptive and regulatory systems, requiring the developing individual to adapt to new routines and to adopt new response patterns.

How life's transitions and turning points are managed can lead to different stress response patterns and, accordingly, different trajectories (Elder, 1985) of behavioral manifestations such as drug use.

Life course research describes and explains stability and change in behavior or attributes over time, and thus life course analyses often focus on the timing, ordering, and duration of major life events and their consequences for later social development. Biological, psychological, cognitive, and social developments occur on different time scales, each with their own significant transitions and turning points (Halfon and Hochstein, 2002). The time frames for these developments also mutually influence each other. For example, although biological processes determine the onset of puberty, puberty is also influenced by social and cultural changes, as evidenced by the varying age of puberty onset and menarche and the associated role changes in different cultures (Worthman, 1999). Historical changes can also influence the timing of life events, such as later age of marriage and childbearing among women, which is related to increased participation of women in the workforce; such changes may also have health-related consequences, including substance use. In particular, the timing of experience may be important in the life course development. For example, some studies have shown that early intervention during the initial "critical period" of a first episode of psychosis improves the chance of recovery in the shorter and longer terms (Birchwood, 1998). Similarly, lost years of experience or missed opportunities (e.g., education, employment) during younger ages because of early onset of deviant behaviors or lifestyles (e.g., drug use, criminal activities) often cannot be easily recaptured or can be recaptured only at a high intervention cost. It appears that many developmental options, choices, and resources are available only during specific development windows, with a disproportionate number presenting in the earlier years of life.

Developmental Criminology

Criminology research closely parallels drug abuse research in its conceptualization of dynamic patterns of long-term behavior as a combination of static and temporal patterns. Concepts in the criminal career (with parallel drug abuse concepts shown in parentheses) include participation in criminal offending (lifetime use), frequency of offending or lambda (frequency of use), crime variety (polydrug use) during a given period, seriousness of offending (severity of use), crime switching over time (drug switching), and desistence (drug use cessation). Criminology has gone further than drug abuse research in mapping dynamic patterns of offending (notably Laub and Sampson, 2001; Loeber and Le Blanc, 1990; Piquero, Farrington, and Blumstein, 2003) with a systematic differentiation of dynamic patterns: acceleration and deceleration in behavior frequency, escalation (also called *aggravation* in crime research) and de-escalation in behavior severity, stabilization and destabilization of behavior, and specialization and diversification of behavior. Notably, problems in measuring desistance from crime are quite similar to problems in cessation of drug abuse. Much depends on the time frame covered and how the end state is defined, and some investigators prefer to focus on change in the rate of offending rather than on desistance per se, which is parallel to the focus on reductions in substance use rather than on cessation or abstinence.

Criminology research has emphasized the strong relationship between age and crime in that involvement in most crimes peaks in adolescence and early adulthood and then declines (Sampson and Laub, 1992, 1993, 2003). Considerable research has focused on the early onset of delinquency and on the stability of criminal and deviant behavior during the life course. Although studies have shown that childhood antisocial behaviors strongly predict adult criminality, it has also been documented that most antisocial children do not become antisocial as adults (Gove, 1985; Robins, 1978). To explain both continuity in childhood deviant behavior and changes during the life course, Sampson and Laub (1992) emphasize the social influences of age-graded transitions and salient life events. By examining the criminological literature on childhood antisocial behavior, adolescent delinquency, and adult crime from the perspective of theory and research on the life course, the age-graded theory of informal social control offers explanations of crime and deviance during the life span (Sampson and Laub, 1992; Laub and Sampson, 1993).

The major thesis of Sampson and Laub's theory relevant to the life course framework applied to drug use is that "social capital" and "turning points" are important concepts in understanding processes of change in the adult life course. Social capital refers to one's social investment in institutional relationships (e.g., work, family) and is intangible in that it is "embodied in the relations among persons" (Laub and Sampson, 1993). In other words, "Social capital is a central factor in facilitating effective ties that bind a person to societal institutions" (Laub and Sampson, 1993, p. 310). The authors link social capital to social control, hypothesizing that individuals with accumulated social capital will be inhibited from criminal behavior (regardless of childhood experience) because of their strong social ties and the obligations and responsibilities associated with those ties, whereas individuals with weak social capital will be freer to be deviant.

Turning points have been conceptualized as an alteration or deflection in a long-term pathway or trajectory that was initiated at an earlier point in time (Laub and Sampson, 1993; Rutter, 1996; Sampson and Laub, 2003). Turning points can modify life trajectories or redirect the paths, despite the connection between childhood and adult experiences. For some individuals, turning points are abrupt (radical turnarounds or changes in life history that separate the past from the future); for most individuals, however, turning points can be "part of a process over time and not as a dramatic lasting change that takes place at any one time" (Pickles and Rutter, 1991, p. 134). Key events often studied or considered as turning points include employment, military service, and marriage (Sampson and Laub, 1992). Turning points can be positive, such as cohesive marriage, meaningful work, and military service, or they can be negative, such as prolonged incarceration, heavy drinking or drug use, and job instability.

More recently, Sampson and Laub (2005; Laub and Sampson, 2003) revisited the concept of turning points from a time-varying view of key life events. They stressed the importance of human agency (or personal choice) in the development of criminal behavior and envisioned development as the constant interaction between individuals and their environments, suggesting the notion of "situated choice," in which the individual agency and structural location within society are interrelated. In other words, what happens in the course of one's life is not all personal choice, nor is it all institution options. Instead, the life course is a dynamic and time-varying combination of the two. Thus, simultaneously studying agency and structural location over time permits discovery of the emergent ways that turning points across the adult life course align with purposive action and stable individual differences within the institutional context. Although considerable development has been made in the criminal career conceptual framework on types of change and the social mechanisms underlying change processes, comparable progress has not taken place in the drug abuse research.

Chronic Illness Management

Research on illness careers has focused on the course of illness and exposure to health care services. Illness concepts (with parallel drug abuse concepts shown in parentheses) include onset of symptom or need (onset of use), onset of disease or disorder (onset of dependent use), recurrence (relapse), chronicity (duration of dependent use), and recovery or remission (cessation). Service system concepts include compliance or adherence with diagnostic and therapeutic interventions, service mix, delay in seeking care (timing), and spacing of health care episodes or long-term disease management. Studies of the illness career have identified stages of illness beginning with recognition of the health problem and health care utilization, continuing through compliance with caregiver advice, outcome (e.g., recovery from or chronicity of illness), and secondary compliance (continuing in a long-term treatment regime; Baltes, Staudinger, and Lindenberger, 1999; Elder, 1978; Pescosolido, 1991; Pescosolido and Boyer, 1999).

Similarities of drug dependence to chronic medical illnesses were explicated by McLellan and colleagues (2000), who compared the diagnoses, heritability, etiology, pathophysiology, and response to treatment of drug dependence with three well-studied and accepted chronic diseases (i.e., type 2 diabetes mellitus, hypertension, and asthma). They also summarized the possible physiological bases for use, abuse, dependence, and relapse. Importantly, they noted that rates of adherence to prescribed interventions for these illnesses are no better than rates of compliance of addicts with treatment plans. These authors asserted that drug dependence is similar to other chronic illnesses in terms of onset and course. Evidence of enduring pathophysiologic changes because of opiate, cocaine, and alcohol dependence helps to explain the tendency to relapse. For example, drug-dependent individuals who have been abstinent for long periods may relapse when they encounter a person, place, or thing that was previously associated with their drug use, producing conditioned physiologic reactions (e.g., withdrawal-like symptoms, craving). It is unclear whether and how such triggered reactions ever subside.

We believe that insights and analytic tools regarding timing and spacing in the illness career will be particularly valuable as drug abuse research turns to the effects of continuing care and cumulative treatment exposure (e.g., the "recovery management" approach) in relation to the timing of an individual's first treatment, how long it takes for him or her to reenter treatment after a relapse, and the mix of services (including formal treatment, monitoring, and self-help activities) to which he or she is exposed over time. Also important for hypothesis generation are findings on the social processes affecting recognition of illness and treatment utilization, such as processes related to access, service quality, and health disparities.

As discussed by Strauss and colleagues (1985), an illness trajectory perspective further expands the intervention focus to include illness management. The term *illness trajectory* refers "not only to the physiological unfolding of a patient's disease but to the total organization of work done over that course, plus the impact of those involved with that work and its organization" (Strauss et al., 1985, p. 8). The concept of trajectory is relevant for understanding chronic illness management, as patients, family, and treatment staff seek to control and cope with illnesses (Strauss et al., 1985, p. 9). The chronic illness trajectory framework (Strauss and Corbin, 1988; Corbin and Strauss, 1991) further emphasizes the need for coordination and linkage with services and to accommodate needs at different stages of chronic illness. Recognizing that a long-standing emphasis on acute care typically drives the health system, the authors argued that the health care system and policy have to change to decrease barriers to services by focusing on trajectory phases rather than specific diseases. The trajectory model of chronic illness has also been specifically applied to mental illness (Rawnsley, 1991), stroke (Burton, 2000), and HIV/AIDS (Corless and Nicholas, 2000). Recently, Wagner and colleagues (Wagner, Austin, and Von Korff, 1996; Wagner et al., 2001; Von Korff et al., 1997) further developed a model of collaborative care, in which patients, in close partnership with health care professionals, are supported with self-care skills for managing their chronic illness.

The Life Course Framework Applied to the Study of Drug Use

The life course framework for the study of drug use focuses on long-term patterns of stability and change, both gradual and abrupt, in relation to transitions across the life span and into and out of roles such as patient, offender, spouse, parent, and/or worker. In addition, a life course perspective incorporates the intersections of individual lives, social change, and social structure. This approach, particularly its emphases on historical contexts and life dynamics, offers an alternative to more historically neutral and static conceptualizations that have dominated many domains of psychosocial research. Considerable parallels in conceptual constructs and analytic techniques exist in studies of the drug use career and the criminal career (as described earlier). In fact, many criminologists consider drug addiction a subset of illegal behaviors. Criminal career researchers are engaged in mapping trajectories of offending, comparing these trajectories across different background characteristics of offenders and measuring

the interplay between criminal justice intervention and change in offending trajectories (Laub and Sampson, 2001; Le Blanc and Loeber, 1998; Nagin and Tremblay, 2001; Nagin et al., 1998; Nagin et al., 2003; Piquero, Farrington, and Blumstein, 2003). Except for recent attention to offender re-entry or similar lines of work, the criminology literature is relatively silent (Farrington, 2003) or pessimistic (Farabee, 2005) about intervention effects, hence the added utility of the illness career approach, which offers richer concepts and approaches for the role of intervention in the life course of chronic conditions such as drug dependence. In our life course drug use framework, we are most interested in developmental transitions, turning points, and trajectories related to drug addiction *in combination with* exposure to treatment and other service systems.

Key concepts in drug use careers include onset, acceleration, regular use, cessation, and relapse and how they vary by drug type and user characteristics. Factors associated with these patterns include individual characteristics, risk and protective factors, and access and response to service system exposure. The issues of service interplay center on utilization and outcomes of services over the long term and reflect the field's increasing realization that various service mixes and "continuing care" strategies have yet to be systematically defined and examined in relation to particular patterns of drug use and relapse over time. The life course drug use framework expands drug use careers to include such key concepts as transitions (to incorporate developmental and social context), turning points (to characterize changes), social capital (to characterize the potential role of social ties), and illness careers (to integrate chronic care management and service interactions). As mentioned earlier, by focusing on the patterns or trajectories across individuals' lives and the ways in which those patterns are shaped by social structures and time, the life course perspective offers a broadened organizing framework that potentially allows for characterizing distinctive patterns of drug use trajectories, identifying critical events and factors contributing to the persistence or change in drug use during the life span and analytically ordering the events that occur during that course.

Next, we apply concepts from the life course perspective to illustrate what is currently known from the drug abuse literature to synthesize existing knowledge within the expanded framework and thus identify gaps and future directions.

Drug Use Trajectories

Research on drug use careers has produced important theoretical and practical insights not apparent when drug abuse is studied only in the short term (Anglin, Hser, and Grella, 1997; Anglin et al., 2001; Gottheil et al., 1998; Hser et al., 1997; Hser, Hoffman et al., 2001; Sobell et al., 1993; Tschacher, Haemmig, & Jacobshagen, 2003; Vaillant, 1988, 1992; Warren, Hawkins, & Sprott, 2003). We provide two examples based on our lengthy follow-up studies.

The first example illustrates long-term patterns of cocaine, methamphetamine, marijuana, and heroin use of 566 drug users randomly selected from a sample of approximately 1,800 drug users recruited in three high-risk settings (600 each from

jails, hospital emergency rooms, and sexually transmitted diseases clinics) in Los Angeles County (Hser, Boyle, & Anglin, 1998). Figure 1 shows patterns of at least weekly use of cocaine, methamphetamine, marijuana, and heroin by these individuals during their lifetimes (Hser, 2002). There were distinct age-related trends for each drug. Marijuana and methamphetamine use showed linear declines as the cohort aged, although declines covered different age periods and occurred at different rates over time. Cocaine use increased from age 20 until the mid-30s and declined after the late 30s. Heroin use, on the other hand, increased with age. Thus, these findings clearly suggest that long-term trajectories of abuse among those who escalate to weekly use or more may differ by drug. Although there could be a "history" effect—where cocaine use became more widely available and thus was used more and in greater amounts, leading to dependence in a period that corresponded to this upsurge among the study cohorts—importantly, drug use peaks at very different ages for such users, compared to users in the general population. Both of these distinctions suggest that early detection and intervention of drug use in the appropriate age groups

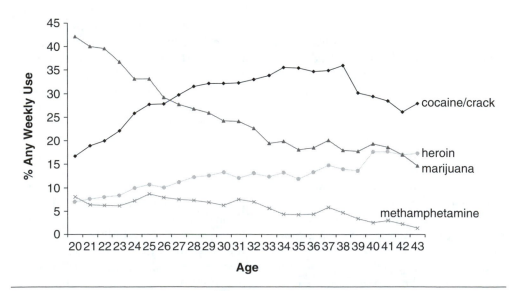

Figure 1   Self-Reported Weekly Use of Illicit Drugs Over Time

should be important policy and practice priorities.

Our second example is based on a 33-year follow-up study of male heroin users in which we found that almost half of those alive at age 50 or older were still using heroin (Hser, Hoffman et al., 2001). Because age of onset was typically about 18 years, the heroin use careers of these men (including periods of temporary abstinence) had spanned 30 to 40 years. Applying a growth mixture modeling strategy (Muthen, 2004; Muthen and Asparouhov, 2008; Nagin, 1999, 2005) to heroin use level (i.e., mean number of days per month using heroin) during the first half of the addiction careers (16 years) since first heroin use, Hser and colleagues (2007) identified three groups with distinctive profiles (Figure 2): (a) the stable high-level heroin users ($n = 278$, 59%), who maintained fairly consistent high levels of heroin use since initiation, (b) decelerated users ($n = 149$, 32%), who started at a high level but decreased their use over time, and (c) early quitters ($n = 44$, 9%), who quickly dropped to no use within 10 years of the initial use. Thus, although some addicts quit using relatively early in their careers,

they constituted only a minority; even among these, it was 8 to 10 years before stable recovery occurred. This series of studies demonstrated that long-term cessation of heroin use is a slow and difficult process for many addicts who experience repeated cycles of abstinence and relapse (Hser, Anglin & Powers, 1993; Hser et al., 1995; Hser et al., 1997).

These examples and other related literature illustrate the heterogeneity of life course drug use trajectories, which for many persisted across a long life span (Hser et al., 2005). In the next section, we apply life course concepts to examine major transitions in drug use trajectories, such as drug use onset, relapse, and cessation, and factors contributing to these changes or lack of changes.

Transitions, Turning Points, and Social Capital

Transitions, turning points, and social capital are important concepts in understanding processes of change in the life course of drug dependence. The life course of drug use involves onset, acceleration, relapse, and cessation demarcated by major changes in drug use trajectories.

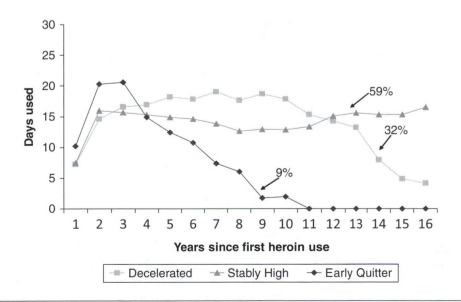

Figure 2   Days Using Heroin: A 33-Year Follow-Up

Research on transitions among the drug use stages has mostly focused on correlates or risks and protective factors; other than for entry into drug treatment, little research has conceptualized or empirically investigated critical events or turning points responsible for major shifts in direction of life trajectories. As Rutter (1996) asserted, although there is convincing evidence of the reality of such changes, their investigation requires careful attention as turning points do not apply to universal age-indexed life transitions. The majority of these critical events concern only small segments of the population, and they derive from major qualitative alterations in experiences. For example, whether marriage produces a positive shift on drug use trajectory depends on the quality, timing, and duration of marriage and is strongly influenced by the drug use patterns of the partner (Anglin, Booth et al., 1987; Anglin, Kao et al., 1987).

As noted above, developmental criminology literature also suggests that trajectories are affected by the degree of social capital available to an individual (Laub and Sampson, 1993). For example, adults will be inhibited from committing crime to the extent that, over time, they accumulate social capital in their work and family lives, regardless of an earlier delinquent background. Thus, the accumulation of social capital can lead to entry into normative systems and assorted resources that serve as pathways to change. It has not yet been empirically demonstrated that social capital works in the same way with drug use trajectories, though there is some indication that it is worth further investigation (Granfield and Cloud, 2001).

Onset of drug use. Most cigarette, alcohol, and drug use begins during adolescence, and an early age of onset or initiation of drug use is one of the best predictors of future drug abuse and dependence. Epidemiological and clinical studies suggest that adolescents who begin drug use at early ages typically use drugs more frequently, escalate to higher levels of use

more quickly, and are more likely to persist in using (Anthony and Petronis, 1995; Yu and Williford, 1992). More specifically, individuals whose drug use starts before high school (age 14 or younger) are more vulnerable to drug problems later in life than are those who start using drugs in high school or college. Initiation of drug use between ages 15 and 18 is common. Drug use usually peaks during late teens and early adulthood, and there is limited initiation of drug use after age 25 (Chen and Kandel, 1995).

Many longitudinal studies have been conducted among general population samples that have assessed participants at relatively early ages and followed them over time to identify risk and protective factors that are related to drug use at later ages. Collectively, these studies have identified an extensive list of risk factors (e.g., family factors such as family history of substance abuse, parental psychological problems, low social attachment; individual factors such as poor self-control, risk taking, sensation seeking; life stress; deviant peer affiliations; environmental factors such as neighborhood disorganization and availability of drugs; genetic factors) and protective factors (e.g., family factors such as supportive relationships, individual factors such as academic involvement and self-esteem) (Hawkins, Catalano & Miller, 1992; West, 2001). Typically, these studies show that initial involvement with drugs may result from peer pressure, drug availability, or other risk factors in an individual's social or family environment. Subsequent escalation to and maintenance of higher levels of drug use are likely to result with contributions from biological, psychological or psychiatric, and environmental characteristics of the individual user. In some cases, vulnerability may be inherited in the form of heightened susceptibility to a certain type of drug. In most cases, however, escalation will be caused by psychological traits or psychiatric conditions, some of which may also be inherited. Although risk and protective factors have been shown to predict drug abuse outcomes at subsequent time points, few studies have tested the flow of such processes over time or determined how variables operate so as to "push" individuals' trajectories toward or away from adverse outcomes (Wills, Walker & Resko, 2005).

Relapse. Even among those who cease use because of their own efforts or as a result of formal treatment interventions, high rates of relapse are typical after any given remission or episode of treatment (Hser et al., 1999; Simpson et al., 1999). Relapse phenomena are difficult to assess across studies, however, because the concept is defined differently by various researchers and clinicians (Gottheil et al., 1998; Tims, Leukefeld & Platt, 2001). Hubbard and Marsden (1986, p. 157) noted that "the understanding of relapse to drug abuse is complicated by current drug abuse patterns that involve multiple use of a wide range of types of licit and illicit drugs, and many patterns of abuse." A basic type of relapse is the return to use of a specific drug that has been used at a previous time point. A second type is the use of a drug to substitute for a previously used primary drug or the development of new patterns of use for the same or for different drugs (Hubbard et al., 2001). Relapse may be defined as a discrete event or as a drawn-out process; considering relapse as part of the treatment and recovery process allows for discussion of an array of pathways to recovery. However defined, high relapse rates have been generally observed across studies.

Many of the risk and protective factors that have been identified with onset appear to be also related to relapse. For example, low socioeconomic status, comorbid psychiatric conditions, and lack of family and social supports are among the most important predictors of relapse following treatment (McLellan et al., 2000; Hser, 2007; Weisner, Ray et al., 2003). Nevertheless, with the following noted exceptions, few studies have sufficiently lengthy follow-up periods to adequately characterize the phenomena involved in the long-term processes of dependence, recovery, and relapse. Based on a 33-year follow-up study, Hser, Hoffman et al. (2001) found that even among those abstinent for as long as 15 years, a quarter had eventually relapsed in subsequent observations. Similarly, Falck, Wang, and Carlson (2006) and Scott, Foss, and Dennis (2003) reported persistent use or high relapse rates among drug users in their long-term follow-up studies. The relapse rates in a 16-year follow-up of individuals with alcohol use disorders were reported by Moos and Moos (2006) to be 38% among those who received help and 57% among those who did not obtain help in the 1st year after recognizing their need for help. In contrast, a long-term follow-up study of veterans who used heroin in Vietnam showed high remission rates and low relapse rates once these veterans returned to the United States (Price, Risk & Spitznagel, 2001). A study of male alcoholics suggested that, unlike with heroin, relapse to alcohol use was rare after abstinence had been maintained for at least 5 years (Vaillant, 1996).

Cessation. Relative to onset and relapse, stable cessation is the least studied phenomenon in drug abuse research. Despite the theoretical and policy importance of understanding why people stop using and are able to maintain abstinence, we do not have robust conceptual models or rich empirical investigations of cessation. Part of the reason is that there is no way to determine if the chosen follow-up period is of sufficient duration to know whether someone has permanently stopped drug use. We can, however, probabilistically identify people who are more or less likely to relapse than others, based on their past and current drug use patterns. It seems obvious that the longer the period of nonuse, the less likely it is that an individual will relapse. Many studies have found that social and personal resources that persons possess can be instrumental in overcoming substance dependence.

Hser, Hoffman et al. (2001) examined life course cessation among heroin addicts and showed that eventual cessation of heroin use is a slow process and may not occur for some older addicts. Opiate use patterns of the cohort were remarkably stable; by 50 to 60 years of age, only about half of the sample interviewed tested negative for heroin. To further identify factors associated with long-term stable recovery, Hser (2007) compared and contrasted the recovery group (defined as being abstinent for at least 5 years prior to the interview at the 33-year follow-up) and the nonrecovery group. The two groups did not differ in deviant behaviors and family or school problems in their earlier lives. Both groups tried formal treatment and self-directed recovery ("self-treatment"), often many times. Although the nonrecovered addicts were significantly more likely to use substances in coping with stressful conditions, to have spouses who also abused drugs, and to lack non-drug-using social support, stable recovery 10 years later was predicted only by ethnicity, self-efficacy, and psychological distress. These findings suggest that in addition to early intervention efforts to curtail heroin addiction, increasing self-efficacy and addressing psychological problems are likely to enhance the odds of maintaining long-term stable recovery. The study findings are consistent with the social capital explanation of drug use and recovery and with similar investigation on desistence of criminal offending. In examining trajectories of offending during the life course of delinquent boys followed from ages 7 to 70, Sampson and Laub (2003) found that although crime declined with age for all offender groups, childhood prognoses poorly accounted for long-term trajectories of offending. Marriage, military service, residential relocation, and employment were identified as turning points that changed their offending trajectories to desistence from crime (Laub and Sampson, 2003). Whether turning points and mechanisms underlying drug use

cessation are similar to crime desistance remains to be examined.

Using a qualitative approach to study natural recovery, Cloud and Granfield (2004) interviewed 46 individuals who overcame their addiction to alcohol and drugs without treatment. The recovery process appeared to be typically triggered by the assorted personal problems (e.g., alienation and feelings of social disconnection, problems in relationships, negative health consequences). In most cases, respondents experienced a turning point that sharply and dramatically disrupted their lives and made them realize the need for personal changes. A variety of distinct turning points, ranging from death of loved ones who abused drugs to responsibilities for children, often provided powerful motivation to terminate addiction. Strategies for sustaining the cessation of addiction generally included engaging in alternative activities (e.g., religious conversion, returning to school, community service), relying on relationships with family and friends, and avoiding drugs, drug users, and the social cues associated with use. The authors argued that much of the impetus and motivation for the study respondents to change was not solely a result of their own psychological will but was associated with conditioning factors in the social environment that supported their desired change. However, sample characteristics may limit the generalizability of these findings. The study participants were well educated and employed and were from relatively stable middle-class backgrounds, and social interactions with others and social capital derived from these relationships were resources or forms of "recovery capital" that increased their capacity to achieve and sustain abstinence.

Although insightful, research on turning points in the life course of drug use has been typically limited to qualitative and/or retrospective recall. A particular event does not universally lead to a turning point or a change in the same direction, and mere possession of higher levels of recovery capital will not necessarily result in cessation of substance dependence. Further research in this direction is needed to fully understand timing, sequence, and context for changes and altered directions in drug use trajectories.

Service Interactions

In real-world settings, overlapping drug, mental health, physical health, and legal problems have increasingly become the norm, but they are typically addressed, if at all, in a fragmented and uncoordinated manner by service agencies. The fact that individuals with drug problems are encountered in medical, criminal justice, welfare, and other service systems is an important reminder that they often have problems and need services in each of these domains.

The life course perspective expands our current understanding of the "interactive, dynamic trajectories" of drug-dependent individuals who participate in diverse social service systems, including addiction treatment, mental health services, HIV prevention, the criminal justice system (CJS), the child welfare system, and primary health care services. Interaction with these social systems can trigger turning points for some individuals, which suggests the potential for social services to identify problematic drug users and introduce and create desirable changes. Considerations of type, timing, duration, and sequencing of service system interactions will be important for structuring these interactions. For example, Weisner, Ray et al. (2003) and Scott, Foss, and Dennis (2003) found that long-term effects of treatment were mediated by the patient's short-term response to treatment plus participation in aftercare and self-help. Similarly, Moosand Moos (2004) found that duration of involvement with services (including treatment, self-help, and periodic check-ins or monitoring) predicted recovery from drinking problems in a long-term time frame. Intensity of services may mediate short-term effects

of a specific service episode; conversely, long-term effects may be mediated by sustained engagement at any level. This is a crucial insight for the health services field in which the policy or practice focus has begun to shift from intensive to "extensive" or longer-term perspective on the course of treatment and recovery or on disease management precepts (Humphreys and Tucker, 2002; McLellan, 2002; McLellan et al., 2005; Moos, 2003; Moos and Moos, 2004; Weisner and Schmidt, 1993, 1995; Weisner et al., 2001; Weisner, 2002). In addition, collaboration between health and social care providers continues to be a well-established policy focus (Allen, Griffith & Lyne, 2004).

Interplay with the drug treatment system. An individual history of drug dependence is most often well established and lengthy before entry into treatment. For various types of drugs, the average time between drug use initiation and initial entry into drug treatment is about 5 to 10 years (Anglin et al., 2001; Hser et al., 1997). Pathways to and reasons for entering treatment may also vary, depending on the individual's stage of use and the consequences of use (Weisner and Matzger, 2002) and interactions with service providers (Weisner, 2001; Weisner and Matzger, 2003). Other issues emerging in a life course perspective are cumulative effects of treatment and the timing of multiple episodes. Long-term abstinence may be significantly more likely for drug users able to quit drug use after one or two treatment episodes than for those with three or more (Dennis et al., 2005), and long-term prospects for recovery may be greater for people who re-enter treatment more promptly after relapsing (Moos and Moos, 2007; Scott, Foss & Dennis, 2003).

Many studies have shown reductions in drug use during and after treatment compared to no treatment or compared to pre-treatment status. Longer treatment retention and successful completion of any given treatment episode are associated with better posttreatment outcomes, but little empirical evidence exists regarding whether there are cumulative treatment effects or effects associated with timing (e.g., early intervention) and structures or forms of service exposure (e.g., extensiveness, integration of services). Empirical evidence is needed to guide the development of effective long-term care strategies.

Interplay with the CJS. The CJS is inundated with drug-crime offenders and violent- and property-crime offenders who have drug problems. Accordingly, the life course of drug use in offender populations is complicated by repeated cycles of arrest, incarceration, community supervision, drug courts, and other CJS behavioral control mechanisms. In the 1990s, treatment was provided to criminal offenders in intensive supervision programs (Petersilia and Turner, 1993), Treatment Alternatives to Street Crime programs (Anglin, Longshore & Turner, 1999; Collins et al., 1982), parolee case management programs such as the Bay Area Services Network in California (Longshore, Turner & Fain, 2005), and system-level innovations such as Breaking the Cycle (Harrell et al., 2003), all geared to addressing drug problems among offenders on probation or parole in the community. The 1990s also saw a rapid increase in the establishment of in-custody (prison and jail) treatment programs. Most recently, through voter initiatives such as Proposition 200 in Arizona and Proposition 36 in California, the emphasis on community supervision and treatment instead of incarceration has been codified in law, applicable not just to offenders residing in particular jurisdictions or sent to particular institutions but also to all persons convicted of eligible drug-related offenses in the state (Longshore et al., 2003).

Studies indicate that retention in treatment is similar for CJS-referred clients and other clients (e.g., Hubbard et al., 1989) and that treatment is effective with CJS clients (e.g., Wexler et al., 1999).

However, those studies have focused on cessation or relapse after single episodes of treatment, not on drug abuse patterns across multiple episodes or from a long-term perspective. Moreover, drug use and crime have mutually reciprocal "multiplier" effects (Murray, 1992; Speckart & Anglin, 1986a, 1986b). Criminal activity may be associated with shorter time to relapse, steeper acceleration to regular use, and/or longer periods of use. Finally, the nature, suitability, and duration of treatment episodes may systematically differ between CJS clients and non-CJS clients.

Interplay with the mental health system. Population surveys and clinical studies have demonstrated that a majority of individuals entering drug treatment have comorbid mental disorders, most commonly mood or anxiety disorders (Kleinman et al., 1990; Rounsaville et al., 1991). Substance users with comorbid disorders have higher rates of treatment utilization than do those without (Kessler et al., 1994; Kessler et al., 1996) and typically seek treatment from a variety of settings, including drug abuse treatment, mental health care, human services, and primary health care (Kessler et al., 1994; Kessler et al., 1996; Regier et al., 1993). Such individuals also have frequent interactions with the CJS (Teplin, Abram & McClelland, 1996; Jordan et al., 1996; Jordan et al., 2002). Furthermore, long-term service costs are higher for individuals with comorbid disorders than for those with only one type of disorder (Dickey and Azeni, 1996; Hoff and Rosenheck, 1998). In general, individuals with comorbid disorders have poor rates of treatment completion and higher rates of posttreatment relapse and rehospitalization (Brown et al., 1998; McLellan et al., 1996; McLellan et al., 1983; Weisner, Matzger & Kaskutas, 2003), although differences in service needs, patterns of treatment utilization, and treatment outcomes have been observed by type of disorder (Compton, Cottler et al., 2003; Grella, 2003).

Results of longitudinal studies of drug abusers with mental illness have been reported only recently (Bartels, Drake & Wallach, 1995; Drake et al., 1996). Grella (2003) found that initiation of mental health treatment preceded initiation of drug treatment by about 10 years among a dually diagnosed cohort sampled from drug treatment, even though these patients had begun regular drug use an average of 6 years prior to entering mental health treatment. Longer stays in residential treatment and participation in outpatient mental health treatment have been associated with lower rates of hospital readmission over 2 years (Moos, King & Patterson, 1996). In addition, greater participation in aftercare services, including mental health treatment and 12-step programs, is associated with better posttreatment outcomes among individuals with co-occurring disorders (Moos et al., 2000; Ouimette, Moos & Finney, 2000; Ritsher et al., 2002). Furthermore, in a 10-year prospective follow-up study of clients with co-occurring severe mental and substance use disorders (Xie, Drake & McHugo, 2006), it was found that approximately one third of clients who were in full remission relapsed in the first year, and two thirds relapsed during the follow-up period. The authors concluded that after attaining full remission, clients with severe mental disorders continue to be at risk of substance abuse relapse for many years.

Research Gaps, Issues, and Future Directions

Our review of the literature indicates that drug users have frequent interactions with a wide range of health and social service providers, in addition to specialty addiction treatment, and their drug use trajectories are embedded within their interactions across these various service systems. New research concepts and tools are needed to map the common and distinctive courses and consequences of long-term use for specific drug types and special populations. Also needed are investigations of the interplay between the life course of drug use and drug treatment and involvement with other service systems, notably the primary health services, criminal justice, and mental health systems. Applying the life course perspective to drug use can improve knowledge of the timing, order, and intensity of service mix in association with outcome. The improved knowledge may facilitate the development of a collaborative model of care (Wagner, Austin & Von Korff, 1996; Wagner et al., 2001; Lester and Gask, 2006) for the management of chronic illness such as drug dependence.

The life course framework expands the drug use *career* concept by explicitly recognizing the chronic aspects of addiction and its management that need to be attended to during the individual life course. The broadened framework also benefits from theoretical developments in other fields that concern phenomena of a chronic nature. Although the life course framework offers a rich ground for future drug research, a life course approach also presents many conceptual and methodological challenges. In this article, we have examined the existing drug dependence literature within the context of the life course perspective and identified gaps requiring future research. Below, we reiterate and highlight three major issues that suggest future research directions.

Developing Chronic Care Strategies

The life course drug use perspective is consistent with the current discussion on reconceptualizing and restructuring the treatment delivery system so as to shape the system around concepts including "continuity of care," "disease management," and "chronic care model" for addiction (McLellan, 2004, 2006; Blue Ribbon Task Force on Health Services Research, 2004). Furthermore, the collaborative model of care (Wagner, Austin &

Von Korff, 1996; Wagner et al., 2001), actively involving patients in their self-care, represents another important model for chronic care. Although these treatment models share a similar emphasis on sustained support for recovery, they need to be operationalized and strategically developed. Our past studies have shown increased success rates associated with successive treatments that provide an orderly progression of service mix (e.g., inpatient, followed by residential, outpatient treatment, and self-help group participation; Khalsa et al., 1993; Hser et al., 2006). Positive findings have also been shown in studies of continuing care intended to maintain progress achieved in the formal phase of treatment and to provide continued support for participation in self-help programs and other pro-recovery activities (McKay, 2001). Similarly, there is some evidence that self-help participation (Etheridge et al., 1997; McKay et al., 2001) or continued monitoring (Dennis, Scott & Funk, 2003) after treatment may sustain the positive effects of the referent treatment.

The life course perspective has implications for future research in defining treatment processes not only as what happens within an episode of care but also, and significantly, as spanning multiple episodes of care to include readmission and continuing care for the substance use disorders. The approach also highlights the need to delineate gaps in our understanding of treatment processes and outcomes emerging as the field embraces the perception of substance use disorders as a chronic or recurring condition. This perspective necessitates that the time frame for evaluating treatment outcomes shifts from that of the single treatment episode to that of the course of the substance use disorder. The many constructs commonly used in treatment outcome research, including "completion," "episode," and "outcome," need to be revisited to be compatible with the chronic disease model of addiction. Rather than focusing on these discrete outcomes, the field needs to move toward performance-based outcomes (McLellan et al., 2005) that describe health-related functioning at different points in time and in relationship to service utilization. Longitudinal intervention studies are needed to more effectively adapt treatment strategies suited to the specific life course stages of drug use and to facilitate long-lasting cessation (McLellan, 2006; McKay, 2005; Rush et al., 1998).

Reciprocal Nature of Drug Use and Service Interaction

Integrative research is needed to address knowledge gaps that currently exist in the research on chronic drug dependence and clinical and service research because drug use and service exposure are mutually and reciprocally influenced. As we have noted, drug users often come in contact with service systems other than drug treatment, and each system (e.g., criminal justice, mental health, welfare, health care) must be able to address not only the problem that brings clients to that system but also their drug use problems. In addition to adopting a longitudinal perspective in assessing drug use trajectories and interactions with a variety of service systems, it is also necessary to develop cross-system capabilities to better serve the individual client and, in doing so, to better serve society (Weisner, 2002).

We have observed how the relationship between drug use and treatment over time is often reciprocal, with drug use being one major determinant for treatment contacts and also the outcome of some of these contacts. Thus, drug use can be both a predictor and an outcome of treatment and other services over time. This is conceptually consistent with the health services literature in which there has been an increased recognition that health status can be both a predictor of health service utilization and a utilization outcome (Gelberg, Andesen & Leake, 2000). Improved understanding of this reciprocal relationship is needed as it may, in fact, be key to improving the design of the drug treatment system (e.g., continuity of care) and increasing treatment utilization, retention, and outcomes.

Methodological Challenges

Similar to challenges in criminology research (Sampson and Laub, 2003), the life course perspective applied to drug research is challenged by several limitations: (a) addiction is typically studied among treatment samples and over constrained portions of the life course (e.g., 6 months after treatment); (b) accurate frequency counts of drug use over time are difficult to obtain; (c) trajectories of drug use are usually identified retrospectively, based on the outcome, rather than prospectively, based on the causal factors presumed to differentiate groups of addicts; and (d) incapacitation and death are typically not accounted for in estimating cessation. These limitations are often because of the logistical and financial difficulties of conducting long-term studies that follow the same individuals over time.

In addition, longitudinal studies of drug use have often failed to measure the timing and sequencing of salient events during the life course. To establish influences on individual development, one must account not only for background factors but also for the changing nature of important life events (e.g., work, marriage, parenthood). Such events, though temporally definable, cannot be treated as static. Quantitative measurement of the timing, duration, and ordering of life transitions has the advantage of permitting substantive applications of statistical models of changes (Hser, Shen et al., 2001).

Recent advancements in statistical methods such as growth curve models and growth mixture models provide promising tools for analyzing longitudinal data. In particular, onset, course, and cessation can be simultaneously assessed using the growth models. The systematic change in an attribute over time can be assessed by the growth curve model, whereas the growth mixture models help to identify subgroups with distinctive trajectories. As noted earlier, however, causal influences are reciprocal during the life course. In explaining dynamic processes in longitudinal research, causality is "best represented by a developmental network of causal factors" (Loeber and Le Blanc, 1990, p. 433) in which dependent variables may also become independent variables over time. Yet, in nonrandomized experiments, controlling for relevant confounders is essential in seeking valid causal inferences. As an example, time-varying treatments pose special challenges because a treatment will often be tailored to the past behavior of the participants. The problem of causal inference for time-varying treatments, assuming no randomization, is extraordinarily challenging. It is a cutting-edge issue on which progress is being made, but it continues to be a challenge as methodologists in this area have not achieved a consensus on the best way to proceed (Raudenbush, 2001). In addition, longitudinal data naturally encounter mortality and survivor bias (e.g., the problems with drawing inferences from longitudinal studies of cohorts of survivors when the most severe are deceased). Both issues may limit or at least complicate the generalizability of these studies and are additional methodological issues needing to be addressed.

Concluding Comments

The merging of disparate life course concepts as applied to the investigation of drug use, criminality, and chronic illness allows a more comprehensive approach for structuring the study of drug use patterns and their interplay with drug treatment and other service systems. By studying both within-individual change and interindividual differences in trajectories during the life course in relation to social transitions and interaction with service systems, we can better identify and facilitate turning points that influence the life course of drug dependence. The life course perspective can help to explain drug use and its interplay with social systems during the life span and to explicate the conceptual issues related to continuity and change in drug use behavior. Rigorous research on the natural course of drug abuse and recovery in diverse populations and service systems in real-world settings can yield findings that substantially improve our understanding of long-term recovery and health services that support recovery. Such research is needed so that long-term intervention strategies involving multisystem efforts for different populations can be devised and informed policy decisions can be made.

REFERENCES

Allen, D., L. Griffiths, and P. Lyne. 2004. Understanding complex trajectories in health and social care provision. *Sociology of Health and Illness* 26 (7): 1008–30.

Anglin, M. D., M. W. Booth, C. F. Kao, L. L. Harlow, and K. Peters. 1987. Similarity of behavior within addict couples. Part II. Addiction-related variables. *International Journal of the Addictions* 22 (7): 583–607.

Anglin, M. D., C. F. Kao, L. L. Harlow, K. Peters, and M. W. Booth. 1987. Similarity of behavior within addict couples. Part I. Methodology and narcotics patterns. *International Journal of the Addictions* 22 (6): 497–524.

Anglin, M. D., Y. Hser, and C. E. Grella. 1997. Drug addiction and treatment careers among clients in the drug abuse treatment outcome study (DATOS). *Psychology of Addictive Behaviors. Special Issue: Drug Abuse Treatment Outcome Study (DATOS)* 11 (4): 308–23.

Anglin, M. D., Y. Hser, C. E. Grella, D. Longshore, and P. Prendergast. 2001. Drug treatment careers: Conceptual overview and clinical, research, and policy application. In *Relapse and recovery processes in the addiction,* ed. J. Platt, C. Leukefeld, and F. M. Tims, 18–39. New Haven, CT: Yale University Press.

Anglin, M. D., D. Longshore, and S. Turner. 1999. Treatment alternatives to street crime: An evaluation of five programs. *Criminal Justice and Behavior* 26 (2): 168–95.

Anthony, J. C., and K. R. Petronis. 1995. Early-onset drug use and risk of later drug problems. *Drug and Alcohol Dependence* 40 (1): 9–15.

Baltes, P. V., U. M. Staudinger, and U. Lindenberger. 1999. Lifespan psychology: Theory and application to intellectual functioning. *Annual Review of Psychology* 50:471–507.

Bartels, S. J., R. E. Drake, and M. A. Wallach. 1995. Long-term course of substance use disorders among patients with severe mental illness. *Psychiatric Services* 46 (3): 248–51.

Birchwood, M. 1998. Early intervention in psychosis: The critical period. In *The recognition and management of early psychosis,* ed. P. McGorry and H. S. Jackson, 226–64. Cambridge, UK: Cambridge University Press

Blue Ribbon Task Force on Health Services Research. 2004. *Report of the Blue Ribbon Task Force on Health Services Research at the National Institute on Drug Abuse.* Bethesda, MD: U.S. Department of Health and Human Services.

Brown, R. A., P. M. Monti, M. G. Myers, R. A. Martin, T. Rivinus, M. E. Dubreuil, and D. J. Rohsenow. 1998. Depression among cocaine abusers in treatment: Relation to cocaine and alcohol use and treatment outcome. *American Journal of Psychiatry* 155 (2): 220–25.

Burton, C. 2000. Living with stroke: A phenomenological study. *Journal of Advanced Nursing* 32:301–9.

Caspi, A., G. H. Elder, and E. Herbener. 1990. Childhood personality and the prediction of life-course patterns. In *Straight and devious pathways from childhood to adulthood,* ed. L. Robins and M. Rutter, 13–35. New York: Cambridge University Press.

Chen, K., and D. B. Kandel. 1995. The natural history of drug use from adolescence to the mid-thirties in a general population sample. *American Journal of Public Health* 85 (1): 41–47.

Chen, K., D. B. Kandel, and M. Davies. 1997. Relationships between frequency and quantity of marijuana use and last year proxy dependence among adolescents and adults in the United States. *Drug and Alcohol Dependence* 46 (1/2): 53–67.

Cloud, W., and R. Granfield. 2004. The social process of exiting addiction: A life course perspective. In *Addiction and life course*, ed. J. Blomqvist, A. Koski-Jannes, and L. Ojesjo, 185–202. Helsinki, Finland: Nordic Council on Alcohol and Drug Research.

Collins, J. J., R. L. Hubbard, J. V. Rachal, E. R. Cavanaugh, and S. G. Craddock. 1982. *Criminal justice clients in drug treatment.* Research Triangle Park, NC: Research Triangle Institute.

Compton, W. M., L. B. Cottler, J. L. Jacobs, A. Ben-Abdallah, and E. D. Spitznagel. 2003. The role of psychiatric disorders in predicting drug dependence treatment outcomes. *American Journal of Psychiatry 160* (5): 890–95.

Corbin, J. M., and A. Strauss. 1991. A nursing model for chronic illness management based upon the trajectory framework. *Scholarly Inquiry for Nursing Practice* 5 (3): 155–74.

Corless, I. B., and P. K. Nicholas. 2000. Long-term continuum of care for people living with HIV/AIDS. *Journal of Urban Health* 77 (2): 176–86.

Dennis, M. L., C. K. Scott, and R. Funk. 2003. An experimental evaluation of recovery management checkups (RMC) for people with chronic substance use disorders. *Evaluation and Program Planning* 26: 339–52.

Dennis, M. L., C. K. Scott, R. Funk, and M. A. Foss. 2005. The duration and correlates of addiction and treatment. *Journal of Substance Abuse Treatment* 28: S51–S62.

Dickey, B., and H. Azeni. 1996. Persons with dual diagnoses of substance abuse and major mental illness: Their excess costs of psychiatric care. *American Journal of Public Health* 86 (7): 973–77.

Drake, R. E., K. T. Mueser, R. E. Clark, and M. A. Wallach. 1996. The course,

treatment, and outcome of substance disorder in persons with severe mental illness. *American Journal of Orthopsychiatry* 66 (1): 42–51.

Elder, G. H., Jr. 1978. Family and life course. In *Transitions: The life courses in historical perspective*, ed. T. K. Harevan, 14–61. New York: Academic Press.

———. 1985. Perspectives in the life course. In *Life course dynamics*, ed. G. H. Elder, Jr., 23–49. Ithaca, NY: Cornell University Press.

Etheridge, R. M., R. L. Hubbard, J. Anderson, S. G. Craddock, and P. M. Flynn. 1997. Treatment structure and program services in the Drug Abuse Treatment Outcome Study (DATOS). *Psychology of Addictive Behaviors* 11 (4): 244–60.

Falck, R., J. Wang, and R. Carlson. 2006. *The natural history of crack-cocaine use: A midwestern perspective.* Paper presented at the Addiction Health Service Research conference, Little Rock, AR, October.

Farabee, D. 2005. *Rethinking rehabilitation: Why can't we reform our criminals?* Washington, DC: AEI.

Farrington, D. P. 2003. Developmental and life-course criminology: Key theoretical and empirical issues—The 2002 Sutherland award address. *Criminology* 2: 221–56.

Gelberg, L., R. M. Andesen, and B. D. Leake. 2000. The behavioral model for vulnerable populations: Application of medical care use and outcomes for homeless people. *Health Services Research* 34: 1273–1302.

George, L. K. 1993. Sociological perspectives on life transitions. *Annual Review of Sociology* 19: 353–73.

Gottheil, E., S. Weinstein, R. Sterling, A. Lundy, and R. Serota. 1998. A randomized controlled study of the effectiveness of intensive outpatient treatment for cocaine dependence. *Psychiatric Services* 49: 782–87.

Gove, W. R. 1985. The effect of age and gender on deviant behavior: A biopsychosocial perspective. In *Gender and the life course*, ed. A. Rossi, 210–34. New York: Aldine.

Granfield, R., and W. Cloud. 2001. Social capital and natural recovery: The role of social resources and relationships in overcoming addiction without treatment. *Substance Use and Misuse* 36 (11): 1543–79.

Grella, C. E. 2003. Contrasting the views of substance misuse and mental health treatment providers on treating the dually diagnosed. *Substance Use and Misuse* 38 (10): 1433–46.

Hagestad, G. O. 1990. Social perspectives on the life course. In *Handbook of aging and the social sciences*, ed. B. H. Binstock and L. K. George, 151–68. San Diego, CA: Academic Press.

Halfon, N., and M. Hochstein. 2002. Life course health development: An integrated framework for developing health, policy, and research. *Milbank Quarterly* 80:433–79.

Harrell, A., O. Mitchell, J. Merrill, and D. Marlowe. 2003. *Evaluation of breaking the cycle*. Washington, DC: Urban Institute.

Hawkins, J., R. Catalano, and J. Miller 1992. Risk and protective factors for alcohol and other drug problems in adolescence and early adulthood: Implications for substance abuse prevention. *Psychological Bulletin* 112: 64–105.

Hoff, R. A., and R. A. Rosenheck. 1998. Long-term patterns of service use and cost among patients with both psychiatric and substance abuse disorders. *Medical Care* 36 (6): 835–43.

Hser, Y. 2002. Drug use careers: Recovery and mortality. In *Substance use by older adults: Estimates of future impact on the treatment system* (DHHS Publication No. SMA 03–3763, Analytic Series A-21), ed. S. P. Korper and C. L. Council, 39–59 Rockville, MD: Substance Abuse and Mental Health Services Administration, Office of Applied Studies.

———. 2007. Predicting long-term stable recovery from heroin addiction: Findings from a 33-year follow-up study. *Journal of Addictive Diseases* 26 (1): 51–60.

Hser, Y., M. D. Anglin, C. Grella, D. Longshore, and M. L. Prendergast. 1997. Drug treatment careers: A conceptual framework and existing research findings. *Journal of Substance Abuse Treatment* 14:543–58.

Hser, Y., M. D. Anglin, and K. Powers. 1993. A 24-year follow-up of California narcotics addicts. *Archives of General Psychiatry* 50: 577–84.

Hser, Y., K. Boyle, and M. D. Anglin. 1998. Drug use and correlates among sexually transmitted disease patients, emergency room patients, and arrestees. *Journal of Drug Issues* 28 (2): 437–54.

Hser, Y., V. Hoffman, C. E. Grella, and M. D. Anglin. 2001. A 33-year follow-up of narcotics addicts. *Archives of General Psychiatry* 58: 503–8.

Hser, Y., D. Huang, C.-P. Chou, and M. D. Anglin. 2007. Trajectories of heroin addiction: Growth mixture modeling results based on a 33-year follow-up study. *Evaluation Review* 31(6): 548–563.

Hser, Y., V. Joshi, M. D. Anglin, and B. Fletcher. 1999. Predicting posttreatment cocaine abstinence for first-time admissions and treatment repeaters. *American Journal of Public Health* 89:666–71.

Hser, Y., D. Longshore, M. L. Brecht, and M. D. Anglin. 2005. Studying the natural history of drug use. In *Epidemiology of drug abuse*, ed. Z. Sloboda, 29–43. New York: Springer.

Hser, Y., H. Shen, C.-P. Chou, S. Messer, and M. D. Anglin. 2001. Analytic approaches for assessing long-term treatment effects: Examples of empirical applications and findings. *Evaluation Review* 25 (2): 233–62.

Hser, Y., M. E. Stark, A. Paredes, D. Huang, M. D. Anglin, and R. Rawson. 2006. A 12-year follow-up of a treated cocaine-dependent sample. *Journal of Substance Abuse Treatment* 30: 219–26.

Hser, Y., K. Yamaguchi, J. Chen, and M. D. Anglin. 1995. Effects of interventions on relapse to narcotics addiction: An event-history analysis. *Evaluation Review* 19 (2): 123–40.

Hubbard, R. L., P. M. Flynn, S. G. Craddock, and B. W. Fletcher. 2001. Relapse after drug abuse treatment. In *Relapse +recovery in addictions,* ed. F. M. Tims, C. G. Leukefeld, and J. J. Platt, 109-21. New Haven, CT: Yale University Press.

Hubbard, R. L., and M. E. Marsden. 1986. Relapse to use of heroin, cocaine, and other drugs in the first year after treatment. In *Relapse and recovery in drug abuse* (NIDA Research Monograph No. 72), ed. F. M. Tims and C. G. Leukefeld, 157–66. Washington, DC: Government Printing Office.

Hubbard, R. L., M. E. Marsden, J. V. Rachal, H. J. Harwood, E. R. Cavanaugh, and H. M. Ginzburg. 1989. *Drug abuse treatment: A national study of effectiveness.* Chapel Hill: University of North Carolina Press.

Humphreys, K., and J. A. Tucker. 2002. Toward more responsive and effective intervention systems for alcohol-related problems. *Addiction* 97 (2): 126–32.

Jordan, B. K., E. B. Federman, B. J. Burns, W. E. Schlenger, J. A. Fairbank, and J. M. Caddell. 2002. Lifetime use of mental health and substance abuse treatment services by incarcerated women felons. *Psychiatric Services* 53 (3): 317–25.

Jordan, B. K., W. E. Schlenger, J. A. Fairbank, and J. M. Caddell. 1996. Prevalence of psychiatric disorders among incarcerated women. II. Convicted felons entering prison. *Archives of General Psychiatry* 53: 513–19.

Kandel, D. B. 2000. Gender differences in the epidemiology of substance dependence in the United States. In *Gender and its effects on psychopathology,* ed. E. Frank, 231–52. Washington, DC: American Psychiatric Press.

Kessler, R. C., K. A. McGonagle, S. Zhao, C. B. Nelson, M. Hughes, S. Eshleman, H. Wittchen, and K. S. Kendler. 1994. Lifetime and 12-month prevalence of DSM-III-R psychiatric disorders in the United States. *Archives of General Psychiatry* 51: 8–19.

Kessler, R. C., C. B. Nelson, K. A. McGonagle, M. J. Edlund, R. G. Frank, and P. J. Leaf. 1996. The epidemiology of co-occurring addictive and mental disorders: Implications for prevention and service utilization. *American Journal of Orthopsychiatry* 66: 17–31.

Khalsa, M. E., A. Paredes, M. D. Anglin, P. Potepan, and C. Potter. 1993. Combinations of treatment modalities and therapeutic outcome for cocaine dependence. In *Cocaine treatment: Research and clinical perspectives* (NIDA Research Monograph 135), ed. F. M. Tims and C. G. Leukefeld, 237–59. Rockville, MD: National Institute on Drug Abuse.

Kleinman, P. H., A. B. Miller, R. B. Millman, G. E. Woody, T. Todd, J. Kemp, and D. S. Lipton. 1990. Psychopathology among cocaine abusers entering treatment. *Journal of Nervous and Mental Disease* 178 (7): 442–47.

Laub, J. H., and R. J. Sampson. 1993. Turning points in the life course: Why change matters to the study of crime. *Criminology* 31 (31): 301–25.

———. 2001. Understanding desistance from crime. In *Crime and justice: A review of research,* ed. M. Tonry, 2–69. Chicago: University of Chicago Press.

———. 2003. *Shared beginnings, divergent lives: Delinquent boys to age 70.* Cambridge, MA: Harvard University Press.

Le Blanc, M., and R. Loeber. 1998. Developmental criminology updated. In *Crime and justice: A review of research,* ed. M. Tonry, 115–97. Chicago: University of Chicago Press.

Lester, H., and L. Gask. 2006. Delivering medical care for patients with serious mental illness or promoting a collaborative model of recovery? *British Journal of Psychiatry* 188 (5): 401–2.

Loeber, R., and M. Le Blanc. 1990. Toward a developmental criminology. In *Crime and justice,* ed. M. Tonry and N. Morris, 375–473. Chicago: University of Chicago Press.

Longshore, D., S. Turner, and T. Fain. 2005. Effects of case management on parolee misconduct: The bay area services network. *Criminal Justice and Behavior* 32 (2): 205–22.

Longshore, D., S. Turner, F. Taxman, A. Harrell, T. Fain, J. Byrne, and B. Taylor. 2003. Evaluation of Operation Drug Test: Findings and implications for pretrial drug testing. *Perspectives: Journal of the American Probation and Parole Association* 27 (3): 24–33.

Lynch, J., and G. D. Smith. 2005. A life course approach to chronic disease epidemiology. *Annual Review of Public Health* 26: 1–35.

McKay, J. R. 2001. Effectiveness of continuing care interventions for substance abusers: Implications for the study of long-term treatment effects. *Evaluation Review* 25 (2): 211–32.

———. 2005. Is there a case for extended interventions for alcohol and drug use disorders? *Addiction* 100 (11): 1594–1610.

McKay, J. R., E. Merikle, F. D. Mulvaney, R. V. Weiss, and J. M. Koppenhaver. 2001. Factors accounting for cocaine two years following initiation of continuing care. *Addiction* 96: 213–25.

McLellan, A. T. 2002. Have we evaluated addiction treatment correctly? Implications from a chronic care perspective. *Addiction* 97 (3): 249–52.

———. 2004. *Toward a continuing care management approach to substance abuse treatment.* Presentation in the ASAM 35th annual Medical–Scientific Conference, Washington, DC, April.

———. 2006. *What if addiction were treated, evaluated and reimbursed as a chronic illness?* Presentation at the UCLA CALDAR Summer Institute on Longitudinal Research, Los Angeles, August.

McLellan, A. T., D. C. Lewis, C. P. O'Brien, and H. D. Kleber. 2000. Drug dependence, a chronic medical illness: Implications for treatment, insurance, and outcomes evaluation. *Journal of the American Medical Association* 284: 1689–95.

McLellan, A. T., L. Luborsky, G. E. Woody, C. P. O'Brien, and K. A. Druley. 1983. Predicting response to alcohol and drug abuse treatments. Role of psychiatric severity. *Archives of General Psychiatry* 40 (6): 620–25.

McLellan, A. T., J. R. McKay, R. Forman, J. Cacciola, and J. Kemp. 2005. Reconsidering the evaluation of addiction treatment: From retrospective follow-up to concurrent recovery monitoring. *Addiction* 100 (4): 447–58.

McLellan, A. T., G. E. Woody, D. Metzger, J. McKay, J. Durrell, A. I. Alterman, and C. P. O'Brien. 1996. Evaluating the effectiveness of addiction treatments: Reasonable expectations, appropriate comparisons. *Milbank Quarterly* 74 (1): 51–85.

Moos, R. H. 2003. Addictive disorders in context: Principles and puzzles of effective treatment and recovery. *Psychology of Addictive Behaviors* 17: 3–12.

Moos, R. H., J. W. Finney, E. B. Federman, and R. Suchinsky. 2000. Specialty mental health care improves patients' outcomes: Findings from a nationwide program to monitor the quality of care for patients with substance use disorders. *Journal of Studies on Alcohol* 61 (5): 704–13.

Moos, R. H., M. J. King, and M. A. Patterson. 1996. Outcomes of residential treatment of substance abuse in hospital- and community-based programs. *Psychiatric Services* 47 (1): 68–74.

Moos, R. H., and B. S. Moos. 2004. Long-term influence of duration and frequency of participation in alcoholics anonymous on individuals with alcohol use disorders. *Journal of Consulting and Clinical Psychology* 72 (1): 81–90.

———. 2006. Rates and predictors of relapse after natural and treated remission from alcohol use disorders. *Addiction* 101: 212–22.

———. 2007. Treated and untreated alcohol use disorders: course and predictors of remission and relapse. *Evaluation Review* 31(6): 564–584.

Murray, D. W. 1992. Drug abuse treatment programs in the Federal Bureau of Prisons: Initiatives for the 1990s. In *Drug abuse treatment in prisons and jails* (NIDA Research Monograph 118), ed. C. G. Leukefeld and F. M. Tims, 62-83. Rockville, MD: National Institute on Drug Abuse.

Muthen, B. 2004. Latent variable analysis: Growth mixture modeling and related techniques for longitudinal data. In *Handbook of quantitative methodology for the social sciences*, ed. D. Kaplan, 345–68. Thousand Oaks, CA: Sage.

Muthen, B., and T. Asparouhov. 2008. Growth mixture analysis: Models with non-Gaussian random effects. In *Advances in longitudinal data analysis*, ed. G. Fitzmaurice, M. Davidian, G. Verbeke, and G. Molenberghs. Boca Raton, FL: Chapman and Hall/CRC Press.

Nagin, D. S. 1999. Analyzing developmental trajectories: Semi-parametric group-based approach. *Psychological Methods* 4:39–177.

———. 2005. *Group-based modeling of development*. Cambridge, MA: Harvard University Press.

Nagin, D. S., A. D'Unger, K. Land, and P. McCall. 1998. How many latent classes of delin-quent/criminal careers? Results from mixed Poisson recession analyses of the London, Philadelphia, and Racine cohorts studies. *American Journal of Sociology* 103:1593–1630.

Nagin, D. S., L. Pagani, E. Richard, and F. Vitaro. 2003. Life course turning points: The effect of grade retention on physical aggression. *Development and Psychopathology* 15:343–61.

Nagin, D. S., and R. E. Tremblay. 2001. Analyzing developmental trajectories of distinct but related behaviors: A group-based method. *Psychological Methods* 6 (1): 18–34.

Office of National Drug Control Policy. 2004. *The economic costs of drug abuse in the United States 1992-2002*. Retrieved on August 7, 2006 from http://www.whitehousedrugpolicy .gov/publications/economic_costs/ e_summary.pdf.

Ouimette, P. C., R. H. Moos, and J. W. Finney. 2000. Two-year mental health service use and course of remission in patients with substance use and posttraumatic stress disorders. *Journal of Studies on Alcohol* 61 (2): 247–53.

Pescosolido, B. A. 1991. Illness careers and network ties: A conceptual model of utilization of compliance. *Advances in Medical Sociology* 2:161–84.

Pescosolido, B. A., and C. A. Boyer. 1999. How do people come to use mental health services? Current knowledge and changing perspectives. In *A handbook for the study of mental health: Social contexts, theories, and systems*, ed. A. V. Horwitz and T. L. Scheid, 392–411. New York: Cambridge University Press.

Petersilia, J., and S. Turner. 1993. *Evaluating intensive supervision probation/parole: Results of a nationwide experiment*. Washington, DC: National Institute of Justice.

Pickles, A., and M. Rutter. 1991. Statistical and conceptual models of "turning points" in developmental processes. In *Problems and methods in longitudinal research: Stability and change*, ed. D. Magnusson, L. R. Bergman, G. Rudinger, and B. Törestad, 133–65. Cambridge, UK: Cambridge University Press.

Piquero, A. R., D. P. Farrington, and A. Blumstein. 2003. The criminal career paradigm: Background and recent developments. In *Crime and justice: A review of research*, ed. M. Tonry, 359–506. Chicago: University of Chicago Press.

Price, R. K., N. K. Risk, and E. L. Spitznagel. 2001. Remission from drug abuse over a 25year period: Patterns of remission and treatment use. *American Journal of Public Health* 91 (7): 1107–13.

Raudenbush, S. W. 2001. Comparing personal trajectories and drawing causal inferences from longitudinal data. *Annual Review of Psychology* 52:501–25.

Rawnsley, M. M. 1991. Chronic mental illness: The timeless trajectory. *Scholarly Inquiry for Nursing Practice: An International Journal* 5 (3): 205–18.

Regier, D., W. Narrow, D. Rae, R. Mandersheid, B. Locke, and F. Goodwin. 1993. The de facto U.S. Mental and addictive disorders service system. *Archives of General Psychiatry* 50:85–94.

Ritsher, J. B., J. D. McKellar, J. W. Finney, P. G. Otilingam, and R. H. Moos. 2002. Psychiatric comorbidity, continuing care and mutual help as predictors of five-year remission from substance use disorders. *Journal of Studies on Alcohol* 63 (6): 709–15.

Robins, L. N. 1978. Sturdy childhood predictors of adult antisocial behavior: Replications from longitudinal studies. *Psychological Medicine* 8:611–22.

Rounsaville, B. J., S. F. Anton, K. Carroll, D. Budde, B. A. Prusoff, and F. Gawin. 1991. Psychiatric diagnosis of treatment-seeking cocaine abusers. *Archives of General Psychiatry* 48:43–51.

Rush, A. J., L. M. Koran, M. B. Keller, J. C. Markowitz, W. M. Harrison, R. J. Miceli, J. A. Fawcett, A. J. Gelenberg, R. M. Hirschfeld, D. N. Klein, J. H. Kocsis, J. P. McCullough, A. F. Schatzberg, and M. E. Thase. 1998. The treatment of chronic depression, part 1. Study design and rationale for evaluating the comparative efficacy of sertraline and imipramine as acute, crossover, continuation and maintenance phase therapies. *Journal of Clinical Psychiatry* 59:589–97.

Rutter, M. 1996. Transitions and turning points in developmental psychopathology: As applied to the age span between childhood and mid-adulthood. *International Society for the Study of Behavioral Development* 19 (3): 603–26.

Sampson, R. J., and J. H. Laub. 1992. Crime and deviance in the life course. *Annual Review of Sociology* 8:63–84.

———. 1993. Life-course desisters? Trajectories of crime among delinquent boys followed to age 70. *Criminology* 41 (3): 555.

———. 2003. *Crime in the making: Pathways and turning points through life.* Cambridge, MA: Harvard University Press.

———. 2005. A life-course view of the development of crime. *Annals of the American Academy of Political and Social Science* 602 (1): 12–45.

Scott, C. K., M. A. Foss, and M. L. Dennis. 2003. Factors influencing initial and longer-term responses to substance abuse treatment: A path analysis. *Evaluation and Program Planning* 26:287–96.

Simpson, D. D., G. W. Joe, B. W. Fletcher, R. L. Hubbard, and M. D. Anglin. 1999. A national evaluation of treatment outcomes for cocaine dependence. *Archives of General Psychiatry* 56 (6): 507–14.

Sobell, L. C., J. A. Cunningham, M. B. Sobell, and T. Toneatto. 1993. A life span perspective on natural recovery (self-change) from alcohol problems. In *Addictive behaviors across the life span: Prevention, treatment and policy issues,* ed. J. S. Baer, G. A. Marlatt, and R. J. McMahon, 35–66. Newbury Park, CA: Sage.

Speckart, G., and M. D. Anglin. 1986a. Narcotics and crime: A causal modeling approach. *Journal of Quantitative Criminology* 2 (1): 3–28.

———. 1986b. Narcotics use and crime: An overview of recent research advances. *Contemporary Drug Problems* 13 (4): 741–69.

Strauss, A., and J. M. Corbin. 1988. *Shaping a new health care system: The explosion of chronic illness as a catalyst for change.* San Francisco: Jossey-Bass.

Strauss, A., S. Fagerhaugh, B. Suczek, and C. Wiener. 1985. *Social organization of medical work.* Chicago: University of Chicago Press.

Teplin, L. A., K. M. Abram, and G. M. McClelland. 1996. Prevalence of psychiatric disorders among incarcerated women: Pretrial jail detainees. *Archives of General Psychiatry* 53 (6): 505–12.

Tims, F. M., C. G. Leukefeld, and J. J. Platt. 2001. *Relapse +recovery in addictions.* New Haven, CT: Yale University Press.

Tschacher, W., R. Haemmig, and N. Jacobshagen. 2003. Time series modeling of heroin and morphine drug action. *Psychopharmacology* 165:188–93.

Vaillant, G. E. 1988. What can long-term follow-up teach us about relapse and prevention of relapse in addiction? *British Journal of Addiction* 83 (10): 1147–57.

———. 1992. Is there a natural history of addiction? In *Addictive states,* ed. C. P. O'Brien and J. H. Jaffee, 41-57. New York: Raven.

———. 1996. A long-term follow-up of male alcohol abuse. *Archives of General Psychiatry* 53: 243–49.

Von Korff, M., J. Gruman, J. Schaefer, S. J. Curry, and E. H. Wagner. 1997. Collaborative management of chronic illness. *Annals of Internal Medicine* 127: 1097–1102.

Wagner, E. H., B. T. Austin, and M. Von Korff. 1996. Organizing care for patients with chronic illness. *Milbank Quarterly* 74: 511–44.

Wagner, E. H., R. E. Glasgow, C. Davis, A. E. Bonomi, L. Provost, D. McCulloch, P. Carver, and C. Sixta. 2001. Quality improvement in chronic illness care: A collaborative approach. *Joint Commission Journal on Quality and Patient Safety* 27 (2): 63–80.

Warner, L. A., R. C. Kessler, M. Hughes, J. C. Anthony, and C. B. Nelson. 1995. Prevalence and correlates of drug use and dependence in the United States. Results from the National Comorbidity Survey. *Archives of General Psychiatry* 52 (3): 219–29.

Warren, K., R. Hawkins, and J. Sprott. 2003. Substance use as a dynamical disease: Evidence and clinical implications of nonlinearity in a time series of daily alcohol consumption. *Addictive Behaviors* 28:369–74.

Weisner, C. 2001. The provision of services for alcohol problems: A community perspective for understanding access. *Journal of Behavioral Health Services and Research* 28 (2): 130–42.

———. 2002. What is the scope of the problem and its impact on health and social systems? In *Changing substance abuse through health and social systems,* ed. W. R. Miller and C. M. Weisner, 3–14. New York: Kluwer Academic/Plenum.

Weisner, C., and H. Matzger. 2002. A prospective study of the factors influencing entry to alcohol and drug treatment. *Journal of Behavioral Health Services and Research* 29 (2): 126–37.

———. 2003. Missed opportunities in addressing drinking behavior in medical and mental health services. *Alcoholism: Clinical and Experimental Research* 27 (7): 1132–41.

Weisner, C., H. Matzger, and L. A. Kaskutas. 2003. How important is treatment? One-year outcomes of treated and untreated alcohol-dependent individuals. *Addiction* 98: 901–11.

Weisner, C., J. Mertens, S. Parthasarathy, C. Moore, and Y. Lu. 2001. Integrating primary medical care with addiction treatment: A randomized controlled trial. *Journal of the American Medical Association* 286: 1715–23.

Weisner, C., G. T. Ray, J. R. Mertens, D. D. Satre, and C. Moore. 2003. Short-term alcohol and drug treatment outcomes predict long-term outcome. *Drug and Alcohol Dependence* 1071 (3): 281–94.

Weisner, C., and L. Schmidt. 1993. Alcohol and drug problems among diverse health and social service populations. *American Journal of Public Health* 83 (6): 824–29.

———. 1995. The community epidemiology laboratory: Studying alcohol problems in community and agency-based populations. *Addiction* 90 (3): 329–41.

West, R. 2001. Theories of addiction (editorial). *Addiction* 96: 3–13.

Wexler, H. K., G. DeLeon, G. Thomas, D. Kressler, and J. Peters. 1999. The Amity prison TC evaluation: Reincarceration outcomes. *Criminal Justice and Behavior* 26 (2): 147–67.

Wills, T., C. Walker, and J. A. Resko. 2005. Longitudinal studies of drug use and abuse. In *Epidemiology of drug abuse,* ed. Z. Sloboda, 177–92. New York: Springer.

Worthman, C. M. 1999. Epidemiology of human development. In *Hormones, health, and behavior: A socio-ecological and lifespan perspective,* ed. C. Panter-Brick and C. M. Worthman, 47–104. New York: Cambridge University Press.

Xie, H., R. Drake, and G. McHugo. 2006. Are there distinctive trajectory groups in substance abuse remission over 10 years? An application of the group-based modeling approach. *Administration and Policy in Mental Health* 33: 423–32.

Yu, J., and W. R. Williford. 1992. The age of alcohol onset and alcohol, cigarette, and marijuana use patterns: An analysis of drug use progression of young adults in New York state. *International Journal of the Addictions* 27 (11): 1313–23.

Yih-Ing Hser is a professor-in-residence at the UCLA Integrated Substance Abuse Programs, Semel Institute for Neuroscience and Human Behavior, David Geffen School of Medicine, University of California, Los Angeles. She has been conducting research in the field of substance abuse and its treatment since 1980 and has extensive experience in research design and advanced statistical techniques applied to substance abuse data. In addition to gender-related issues in substance abuse and treatment, she has published in the areas of treatment evaluation, epidemiology, natural history of drug addiction, and innovative statistical modeling development and application. She is the director of the Center for Advancing Longitudinal Drug Abuse Research.

Douglas Longshore, PhD, was a sociologist at the UCLA Integrated Substance Abuse Programs. He was the principal investigator of the statewide evaluation of the Substance Abuse and Crime Prevention Act (SACPA, commonly known as Proposition 36). His interests included intervention with drug-using criminal offenders, motivational factors in treatment and recovery, and racial/ethnic and cultural aspects of treatment and recovery. He passed away on December 30, 2005, from cancer.

M. Douglas Anglin, PhD, is a professor-in-residence in the Department of Psychiatry and Biobehavioral Sciences at University of California, Los Angeles. He has been conducting research on substance abuse and treatment evaluation since 1972 and is author or coauthor of more than 150 published articles. He has been principal investigator on more than 30 federally funded studies. He is the associate director of the UCLA Integrated Substance Abuse Programs.

MOTIVATIONAL INTERVIEWING AND SOCIAL WORK PRACTICE

STÉPHANIE WAHAB

UNIVERSITY OF UTAH, SALT LAKE CITY

Abstract

- *Summary*: Motivational interviewing was proposed as an alternative model to direct persuasion for facilitating behavior change. Social work behavior change interventions have traditionally focused on increasing skills and reducing barriers. More recent recommendations tend to encourage practitioners to explore a broad range of issues, including but not limited to skills and barriers. The article defines and explains motivational interviewing by presenting its essential *spirit* and techniques, and provides a brief case example within a domestic violence context.

- *Findings*: This article proposes motivational interviewing as an intervention appropriate for social work practice concerned with behavior change by arguing that motivational interviewing is an exciting intervention model for numerous social work settings due to its consistency with core social work values, ethics, resources, and evidence-based practice.

- *Applications*: Social workers may strive to practice and test motivational interviewing in addictions settings, as well as within other critical social work arenas including but not limited to health, domestic violence, batterer treatment, gambling, HIV/AIDS prevention, dual disorders, eating disorders, and child welfare.

Keywords: ambivalence; intrinsic motivation; motivational interviewing; practice resistance

SOURCE: "Motivational Interviewing and Social Work Practice" by Stéphanie Wahab. In the 2005 issue of *Journal of Social Work,* 5(1), 45–60. Used with permission.

INTRODUCTION

Of the 'four forces' of social work (psycho-dynamic, cognitive-behavioral, existential-humanistic and transpersonal (Derezotes, 2000)), cognitive behavioral therapy (CBT) has significantly informed numerous social work interventions concerned with behavior change both with individuals and with groups. Traditionally, behavior change interventions have specifically focused on increasing skills and reducing barriers. Practice knowledge now indicates that simply telling people what to do, or how to do it, is rarely effective in supporting people to change their desired behaviors. More recent recommendations tend to encourage practitioners to explore a broad range of issues. In fact, leading theoretical approaches such as the information-motivation-behavioral skills model (Fisher and Fisher, 1992), the transtheoretical model (Prochaska and DiClemente, 1984), and the health belief model (Rosenstock et al., 1994) highlight motivational constructs as key elements of the behavior change process. Also reflected in the behavior change literature is a significant finding that the way (the spirit) in which clinicians interact with clients has a significant effect on clients' motivation and resistance to change (Miller et al., 1988; Brown and Miller, 1993).

WHAT IS MOTIVATIONAL INTERVIEWING?

Motivational interviewing (MI) was proposed as an alternative model to direct persuasion for facilitating behavior change by Miller in the early 1980s (Miller, 1983, 1985). The original conceptualization of MI evolved from Miller's work in the treatment of problem drinkers and was elaborated and developed more fully with the assistance of his colleague Dr. Stephen Rollnick in 1991 (Miller and Rollnick, 1991). Miller and Rollnick (2002) define MI as 'a client-centered, directive method for enhancing intrinsic motivation to change by exploring and resolving ambivalence' (p. 25).

Although several models such as the drinker's check-up (DCU) (Miller and Sovereign, 1989), motivational enhancement therapy (MET) (Project Match Research Group, 1993), brief motivational interviewing (Rollnick et al., 1992) and brief interventions (Holder et al., 1991) were derived from and are similar to MI, MI is distinct from these methods in its time, intensity and structure.

MI is grounded in the transtheoretical model (TM) (Prochaska and DiClemente, 1982) and informed by seven distinct theories: conflict and ambivalence (Orford, 1985), decisional balance (Janis and Mann, 1977), health beliefs (Rogers, 1975), reactance (Brehm and Brehm, 1981), self-perception theory (Bem, 1967), self-regulation theory (Kanfer, 1987), and Rokeach's value theory (Rokeach, 1973). Briefly, the transtheoretical model conceptualizes behavior change as a process with various stages. Change is understood as a series of stages of change. The stages represent distinct categories along a continuum of motivational readiness. These categories include precontemplation, contemplation, preparation, action, maintenance and relapse. According to Prochaska and DiClemente (1982) precontemplation is the state in which an individual is not yet considering the possibility of change. Contemplation is the stage defined by ambivalence about changing or initiating a behavior. Preparation is a state characterized by an intention to change in the immediate future, usually within the next month. Action is the stage where the individual takes action in order to achieve a behavior change. Maintenance is the stage where the individual strives to maintain and integrate a behavior that has been successfully started or changed. Relapse is the stage when an individual re-engages the undesired behavior and/or stops the desired behavior. While the TM informs MI, we must be cautious not to mistake one for the other. Even though current literature (Miller and Rollnick, 2002) and training by the MI leaders (Miller and Rollnick) no longer stress the significance of the TM for MI as much as they used to (because it does not necessarily capture the many nuances of the individual change process), they continue to agree that the TM can provide a helpful heuristic for helping clinicians understand the need to tailor what they do to the client's readiness profile.

The overall intention of MI is to support people to move along a continuum of behavior change by creating a supportive, non-judgmental, directive environment to facilitate the exploration of one's motivations, readiness and confidence levels for change, as well as ambivalence to change (Miller and Rollnick, 2002). The intention behind assessing motivation, readiness and confidence levels for change is to tailor the intervention accurately to the client's stage of change at any given moment. A client who is considered a 'precontemplator' (Prochaska and DiClemente, 1982) would be unlikely to be responsive to an action-oriented intervention. Similarly, someone who is ready to act or change their behavior(s) may not be supported and encouraged by an intervention that focuses on getting ready for change. In addition, an individual who is ready and motivated to change their behavior, and does not feel confident that they can carry out the change, will require different supports and resources than if their barrier resides in their motivation level. More specifically, it is possible to be motivated and ready to change yet not confident about one's ability to successfully carry out the change.

THE *SPIRIT* OF MOTIVATIONAL INTERVIEWING

What is referred to as the MI spirit is the style, the way, the intention and the gestalt of the practitioner's disposition with the client. The spirit is different from the technique in that it transcends the mechanisms of the practice by supporting and providing the foundation for the skills and techniques. While the skills and techniques can be taught, the spirit is more elusive and comes from within the clinician. MI trainers often aim to elicit and evoke the MI spirit within trainees by modeling it themselves. Rollnick and Miller (1995) point to seven particular elements of the MI spirit:

1. Motivation to change is elicited from the client, and not imposed from without.

2. It is the client's task, not the counselor's, to articulate and resolve his or her ambivalence.

3. Direct persuasion is not an effective method for resolving ambivalence.

4. The counseling style is generally a quiet and eliciting one.

5. The counselor is directive in helping the client to examine and resolve ambivalence.

6. Readiness to change is not a client trait, but a fluctuating product of interpersonal interaction.

7. The therapeutic relationship is more like a partnership or companionship than expert/recipient roles.

The spirit of MI involves an availability and willingness to be present enough with a client to glimpse their inner world. Consequently, empathic and reflective listening are foundational skills to this practice. It has been said that one never masters the art of reflective listening, but rather, develops and nurtures the ability through a lifetime. Without the ability to engage in reflective listening, it is impossible to practice MI (Miller and Rollnick, 2002).

While MI draws from CBT models, it also embodies elements and influence from the third (existential-humanistic) and fourth (transpersonal) forces. The client-centered approach to MI supports the third force's focus on unconditional positive regard (Rogers, 1957, 1959), acceptance, and the here and now. It has been argued (Miller and Rollnick, 2002) that the spirit and techniques of MI are grounded in the Rogerian (1957, 1959) concepts of 'acceptance' and 'unconditional positive regard'. Rogers surmised that by creating an accepting, non-judgmental, empathic relationship setting, the therapist constructs the circumstances that facilitate change. Miller (2000), who has spent a significant portion of his career researching 'what triggers change', postulates that love, referenced as *agape*, might be the key ingredient that facilitates behavior change. In fact, in a study of individuals who had experienced sudden transformational change, Miller and C'de Baca (1994) reported that a majority of the participants in the study mentioned that they had felt completely loved and accepted during their transformational experiences. While not all clients choose to explore the spiritual elements of their behaviors, the client-centered approach coupled with the spirit of MI create a space for transpersonal and existential experiences and exploration to take place within the context of behavior change interventions.

MI fidelity tools such as the motivational interviewing skills code (MISC) (Miller et al., 2003) and the motivational interviewing treatment integrity code (MITI) (Moyers et al., 2005) allow practitioners and researchers to evaluate the integrity of the spirit of MI. They may also serve as tools for self-evaluation by clinicians learning MI, and as feedback mechanisms to improve MI competence in training. While clinicians, program and grant funders may be drawn to CBTs because of the clarity and ease associated with measuring the respective outcome variables, clinicians may be encouraged to move beyond simply task-centered approaches now that MI tools have been developed to evaluate third and fourth force constructs such as empathy and understanding. Both the MISC and MITI have been evaluated and tested (see above-referenced studies for reliability estimates).

MOTIVATIONAL INTERVIEWING SKILLS AND TECHNIQUES

Unlike confrontive techniques, MI aims to support the client to generate reasons, plans, and motivations for change. Within MI, practitioners do not impose diagnostic labels, engage clients in a punitive or coercive fashion, argue that the client has a problem, attempt to convince or force the client to change, or create change plans for the client, nor does the practitioner do most of the talking. Rather, the MI clinician facilitates a process where clients convince themselves to consider and engage in behavior change. They do so specifically by engaging the four basic principles of MI: 1) express empathy; 2) develop discrepancy; 3) roll with resistance; and 4) support self-efficacy (Miller and Rollnick, 2002). The principles are operationalized by assessing motivation, confidence and readiness; exploring ambivalence; enhancing client motivation; rolling with resistance; supporting self-efficacy; and strengthening commitment.

A GOOD FIT WITH SOCIAL WORK

Evidence-Based Practice

Currently, there are more than 73 publications of international clinical trials that have evaluated MI (Miller, personal communication, 28 October, 2004) and its effectiveness in a variety of settings (see www.motivationalinterview.org for a listing of these studies). Contemporary MI practices occur on five continents and demonstrate the feasibility of adapting MI to a variety of risk behaviors and populations (Dunn et al., 2001). Studies have been conducted in the US, Canada, England, Norway, Switzerland, Italy, Zambia and South Africa among other countries. In addition, MI has been used and tested with adolescents and adults in settings and problem areas that include but are not limited to problem drinkers (Miller et al., 1993; Senft et al., 1995; Bosari and

Carey, 2000; Murphy et al., 2004),[1] drug users (Saunders et al., 1995; Longshore and Grills, 2000; Stotts, et al., 2001; Babor, 2004), smokers (Butler et al., 1999; Cigrang et al., 2002; Stotts et al., 2002), psychiatric patients (Kemp et al., 1996; Swanson et al., 1999), gamblers (Hodgins et al., 2001), batterers (Kennerley, 2000; Kistenmacher, 2000), HIV risk reduction (Carey et al., 1997; Picciano et al., 2001; Koblin et al., 2004), nutrition and minority populations (Longshore and Grills, 2000; Resnicow et al., 2001), in probation settings (Harper and Hardy, 2002).

Dunn et al. carried out the most comprehensive and systematic review of the effects of MI. They focused on four particular practice domains in which MI was utilized: substance abuse, HIV risk, smoking and diet/exercise. They found that:

> there was substantial evidence that MI is an effective substance abuse intervention method when used by clinicians who are non-specialists in substance abuse treatment, particularly when enhancing entry to and engagement in more intensive substance abuse treatment. (2001: 1)

Dunn et al. (2001) were unable to judge the effectiveness of MI in the other three domains due to 'inadequate data', and note that the reason for the cumulative evidence for the effectiveness of MI in the substance abuse domain is due to the large number of studies on the topic.

MI in Social Work

Social workers have quickly joined the ranks of practitioners who are both utilizing and evaluating MI interventions. Smyth (1996) considers the use of MI to help engage and motivate clients to make the changes necessary for recovery from dual disorders. Hohman (1998) suggests MI for child welfare workers who work with substance abusers, as a useful intervention technique, by applying it to a case

study. Rutledge et al. (2001) describe the principles of MI and discuss its application, with case examples drawn from a pilot trial of motivational enhancement therapy (MET), for HIV risk reduction among 'men who have sex with men' (MSM). Finally, Harper and Hardy (2002) tested the use of MI as a method to improve 'effective practice with offenders who had a drug/alcohol problem' (p. 394). Sixteen probation officers were trained in MI. Probation officers recruited offenders ($n = 65$) who they knew had drug and alcohol problems. Offenders were administered the CRIME-PICS II (Frude et al., 1994), before and after the MI training for officers. The findings indicate that offenders who were supervised by MI-trained officers, demonstrated more significant attitudinal changes (measured by the CRIME-PICS) than offenders not supervised by MI-trained officers. While offenders in the control group also demonstrated significant changes, changes occurred across two scales, rather than four scales (as they did for the intervention group). In addition, they found a significant decrease in the score for drinking and drugs on a probation inventory, amongst offenders in the intervention group, which was not affected in the control group. Although the application of MI has yet to be systematically used and tested within the social work profession, it is clear by their participation in MI training that social workers are increasingly interested in the intervention. Additional rigorous research on the use of MI within various social work settings could significantly contribute to the growing body of literature on the effectiveness of MI, particularly since social workers tend to bring unique and empowerment-based approaches to multi-disciplinary practice settings.

While there has been and continues to be extensive speculation on why and how MI works, researchers and practitioners, including Miller and Rollnick, remain speculative about what exactly makes MI effective when it is effective (Rollnick and

Miller, 1995; Noonan and Moyers, 1997). Speculations about why MI works have thus far revolved around constructs such as empathy, self-efficacy, cognitive dissonance, motivation, love, and change talk.

Social Work Codes of Ethics

While we do not yet know exactly why or how MI works when it does work (Miller and Rollnick, 2002), MI researchers and practitioners alike claim that the therapeutic relationship is a key component to its efficacy. Empathy, one of the four basic MI principles, appears to have particular significance for behavior outcome measures (Miller et al., 1980). MI's emphasis on, and valuing of, the therapeutic relationship is consistent with the value social work places on human relationships. The four basic MI principles (mentioned earlier) underscore and support the value social work places on the *dignity and worth of the person* (NASW, 1996) also supported by the Australian Association of Social Workers, L'Association Nationale des Assistants de Service Social, and the British Association of Social Workers, as well as the International Federation of Social Workers.

Respect for Self-Determination and Autonomy

MI's client-centered approach to behavior change supports the social work ethical standards of *self-determination* by allowing and encouraging clients to set the agenda and pace for change. Although directive, the client-centered nature of MI requires that practitioners respect and accept clients' choices regarding their behaviors; including the choice not to change.

Brief Intervention

Another benefit (and interest) to social work practice is the 'brief intervention' model of MI. The literature on brief interventions supports both its cost-effectiveness (Holder et al., 1991; Langenbucher, 1994) and effectiveness in addictions treatment (Oliansky et al., 1997). Miller and Rollnick

(1991) note that research teams in numerous countries have found that brief interventions, lasting one to three sessions, are 'comparable in impact to more extensive treatments for alcohol problems' (p. 31). Similarly, the WHO Brief Intervention Study Group (1996) concluded that brief interventions in alcohol treatment 'are remarkably robust and should generalize to a variety of different health care settings and sociocultural groups' (p. 954). While Dunn et al.(2001) note that more research is needed to evaluate the cost-effectiveness of MI, the time-limited nature of brief interventions, such as MI, holds the potential to respond to client needs, demands for treatment, and agency resource limitations simultaneously. In a time where funding and budget cut-backs are the norm, providers and third party payers are hungry for time- and resource-effective interventions.

Diverse Populations

As social workers continue to refine their attention to cross-cultural issues and practice competencies, MI may prove to support those endeavors. Two studies have tested the use of MI with minority populations and found positive results. Resnicow et al. (2001) incorporated MI in their multicomponent intervention to increase fruit and vegetable consumption among African Americans. At baseline, 1011 participants were recruited from 14 different churches. Participants were randomly assigned to three treatment conditions, one of which included three counseling calls that were informed by MI. Their results showed that fruit and vegetable intake was significantly greater in the MI group than in the comparison and self-help groups. Although the MI intervention was not 'classic' MI (Resnicow et al., 2001: 7), their findings provide cause to believe that MI may hold potential to be effective with diverse racial and ethnic groups. The second study, by Longshore and Grills (2000), tested MI in conjunction with didactic counseling in a 'culturally congruent' setting (p. 1231), to promote recovery from illegal drug use among African Americans. Two hundred and twenty-two drug users were randomly assigned to a control condition or a 'culturally congruent' setting where they received didactic counseling and MI. Their findings showed that participants assigned to the intervention group reported more favorable change in their motivation to seek help. In addition, they were significantly more involved in the experience, were more self-disclosing, and participated more actively. Because MI was used in conjunction with didactic counseling and a culturally congruent setting, it is difficult to know which elements facilitated the positive outcomes. Like the Resnicow et al. (2001) project, this study provides social work practitioners and researchers with questions and additional reason to consider the use of MI.

Example of the Use of Motivational Interviewing in a Domestic Violence Context

As case examples for the use of MI in substance abuse settings are already provided in the literature (for example, Hohman, 1998), what follows is a case example of the use of MI within a domestic violence context. The following case example takes place with an MI-trained counselor in a battered women's shelter. The skills utilized in this example represent some of the techniques practiced in Phase I of MI (Miller and Rollnick, 2002).

Delores is a 36-year-old woman, originally from Ixtapa, Mexico. She currently lives in Salt Lake City, Utah, with her husband. She has three children with her husband; the children currently live with her parents in Mexico. She entered a confidential battered women's shelter due to emotional and physical violence she had been experiencing from her husband. She feared for her safety as well as her life. The most recent incident of abuse occurred the day prior to entering the shelter. Her husband beat her severely

with a gun and left her for dead. A neighbor heard her screams and called 911. By the time the police and ambulance arrived, the husband was gone and Delores was unconscious. She was taken to the hospital, treated and released 24 hours later. She did not want to return home at that time. With the assistance of a hospital social worker she gained entry into a confidential battered women's shelter.

Upon reviewing the intake notes of Delores' initial interview prior to entering the shelter, the counselor discovered that this was not the first time that Delores had been severely beaten by her husband. She had already been sent to the emergency room three times within that same year due to her husband's violence. She had left him on two prior occasions for extended visits with friends and family in order to recover and attain safety for a short while. She had never stayed in a battered women's shelter in the past, nor had she ever pressed charges against her husband. She feared deportation and did not want to return to live in Mexico.

Social worker (SW):	I'm glad to see you found your way to a safe place. I imagine that you may have many mixed feelings about being here. Could I spend some time exploring your situation with you? [Ask Permission. Wait for response.] What incident brought you to the shelter? [Appreciation. Open-ended question.]
Deolores (DE):	Well, my husband hit me. I made him angry by disobeying him. I didn't have dinner ready on time. He had made plans with his friends to go out and told me that dinner had to be ready by 5 p.m. I had been at the neighbor's house helping her with her children when I realized that it was 5:15 p.m. and I hadn't started dinner. I ran home and he was waiting for me when I ran in the door. I could tell he was very upset.
SW:	You were nervous about being late. What happened next? [Reflection. Open-ended question. Explore.]

DE: He just came up to me and started hitting me and beating me. I fell to the ground and was begging for him to stop. He pulled me by the hair across the room and kicked me. I realized that the more I cried, the more he hit. I tried not to make too much noise because I didn't want him to get more angry and I was afraid the police would come. I didn't want them to take him to jail. I think I blacked out because I don't remember anything else. Next thing I knew I was in the hospital. [She begins to cry.]

SW: Even though he was hurting you, you were worried and concerned about what . . . would happen to him. [Reflecting emotion.] . . .

DE: Yes, I didn't want him to get in trouble. I love him. The police don't like   Mexicans in Utah and I was afraid that they would do something bad to him. I was afraid for the both of us.

SW: It sounds like you were worried that things would be worse if the police intervened. [Paraphrase.]

DE: Yes, I'm so glad that he didn't get arrested. That would have been bad! I don't even know how long I will stay here. I just want my face and bruises to heal. I want time to think, and I want him to cool off a bit. I'll go back when I'm good and ready.

The worker did not react to Delores' comment about going back to her husband. She continued to explore Delores' history of abuse with her husband, as well as the help that she had sought from friends and family through the years. Delores never used the word abuse to refer to her husband's violence. Consequently, the worker mirrored her language and did not use words such as violence or abuse when referring to what happened. The worker continued to explore Delores' feelings about her husband, as well as her thoughts about what she wants for herself.

SW: So, it sounds like even though your husband has hit you on numerous occasions, you still have strong feelings for him. You love him. [Summarize. Paraphrase. Reflect emotion.]

DE: He is a great man. It may not seem like it sometimes, but he loves me and is a good friend. He is good to the children. We've been together a long time.

SW: You have a complicated history and despite the violence he has some qualities that are important to you. [Pause.] You mentioned that once you heal and he has time to cool off you are going to be ready to return to him. Tell me a little bit about the advantages of going back to him. [Amplified reflection followed by a paraphrase. Begin to explore ambivalence.]

DE: For starters, things will be really good for a while when I go back, they always are for a while. Second, I won't have to worry about how I'm going to send money back to my parents for the kids. I'll be able to see my friends, and I won't have to start from scratch like I would if I didn't go back. Most of all, I won't have to worry about having to go back to Mexico right away.

SW: So when you return, a honeymoon phase, financial security, your friends and being able to stay in the US are the positive aspects of going back. What other reasons? [Rephrase followed by an open-ended question.]

DE: No, I think that is about all.

SW: You have mentioned some of the advantages, what would you say are some of the disadvantages to going back to your husband? [Explore ambivalence.]

DE: Well, I have one friend who will be very mad and she may not want to talk to me if I go back to him. Also, chances are I will piss him off again at some point and he might hit me. Next time it might even be worse. It seems to get worse every time. I wouldn't be surprised if he kills me one day.

SW: So, the concern for your safety and life are some of the negatives. [Amplified reflection.] You have expressed important reasons to go back and important reasons not to go back. [Summary reflection.]

DE: Yes, I think the positives outweigh the negatives. That may seem crazy to you, but it makes sense to me.

SW: On the one hand, financial, social, and immigration issues are taken care of if you go back. On the other hand, if you go back, he may kill you someday. [Double-sided reflection.] Right now you are willing to take the risk of losing your life because the positives outweigh the negatives. [Amplified reflection. Develop discrepancy.]

SW: Where does this leave you now? [Support self-determination. Develop discrepancy. Elicit self-motivational statements.]

DE: I don't know really? I guess I just need time to think.

The worker does not press Delores to make a decision, nor does she suggest that she not go back. Instead, she supports Delores' expression of need for time and allows her to sit with the positives and negatives of going back.

SW: This is a difficult time for you. You love your husband and don't want him to get in trouble. You feel like there are advantages and disadvantages to going back. Right now, you want time to think and heal before you decide what to do next. Whatever you decide to do is your choice. I'm confident that you will make the best choice for

yourself. I believe that you are the expert on your life and current situation. I/we will be here to support you in your process. [Express empathy. Summarize. Support self-determination and choice. Express confidence and support.]

In the following session, instead of focusing on Delores' expression of intent to return to her husband, the worker explores, in more depth, what Delores wants for herself and her family. She never gives advice or unsolicited feedback. Instead, she uses a lot of reflective listening and summarizing to act as a mirror for Delores. It is only if and when Delores feels safe, accepted and supported for who she is, that she will be able to consider doing something different. Since 'going back' does not seem like a pressing issue for Delores, the worker asks Delores what she would like to focus on and seek assistance for while she is in the shelter. She allows Delores to set the plan for work and supports her choices, without (positive or negative) judgment.

Central to the MI client-centered spirit and techniques is the consistent emphasis on client autonomy and self-determination. The client has the freedom and responsibility to contemplate and engage in change. When a client is motivated and already engaged in behavior change, the MI practitioner works to support and encourage the client's commitment to change. When an individual is motivated, confident and ready for change, a practitioner engages MI Phase II techniques (Miller and Rollnick, 2002) that include working with a menu of options, reflecting change talk, supporting self-efficacy, negotiating a change plan, and strengthening commitment.

Conclusion

In conclusion, the literature both within and outside the social work profession suggests that MI may be an intervention worthy of additional social work attention and exploration. As the use of MI within the alcohol and drug addictions fields has been widely tested, social workers may both strive to incorporate MI in such practice settings, and add to the body of literature by using and testing MI within other critical social work areas including but not limited to health, domestic violence, batterer treatment, gambling, HIV prevention, dual disorders, eating disorders, adolescents, the homeless, and child welfare.

The potential benefits of incorporating MI in social work practice settings that have been explored in this paper include its consistency with certain social work values (client-centered, right to self-determination, respect for diversity and respect for the inherent worth of the individual) and ethics (importance of human relationships, respect, and practice-based interventions), its brief intervention structure, and the empirical support for its use with certain populations. In addition, the fact that MI is already being used and tested in a number of practice settings both across and within social work speak to its flexibility and practicality for social workers who work with individuals who present with varying levels of motivation to change a variety of different behaviors. The potential to utilize MI within multicultural settings is promising for social work, as well as supporting our profession's commitment to working with and across difference with respect, sensitivity and efficiency. Finally, a search of the Computer Retrieval of Information on Scientific Projects (CRISP) database (http://crisp.cit.nih.gov) indicates that some 68 research projects using and testing MI have received federal funding, a promising statistic for MI practitioners and researchers.

Despite all the perceived benefits to adopting MI in social work settings, social workers may also encounter some challenge. Although MI trainers are widely available in North America and Europe, agencies and organizations may not always have the financial resources to provide appropriate training and supervision. In addition, because MI is much more than a set of skills and techniques—rather, a way of being with individuals—practitioners and agencies must be able and willing to embrace, live and support the MI spirit (Miller, 2000). Teaching and practicing with the MI spirit may be challenging for those who do not embrace epistemologies that regard human beings as experts on their own lives, entitled to self-determination, respect and acceptance. Finally, although directive in its practice, MI counselors engage in minimal problem solving, action planning and advice giving, activities that are often central to social work practices and interventions. Learning to allow clients to make their own choices, even in the face of their attachment to their potentially life-threatening behaviors (substance use, violence, etc.), frequently proves challenging for those who wish to help.

Note

1. See Noonan and Moyers (1997) for a review of the evidence supporting the efficacy of MI with problem drinkers.

References

Babor, T. F. (2004) 'Brief Treatments for Cannabis Dependence: Findings from a Randomized Multisite Trial', *Journal of Consulting and Clinical Psychology* 72: 455–66.

Bem, D. (1967) 'Self-perception: An Alternative Interpretation of Cognitive Dissonance Phenomena', *Psychological Review* 74(3): 183–200.

Bosari, B. and Carey, K. B. (2000) 'Effects of a Brief Motivational Intervention with College Student Drinkers', *Journal of Consulting and Clinical Psychology* 68(4): 728–33.

Brehm, S.S. and Brehm, J. W. (1981) *Psychological Reactance: A Theory of Freedom and Control.* New York: Academic Press.

Brown, J. M. and Miller, W. R. (1993) 'Impact of Motivational Interviewing on Residential Alcoholism Treatment', *Psychology of Addictive Behaviors* 7(4): 211–18.

Butler, C., Rollnick, S., Cohen, D., Russell, I., Bachmann, M. and Stott, N. (1999) 'Motivational Consulting Versus Brief Advice for Smokers in General Practice: A Randomized Trial', *British Journal of General Practice* 49(445): 611–16.

Carey, M. P., Maisto, S. A., Kalichman, S. C., Forsyth, A. D., Wright, E. M. and Johnson, B. T. (1997) 'Using Information, Motivational Enhancement, and Skill Training to Reduce the Risk of HIV Infection for Low-income Urban Women: A Second Randomized Clinical Trial', *Journal of Consulting and Clinical Psychology* 65(4): 531–41.

Cigrang, J. A., Severson, H. H. and Peterson, A. L. (2002) Pilot Evaluation of a Population-based Health Intervention for Reducing Use of Smokeless Tobacco', *Nicotine Tobacco Research* 4(1): 127–31.

Derezotes, D. S. (2000) *Advanced Generalist Social Work Practice*. Thousand Oaks, CA: Sage.

Dunn, C., Deroo, L. and Rivara, F. P. (2001) 'The Use of Brief Interventions Adapted from Motivational Interviewing Across Behavioral Domains: A Systematic Review', *Addiction* 96(12): 1725–42.

Fisher, W. and Fisher, W. A. (1992) 'Understanding and Promoting Aids Preventive Behavior: A Conceptual Model and Educational Tools', *Canadian Journal of Human Sexuality* 1(3): 99–106.

Frude, N., Honess, T. and Maguire, M. (1994) *CRIME-PICS II*. Cardiff: Michael and Associates.

Harper, R. and Hardy, S. (2002) 'An Evaluation of Motivational Interviewing as a Method of Intervention with Clients in a Probation Setting', *British Journal of Social Work* 30(3): 393–400.

Hodgins, D. C., Currie, S. R. and el-Guebaly, N. (2001) 'Motivational Enhancement and Self-help Treatments for Problem Gambling', *Journal of Consulting and Clinical Psychology* 69(1): 50–7.

Hohman, M. M. (1998) 'Motivational Interviewing: An Intervention Tool for Child Welfare Caseworkers Working with Substance-abusing Parents', *Child Welfare* 77(3): 275–89.

Holder, H., Longabaugh, R., Miller, W. R. and Rubonis, A. V. (1991) 'The Cost-effectiveness of Treatment for Alcoholism: A First Approximation', *Journal of Studies on Alcohol* 52(6): 517–40.

Janis, I. L. and Mann, L. (1977) *Decision-making: A Psychological Analysis of Conflict, Choice, and Commitment.* New York: Free Press.

Kanfer, F. H. (1987) 'Self-regulation and Behavior', in H. Heckhausen, P. M. Gollwitzer and F. E. Weinert (eds) *Jenseits des Rubikon*, pp. 286–99. Heidelberg: Springer-Verlag.

Kemp, R., Hayward, P. and Applewhaite, G. (1996) 'Compliance Therapy in Psychotic Patients: Randomized Controlled Trial', *British Medical Journal* 312(1): 345–9.

Kennerley, R. J. (2000) *The Ability of a Motivational Pre-group Session to Enhance Readiness for Change in Men who Have Engaged in Domestic Violence.* Dissertation abstract. Dissertation Abstracts International Sec.B The Sciences and Engineering, 60, 7B, 3569, US: Univ. Microfilms International.

Kistenmacher, B. R. (2000) *Motivational interviewing as a mechanism for change in men who batter: a randomized controlled trial.* Dissertation Abstracts International, 61, 09B, 4989, Accession No: AAI9987427.

Koblin, B., Chesney, M., Coates, T. and EXPLORE Study Team (2004) 'Effects of a Behavioural Intervention to Reduce Acquisition or HIV Infection among Men who have Sex with Men: The EXPLORE Randomised Controlled Study', *Lancet* 364(9428): 41–50.

Langenbucher, J. (1994) 'Rx for Health Care Costs: Resolving Addictions in the General Medical Setting', *Alcoholism:*

Clinical and Experimental Research 18(5): 1033–6.

Longshore, D. and Grills, C. (2000) 'Motivating Illegal Drug Use Recovery: Evidence for a Culturally Congruent Intervention', *Journal of Black Psychology* 26(3): 288–301.

Miller, W. R. (1983) 'Motivational Interviewing with Problem Drinkers', *Behavioral Psychotherapy* 11(2), 147–72.

Miller, W. R. (1985) 'Motivation for Treatment: A Review with Special Emphasis on Alcoholism', *Psychological Bulletin* 98(1), 84–107.

Miller, W. R. (2000) 'Rediscovering Fire: Small Interventions, Large Effects', *Psychology of Addictive Behaviors* 14(1): 6–18.

Miller, W., Benefield, R. G. and Tonigan, J. S. (1993) 'Enhancing Motivation for Change in Problem Drinking: A Controlled Comparison of Two Therapist Styles', *Journal of Consulting Clinical Psychology* 61(3): 455–61.

Miller, W. R. and C'de Baca, J. (1994) 'Quantum Change: Toward a Psychology of Transformation', in T. Heatherton and J. Weinberger (eds) *Can Personality Change?*, pp. 253–80. Washington, DC: American Psychological Association.

Miller, W. R., Moyers, T. B., Ernst, D. and Amrhein, P. (2003) *The Motivational Interviewing Skills Code (MISC) Manual (Version 2.0)*. URL (consulted 25 October 2004): http://casaa.unm .edu/download/ misc.pdf.

Miller, W. R and Rollnick, S. (1991) *Motivational Interviewing: Preparing People to Change Addictive Behavior*. New York: Guilford.

Miller, W. R. and Rollnick, S. (2002) *Motivational Interviewing: Preparing People for Change* (2nd edn). New York: The Guilford Press.

Miller, W. R. and Sovereign, R. G. (1989) 'The Check-up: A Model for Early Intervention in Addictive Behaviors', in T. Loberg, W. R. Miller, P. E. Nathan and G. A. Marlatt (eds) *Addictive Behaviors: Prevention and Early Intervention*, pp. 219–31. Amsterdam: Swets and Zeitlinger.

Miller, W. R., Sovereign, R. G. and Krege, B. (1988) 'Motivational Interviewing with Problem Drinkers: II. The Drinker's Check-up as a Preventative Intervention', *Behavioral Psychology* 16(4): 251–68.

Miller, W. R., Taylor, C. A. and West, J. C. (1980) 'Focused Versus Broad Spectrum Behavior Therapy for Problem Drinkers', *Journal of Consulting and Clinical Psychology* 48(5): 590–601.

Moyers, T. B., Martin, T., Manuel, J. K., Hendrickson, S. M. L. and Miller, W. R. (2005) 'Assessing Competence in the Use of Motivational Interviewing', *Journal of Substance Abuse Treatment* 28: 19–26.

Murphy, J. E., Benson, T. A., Vuchinich, R. E., Deskins, M. M., Eakin, D. and Flood, A. M. (2004) 'A Comparison of Personalized Feedback for College Student Drinkers Delivered With and Without a Motivational Interview', *Journal of Studies on Alcohol* 65: 200–3.

NASW (1996) *Code of Ethics*. Washington, DC: NASW Press.

Noonan, W. C. and Moyers, T. B. (1997) 'Motivational Interviewing', *Journal of Substance Misuse* 2(8): 8–16.

Oliansky, D. M., Wildenhaus, K. J., Manlove, K., Arnold, T. and Schoener, E. P. (1997) 'Effectiveness of Brief Interventions in Reducing Substance Use Among At-risk Primary Care Patients in Three Community-based Clinics', *Substance Abuse* 18(3): 95–103.

Orford, J. (1985) *Excessive Appetites: A Psychological View of Additions*. New York: Wiley.

Picciano, J. F., Roffman, R. A., Kalichman, S. C., Rutledge, S. E. and Berghuis, J. P. (2001) 'A Telephone-based Brief Intervention Using Motivational Interviewing Enhancement to Facilitate HIV Risk Reduction Among MSM: A Pilot Study', *AIDS and Behavior* 5(3): 251–62.

Prochaska, J. O. and DiClemente, C. C. (1982) 'Transtheoretical Therapy: Toward a More Integrative Model of Change', *Psychotherapy: Theory, Research, and Practice* 19(3): 276–88.

Prochaska, J. O., and DiClemente, C. C. (1984) *The Transtheoretical Approach:*

Crossing Traditional Boundaries of Therapy. Homewood, IL: Dow Jones/Irwin.

Project Match Research Group (1993) 'Project MATCH: Rationale and Methods for a Multisite Clinical Trial Matching Patients to Alcoholism Treatment', *Alcoholism: Clinical and Experimental Research* 17(6): 1130–45.

Resnicow, K., Jackson, A., Wang, T., De, A. K., McCarty, F., Dudley, W. N. and Baranowski, T. (2001) 'A Motivational Interviewing Intervention to Increase Fruit and Vegetable Intake through Black Churches: Results of the Eat for Life Trial', *American Journal of Public Health* 91(10): 1686–93.

Rogers, C. R. (1957) 'The Necessary and Sufficient Conditions for Therapeutic Personality Change', *Journal of Consulting Psychology* 21(2): 95–103.

Rogers, C. R. (1959) 'A Theory of Therapy, Personality, and Interpersonal Relationships as Developed in the Client-centered Framework', in S. Koch (ed.) *Psychology: The Study of a Science. Vol. 3. Formulations of the Person and the Social Context*. New York: McGraw Hill.

Rogers, R. W. (1975) 'A Protection Motivation Theory of Fear Appeals and Attitude Change', *Journal of Psychology* 91(1): 93–114.

Rokeach, M. (1973) *The Nature of Human Values*. New York: Free Press.

Rollnick, S., Bell, A. and Heather, N. (1992) 'Negotiating Behavior Change in Medical Settings: The Development of Brief Motivational Interviewing', *Journal of Mental Health* 1(1): 25–37.

Rollnick, S. and Miller, W. R. (1995) 'What is Motivational Interviewing?', *Behavioral and Cognitive Psychotherapy* 23(4): 325–34.

Rosenstock, I. M., Strecher, V. J. and Becker, M. H. (1994) 'The Health Belief Model And HIV Risk Behavior Change', in R. J. DiClemente and J. L. Peterson (eds) *Preventing AIDS: Theories and Methods of Behavioral Interventions*, pp. 5–24. New York: Plenum.

Rutledge, S. E., Roffman, R. A., Mahoney, C., Picciano, J. F., Berghuis, J. P. and Kalichman, S. C. (2001) 'Motivational

Enhancement Counseling Strategies in Delivering a Telephone-based Brief HIV Prevention Intervention', *Clinical Social Work Journal* 29(3): 291–306.

Saunders, B., Wilkinson, C. and Phillips, M. (1995) 'The Impact of a Brief Motivational Intervention with Opiate Users Attending a Methadone Programme', *Addiction* 90(3): 415–24.

Senft, R. A., Polen, M. R., Freeborn, D. K. and Hollis, J. F. (1995) *Drinking Patterns and Health: A Randomized Trial of Screening and Brief Intervention in a Primary Care Setting*. Final Report to the National Institute on Alcohol Abuse and Alcoholism. Portland, OR: Center for Health Research, Kaiser Permanente.

Smyth, N. J. (1996) 'Motivating Persons with Dual Disorders: A Stage Approach', *Families in Society: The Journal of Contemporary Human Services* 77(10): 605–14.

Stotts, A. L., DiClemente, C. C. and Dollan-Mullen, P. (2002) 'One-to-one: A Motivational Intervention for Resistant Pregnant Smokers', *Addictive Behaviors* 27(2): 275–92.

Stotts, A. M., Schmitz, J. M., Rhoades, H. M. and Grabowski, J. (2001) 'Motivational Interviewing with Cocaine-dependent Patients: A Pilot Study', *Journal of Consulting and Clinical Psychology* 69(5): 858–62.

Swanson, A. J., Pantalon, M. V. and Cohen, K. R. (1999) 'Motivational Interviewing and Treatment Adherence Among Psychiatric and Dually-diagnosed Patients', *Journal of Nervous and Mental Diseases* 187(10): 630–5.

WHO Brief Intervention Study Group (1996) 'A Cross-national Trial of Brief Interventions with Heavy Drinkers', *American Journal of Public Health* 86(7): 948–55.

Stéphanie Wahab, PhD, has been an Assistant Professor at the University of Utah's College of Social Work since 2000. Her areas of specialization are qualitative research, commercial sex work, motivational interviewing, diversity and social justice, and domestic violence. Recent publications have appeared in *Affilia, Journal of Sociology and Social Welfare, International Journal in Psychiatry in Medicine, Cancer Control Journal (Cancer, Culture and Literacy Supplement), Qualitative Inquiry,* and *Qualitative Social Work.* She has been a motivational interviewing trainer since 1999 and belongs to the international Motivational Interviewing Network of Trainers. Address: University of Utah, College of Social Work, 395 S. 1500 E, Salt Lake City, Utah 84112–0260, USA.

12

Motivational Interviewing to Affect Behavioral Change in Older Adults

Sherry M. Cummings

R. Lyle Cooper

Kim McClure Cassie
University of Tennessee

This article reviews and assesses the existing research literature on the efficacy of motivational interviewing (MI) to promote lifestyle changes and improve functioning among older adults confronting serious health challenges. A comprehensive literature review was conducted of intervention studies that tested the use of MI to achieve behavioral change among older adults with acute and chronic illnesses. Although limited in number, the studies revealed a significant improvement in physical activity, diet, cholesterol, blood pressure and glycemic control, and increased smoking cessation following MI. MI and its derivatives can be useful in dealing with a range of health issues faced by older adults. Further research to extend findings and address methodological issues is recommended. The integration of MI into social work courses focused on practice with older adults should be considered.

Keywords: motivational interviewing; older adults; evidence-based interventions

Authors' Note: Correspondence may be addressed to Sherry M. Cummings, University of Tennessee, College of Social Work, 193E Polk Ave., Nashville, TN 37210; e-mail: scumming@utk.edu.

SOURCE: "Motivational Interviewing to Affect Behavioral Change in Older Adults" by Sherry M. Cummings, R. Lyle Cooper, and Kim McClure Cassie. In the 2009 issue of *Social Work Practice*, *19*(2), 195–204. Used with permission.

The inexorable growth of the older population is now common knowledge. At present, there are 37 million persons 65 years of age and older in the United States. By 2030, the number of older adults will more than double to about 80 million (U.S. Census Bureau, 2004). Later life is often accompanied by an increase in acute illnesses and chronic medical conditions, which can result in physical and emotional pain for older individuals and escalating medical costs for society. Medical professionals treat the physical aspects of illness, and the role of the social worker is to address the behavioral aspects and psychosocial dimensions of disease management. Many acute and chronic illnesses experienced in later life can be prevented or managed, at least in part, through lifestyle alterations (Beers, 2004). However, modifying one's behavior often presents overwhelming challenges that many individuals cannot successfully confront on their own. Social workers can play a vital role in promoting health and preventing disability among older adults through the application of evidence-based treatments that target behavioral change and enable clients to effectively deal with health-related conditions. The majority of evidence-based interventions used to treat medical conditions among older adults are pharmaceutical in nature. However, as the number of older adults continues to grow, it is essential that social work practitioners have knowledge of effective psychosocial strategies that address the behavioral and psychological aspects of disease management.

Motivational interviewing (MI) is an intervention that employs a client-centered counseling style for achieving behavior change by facilitating exploration and resolution of ambivalence (Miller & Rollnick, 2002). Although a substantial body of literature exists affirming the efficacy of this approach, very little of the literature focuses on older adults. The purpose of this article is to review and assess the existing research literature on the efficacy of MI for promoting lifestyle changes and improved functioning among older adults confronting serious health challenges (Table 1).

MAJOR ILLNESS AMONG OLDER ADULTS AND EFFECT OF BEHAVIORAL CHANGES

As individuals age, their risk for developing disease and disability substantially increases. Disease and impairment can significantly restrict independence, increase the need for support, and lead to death. The leading causes of death among persons 65 years of age and older are heart disease, cancer, and stroke, which account for 62% of all fatalities for this population (Federal Interagency Forum on Aging-Related Statistic, 2006). Other chronic conditions among older adults that cause significant levels of impairment and commonly cause death include diabetes and chronic obstructive pulmonary disease (COPD; American Diabetes Association, 2007; American Lung Association, 2006). Research clearly demonstrates the relationship between personal health habits and disease (Beers, 2004). Specific lifestyle factors, such as smoking, diet, exercise, and alcohol consumption, have been consistently associated with disease and disability among older adults.

Smoking is the most common cause of COPD and lung cancers and is a leading risk factor for mouth, neck, and head cancers and for coronary artery disease and stroke (National Cancer Institute, 2007). Smoking cessation is considered a critical treatment for COPD. Experts also suggest that smoking cessation is one of the most important behaviors in which a person can engage to prevent heart attack and stroke (Beers, 2004). Likewise, healthy eating habits are necessary for older individuals to prevent or control diseases/conditions such as high blood pressure, diabetes, heart disease, stroke, osteoporosis, and certain cancers (Beers, 2004). Poor diet is related to obesity, which carries an increased risk of cardiovascular and pulmonary conditions and can exacerbate

Table 1 Description of Studies Examined

Author(s)	Targeted Behavior	N	Treatment	Frequency/Duration	Treatment Group Outcome	Population
Bennett et al. (2007)	Physical activity	56	Face to face MI session with master's-level physical activity specialist. Follow-up motivational interviewing (MI) by phone.	One face-to-face/24 minutes; three phone calls (2 weeks, 2 months, 4.5 months)/10 minutes	Increased physical activity	Long-term cancer survivors group mean age, 56 years (standard deviation [SD] = 9)
Bennett et al. (2005)	General health	111	Face-to-face MI with bachelor's-level registered nurse, and follow-up phone calls	One face-to-face/1 hour; monthly phone calls (over 6–9 months)/3–45 minutes	Less health distress and health interference	Community-dwelling adults aged 60+ years in Oregon with chronic diseases
Borrelli et al. (2005)	Smoking cessation	98	Face-to-face MI and follow-up MI phone calls	Three face-to-face/20–30 minutes; phone calls (number not specified)/5 minutes	Twice as likely to report continued abstinence	Smokers receiving home health care in Rhode Island. Mean age, 57 years (SD = 14)
Brodie & Inoue (2005)	Physical activity	92	Two treatment groups. One was advised to exercise and received MI. The other only received MI.	Eight sessions for both groups/1 hour	Increased walking distances	Adults aged 65+ years with chronic heart failure in United Kingdom
Gordon et al. (2003)	Alcohol consumption	301	MI with bachelor-level interventionist at primary care physician's office	One initial session/45–60 minutes; two additional contacts/10–15 minutes; other details lacking	Trend toward decreased alcohol consumption, but no statistically significant differences	Young adults (21–64 years old) compared with older adults (65+ years old) in Pennsylvania
Hokanson et al. (2006)	Smoking cessation	114	Face-to-face MI, follow-up phone sessions, and nicotine replacement therapy	One face-to-face/20–30 minutes; three to six phone calls/no duration details	Short-term decrease in smoking in past 7 days and daily smoking patterns	Adults with type 2 diabetes; group mean age, 54 years (SD = 9)
Hyman et al. (2007)	Smoking cessation, improved diet and exercise	230	Face-to-face MI counseling and follow-up MI phone calls	Three face-to-face every 6 months/duration not specified; seven follow-up phone calls/15 minutes	Decreased sodium intake, increased smoking cessation	African American smokers in United Kingdom with hypertension
Jackson et al. (2007)	Physical activity	40	Face-to-face MI with dietician	One face-to-face session/20–30 minutes	Increased physical activity	Adults with type 2 diabetes, aged 34–75 years, mean age of treatment group, 58 years (SD = 11)
Kolt et al. (2007)	Physical activity	186	MI phone calls with exercise counselor	Eight phone calls over 3 months/10–16.5 minutes	Increased physical activity and functioning	Adults 65+ years old in New Zealand

(Continued)

Table 1 (Continued)

Author(s)	Population	Targeted Behavior	N	Treatment	Frequency/Duration	Treatment Group Outcome
Kreman et al. (2006)	Rural Caucasians with high cholesterol. Mean age, 54 years ($SD = 6$)	Improved diet and exercise	24	Phone-based MI	One phone session/ 30–45 minutes	Decreased total cholesterol and high density lipoproteins
McHugh et al. (2001)	Adults in United Kingdom awaiting coronary artery bypass graft surgery. Mean age, 61 years; range, 35–77 years old	Cardiovascular risk factors	120	Health education and MI from nurse in home	Monthly (other details not available)	Improved smoking cessation, weight, physical activity, total cholesterol, and blood pressure
Sims et al. (1998)	Adults 65+ years old in United Kingdom	Physical activity	20	Initial MI session and follow-up phone calls with primary care nurse	Initial MI session details lacking; follow-up calls occurred 2 and 6 weeks after initial session	No statistically significant difference
Smith et al. (1997)	Females over 50 years old with type 2 diabetes	Weight loss	21	MI with psychologist	Three sessions/duration not specified	Improved glucose control, increased program adherence, increased exercise frequency
Wakefield et al. (2004)	Adults with cancer in Australia. Mean age, 53 years ($SD = 14$)	Smoking cessation	137	MI with counselor, nicotine replacement therapy, counseled smoking family members to quit	11 sessions/18 minutes	More likely to use nicotine replacement therapy and written materials, no difference in cessation rates
West et al. 2007	Overweight females with diabetes. Mean age, 53 years ($SD = 10$)	Weight loss, glycemic control	217	Independent MI with licensed clinical psychologist	Quarterly sessions/45 minutes	Short-term weight loss, improved glycemic control, less effective with African Americans

other conditions including diabetes, arthritis, and hypertension (Hooyman & Kiyak, 2008). Last, those who consume alcoholic beverages in greater quantities than suggested for older adults (e.g., more than one or two drinks/day) suffer from increased rates of head, neck, and liver cancer; cardiovascular disease; stroke; falls; and fractures (Fingerhood, 2000; National Institute on Alcohol Abuse and Alcoholism, 2005). In spite of the above evidence, many individuals are unable to surmount the emotional, psychological, and practical challenges related to needed behavioral change and, therefore, suffer severe deleterious consequences of poor health control.

MOTIVATIONAL INTERVIEWING

MI is a client-centered directive form of counseling focused on the resolution of ambivalence to enable client behavior change. According to MI, all persons considering behavior change experience an internal conflict regarding the pros and cons of change. This internal conflict, or ambivalence, must be resolved for a client to make a decision to change his or her behavior. It is the role of the MI therapist to help the client overcome his or her negative perception of change in favor of a positive recognition of the benefits of change. Toward this end of ambivalence resolution, several practices are employed including developing discrepancy (between stated life goals and current behavior), supporting self-efficacy, expression of empathy, and avoiding argumentation. These strategies are all employed to enable the practitioner to engage the client in change talk. Change talk is the client's verbal expression of the positive effects of engaging in behavioral change. Foundational to all of these skills is working within the "spirit" of MI (Miller & Rollnick, 2002).

The spirit of MI refers to the clinician's way of being with clients. This emphasis sprung originally from Roger's (1961) ideas regarding the importance of relationship in the counseling interaction. Miller and Rollnick (2002) have defined this spirit as a focus on the practitioner's collaboration with clients in an effort to evoke both reasons to change and specific methods of engaging in change, rather than imposing methods on the client. In addition, the spirit of MI focuses on recognizing and honoring client autonomy. Collaboration is expressed by developing a partner-like relationship with clients. The MI therapist seeks to draw out the client's intrinsic motivation to and capacity for change. Of course, this also indicates the therapist's strong belief the clients are motivated and capable of change. Finally, the spirit of MI dictates a belief in client autonomy and further allocation to the client of responsibility for change.

To examine the effect of MI on lifestyle changes and functioning among older adults, a comprehensive literature review was conducted in June 2007. PubMed, PsychINFO, Social Science Abstracts, Social Service Abstracts, and Sociological Abstracts were the databases searched. Search terms included MI or motivational enhancement therapy and elder, old adult*, aged, heart disease, chronic illness, diabetes, chronic diseases, smoking, diet, exercise, alcohol, hyperlipidemia, or hypertension. Only articles meeting the following criteria were included in this review: the average age of the sample must exceed 50 years, and the research design must be a randomized controlled study. A total of 15 studies investigating the effect of MI among older adults were identified and included in this review. Studies addressed diet, exercise, and weight control; chronic disease management; smoking; and alcohol consumption.

Diet, Exercise, and Weight Control

Debilitating conditions among older adults such as diabetes, heart disease, and some forms of cancer are often related to lifestyle choices and behaviors that are associated with inactivity, poor nutrition, and obesity. As such, it is not surprising that the preponderance of research related to the use of MI with older adults has been focused on the areas of diet, exercise, and weight control.

Three studies examined the use of MI to assist older adults suffering from adult-onset diabetes with weight and glycemic control issues. The most extensive study identified on this topic was conducted by West, DiLillo, Bursac, Gore, and Greened (2007). Researchers randomly assigned 217 overweight women with type 2 diabetes mellitus who were being treated with oral medications into either a treatment group or an attention-only control group. Both groups participated in a weight management program. Participants were recruited from 2000 to 2002 in Alabama. The average age of participants was 53 years (standard deviation [SD] = 10). The treatment group also received individual MI sessions lasting about 45 minutes with a licensed clinical psychologist before the first weight management program and then quarterly at 3, 6, 9, and 12 months. The clinical psychologist received weekly supervision of their MI skills, and audiotapes of intervention sessions were randomly reviewed. The attention-only control group met with health educators for the same amount of time to discuss female health issues. Findings revealed that individuals in both groups lost weight and experienced improved glycemic control ($p < .02$), but outcomes among individuals receiving MI were significantly better. Both groups regained weight. The weight regain began to occur at 6 months in the control group but was delayed until 12 months in the treatment group. Of note, in this study, MI appeared to be less effective among African Americans ($p < .001$). Overall, African Americans lost less weight than Caucasians, regardless of the group to which they were assigned.

Two smaller studies examining the use of MI among older adults with adult-onset diabetes yielded similar results. Jackson, Asimakopoulou, and Scammell (2007) randomly assigned 40 adults with type 2 diabetes mellitus, recruited from an outpatient clinic in the United Kingdom, into a treatment or control group to examine the effect of MI on physical activity. Participants' ages ranged from 34 to 75 years, with an average of 58 years in the intervention group and 62 years in the control group. Individuals in both groups received standard care and information, but individuals in the treatment group also received one face-to-face MI session at an outpatient clinic with a dietician who was trained in MI. Specific details regarding interventionist training were not provided. At 6 weeks, both groups reported increased physical activity. Frequency and duration of physical activity were significantly higher in the treatment group ($p <. 01$). Weight loss was not reported.

In a similar study, Smith, Heckemeyer, Kratt, and Mason (1997) examined the effect of MI on adherence with a weight control program among 21 females with non-insulin-dependent diabetes mellitus. The average age of participants was 62.4 years ($SD = 7$ years). Participants were randomly assigned into treatment or control group. Both groups participated in a weekly weight control program. Individuals in the treatment group also received three MI sessions with a psychologist experienced in MI. Training specifics were not provided. The treatment group had a statistically significant improvement in glucose control ($p < .05$), and statistically significant differences were found in attendance ($p < .01$), food dairy completion ($p < .01$), and blood glucose monitoring ($p < .05$), with better outcomes found in the treatment group. However, no difference was noted in weight loss between the two groups.

Diet, exercise, and weight control are especially important among individuals with heart disease. Two studies were identified that examined the use of MI among individuals with, or at risk for, heart disease. Brodie and Inoue (2005) studied the effect of MI on physical activity among 92 adults with chronic heart failure. Participants were recruited from patients receiving care at two hospitals in the United Kingdom. Participants ranged in age from 65 to 94 years (average = 79 years). Participants were randomly assigned into one of three groups: group one received standard care from a heart failure specialist nurse (nursing training in MI was not specified), group two was advised to exercise and participate in a MI program, and group three actually received MI from a researcher. In both groups two and three, the MI program consisted of eight 1-hour sessions. After 5 months, all groups significantly increased walking distances ($p < .001$). However, no significant difference in outcomes was found among the three groups.

A smaller study was conducted by Kreman, Yates, Agrawal, Fiandt, Briner, and Shurmur (2006) among 24 Caucasian rural livestock producers in the United States with high cholesterol—a known risk of heart disease. The average age of participants was 54 years and ranged from 39 to 67 years. The effect of a telephone-based MI intervention to encourage participants to improve their diet and exercise was examined. Participants were equally distributed and randomly assigned to either a treatment group receiving MI or an education- and attention-only control group. Both groups received standard educational material from the American Heart Association. A nurse, trained in MI, placed a phone call lasting 30–45 minutes to participants in both groups. Training specifics were not provided. The nurse used MI to motivate and encourage positive behaviors among the treatment group. When speaking with individuals in the control group, the nurse read a scripted review of the written materials and answered participant questions. Three months later, the treatment group had experienced a statistically significant decrease in their total cholesterol ($p = .017$), whereas the control group did not experience a significant decrease ($p = .10$).

Among 56 long-term cancer survivors, Bennett, Lyons, Winters-Stone, Nail, and Scherer (2007) examined the effect of MI

on increased physical activity. Participants ranged in age from 37 to 85, with an average age of 56 in the intervention group and 60 in the control group. Participants were randomly assigned to either a treatment or a control group. The treatment group received an initial face-to-face MI session with a master's-level physical activity specialist lasting about 24 minutes. The interventionist received 14 hours of training on group and individual MI techniques. Follow-up phone calls lasting about 10 minutes were made to individuals in the treatment group at 2 weeks, 2 months, and 4.5 months. The control group received two calls lasting less than 4 minutes reminding participants to come in for measurement. Although the treatment group was initially more inactive than the control group ($p = .04$), at 6 months they were significantly more active than those in the control group ($p < .01$).

Two additional studies were identified that examined the effect of MI on physical activity among participants with no specified diagnosis. Kolt, Schofield, Kerse, Garrett, and Oliver (2007) examined the effect of a telephone-based MI program on physical activity among 186 older adults. Participants were recruited from the primary care offices in New Zealand in 2003–2004. All participants were over the age of 65 years. The average age of the control group was 74.3 years ($SD = 5.9$), and it was 74.1 years ($SD = 6.2$) in the intervention group. Participants were equally divided and randomly assigned into a treatment and control group. The treatment group received eight scripted MI phone calls, lasting 10–16.5 minutes each, with an exercise counselor over 3 months. The specific training of the MI counselor was not discussed. The control group received no intervention. At the conclusion of the intervention, the treatment group reported a significant increase in physical activity ($p = .007$) and a statistically significant higher level of physical functioning ($p = .04$) than the control group.

Sims, Smith, Duffy, and Hilton (1998) also examined the effect of MI on physical activity among 20 older adults recruited from a suburban practice in the United Kingdom. The average age of participants was 72.2 years ($SD = 4.26$). After randomly assigning participants to a treatment or control group, the treatment group received both one MI session with a primary care nurse who had attended a 2-day MI training and two follow-up phone calls 2 and 6 weeks later, whereas individuals in the control group received usual care. Training specifics were not provided. No significant differences were observed between the two groups at the conclusion of the study.

Chronic Disease Management

Three studies were identified that examined the effect of MI on behaviors associated with the management of chronic diseases. A sample of 230 African American smokers with hypertension and a high risk of cardiovascular disease from an urban area in the southwestern United States were studied by Hyman, Pavilk, Taylor, Goodrick and Moye (2007) to determine the effect of MI on smoking, diet, and exercise. Participants were recruited from two primary care clinics in 2002–2004. Participants ranged in age from 45 to 64 years, with an average age of about 53 years. Subjects were randomly assigned to one of three groups. The simultaneous-treatment group was encouraged to stop smoking, decrease sodium intake, and increase physical activity altogether. Participants in the sequential treatment group were encouraged to address one problem behavior (smoking, sodium intake, or inactivity) at a time, with focus shifting to a different problem behavior every 6 months. The usual-care control group only received phone calls reminding them of measurement appointments. Both treatment groups received face-to-face counseling every 6 months with a health educator at a health clinic and MI phone calls lasting about 15 minutes at

2, 4, 6, 8, 10, 12, 16, and 20 weeks. Details regarding the training of interventionists are unknown. Researchers concluded that intervention aimed at addressing multiple behavior problems simultaneously was more successful than the sequential introduction of issues or usual care. At 6 months, individuals in the simultaneous treatment group had a greater decrease in sodium than did those in the control group ($p = .01$). At 18 months, smoking cessation was highest among the simultaneous group and approached significance (20% compared with 17% in the sequential group and 10% in the control group; $p = .08$).

McHugh, Lindsay, Hanlon, Hutton, Brown, Morrison, and Wheatley (2001) assessed the effect of MI on smoking, physical activity, weight, cholesterol levels, and blood pressure among 120 persons awaiting coronary artery bypass graft surgery. Participants were recruited from 47 physician's practices in the United Kingdom. The study was conducted in 1997 and 1998. Participant ages ranged from 35 to 77 years, with an average age of 63 in the control group and 61 in the intervention group. Participants were randomly assigned to either a treatment group receiving monthly health education and MI from nurses or a control group receiving usual care. Specific details regarding nurse training in MI were not provided. Significantly better outcomes were observed among the treatment group in the areas of smoking cessation ($p < .001$), weight ($p = .01$), physical activity ($p < .001$), and blood pressure ($p < .001$).

Bennett and colleagues (2005) examined the effect of MI on the health of 111 community-dwelling individuals with chronic diseases, including diabetes, lung disease, heart disease, arthritis, and neuromuscular disease in Oregon. The average age of participants in the intervention group was 71.2 years ($SD = 7.8$), and it was 69.2 years ($SD = 7.1$) in the control group. Participants were randomly assigned to either a control group receiving usual care from their physician or a treatment group receiving MI through a 1-hour face-to-face initial meeting with a bachelor's-level registered nurse and an average of seven phone calls lasting 3–45 minutes each over 6 months. Nurse interventionists received 24 hours of training in MI, which included instruction and role-playing. Longer phone calls occurred earlier in the program, and shorter phone calls later. At the conclusion of the study, the intervention group reported significantly less health distress ($p = .05$) and less illness interference ($p = .04$) than the control group.

Smoking Cessation

Three studies were identified that examined the use of MI on smoking cessation among older adults. Wakefield, Olver, Whitford, and Rosenfeld (2004) examined differences in cessation rates among 137 adults diagnosed with cancer. Participants were recruited from a single Australian hospital in 1999–2000. The average age of participants in the intervention group was 52.6 years ($SD = 13.8$), and it was 51.9 years ($SD = 11.5$) in the control group. Participants were randomly assigned to either a control group receiving standard written information about smoking cessation and referrals to a cessation hotline or a treatment group receiving an average of 11 contacts lasting about 18 minutes each with a counselor trained in MI, along with written materials. Specifics regarding counselor training were not provided. Individuals in the treatment group who smoked 15 cigarettes a day or more were offered nicotine replacement therapy (NRT). Six months postintervention, researchers found that the treatment group was more likely to use NRT ($p = .04$) and the written materials that were provided to them ($p = .04$), but no statistically significant differences in cessation rates were found between the treatment and control groups.

More positive results were reported by Hokanson, Anderson, Hennrikus, Landon, and Kendall (2006) in their evaluation of the effect of MI on smoking cessation among 114 smokers with adult-onset diabetes mellitus. Participants were recruited from a diabetes center in Minneapolis, Minnesota, in 2001–2004. The average age of participants in the treatment group was 54 years ($SD = 9$), and it was 53 years ($SD = 9$) in the control group. Participants were randomly assigned to either a treatment group or to a usual-care control group. The treatment group received one initial face-to-face session using MI and three to six brief follow-up phone sessions. Interventionists attended 12 hours of training on MI and smoking cessation, and ongoing support was available. If a participant in the treatment group did not express an interest in smoking cessation after two or three follow-up phone calls the counselor stopped calling and instructed them to call as needed. It is unclear whether or not these individuals were included in the follow-up analysis. Those expressing an interest in smoking cessation received more frequent follow-up phone calls. NRT was also offered to interested individuals in the treatment group. The usual-care control group received standard written information and referrals to local smoking cessation programs. Three months postintervention, fewer treatment group participants reported smoking than did those in the usual care group ($p = .077$). Fewer treatment group participants reported smoking daily compared to the usual-care group ($p = .048$). At 6 months, however, no significant differences were noted between the two groups.

Borrelli, Novak, Hecht, Emmons, Papandonatos, and Abrams (2005) reported similar results. Ninety-eight nurses from the Visiting Nurse Association in Rhode Island were randomly assigned to deliver either an MI intervention or standard care to 273 adult smokers receiving home case services from the association. Recruitment and intervention occurred from 1998 to 2003. The average age of participants was 57.2 years ($SD = 14.3$). Smokers in both groups received written materials especially designed for older and medically ill smokers. In addition, the treatment group received three in-person home visits lasting 20–30 minutes and follow-up phone calls employing MI from nurses trained in MI. Training involved role-playing and was delivered in small groups by a licensed clinical psychologists and a nurse educator. Individuals in the standard-care control group received only one visit lasting 5–10 minutes from the home health nurse, who focused on providing participants with standardized cessation guidelines. The treatment group reported significantly more attempts to stop smoking ($p < .05$) and a significant decrease in the number of cigarettes smoked daily ($p < .05$) when compared with the control group. Participants in the treatment group were twice as likely to report continuous abstinence compared with the control group as well. Unlike the study conducted by Hokanson and colleagues (2006), the effects of this MI-enhanced smoking cessation intervention were more long lasting. Borrelli and colleagues reported that at 2 months, 6 months, and 12 months postintervention, the statistically significant differences remained between the treatment and control group ($p < .05$).

Alcohol Consumption

Only one study was identified that examined the effect of MI on alcohol consumption among older adults. Gordon and colleagues (2003) examined the effect of brief interventions on hazardous drinking behavior among older adults aged 65 years or more (n = 45). Participants were recruited from 12 physicians' waiting rooms in western Pennsylvania from 1995 to 1997. Men who reported drinking 16 or more alcoholic beverages a week, women who reported drinking 12 or more alcoholic beverages a week, and individuals scoring eight or higher on the Alcohol Use Disorders Identification Test were considered hazardous drinkers.

Participants were randomly assigned to one of three groups: MI, brief advice, or usual care. Individuals receiving MI met with a bachelor's-level interventionist at their primary care physician's office for 45–60 minutes, where an interventionist used MI techniques to assist participants in creating goals to decrease alcohol consumption. The interventionist received a technique manual with training, supervision, and feedback. Participants were contacted on two additional occasions to encourage continued progress toward their stated goals. Individuals receiving brief advice also met with an interventionist at their physician's office, where participants were told of the consequences of hazardous drinking behavior and advised to reduce their drinking. The initial session lasted only 10–15 minutes with no follow-up sessions. The usual-care group received standard care from their physician and had no contact with interventionists. Among the older adults, researchers found a trend toward decreased alcohol consumption, but one intervention did not appear to be more affective than the other, and neither intervention was statistically different from the standard care group.

Summary

MI has been used to address a number of behavior problems associated with lifestyle choices among older adults. In the area of diet, exercise, and weight control, MI has been found to produce significant changes among older adults including short-term weight loss, increased frequency and duration of physical activity, decreased health distress, decreased sodium intake, improved glucose control, decreased blood pressure, and improved adherence to weight control programs. With regard to smoking cessation, all but one study found MI to be effective at increasing smoking cessation rates. Although racial and ethnic diversity was limited, at least one study reported that MI was less effective among African Americans. The studies reviewed produced conflicting results concerning the effectiveness of MI in helping clients achieve long-term sustained improvements in lifestyle and health behaviors. These variations in findings may be related to differences in the treatment dosage (amount of treatment) applied and the specific model of MI employed.

DISCUSSION AND APPLICATIONS TO SOCIAL WORK

Although limited in number, MI studies conducted with older adults do highlight the potential of this approach for achieving important behavioral changes in older clients. Given the serious negative effects that problematic behaviors exert on the health and well-being of older adults, such evidence should be seriously considered. These studies suggest that MI techniques are both acceptable to older adults and capable of producing change in a variety of health behaviors in a relatively brief period of time. Further, the studies conducted by Kolt and colleagues (2007) and Kreman et al. (2006) indicate that the effectiveness of MI treatment can be extended to telephone-based approaches. Several of the other studies reviewed earlier also used telephone contact as part of their intervention approach. Because of the functional impairments experienced by many adults as they age, interventions that can be conducted either partially or completely in the home environment are especially important to note.

The findings of this review indicate that MI and its derivatives can be useful in dealing with a range of issues faced by older adults. Given this, the integration of MI into social work courses focused on practice with older adults should be considered. Aging-related textbooks and course syllabi often discuss the usefulness of cognitive behavioral, problem-solving, reminiscence, and remotive therapies with older adults (Hooyman & Kiyak, 2008; Kropf & Tompkins, 2002). Few, however, make mention of MI. One of the most significant features of MI is the brief time period within which documented changes have occurred in clients' lives. Considering that gerontological social workers operate in a variety of setting (e.g., hospitals, medical clinics, senior centers, etc.) that often necessitate brief interventions, equipping students to provide promising brief treatments, such as MI, in fast paced environments is warranted. In addition, making training available for current practitioners working with older clients is also indicated.

Although MI approaches with older adults do hold promise, continued investigation is required. Beyond the need for a greater base of evidence concerning the efficacy of MI conducted with older adults, several of the findings noted raise issues that deserve further attention in future MI research studies. These include discussion of the half-life and dosing effects of MI, the fidelity of MI interventions, the utility of addressing multiple damaging health behaviors simultaneously, and racial differences in health outcomes. Several of the studies mentioned here indicate that treatment groups receiving MI experienced significant differences in behavior change at early follow-up points but that these changes dissipated over time (short half-life). However, among two of the most comparable studies (Borrelli et al., 2005; Hokanson et al., 2006) the MI "dose" (amount of treatment) delivered seemed to affect the half-life of the intervention. MI has long been touted for its brevity. However, this review suggests that there may be a minimum dose that is needed to enhance long-term efficacy with older adults. The studies reviewed here do not provide sufficient information to determine what dosage is needed to provide a sufficient behavior-change half-life. Further investigation is needed to determine the amount of treatment time needed to secure long-term behavioral change.

Although the majority of the studies reviewed here reported positive outcomes, conflicting findings do exist. One issue likely explaining some of the outcome differences noted in this review is the variation in the MI modalities employed. MI has been adapted to fit many different settings and to address a wide variety of problems. In their discussion of MI adaptations, Miller and Rollnick (2002) described two common interventions that, similar to MI, focus on motivation and behavioral change but differ in the nature of the client–worker relationship and in the type of change targeted. Behavior change counseling is a brief (5–30 minute) intervention that has a goal of building motivation to change and uses a more collaborative worker–client relationship. Brief advice is described as a very brief (5–15 minute) intervention in which the interventionist is in the role of an expert advice giver and the client is a passive receiver. The goal of MI is to not only initiate or establish motivation to change but also to develop the commitment to change. Without clear descriptions of the interventions employed in MI research studies, it is not possible to determine their adherence to the basic MI model or to effectively compare the findings. To enhance knowledge concerning MI effectiveness, it is critical that future studies provide a clear description of the intervention employed.

Hyman and colleagues (2007) compared a MI approach that addressed multiple symptoms contributing to chronic illness simultaneously to an approach that addressed these symptoms sequentially. As noted above, the simultaneous approach was superior across all measures. In social work practice, it is the exception rather than the rule that clients served are struggling to overcome one isolated issue. Typically, the problems people deal with are multicausal and comorbid. As discussed earlier, an essential change mechanism is enabling clients to develop a discrepancy between stated life goals and current behavior. In theory, then, addressing multiple problems that all impinge on the respondent's life goals would be the most expedient and effective course of action. The findings of Hyman

and colleagues (2007) provide beginning support for this.

Finally, one study indicated disparities in outcomes for older African American and Caucasian adults (West et al., 2007). Although this disparity was found in only one study, it is not clear whether demographic variables, such as race, were considered in other studies. Little information exists concerning the differential effect of MI by race or gender. This, however, is certainly an important issue. Given that social workers frequently serve low-income individuals and that racial/ethnic minorities and women are overrepresented in this population, studies that examine the effectiveness of MI with these groups are needed.

The studies contained in this review possessed several limitations such as small sample size, unspecified participant motivation to change, reliance on self-reported measures, and lack of participant diversity. Likewise, it should be noted that assessing the efficacy of a specific therapeutic approach by means of narrative review of the intervention literature does have its limitations. Meta-analysis, which provides a statistical amalgamation, summarization, and review of quantitative studies, can provide more objective evaluation of the evidence and a more precise estimate of treatment effect than can traditional narrative reviews (Egger & Davey Smith, 1997). However, to conduct a meaningful meta-analysis, a sizable number of primary research studies must first exist. Research on MI to promote behavioral change in older adults is still in the early stages.

In sum, existing studies of MI with older adults do provide beginning evidence of the effectiveness of this approach for affecting needed behavioral change among older adults with acute and chronic illnesses. The narrative review provided here suggests that MI with older adults can provide beneficial outcomes in terms of weight loss, smoking cessation, and improved diet and that continued MI intervention studies—and future statistical reviews of these studies—is warranted. Given the emerging body of evidence concerning MI and the serious negative consequences that problematic behaviors can have on the health and functioning of older adults, efforts should be made to introduce social work students and professionals to MI principles and techniques. Ongoing research is needed, however, to confirm and extend research findings. Because of the tremendous health, quality-of-life, and medical cost benefits that can be achieved through needed behavioral and lifestyle changes, ongoing research and the education of social work students and professionals on the use of MI with older adults is recommended.

REFERENCES

American Diabetes Association (2007). *Total prevalence of diabetes & prediabetes.* Retrieved April 27, 2007, from http://diabetes.org/diabetes-statistics/prevalence.jsp.

American Lung Association (2006). *Chronic obstructive pulmonary disease fact sheet.* Retrieved August 24, 2007, from http://www.lungusa.org/site/pp.asp?c=dvLUK9O0E&b=35020.

Beers, M. H. (2004). *The Merck manual of health & aging.* Whitehouse Station, NJ: Merck.

Bennett, J. A., Lyons, K. S., Winters-Stone, K., Nail, L. M., & Scherer, J. (2007). Motivational interviewing to increase physical activity in long-term care cancer survivors. *Nursing Research, 56,* 18–27.

Bennett, J. A., Perrin, N. A., Hanson, G., Bennett, D., Gaynor, W., Flaherty-Robb, M., et al. (2005). Healthy aging demonstration project: Nurse coaching for behavior change in older adults. *Research in Nursing & Health, 28,* 187–197.

Borrelli, B., Novak, S., Hecht, J., Emmons, K., Papandonatos, G., & Abrams, D. (2005). Home health care nurses as a new channel for smoking cessation treatment: Outcomes from project CARES (community-nurse assisted research and education on smoking). *Preventive Medicine, 41,* 815–821.

Brodie, D. A., & Inoue, A. (2005). Motivational interviewing to promote physical activity for people with chronic heart failure. *Journal of Advanced Nursing, 50,* 518–527.

Egger, M., & Davey Smith G. (1997). Meta-analysis: Potentials and promise. *British Medical Journal, 315,* 1371–1374.

Federal Interagency Forum on Aging-Related Statistics (2006). *Older Americans update 2006: Key indicators of well-being.* Hyattsville, MD: Author, 2006.

Fingerhood, M. (2000). Substance abuse in older people. *Journal of the American Geriatrics Society, 48,* 985–995.

Gordon, A. J., Consigliore, J., Maisto, S. A., McNeil, M., Kraemer, K. L., & Kelley, M. E. (2003). Comparison of consumption effects of brief interventions for hazardous drinking elderly. *Substance Use & Misuse, 38,* 1017–1035.

Hokanson, J. M., Anderson, R. L., Hennrikus, D. J., Landon, H. A., & Kendall, D. M. (2006). *The Diabetes Educator, 32,* 562–570.

Hooyman, N., & Kiyak, H. A. (2008). *Social gerontology* (8th ed.). Needham Heights, MA: Allyn & Bacon.

Hyman, D. J., Pavlik, V. N., Taylor, W. C., Goodrick, G. K., & Moye, Lemuel. (2007). Simultaneous vs. sequential counseling for multiple behavior change. *Archives of Internal Medicine, 167,* 1152–1158.

Jackson, R., Asimakopoulou, K., & Scammell, A. (2007). Assessment of the transtheoretical model as used by dietitians in promoting physical activity in people with type 2 diabetes. *Journal of Human Nutrition & Dietetics, 20,* 27–36.

Kolt, G. S., Schofield, G. M., Kerse, N., Garrett, N., & Oliver, M. (2007). Effect of telephone counseling on physical activity for low-active older people in primary care: A randomized, controlled trial. *Journal of the American Geriatrics Society, 55,* 986–992.

Kreman, R., Yates, B. C., Agrawal, S., Fiandt, K., Briner, W., & Shurmur, S. (2006). The effects of motivational interviewing on physiological outcomes. *Applied Nursing Research, 19*, 167–170.

Kropf, N. P., & Tompkins, C. J. (2002). *Teaching aging: Syllabi, resources, & infusion materials for the social work curriculum.* Alexandria, VA: Council on Social Work Education.

Miller, W. R., & Rollnick, S. (2002). *Motivation interviewing: Preparing people for change* (2nd ed.). New York: Guilford Press.

McHugh, F., Lindsay, G. M., Hanlon, P., Hutton, I., Brown, M. R., Morrison, C., et al. (2001). Nurse led shared care for patients on the waiting list for coronary artery bypass surgery: A randomized controlled trial. *Heart, 86*, 317–323.

National Cancer Institute (2007). *What you need to know about lung cancer.* National Cancer Institute (NCI) booklet [NIH Publication No. 07-1553]. Retrieved July 26, 2007, from http://www.cancer.gov/cancertopics/wyntk/lung.

National Institute on Alcohol Abuse and Alcoholism (2005). *Social work education for the prevention and treatment of alcohol use disorders.* Retrieved May 22, 2008, from http://pubs.niaaa.nih.gov/publications/Social/Module10COlderAdults/

Module%2010%20C%20Older%20Adults.ppt.

Rogers, C. (1961). *On becoming a person: A therapist's view of psychotherapy.* New York: Houghton Mifflin.

Sims, J., Smith, F., Duffy, A., & Hilton, S. (1998). Can practice nurses increase physical activity in the over 65s? Methodological considerations from a pilot study. *British Journal of General Practice, 48*, 1249–1250.

Smith, D. E., Heckemeyer, C. M., Kratt, P. P., & Mason, D. A. (1997). Motivational interviewing to improve adherence to a behavioral weight-control program for older obese women with NIDDM. *Diabetes Care, 20*, 52–54.

U.S. Census Bureau. *U.S. Census Bureau, Statistical Abstract of the United States: 2004-2005.* Retrieved May 22, 2008, from http://www.census.gov/prod/2004pubs/ 04statab/pop.pdf.

Wakefield, M., Olver, I., Whitford, H., & Rosenfeld, E. (2004). Motivational interviewing as a smoking cessation intervention for patients with cancer. *Nursing Research, 53*, 396–405.

West, D. S., DiLillo, V., Bursac, Z., Gore, S. A., & Greene, P. G. (2007). Motivational interviewing improves weight loss in women with type 2 diabetes. *Diabetes Care, 30*, 1081–1087.

13

TREATMENT APPROACHES FOR DRUG ADDICTION

NATIONAL INSTITUTE ON DRUG ABUSE

Drug addiction is a complex but treatable disease. It is characterized by compulsive drug craving, seeking, and use that persist even in the face of severe adverse consequences. For many people, drug abuse becomes chronic, with relapses possible even after long periods of abstinence. In fact, relapse to drug abuse occurs at rates similar to those for other well-characterized, chronic medical illnesses such as diabetes, hypertension, and asthma. As a chronic, recurring illness, addiction may require repeated episodes of treatment before sustained abstinence is achieved. Through treatment tailored to individual needs, people with drug addiction can recover and lead productive lives.

The ultimate goal of drug addiction treatment is to enable an individual to achieve lasting abstinence, but the immediate goals are to reduce drug abuse, improve the patient's ability to function, and minimize the medical and social complications of drug abuse and addiction. Like people with diabetes or heart disease, people in treatment for drug addiction will also need to change their behavior to adopt a more healthful lifestyle.

In 2006, 23.6 million persons aged 12 or older needed treatment for an illicit drug or alcohol use problem (9.6 percent of the persons aged 12 or older). Of these, 2.5 million (10.8 percent of those who needed treatment) received treatment at a specialty facility. Thus, 21.2 million persons (8.6 percent of the population aged 12 or older) needed treatment for an illicit drug or alcohol use problem but did not receive it. These estimates are similar to the estimates for 2005.*

Untreated substance abuse and addiction add significant costs to families and communities, including those related to violence and property crimes, prison

Authors' Note: This is a fact sheet covering research findings on effective treatment approaches for drug abuse and addiction. If you are seeking treatment, please call 1-800-662-HELP(4357) for information on hotlines, counseling services, or treatment options in your State. This is the Center for Substance Abuse Treatment's National Drug and Alcohol Treatment Service. Drug treatment programs by State also may be found online at www.findtreatment.samhsa.gov.

SOURCE: National Institute of Health, U.S. Department of Health and Human Services. Used with permission.

225

expenses, court and criminal costs, emergency room visits, healthcare utilization, child abuse and neglect, lost child support, foster care and welfare costs, reduced productivity, and unemployment.

The cost to society of illicit drug abuse alone is $181 billion annually.[1] When combined with alcohol and tobacco costs, they exceed $500 billion including healthcare, criminal justice, and lost productivity.[2,3] Successful drug abuse treatment can help reduce these costs in addition to crime, and the spread of HIV/AIDS, hepatitis, and other infectious diseases. It is estimated that for every dollar spent on addiction treatment programs, there is a $4 to $7 reduction in the cost of drug-related crimes. With some outpatient programs, total savings can exceed costs by a ratio of 12:1.

BASIS FOR EFFECTIVE TREATMENT

Scientific research since the mid-1970s shows that treatment can help many people change destructive behaviors, avoid relapse, and successfully remove themselves from a life of substance abuse and addiction. Recovery from drug addiction is a long-term process and frequently requires multiple episodes of treatment. Based on this research, key principles have been identified that should form the basis of any effective treatment program:

- No single treatment is appropriate for all individuals.

- Treatment needs to be readily available.

- Effective treatment attends to multiple needs of the individual, not just his or her drug addiction.

- An individual's treatment and services plan must be assessed often and modified to meet the person's changing needs.

- Remaining in treatment for an adequate period of time is critical for treatment effectiveness.

- Counseling and other behavioral therapies are critical components of virtually all effective treatments for addiction.

- For certain types of disorders, medications are an important element of treatment, especially when combined with counseling and other behavioral therapies.

- Addicted or drug-abusing individuals with coexisting mental disorders should have both disorders treated in an integrated way.

- Medical management of withdrawal syndrome is only the first stage of addiction treatment and by itself does little to change long-term drug use.

- Treatment does not need to be voluntary to be effective.

- Possible drug use during treatment must be monitored continuously.

- Treatment programs should provide assessment for HIV/AIDS, hepatitis B and C, tuberculosis, and other infectious diseases, and should provide counseling to help patients modify or change behaviors that place themselves or others at risk of infection.

- As is the case with other chronic, relapsing diseases, recovery from drug addiction can be a long-term process and typically requires multiple episodes of treatment, including "booster" sessions and other forms of continuing care.

EFFECTIVE TREATMENT APPROACHES

Medication and behavioral therapy, alone or in combination, are aspects of an overall therapeutic process that often begins with detoxification, followed by treatment and relapse prevention. Easing withdrawal symptoms can be important in the initiation of treatment; preventing relapse is necessary for maintaining its effects. And sometimes, as with other chronic conditions, episodes of relapse may require a return to prior treatment components. A continuum of care that includes a customized treatment regimen, addressing all aspects of an individual's life, including medical and mental health services, and follow-up options (e.g., community- or family-based recovery support systems) can be crucial to a person's success in achieving and maintaining a drug-free lifestyle.

Medications can be used to help with different aspects of the treatment process.

Withdrawal: Medications offer help in suppressing withdrawal symptoms during detoxification. However, medically assisted withdrawal is not in itself "treatment"—it is only the first step in the treatment process. Patients who go through medically-assisted withdrawal but do not receive any further treatment show drug abuse patterns similar to those who were never treated.

Treatment: Medications can be used to help re-establish normal brain function and to prevent relapse and diminish cravings throughout the treatment process. Currently, we have medications for opioid (heroin, morphine) and tobacco (nicotine) addiction, and are developing others for treating stimulant (cocaine, methamphetamine) and cannabis (marijuana) addiction.

Methadone and buprenorphine, for example, are effective medications for the treatment of opiate addiction. Acting on the same targets in the brain as heroin and morphine, these medications suppress withdrawal symptoms, and relieve craving for the drug. This helps patients to disengage from drug-seeking and related criminal behavior and be more receptive to behavioral treatments.

Buprenorphine: This is a relatively new and important treatment medication. National Institute on Drug Abuse (NIDA)-supported basic and clinical research led to its development (Subutex or, in combination with naloxone, Suboxone), and demonstrated it to be a safe and acceptable addiction treatment. While these products were being developed in concert with industry partners, Congress passed the Drug Addiction Treatment Act (DATA 2000), permitting qualified physicians to prescribe narcotic medications (Schedules III to V) for the treatment of opioid addiction. This legislation created a major paradigm shift by allowing access to opiate treatment in a medical setting rather than limiting it to specialized drug treatment clinics. To date, nearly 10,000 physicians have taken the training needed to prescribe these two medications, and nearly 7,000 have registered as potential providers.

Behavioral treatments help patients engage in the treatment process, modify their attitudes and behaviors related to drug abuse, and increase healthy life skills. Behavioral treatments can also enhance the effectiveness of medications and help people stay in treatment longer.

Outpatient behavioral treatment encompasses a wide variety of programs for patients who visit a clinic at regular intervals. Most of the programs involve individual or group drug counseling. Some programs also offer other forms of behavioral treatment such as:

- *Cognitive Behavioral Therapy*, which seeks to help patients recognize, avoid, and cope with the situations in which they are most likely to abuse drugs.

- *Multidimensional Family Therapy*, which addresses a range of influences on the drug abuse patterns of adolescents and is designed for them and their families.

- *Motivational Interviewing*, which capitalizes on the readiness of individuals to change their behavior and enter treatment.

- *Motivational Incentives* (contingency management), which uses positive reinforcement to encourage abstinence from drugs.

Residential treatment programs can also be very effective, especially for those with more severe problems. For example, therapeutic communities (TCs) are highly structured programs in which patients remain at a residence, typically for 6 to 12 months. Patients in TCs may include those with relatively long histories of drug addiction, involvement in serious criminal activities, and seriously impaired social functioning. TCs are now also being designed to accommodate the needs of women who are pregnant or have children. The focus of the TC is on the resocialization of the patient to a drug-free, crime-free lifestyle.

Treatment Within the Criminal Justice System can succeed in preventing an offender's return to criminal behavior, particularly when treatment continues as the person transitions back into the community. Studies show that treatment does not need to be voluntary to be effective. Research suggests that treatment can cut drug abuse in half, drastically decrease criminal activity, and significantly reduce arrests.[4]

Other information sources For more detailed information on treatment approaches for drug addiction and examples of specific programs proven effective through research, view NIDA's *Principles of Drug Addiction Treatment: A Research-Based Guide* at www.nida.nih.gov/PODAT/PODAT Index.html (English) or www.nida.nih.gov/PODAT/Spanish/PODAT Index.html (Spanish).

For information about treatment for drug abusers in the criminal justice system, view NIDA's *Principles of Drug Abuse Treatment for Criminal Justice Populations: A Research-Based Guide* at **www.drugabuse.gov/DrugPages/cj.html**.

Data Sources

*Data are from the National Survey on Drug Use and Health (formerly known as the National Household Survey on Drug Abuse), which is an annual survey of Americans age 12 and older conducted by the Substance Abuse and Mental Health Services Administration. This survey is available online at www.samhsa.gov and from the National Clearinghouse for Alcohol and Drug Information at 800-729-6686.

[1]Office of National Drug Control Policy. The Economic Costs of Drug Abuse in the United States: 1992–2002.

Washington, DC: Executive Office of the President (Publication No. 207303), 2004.

[2]Harwood, H. Updating Estimates of the Economic Costs of Alcohol Abuse in the United States: Estimates, Update Methods, and Data Report. Prepared by the Lewin Group for the National Institute on Alcohol Abuse and Alcoholism, 2000.

[3]Centers for Disease Control and Prevention. Annual Smoking–Attributable Mortality, Years of Potential Life Lost, and Productivity Losses — United States, 1997–2001. *Morbidity and Mortality Weekly Report* 54(25):625–628, July 1, 2005.

[4]The National Treatment Improvement Evaluation Study (NTIES): Highlights. DHHS Publication No. (SMA) 97-3159. Rockville, MD: U.S. Department of Health and Human Services, Substance Abuse and Mental Health Services Administration, Center for Substance Abuse Treatment, Office of Evaluation, Scientific Analysis and Synthesis, pp. 241–242. 1997.

14

METHAMPHETAMINE ABUSE IN THE UNITED STATES

Contextual, Psychological, and Sociological Considerations

MICHAEL T. SHREM

PERRY N. HALKITIS

NEW YORK UNIVERSITY

Abstract

Emerging behavioral research on methamphetamine suggests a growing public health concern no longer limited to specific regions of the United States. Given that current evidence-based treatments for addressing methamphetamine addiction have had limited success, there remains a need to further examine the efficacy of these approaches. Here, we synthesize the psychological research literature regarding the prevalence and correlates of methamphetamine use across all segments of the U.S. population, analyze the role that use of the drug plays in

Acknowledgments. This manuscript is informed, in part, by two of Dr. Halkitis' research investigations, Project BUMPS (NIDA Contract # R01DA13798) and Project Tina (funded by the 1999 American Psychological Foundation Placek Award). The authors would like to further acknowledge Kelly Green for her editorial assistance.

Competing Interests: None declared.

Author's note: Correspondence should be directed to: Perry N. Halkitis, PhD, New York University, 82 Washington Square East, Pless 553, New York, NY 10003, USA. [Tel. +1 212 998 5373; Fax +1 212 995 4048; e-mail: Pnh1@nyu.edu]

SOURCE: "Methamphetamine Abuse in the United States: Contextual, Psychological and Sociological Considerations" by Michael T. Shrem and Perry N. Halkitis. In the 2008 issue of *Journal of Health Psychology, 13*(5), 669–679. Used with permission.

relation to sexual risk-taking and consider implications for therapeutic interventions to address this drug addiction.

Keywords: addiction; methamphetamine; sexual risk-taking; treatment

INTRODUCTION

Methamphetamine use continues to evolve as part of a growing epidemic that has historically been rooted within the Western and Midwestern regions of the United States (Rawson, Anglin, & Ling, 2002). Recent trends have highlighted the emergence of methamphetamine within major cities on the East coast (Halkitis, Fischgrund, & Parsons, 2005; Halkitis, Parsons, & Stirratt, 2001; Halkitis, Parsons, & Wilton, 2003; Jacobs, 2002; Rawson et al., 2002), signifying the drug's outreach as having exceeded its original geographic specificity, and highlighting the importance of it being viewed as a long-term and widespread public health problem.

Methamphetamine, a stimulant colloquially known as 'crystal meth', 'crank', 'ice', 'chalk' or 'Tina', is a highly addictive substance that can be snorted, smoked, ingested orally or rectally and injected. It is a methyl derivative of amphetamine, and is a powerful psychostimulant that directly affects the autonomic nervous system and central nervous system even when taken in small amounts. Chronic use of high doses of methamphetamine may cause permanent neurological damage, as intense exposure has been shown to cause irreversible damage to neural-cell endings in rats, pigs, cats, and nonhuman primates (Halkitis, 2004). Long-term methamphetamine use has also been associated with the reduction of dopamine transporters that negatively affect motor coordination and memory (Nordahl, Salo, & Leamon, 2003), as well as reductions in serotonin levels, the brain chemical most associated with experiencing pleasure. Other long-term effects of methamphetamine use include weight loss, Parkinson's-like symptoms, deterioration of gums and teeth, toxicity of the kidneys and liver, prenatal complications and birth defects. In addition, the continuous

stimulation of the nervous system caused by methamphetamine has been shown to induce negative psychological states that include anxiety, confusion, insomnia, aggression, depression, paranoia, psychosis, and suicidal ideation (Perdue, Hagan, Thiede, & Velleroy, 2003; Rawson et al., 2000; Swalwell & Davis, 1999).

Much research supports a close association between methamphetamine use and sexual risk-taking especially within the gay community, where use of the drug has been on the rise for the last decade, seriously hampering HIV prevention efforts (Halkitis et al., 2001, 2003; Halkitis, Green, & Mourgues, 2005a; Harris, Thielde, McGough, & Gordon, 1993; Sorvillo et al., 1995). Furthermore, because of the hyper-sexual-inducing qualities of this substance, use of methamphetamine may exacerbate the transmission of other pathogens such as syphilis, gonorrhea and hepatitis, which have been transmitted at increased rates over the last several years in large metropolises such as New York City (Centers for Disease Control and Prevention, 2002; de Luise, Brown, Rubin, & Blank, 2000).

Significant comorbidity exists between psychopathology and use of methamphetamine (Conway, Swendsen, Rounsaville, & Merikangas, 2002; Matsumoto, Miyakawa, Yabana, Iizuka, & Kishimoto, 2000; Shoptaw, Peck, Reback, & Rotheram-Fuller, 2003), highlighting the importance of disentangling the personality, developmental and contextual factors which contribute to use of this drug. For example, psychiatric comorbidity, including depression, personality disorders and psychoses were found in almost 50 percent of the sample participants diagnosed with methamphetamine dependency (Committee on Opportunities in Drug Abuse Research, 1996, p. 108). Furthermore, some trait models of addiction have emphasized personality characteristics as the major contributing factor toward drug dependence (Petraitis, Flay, & Miller, 1995; Russell & Mehrabian, 1977), creating greater behavioral disinhibition/impulsivity, negative emotionality (i.e., high reactivity, pessimism) and positive emotionality (i.e., extraversion, sociability, agreeableness). Other models of addiction have focused on the synergistic effect of personality and primary socialization sources, including family, schools, the media and peer groups (Oetting, Deffenbeacher, & Donnermeyer, 1998).

The past decade has witnessed alarmingly widespread increases in methamphetamine use across all segments of the United States population, including increased use among adolescents (Johnston, O'Malley, & Bachman, 2003). Moreover, the negative physical and psychological effects of methamphetamine are not merely limited to users of the drug. Children of parents who use or produce methamphetamine are at significant risk for physical and emotional abuse, as well as neglect, malnourishment, parental abandonment and methamphetamine addiction (Swetlow, 2003). The effects of the current methamphetamine epidemic in the United States are far-reaching for our society, thus warranting scrutinized investigation that can better inform social policy and treatment efficacy, and provide a lens from which to consider the potential impact of this drug should it spread to Western Europe and non-industrialized sections of our world.

In what follows, we examine methamphetamine use in the United States from historical, sociological, and behavioral perspectives, with a specific emphasis on the psychological and contextual factors related to use of methamphetamine, and its impact on the mental health of individuals, with consideration to matters of treatment and public health.

HISTORICAL CONSIDERATIONS OF METHAMPHETAMINE

First synthesized by German scientists in the late 19th century, amphetamines, the general class of stimulants that includes methamphetamine, have had a history of pharmaceutical and recreational uses both domestically and abroad. In the United States, amphetamines were first introduced in the 1930s, when they were marketed as bronchial inhalers used to treat nasal congestion for allergies, asthma, and colds (Anglin, Burke, Perrochet, Stamper, & Dawd-Noursi, 2000). In 1937, an amphetamine tablet was introduced to treat narcolepsy (a spontaneous sleep disorder), and subsequent medical uses included reducing activity in hyperactive children and as an appetite suppressant targeted toward women trying to lose weight (Matsumoto et al., 2000). Amphetamines were first used as a recreational drug in the United States during the Depression and Prohibition by individuals looking for an alcohol substitute. They were also widely used during the Second World War among German, Japanese, and American troops, as a sleep inhibitor in order to keep the troops awake, alert, and energized. Amphetamines were similarly used by American soldiers throughout the Vietnam War to enhance performance and productivity. It has been documented that American soldiers used more amphetamines during the Vietnam War than the rest of the world's total use during the Second World War (Miller, 1997).

Popular and legal medical amphetamines were first linked to the production of methamphetamine during the original 'street speed scene' occurring in San Francisco in the 1950s. Methamphetamine was first illegally produced by outlawed 'biker clubs', many of whose members were veterans of war (i.e., the Second World War, and later the Korean and Vietnam Wars). Fueled by the demand for pharmaceutical amphetamine, illicitly manufactured powdered methamphetamine was first developed and used by the various members of the 'counter-culture street scene'. Since that time, there has been what can be considered three endemic periods of increased methamphetamine use: post-Second World War, the late 1960s through the 1970s and, most recently, the resurgence of methamphetamine use beginning in the mid-1990s.

There are several factors that distinguish the current period of increased methamphetamine prevalence from the previous epochs. First, while methamphetamine use has historically been limited geographically to the Pacific Rim, there has been a rapid spread of the drug's use to other geographic epicenters, including major eastern cities and Midwestern states (Halkitis et al., 2001, 2003). Second, new production methods using household and store-bought materials, as well as the rise of the Internet as a disseminator of information, provide increased access to the means for production, creating serious psychological and health-based implications for children living in these home-based laboratories, as well as those living in the surrounding areas. Third, the current epidemic comes at a time when HIV prevalence continues to be a major health threat within the U.S. population, and there is strong evidence supporting the relationship between methamphetamine use, increased sexual risk and HIV seroconversion, highlighting the increased risk factors inherent to this particular time frame (Frosch, Shoptaw, Huber, Rawson, & Ling, 1996; Halkitis, Green, & Carragher, 2006; Halkitis, Shrem, & Martin, 2005c; Reback & Ditman, 1997).

METHAMPHETAMINE USE ACROSS POPULATIONS

Methamphetamine use affects adult and adolescent populations and appears to transcend sociodemographic lines. Below we outline our current understanding of use in these segments of the population and consider correlates of use within each developmental cohort.

Adults

There are several indicators highlighting the increasing trend in methamphetamine use among the adult U.S. population. According to the National Survey on Drug Use and Health that samples the civilian, noninstitutionalized population of the United States (U.S. Department of Health & Human Services, 2003), 12.4 million Americans (5.2% of the population) reported having tried methamphetamine at least once in their lifetime. This number shows a marked increase from the 1994 estimate of 3.8 million. In the most recent sample, approximately 1.3 million (0.6%) reported using in the previous year and 607,000 (0.3%) reported use within the month prior to the survey. While the survey assessed individuals ages 12 and older, the majority of users were found to be adults between the ages of 18 and 34. Even more alarming, the Drug Abuse Warning Network (DAWN) reported progressively increasing methamphetamine-related episodes from hospital emergency departments in 21 metropolitan areas, ranging from 10,447 reports in 1999 to 17,696 reports in 2002 (Office of National Drug Control Policy, 2004). A further indication of more frequent use among adults is the increasing numbers of individuals seeking drug treatment for methamphetamine use. For example, in San Diego, an area known for its high prevalence of methamphetamine, approximately 37 percent of the drug treatment admissions were for stimulant use that included methamphetamine.

Behavioral characteristics associated with chronic methamphetamine use among adult populations include violent and aggressive behaviors, sexual risk-taking and impulsivity. In assessing a sample of 86 methamphetamine users, Wright and Klee (2004) found that 47 percent of their sample had reported committing a violent crime, and 62 percent reported ongoing problems with aggression related to their methamphetamine use. In another sample of 1,016 methamphetamine users seeking drug treatment, 80 percent of the women reported being a victim of domestic abuse or violence from their partner, and 73.3 percent of the overall sample reported a history of physical or sexual abuse at the hands of parents, siblings, partners, friends and/or strangers (Cohen et al., 2003). While methamphetamine has a reputation for inducing aggressive and violent behaviors, many abusers of the drug appear to have developmental histories of physical and sexual abuse that is often linked to abusive behavioral patterns in adulthood.

Heterosexual adult users. While much recent attention has been given to the sexual risk-taking of gay and bisexual methamphetamine using men, there has been little research with regard to the sexual risk-taking of heterosexual male and female methamphetamine users. However, in a recent study of HIV-negative, methamphetamine dependent heterosexual men and women, Semple, Patterson and Grant (2004) reported the mean number of unprotected vaginal sexual acts within the last two months to be approximately 22 (SD = 26.6). In this sample, one-third reported having anal sex using condoms only 25 percent of the time. While there is no non-methamphetamine using control group for comparison, the substance does appear to be related to sexual risk behaviors among the heterosexual population; these statistics parallel similar patterns among gay and bisexual men (Halkitis et al., 2001). Further research, modeled after current work within the gay and bisexual community, is recommended in order to assess the behavioral and contextual characteristics specific to heterosexual methamphetamine using HIV-positive and HIV-negative men and women.

In addition, there is a dearth of literature on the psychological profiles of heterosexual methamphetamine using men and women. However, recent data reported from the Methamphetamine Treatment Project (MTP), a multisite outpatient treatment study of adult methamphetamine using men and women, suggests that users of the drug also have a host of comorbid psychiatric conditions, including high levels of anxiety, depression, suicidality and psychotic symptoms (Zweben et al., 2004). This sample also reported

greater difficulty modulating their anger with a greater frequency of assault and weapons charges. Similarly, in a recent report released by the Centers for Disease Control & Prevention (2006), heterosexual male methamphetamine users were found to be more likely to have multiple sexual partners, have casual female partners, have female partners who inject drugs and have had anal intercourse with their female partners. Characteristically, men and women report their motivations for using methamphetamine to include wanting to get high, to gain more energy and to party (U.S. Department of Justice, 2003), again paralleling findings among gay and bisexual men (Halkitis et al., 2003). Women are more likely to report additional reasons for use including weight loss, increased sense of attractiveness and coping with difficult emotions (Gorman et al., 2003); there is further evidence among women that methamphetamine use is also likely to be seen among those with eating disorders (Matsumoto et al., 2000).

Gay and bisexual male adult users. Methamphetamine use is not confined to gay and bisexual men, however the majority of literature supports the increasing trend of methamphetamine use within this segment of the population, and much of the psychological research over the last decade is focused on the interplay of methamphetamine use and HIV in gay men (Hall, 1996; Mendelson & Harrison, 1996; Halkitis et al., 2003, 2005b). While methamphetamine prevalence rates have historically been documented to range between 5 percent and 25 percent of the gay and bisexual men surveyed, more current investigations, including the Seropositive Urban Men's Study (SUMS), a study of HIV-positive men who have sex with men (MSM), estimate the rate of methamphetamine use to be 11 percent, with respective rates of 17 percent and 7 percent in San Francisco and New York (Purcell, Parsons, Halkitis, Mizuno, & Woods, 2001). It should be noted that these data were collected in 1997, and in that time we have seen escalations in methamphetamine use along the East coast of the United States. For example, more current data indicate increasing frequencies of methamphetamine use among gay and bisexual men in New York City regardless of race, ethnicity, socioeconomic status (SES) or HIV status (Halkitis et al., 2003, 2005b). Furthermore, in a sample of gay and bisexual men frequenting gay social venues, Halkitis and Parsons (2002) estimated that 10 percent of their sample were using methamphetamine, and that 25 percent of the methamphetamine users in their sample reported first using the substance within the three months prior to their participation in the study, confirming the time frame of methamphetamine's emergence in New York City to be sometime in the mid- to late 1990s. In addition, a more recent longitudinal investigation found that among a sample of 450 club drug using gay and bisexual men, 64.6 percent (n = 293) reported using methamphetamine in the four months prior to assessment with a mean use of 11.76 days (SD = 19.24) (Halkitis et al., 2005b). These results further indicate increasing trends of methamphetamine use within certain segments of the population in New York City. Use among gay and bisexual men in the Western and Midwestern areas of the United States has a longer history (Freese, Obert, Dickow, Cohen, & Lord, 2000; Rawson et al., 2002). The San Francisco Department of Health (2004) recently estimated that 17 percent to 22 percent of gay men had used methamphetamine in the past 12 months.

The danger inherent to the drastic increases in methamphetamine use currently underway among gay and bisexual men is twofold, and shines the spotlight on what Halkitis et al. (2001) refer to as a 'Double Epidemic', the devastating physiological and psychological consequences of methamphetamine use, as well as its contribution to the increasing risk for HIV transmission. While research demonstrates that methamphetamine use is linked with high-risk sex among gay and bisexual men (Frosch et al., 1996; Halkitis et al., 2003, 2005b; Parsons & Halkitis, 2002; Paul, Stall, & Davis, 1993; Reback & Ditman, 1997; Stall, McKusick, Wiley, Coates, & Ostrow, 1986; Stall & Wiley, 1988, Woody et al., 1999), it appears to be layered with complex behavioral and psychologically driven motivations that vary depending on the contextual factors and the personality traits of those who use the drug (Halkitis et al., 2006). Across the board, behavioral motivations and outcomes for methamphetamine use within this demographic include social and sexual disinhibition, enhanced sexual desire, low rates of condom use, prolonged sexual activity and increased multiple and casual/anonymous sexual partners (Gorman, 1998; Hando & Hall, 1994; Molitor, Truax, Ruiz, & Sun, 1998). Psychological correlates of its use appear to be avoidant coping, including the avoidance of unpleasant emotions and physical pain, as well as a means to increase pleasant times with others (Halkitis & Shrem, 2006; Halkitis et al., 2005a, 2006).

At the same time, there appear to be differing motivations associated with use based on HIV serostatus. In examining a convenience sample of HIV-positive men who have sex with men (MSM), Semple, Patterson and Grant (2002) found that methamphetamine use was associated with sexual enhancement, as well as cognitive escapism from the negative feelings participants had associated with their HIV serostatus. Similarly, Halkitis et al. (2006) found that HIV-positive men were more likely to use methamphetamine to deal with social pressures and to avoid conflict with others. These studies suggest that there is most clearly an interaction between methamphetamine use and HIV serostatus, and this relationship confirms previously discussed ideas concerning the synergy of HIV and drug use epidemics. Compounding the dangers of methamphetamine use further are the barriers to HIV medication adherence caused by methamphetamine abuse. These include disruptions in sleeping and eating patterns, fears of mixing HIV medications with methamphetamine, and as a strategy for coping with the demanding nature of HIV medication schedules (Halkitis, Kutnick, & Slater, 2005b; Reback, Larkins, & Shoptaw, 2003).

While the overall rate of HIV infections among MSM has declined since the early years of the epidemic, there have been drastic increases over the last four years, with gay and bisexual men continuing to be at high risk for infection, accounting for 55 percent of estimated new AIDS diagnoses in 2002 (Centers for Disease Control and Prevention, 2002). While there appears to be a strong link between methamphetamine and sexual risk behaviors, there remains some question as to the direction of the relationship between the two. In examining 49 methamphetamine using gay/bisexual men, Halkitis et al. (2005c) found equivalent rates of unprotected sexual intercourse under conditions of methamphetamine use, other drug use (i.e., ecstasy, cocaine) and sobriety. These results may suggest that, in many instances, the same type of individual that actively engages in sexual risk behaviors is also drawn toward using methamphetamine. One hypothesis may be that sensation-seeking individuals are attracted to both the riskiest types of sexual behaviors, as well as the type of high that methamphetamine produces.

Adolescents

Both empirical and anecdotal evidence support increasing trends of methamphetamine use among school age and adolescent populations. While rates of methamphetamine use remained relatively stable between 1989 and 1992, recent data examining the prevalence of use among high school students show an increase of almost 50 percent over the last decade (Oetting et al., 2000). More specifically, data drawn from the National High School Senior Survey, a longitudinal investigation examining the prevalence of drug use among a sample of 15,929 public and private high school students, show that 4.4 percent of teens have tried methamphetamine in their lifetime. In terms of developmental stage, 6.2 percent of high school seniors report lifetime use, followed by 5.2 percent of 10th grade students and 3.9 percent of 8th grade students. Another nationwide report estimates even higher rates of high school student lifetime use at 7.6 percent, with high school boys reporting more frequent lifetime use than high school girls (8.3% vs 6.8%). These numbers represent a significant increase from the rate of 3.3 percent reported in 1991 (US Department of Justice, 2003). Demographic data from this sample showed American Indian and Hispanic teenagers as the most likely users of methamphetamine, followed by Asian Americans, Whites and Blacks. Overall, these data may underestimate the prevalence of methamphetamine among school age adolescents as they were collected solely from secondary school classrooms, and do not reflect methamphetamine use by high school dropouts. Research suggests that dropouts are more likely to engage in drug use than high school seniors (Gfroerer, 1993). Adolescents in school may also be less likely to report their drug use due to social desirability issues that they may associate with reporting accurately and honestly. In addition, methamphetamine use among teens and adolescents appears to be more severe in the midwestern regions of the country. Anecdotally, an expert of Juvenile Courts Services in Marshall County, Iowa, estimates that an alarming 33 percent of the county high school students had tried the drug (Koch Institute, http://www.kci.org/meth_info/ national_trend.htm).

There are sparse empirical data on the social, psychological and behavioral precursors, and risk factors specific to methamphetamine-using adolescents, highlighting the need for additional research in this area. The little work that has been done suggests that psychosocial precursors to methamphetamine use include a history of family instability and erratic home environments that include physical and sexual abuse, exposure to drug use and pre-existing adjustment and psychiatric disorders (Brook, Szandorowska, & Whitehead, 1976). Further, in a sample of 882 adult methamphetamine arrestees, 10 percent indicated that either their parents or other family members had introduced them to the drug, and 29 percent reported their parents to be substance users when they were children. Among this sample, the majority of whom reported their initial use to be in high school, stated that their motivations for initial use included experimentation (34%), peer pressure (25%), to get high (18%) and for increased energy (17%).

Socialization factors and risk perceptions may have a significant influence on adolescent methamphetamine use as well. Methamphetamine has historically received relatively sparse media coverage compared to alcohol, marijuana, and cocaine, and as a result, adolescents may not be as aware of the consequences of methamphetamine use. For example, a longitudinal survey of high school students shows a significant reduction in the perception of risk factors associated with methamphetamine and other drug use, and these decreases were positively correlated with more frequent rates of use (Johnston et al., 2003). Additionally, the social effects of methamphetamine lead many adolescents to start using the drug in party scenes to relieve social inhibitions, and improve self-confidence and self-esteem (Moss & Tarter, 1993). Other adolescents have reported feeling happier, being more aware of their surroundings, and possessing the ability to think faster when using methamphetamines (Moss & Tarter, 1993). The sexual characteristics of the drug may dissuade sexual inhibitions as well, resulting in more frequent sexual experimentation, which may lead to increased risk for sexually transmitted diseases and unwanted teenage pregnancy.

Children

Methamphetamine affects the well-being of children on multiple levels. Its ease of production using store-bought materials has led to a greater number of 'local entrepreneurs' producing the drug in clandestine laboratories, typically found in home kitchens, bathrooms, basements and abandoned buses. The latest data from a 2002 U.S. Department of Justice report show that a total of 2023 children were found residing in home-based methamphetamine laboratories, up from 976 children in 2001, and 216 in 2000 (Swetlow, 2003). This trend may be reflective of either an increase in production sites, and/or stronger law enforcement efforts launched at curtailing the production of methamphetamine, resulting in the discovery of more methamphetamine producing laboratories. In addition, 1,373 children were reported exposed to some form of chemical contamination. Limited exposure to the chemicals used for production can result in headaches, nausea, and dizziness. High exposure and chronic exposure may lead to more serious physical problems including respiratory damage, chemical burns, cancer, brain damage, and may also negatively impact the liver, kidney, spleen, and immunologic system. Children living in these homes are also at greater risk for exposure to discarded needles and drug paraphernalia, fires and explosions, and hazardous life-style conditions (e.g., explosives, booby traps, loaded weapons, unsanitary living conditions).

The psychological repercussions for children living in these homes are devastating as well. Children raised in these environments experience stress and trauma that retard their emotional and cognitive functioning resulting in a host of behavioral problems that are not limited to, but may include, low self-esteem, shame, poor social skills and peer relations, increased risk for teenage pregnancy, and school failure (Oishi, West, &

Stuntz, 2000). In addition, because many of these methamphetamine-producing parents are users of the drug as well, these children are at increased risk for physical and sexual abuse, resulting in the greater likelihood of an attachment disorder, which manifests itself in the inability to trust, form meaningful relationships, and an impaired ability to adapt (Drug Endangered Children Resource Center, 1999). In addition, children with attachment disorders are at greater risk for antisocial and illegal behaviors as they enter adulthood (Fonagy et al., 1997).

Prenatal exposure to methamphetamine also poses serious health risks to newborn children. For example, the state of Iowa estimates that drugs affect 4,000 new infants each year, citing that in 90 percent of these cases the drug is methamphetamine (Lucas, 1997). The results to the newborn can be devastating, and may include premature birth, growth retardation, abnormal reflexes, extreme irritability, physical trembling, feeding difficulties, aversion to touch, and other withdrawal type symptoms. The prenatal exposure to methamphetamine may also have longitudinal effects. A study that followed children who had intrauterine exposure to methamphetamine were found in adolescence to exhibit higher levels of aggression and school failure, and have greater difficulty adjusting to their environment (Lucas, 1997). These children are at great physical and psychological risk, and as methamphetamine prevalence remains on the rise, there is little reason to believe that the increasing trend in the number of children exposed to these conditions will subside, furthering the urgency for effective and immediate prophylactic and therapeutic intervention.

TREATMENT CONSIDERATIONS FOR METHAMPHETAMINE ADDICTION

The complex interaction between intrapsychic, environmental and behavioral factors makes methamphetamine dependence a difficult disorder to treat. Exacerbating the obstacles to recovery are severe withdrawal symptoms that include severe anhedonia and depression, as well as intense cravings for the drug that can be spurred on by environmental cues operating on the principles of classical stimulus–response conditioning (Rawson et al., 2002). These symptoms are antithetical to the intense 'rush' and feelings of empowerment that methamphetamine provides. What logically follows is a vicious cycle whereby methamphetamine users revert back to their use to combat the intense dysphoric experience associated with withdrawal. In reality, they are perpetuating their dependence and increasing the likelihood that they will experience more frequent depressive symptomatology, further intensifying their craving for the drug, influencing them to return to it as a form of self-medication to alleviate their depressive withdrawal symptoms.

Our comprehensive review of the literature demonstrates the debilitating effects of methamphetamine as transcending age, race, gender, and sexual orientation, as it is layered with complex psychological states and behavioral interactions. As the field of psychology continues to move toward structured evidence-based treatments in which the main focus is to target maladaptive behaviors, emphasizing the restructuring of cognitive processes and providing proactive coping strategies, it seems critical to the efficacy of any treatment approach to keep a watchful eye on the more dynamic and affective processes underlying drug using behaviors, particularly if it is determined that the psychiatric disorder predates the drug using behaviors. While there is a great deal of merit and empirical support for the efficacy of current manualized treatment protocols in transforming maladaptive behaviors, including methamphetamine use, specific drug using behaviors do not exist in a vacuum, and contribute and interact within a larger landscape that makes up the individual personality. This has been demonstrated by the comorbid psychological conditions, traumatized developmental histories and anti-social behaviors so often associated with methamphetamine abuse. Other factors such as sexual identity, cultural identity, adolescent identity, HIV serostatus, and gender interact with the psychological motivations to use methamphetamine and can also be overlooked when therapists are encouraged to adhere to rigid and inflexible treatment protocols.

Several recommendations should be considered for further investigation. First, in order to best understand the individual behavioral motivations, it is essential to know the 'whole' person, and treatment protocols could be informed by a complete developmental history and assessment of personality in determining best practices for treatment. Also, previous research has demonstrated marked behavioral, contextual, and psychological differences based on the frequency, intensity, and method of administration associated with methamphetamine use (Semple, Patterson, & Grant, 2003). It is recommended that these factors be assessed prior to therapeutic intervention to determine the progression of methamphetamine use and its interrelationship with maladaptive behaviors, negative psychological states, and severity of withdrawal symptoms that so often influence treatment retention. Finally, methamphetamine use is often used to manage negative affective states, providing an illusion of control over what might otherwise be considered unpredictable and overwhelming feelings. In addition, chronic methamphetamine use has the ability to distort cognitive functioning and impact an individual's ability to recognize and appropriately express emotions. While newer treatments have begun utilizing person-centered, group and family therapeutic approaches, consideration also could be given to the integration of insight-oriented therapeutic components into treatment protocols in order to provide therapeutic flexibility when dealing with these psychologically complex and multidimensional issues.

Recently, mindfulness meditation has emerged as a core psychotherapeutic technique adaptable to both cognitive and psychodynamic approaches. Mindfulness has been described as a state of detached awareness, where an individual is able to sit with stillness, examining all aspects of themselves in a nonjudgmental and non-threatening way. As a therapeutic modality, mindfulness promotes psychological flexibility and insight, and integrates many of the free associations and cognitive restructuring that is common to both directive and nondirective clinical approaches (Martin, 1997).

While mindfulness-based therapies have proven to be beneficial in other areas, including stress and anxiety reduction, the treatment of borderline personality disorder, depression relapse, and in the rehabilitation of physically ill patients, with the exception of Marlatt (2002), limited attention has been given to its potential in the area of addiction. Based on the psychological motivations to use methamphetamine as an escape, to cognitively disassociate and avoid dealing with negative emotions and manage social anxiety, the detached awareness associated with mindfulness may provide a safe way for these individuals to examine their thoughts, feelings, behaviors, and perceptions. In addition, mindfulness has been described as a consciousness-absorbing process, and is associated with neurological plasticity and benefits that include the promotion of positive emotions (Davidson et al., 2004; Goleman, 2003). These features may provide an alternative experience to the euphoric states associated with methamphetamine use, and could help counteract the neurological and chemical imbalances caused by chronic methamphetamine use, helping to relieve the depressive and aggressive symptomatology associated with withdrawal. Thus, future research regarding the treatment of methamphetamine should assess the efficacy of mindfulness-based therapies in affecting change.

REFERENCES

Anglin, M. D., Burke, C., Perrochet, B., Stamper, E., & Dawd-Noursi, S. (2000). History of the methamphetamine problem. *Journal of Psychoactive Drugs, 32*(2), 137–141.

Brook, R., Szandorowska, B., & Whitehead, P. C. (1976). Psychosocial dysfunctions as precursors to amphetamine abuse among adolescents. *Addictive Diseases: An International Journal, 2*(3), 465–478.

Centers for Disease Control and Prevention. (2002). Primary and secondary syphilis among men who have sex with men—New York City. *Morbidity and Mortality Weekly Report, 51*, 853–856.

Centers for Disease Control and Prevention. (2006). Methampetamine use and HIV risk behaviors among heterosexual men: Preliminary results from five Northern California counties, December 2001–November 2002. *Morbidity and Mortality Weekly Report, 55*(1), 273–277.

Cohen, J. B., Dickow, A., Horner, K., Zweben, J. E., Balabis, J., Vandersloot, D., & Reiber, C. (2003). Abuse and violence history of men and women in treatment for methamphetamine dependence. *American Journal of Addiction, 12*, 377–385.

Committee on Opportunities in Drug Abuse Research (Division of Neuroscience and Behavioral Health & Institute of Medicine). (1996). *Pathways of addiction: Opportunities in drug abuse research.* Washington, DC: National Academy Press.

Conway, K. P., Swendsen, J. D., Rounsaville, B. J., & Merikangas, K. R. (2002). Personality, drug of choice, and comorbid psychopathology among substance abusers. *Drug & Alcohol Dependence, 65*(3), 225–234.

Davidson, R., Kabat-Zinn, J., Schumacher, J., Rosenkranz, M., Muller, D., Santorelli, S., et al. (2004). Alterations in brain and immune function produced by mindfulness meditation. *Psychosomatic Medicine, 66*, 564–570.

de Luise, C., Brown, J., Rubin, S., & Blank, S. (2000). *Emerging patterns in primary and secondary syphilis among men: NYC: January—September 2000.* New York City: Department of Health & Mental Hygiene.

Drug Endangered Children Resource Center. (1999). *Medical protocols for children found at methamphetamine lab sites.* Los Angeles, CA: Drug Endangered Children Resource Center.

Fonagy, P., Target, M., Steele, M., Steele, H., Leigh, T., Levinson, A., et al. (1997). Morality, disruptive behavior, borderline personality disorder, crime and their relationship to security of attachment. In L. Atkinson & K. J. Zucker (Eds.), *Attachment and psychopathology* (pp. 223–274). New York: Guilford Press.

Freese, T. E., Obert, J., Dickow, A., Cohen, J., & Lord, R. H. (2000). Methamphetamine abuse: Issues for Special Populations. *Journal of Psychoactive Drugs, 32*(2), 177–182.

Frosch, D., Shoptaw, S., Huber, A., Rawson, R. A., & Ling, W. (1996). Sexual HIV risk among gay and bisexual male methamphetamine abusers. *Journal of Substance Abuse Treatment, 3*, 483–486.

Gfroerer, J. (1993). *An overview of the national household survey on drug abuse and related methodological research.* Proceedings of the Survey Research Section of the American Statistical Association, Joint Statistical Meetings, Boston, MA, August.

Goleman, D. (2003). *Destructive emotions. How can we overcome them?* New York: Bantom Dell.

Gorman, M. (1998). A tale of two epidemics: HIV and stimulant use. *FOCUS, 13*, 1–8.

Gorman, E. M., Clark, C. W., Nelson, K. R., Applegate, T., Amato, E., & Scrol, A. (2003). A community social work study of methamphetamine use among women: Implications for social work practice, education and research. *Journal of Social Work Practice in the Addictions, 3*(3), 41–62.

Halkitis, P. N. (2004). *Methamphetamine: Strategies for prevention, harm reduction and treatment.* Paper presented at the Boston Department of Health, Boston, MA, April.

Halkitis, P. N., Fischgrund, B. N., & Parsons, J. T. (2005). Explanations for methamphetamine use among gay and bisexual men in New York City. *Substance Use and Misuse, 40,* 1–15.

Halkitis, P. N., Green, K. A., & Carragher, D. (2006). Methamphetamine use, sexual behavior, & HIV seroconversion. *Journal of Gay and Lesbian Psychotherapy, 10*(3/4), 95–109.

Halkitis, P. N., Green, K. A., & Mourgues, P. (2005a). Longitudinal investigation of methamphetamine use among gay and bisexual men in New York City: Findings from Project BUMPS. *Journal of Urban Health, 82*(1, Supp. 1), i18–i25.

Halkitis, P. N., Kutnick, A., & Slater, S. (2005b). The social realities of adherence to protease inhibitor regimens: Substance use, health care, & psychological states. *Journal of Health Psychology, 10*(4), 545–558.

Halkitis, P. N., & Parsons, J. T. (2002). Recreational drug use and HIV sexual risk behavior among men frequenting urban gay venues. *Journal of Gay and Lesbian Social Services, 14*(4), 19–38.

Halkitis, P. N., Parsons, J. T., & Stirratt, M. J. (2001). A double epidemic: Crystal methamphetamine drug use in relation to HIV transmission among gay men. *Journal of Homosexuality, 41*(2), 7–35.

Halkitis, P. N., Parsons, J. T., & Wilton, L. (2003). An exploratory study of contextual and situational factors related to methamphetamine use among gay and bisexual men in New York City. *Journal of Drug Issues, 33*(2), 413–432.

Halkitis, P. N., & Shrem, M. T. (2006). Psychological differences between binge and chronic methamphetamine using gay and bisexual men. *Addictive Behaviors, 31,* 549–552.

Halkitis, P. N., Shrem, M. T., & Martin, F. (2005c). Sexual behavior patterns of methamphetamine using gay and bisexual men in New York City. *Substance Use and Misuse, 40,* 703–719.

Hall, W. (1996). What have population surveys revealed about substance use disorders and their co-morbidity with other mental disorders? *Drug & Alcohol Review, 15*(2), 157–170.

Hando, J., & Hall, W. (1994). HIV risk-taking behavior among amphetamine users in Syndey, Australia. *Addiction, 89,* 79–85.

Harris, N. V., Thiede, H., McGough, J. P., & Gordon, D. (1993). Risk factors for HIV infection among injecting drug users: Results of blinded surveys in drug treatment centers, King County, Washington 1988–1991. *Journal of Acquired Immune Deficiency Syndromes, 6,* 1275–1282.

Jacobs, A. (2002). In clubs, a potent drug stirs fears of an epidemic. *New York Times,* 29 January, p. B1.

Johnston, L. D., O'Malley, P. M., & Bachman, J. G. (2003). *Monitoring the future of: National results on adolescent drug use; overview of key findings.* Bethesda, MD: National Institute on Drug Abuse.

Koch Institute. http://www.kci.org/meth_info/national_trend.htm.

Lucas, S. E. (1997). *Proceedings of the national consensus meeting on the use, abuse and sequalae of abuse of methamphetamine with implications for prevention, treatment and research.* Publication No. SMA 96–801 3. Rockville, MD: U.S. Department of Health and Human Services.

Marlatt, G. (2002). Buddhist philosophy and the treatment of addictive behavior. *Cognitive and Behavioral Practice, 9,* 44–50.

Martin, J. (1997). Mindfulness: A proposed common factor. *Journal of Psychotherapy Integration, 7*(4), 291–312.

Matsumoto, T., Miyakawa, T., Yabana, T., Iizuka, H., & Kishimoto, H. (2000). A clinical study of comorbid eating disorders in female methamphetamine abusers: First report. *Seishin Igaku, 42*(11), 1153–1160.

Mendelson, B., & Harrison, L. (1996). Drug trends in Denver and Colorado. *Proceedings of the community epidemiology work group public health service, NIDA, 2*, 52–67.

Miller, M. A. (1997). History and epidemiology of methamphetamine abuse in the United States. In H. Klee (Ed.), *Amphetamine misuse* (pp. 113–133). Amsterdam: Harwood Academic Publishers.

Molitor, F., Truax, S., Ruiz, J., & Sun, R. (1998). Association of female methamphetamine use during sex with risky sexual behaviors and HIV infection among non-injectors drug users. *Western Journal of Medicine, 168*(2), 93–97.

Moss, H. B., & Tarter, R. E. (1993). Substance abuse, aggression, and violence: What are the connections? *American Journal on Addictions, 2*(2), 149–160.

Nordahl, T. E., Salo, R., & Leamon, M. (2003). Neuropsychological effects of chronic methamphetamine use on neurotransmitters and cognition: A review. *Journal of Neuropsychiatry and Clinical Neurosciences, 13*(3), 317–325.

Oetting, E. R., Deffenbeacher, J. L., & Donnermeyer, J. F. (1998). Primary socialization theory: The role played by personal traits in the etiology of drug use and deviance II. *Substance Use & Misuse, 33*(6), 1337–1366.

Oetting, E. R., Deffenbeacher, J. L., Taylor, M. J., Luther, N., Beauvais, F. M., & Edwards, R. W. (2000). Methamphetamine use by high school students: Recent trends, gender, and ethnicity differences, and use of other drugs. *Journal of Child and Adolescent Substance Abuse, 10*, 33–50.

Office of National Drug Control Policy. (2004). *Methamphetamine: Facts and figures.* Retrieved March 9, 2004, from http://www.white housedrugpolicy.gov/DrugFact/ methamphetamine/index.html.

Oishi, S. M., West, K. M., & Stuntz, S. (2000). *Drug endangered children health and safety manual.* West Los Angeles, CA: Drug Endangered Children Resource Center, May.

Parsons, J. T., & Halkitis, P. N. (2002). Sexual and drug-using practices of HIV-positive men who frequent public and commercial sex environments. *AIDS Care, 14*(6), 815–826.

Paul, J. P., Stall, R., & Davis, F. (1993). Sexual risk for HIV transmission among gay/bisexual men in substance-abuse treatment. *AIDS Education & Prevention, 5*, 11–24.

Perdue, T., Hagan, H., Thiede, H., & Velleroy, L. (2003). Depression and HIV risk behavior among Seattle-area injection drug users and young men who have sex with men. *AIDS Education and Prevention, 15*(1), 81–92.

Petraitis, J., Flay, B. R., & Miller, T. Q. (1995). Reviewing theories of adolescent substance use: Organizing pieces in the puzzle. *Psychological Bulletin, 117*, 67–86.

Purcell, D. W., Parsons, J. T., Halkitis, P. N., Mizuno, Y., & Woods, W. J. (2001). Substance use and sexual transmission risk behavior of HIV-positive men who have sex with men. *Journal of Substance Abuse, 13*(1–2), 185–200.

Rawson, R. A., Anglin, M. D., & Ling, W. (2002). Will the methamphetamine problem go away? *Journal of Addictive Diseases, 21*, 5–19.

Rawson, R., Huber, A., Brethen, P., Obert, J., Gulati, V., Shoptaw, S., & Ling, W. (2000). Methamphetamine and cocaine users: Differences in characteristics and treatment retention. *Journal of Psychoactive Drugs, 32*(2), 233–238.

Reback, C., & Ditman, D. (1997). *The social construction of a gay drug: Methamphetamine use among gay and bisexual males in Los Angeles.* Report funded by the City of Los Angeles.

Reback, C. J., Larkins, S., & Shoptaw, S. (2003). Methamphetamine abuse as a barrier to HIV medication adherence among gay and bisexual men. *AIDS Care, 15*(6), 775–785.

Russell, J. A., & Mehrabian, A. (1977). Environmental effects on drug use. *Environmental Psychology & Nonverbal Behavior, 2*(2), 109–123.

San Francisco Department of Health. (2004). www.dph.sf.ca.us/PHP/AIDSSurvUnit.htm.

Semple, S., Patterson, T. L., & Grant, I. (2002). Motivations associated with methamphetamine use among HIV+men who have sex with men. *Journal of Substance Abuse Treatment, 22*(3), 149–156.

Semple, S., Patterson, T. L., & Grant, I. (2003). Binge use of methamphetamine among HIV-positive men who have sex with men: Pilot date and HIV prevention implications. *AIDS Education & Prevention, 15*(2), 133–147.

Semple, S., Patterson, T. L., & Grant, I. (2004). The context of sexual risk behaviour among heterosexual methamphetamine users. *Addictive Behaviors, 29*(4), 807–810.

Shoptaw, S., Peck, J., Reback, C. J., & Rotheram-Fuller, E. (2003). Psychiatric and substance dependence comorbidities, sexually transmitted diseases, and risk behaviors among methamphetamine-dependent gay and bisexual men seeking outpatient drug abuse treatment. *Journal of Psychoactive Drugs, 35*, 161–168.

Sorvillo, F., Kerndt, P., Cheng, K., Beall, G., Turner, P. A., Beer, V. L. et al. (1995). Emeriging patterns of HIV transmission: The value of alternative surveillance methods. *AIDS, 9*, 625–629.

Stall, R., McKusick, L., Wiley, J., Coates, T. J., & Ostow, D. G. (1986). Alcohol and drug use during sexual activity and compliance with safe sex guidelines for AIDS: The AIDS behavioral research project. *Health Education Quarterly, 13*(4), 1986, 359–371.

Stall, R., & Wiley, J. (1988). A comparison of alcohol and drug use patterns of homosexual and heterosexual men: The San Francisco men's health study. *Drug & Alcohol Dependence, 22*(1–2), 63–73.

Swalwell, C., & Davis, G. (1999). Methamphetamine as a risk factor for acute aortic dissection. *Journal of Forensic Science, 44*, 23–26.

Swetlow, K. (2003). *Children at clandestine methamphetamine labs: Helping meth's youngest victims.* Retrieved November 1, 2003 from http://www.ojp.usdoj.gov/ovc/publications/bulletins/children/welcome.html.

United States Department of Justice. (2003). *Meth awareness.* Washington, DC: United States Department of Justice. Retrieved May 5, 2004, from http://www.usdoj.gov/methawareness.

United States Department of Health and Human Services (Substance Abuse and Mental Health Services Administration). (2003). *National survey on drug use and health: Results.* Retrieved November 1, 2004 from http://www.oas.samhsa.gov/nhsda/2k3nsduh/2k3Results.htm#toc.

Woody, G. E., Donnell, D., Seage, G. R., Metzger, D., Marmor, M., Koblin, B. A. et al. (1999). Non-injection substance use correlates with risky sex among men having sex with men: Data from HIVNET. *Drug & Alcohol Dependence, 53*(3), 197–205.

Wright, S., & Klee, H. (2004). Violent crime, aggression, and amphetamine: What are the implications for drug treatment services? *Drugs: Education, Prevention & Policy, 8*, 73–90.

Zweben, J. E., Cohen, J. B., Christian, D., Galloway, G. P., Salinardi, M., Parent, D., & Iguchi, M. (2004). Psychiatric symptoms in methamphetamine users. *American Journal on Addictions, 13*(2), 181–190.

Michael T. Shrem, PsyD, was a Research Assistant at the Center for Health, Identity, Behavior & Prevention Studies at New York University at the time this manuscript was authored.

Perry N. Halkitis, PhD, is Professor of Applied Psychology and Director of the Center for Health, Identity, Behavior & Prevention Studies, the Steinhradt School of Culture, Education and Human Development, New York University.

CRITICAL THINKING QUESTIONS

Reading 10

1. Do you get the impression that the authors of this selection are arguing against treatment? Why or why not?

2. According to the authors, we can learn of factors that can be incorporated into treatment through a study of natural recovery. What are some of these factors?

3. Discuss the significance of the unexpectedly quick recovery of U.S. soldiers following heavy drug use in the Vietnam War?

4. Drawing on the principle of evidence-based practice, how would you design a research investigation to measure the prevalence that natural recovery occurs among youths?

Reading 11

1. How is the *spirit* of MI different from the technique?

2. Differentiate motivational from confrontational strategies.

3. Consider how an intervention designed to treat substance-abusing clients can also be used for victims of domestic violence.

Reading 12

1. Compare the approach the authors of this paper take to examine the merits of motivational interviewing with Wahab's approach in the previous reading. Do you prefer one to the other?

2. Note the method used by the authors to obtain evidence-based research papers. Discuss other possible research areas for which this contemporary method of locating relevant literature might be productive.

3. Summarize the findings of 230 African American smokers used with two treatment approaches. Was the use of a control group necessary? Discuss the significance of the findings for treatment providers.

4. Of the studies from the research literature summarized in this article, which one did you find the most significant? Discuss the reasons for your choice.

5. From an evidence-based standpoint what were some of the limitations of the various studies examined, according to the authors?

Reading 13

1. Describe the various medications singled out in the NIDA report.

2. Check out NIDA on their website (www.drugabuse.gov) and describe the possible uses of this resource.

3. What are the advantages of Buprenorphine over methadone?

4. Review the various treatments described in the reading and consider the social and economic advantages to society in increased treatment availability.

Reading 14

1. Which of the long-term effects of methamphetamine (meth) do you find the most disturbing personally? How do the authors explain the sexual risk-taking associated with users of this drug?

2. What did you learn from this article that was the most surprising?

3. Compare the use of meth today with its use historically.

4. Discuss gender and sexual identity differences in the use of this drug.

5. Note the references to *anhedonia* during abstinence. What does this term mean?

PART V

POLICY CONSIDERATIONS

The key American values are generally listed as moralism, individualism, competition, and equal opportunity. Given these core values, the United States can be expected to respond to illicit drug use and alcoholism without a great deal of compassion. And it is true that the U.S. has the highest incarceration rate in the world and the highest incarceration rate for drug-related violations in the world.

And yet, even while the prison population continues to grow, there are some welcome changes in the wind. For one, there is a growing acceptance by the public of alternative responses to persons in trouble with drugs other than imprisonment. We are speaking of harm reduction policies to help people survive and overcome their difficulties. A second major and related development is the proliferation of drug courts across the nation. These courts are not courts in the usual sense, but they are often overseen by judges who monitor the progress and treatment of drug addicts who have been convicted of drug-related crime. This section on policy considers such innovations and the evidence that is presented pertaining to their effectiveness. What these approaches have in common is that they are pragmatic rather than moralistic, and based on a belief that when given the support they need, people can change for the better.

Harm reduction concepts, when put into practice, can be controversial. So it is with programming to provide decent housing for homeless alcoholics and drug addicts. Often these people have a mental disorder as well. A new model that is becoming more common in cities of the Pacific Northwest is known as Housing First (as opposed to Treatment First). In a landmark study provided in Reading 15, Padgett, Gulcur, and Tsemberis provide empirical evidence to show that abstinence-only programming has no advantage in helping addicted homeless people recover over this more flexible model. The policy implications of this research are profound.

Reading 16 provides a theoretical framework on harm reduction and shows how this framework can be applied to reduce high-risk behaviors in youth. This contribution, in effect, takes motivational interviewing strategies as described in the previous section, into the harm reduction realm.

This anthology concludes on a positive note with a critical examination of one of the most promising developments in recent years, the drug court. Utilizing advanced statistical analysis, DeMatteo, Marlowe, and Festinger, similar to harm reduction theorists, examine drug court operations as a form of prevention. The significance of the drug court is that it represents a joining of the criminal justice system and community services to help drug addicts find their way to a sober and healthy life. The authors' argument for matching clients to programs such as this is well taken as is their openness to pharmacological interventions to reduce craving. If you read their paper closely, however, you will note both consistencies and inconsistencies among the three readings in this section, mainly because the intensive supervision and zero tolerance aspects of the drug court contradict principles centered on boosting self-motivation.

15

HOUSING FIRST SERVICES FOR PEOPLE WHO ARE HOMELESS WITH CO-OCCURRING SERIOUS MENTAL ILLNESS AND SUBSTANCE ABUSE

DEBORAH K. PADGETT

NEW YORK UNIVERSITY, SCHOOL OF SOCIAL WORK

LEYLA GULCUR AND SAM TSEMBERIS

PATHWAYS TO HOUSING

The literature on homeless adults with severe mental illness is generally silent on a critical issue surrounding service delivery—the contrast between housing first and treatment first program philosophies. This study draws on data from a longitudinal experiment contrasting a housing first program (which offers immediate permanent housing without requiring treatment compliance or abstinence) and treatment first (standard care) programs for 225 adults who were homeless with mental illness in New York City. After 48 months, results showed no significant group differences in alcohol and drug use. Treatment first participants were significantly more likely to use treatment services. These findings, in combination with previous reports of much higher rates of housing stability in the housing first group, show that "dual diagnosed" adults can remain stably housed without increasing their substance use. Thus, housing first programs favoring immediate housing and consumer choice deserve consideration as a viable alternative to standard care.

Keywords: homelessness; serious mental illness; dual diagnosis; psychiatric rehabilitation

SOURCE: "Housing First Services for People Who Are Homeless With Co-Occurring Serious Mental Illness and Substance Abuse" by Deborah K. Padgett, Leyla Gulcur, and Sam Tsemberis. In the 2006 issue of *Research on Social Work Practice*, 16(1), 74–83. Used with permission.

Homelessness in the United States, traceable to a famine in housing markets beginning in the early 1980s, afflicts thousands of persons who are psychiatrically disabled who lack adequate community-based care (Baumohl, 1996; Lovell & Cohn, 1998). Many are visible as they lead troubled lives on the streets; however, a growing number are likely to be incarcerated—the largest de facto psychiatric facility in the country is the Los Angeles County Jail (Butterfield, 2003). Regardless of whether the problem is viewed as one of individual pathology or systemic failure, the plight of people with mental illness and who are homeless remains one of the least understood and most contested service delivery problems in mental health today (Gonzalez & Rosenheck, 2002; McGray, 2004; Substance Abuse and Mental Health Services Administration [SAMHSA], 2003).

Social workers join other providers and advocates in lamenting the lack of service integration and the scarcity of resources available to meet the needs of adults who are homeless with mental illness who also abuse substances. However, the literature of social work and other professions is generally silent on a policy-relevant and practice-relevant debate surrounding service delivery for this population. The point of contention stems from fundamental differences in how people with mental illness who are homeless are viewed and in how consumer choice is defined and incorporated into a program's service delivery philosophy. Put another way, there are two contrasting paradigms in services for persons who are homeless with serious mental illness; one the traditional continuum of care approach favoring treatment first and the other a consumer-driven movement (housing first) that has gained momentum in recent years (Carling, 1990; Culhane, Metraux, & Hadley, 2001; Tsemberis, 1999).

Among a number of differences between them, a contrast of interest in this report lies in how they deal with substance abuse and whether abstinence is a precondition to independent housing and other services. Approximately 50% to 70% of persons who are homeless with mental illness abuse substances (Drake, Osher, & Wallach, 1991; SAMHSA, 2003), and these estimates are widely considered underreports because of denial, distrust, and fear of the consequences of divulging illegal behaviors (Drake, Yovetich, Bebout, Harris, & McHugo, 1997).

Housing first programs rank stable housing as the first and highest priority vis-à-vis abstinence from substance use and/or abuse, thus practicing a harm reduction approach (Inciardi & Harrison, 2000). Treatment first programs reverse this sequence and require detoxification and sobriety before giving access to services such as independent housing. For these programs, consumers' choice in adherence to mental health treatment and abstinence requirements must be relinquished for their own sake until they are deemed ready for independent living.

Our primary goals in this article are twofold: (a) to describe the historic development and core components of these two distinct service alternatives (treatment first and housing first) and (b) to provide findings related to substance and services use from the only randomized experiment designed to compare their effectiveness—the New York Housing Study.

BACKGROUND

The Treatment First Approach for People Who Are Homeless With Mental Illness

The era of deinstitutionalization opened the door to independent living for persons with diagnoses such as schizophrenia and bipolar disorder; however, these individuals still needed an array of support services as they made the transition from psychiatric hospital to community (Dixon, Krauss, Kernan, Lehman, & DeForge, 1995). Among these were medication management, psychological counseling, education, and job training. For a large subgroup, abuse of drugs and/or alcohol complicated matters considerably (Drake et al., 1997). Persons with mental illness who became homeless were disproportionately individuals who were "dual diagnosed" whose lives became a continual struggle to find shelter and avoid being victimized (Drake et al., 1991; Padgett & Struening, 1992).

The well-intentioned but underfunded system of public sector mental health services that evolved after the 1960s rarely interacted with drug and alcohol (D/A) treatment programs designed with clients without mental illness in mind. However, both service systems had one thing in common: They were predicated on assumptions of the need for structure and control. Different funding streams, staff expertise, and service philosophies notwithstanding, the mental health, D/A, and homeless services systems share a "hurdle" approach in which gaining access to services requires relinquishing control and choice. In exchange for a bed and supportive services, consumers and/or clients submitted to rules requiring treatment compliance, abstinence, curfews, limited visitation, and a loss of privacy (Miller & Flaherty, 2000). From the perspective of a person who was dually diagnosed living on the street, this threshold for entry can seem daunting at best. It is also a high-stakes gamble because rule breaking usually leads to expulsion and a return to the streets.

Evaluations of treatment first programs have produced modest results in achieving housing stability (Lipton, Siegel, Hannigan, & Samuels, 2000); however, program attrition and a return to the "institutional circuit" (Hopper, Jost, Hay, Welber, & Haugland, 1997) remain a problem when trying to ascertain change over time. Recent innovations in programs designed specifically for persons with dual diagnoses have shown promising results for integrated treatment models (Drake et al., 1997; Bebout, Drake, Xie, McHugo, & Harris, 1997; Minkoff, 2001) and Double Trouble in Recovery 12-step

groups (Magura, Laudet, Mahmood, Rosenblum, & Knight, 2002). Indeed, the cumulative findings have made integrated treatment for persons who are dual diagnosed the "state of the art" in terms of effectiveness (Tsuang, Fong, & Ho, 2003).

When integrated treatment was linked to housing options in a randomized trial, positive outcomes were associated with supervised living and on-site clinical services (McHugo et al., 2004). However, no study of integrated treatment to date has tested its comparative effectiveness as part of the consumer choice model as is the focus of the current study.

Reversing the Continuum: The Pathways Model of Housing First for Adults Who Are Psychiatrically Disabled and Homeless

By the early 1990s, a consumer-centered approach surfaced that reversed the treatment first continuum. Its proponents argued for "supported housing," with tenets of consumer choice, ongoing support services, and community integration (normal housing, not "treatment" residences; Carling, 1990; Ridgeway & Zipple, 1990; Srebnik, Livingston, Gordon, & King, 1995). They described treatment first approaches as "supportive housing" with on-site (or proximal) staff and rules governing behavior ranging from curfews to visitation to abstinence. Most involve congregate living with other consumers who are homeless and function as transitional housing; that is, therapeutic environments designed to foster independent living skills enabling clients to graduate to living on their own. In contrast, housing first is a type of "supported housing" that separates treatment from housing, considering the former voluntary and the latter a fundamental need and human right. As such, it provides scatter-site housing without on-site staff supervision and generally promotes harm reduction rather than requiring abstinence.

Although confusion can arise regarding what are considered essential and defining program components in supported versus supportive housing (Fakhoury, Murray, Shepherd, & Priebe, 2002), housing first shares a bottom-line commitment to consumer choice and to immediate and continuing access to scatter-site independent housing. To our knowledge, the agency model that is the subject of the current study—Pathways to Housing, Inc.—stands alone in embodying the following elements: (a) immediate independent permanent housing that is not contingent on treatment compliance and is retained regardless of the client's temporary departure because of inpatient treatment or incarceration; (b) choice and harm reduction with respect to mental health treatment and substance use; (c) integrated Assertive Community Treatment (ACT) services (Drake et al., 1998) that work in conjunction with housing staff and a nurse practitioner to address ongoing housing and health needs.

The New York Housing Study

With its funding of a national multisite study of housing alternatives for persons who are homeless with mental illness, the federal agency SAMHSA chose the Pathways to Housing (PTH) program as the experimental condition for the New York City site (Shern et al., 2000). The New York Housing Study (NYHS), which began in 1996, was a 4-year randomized trial comparing the PTH version of housing first with treatment first continuum of care programs in the New York City area.

Published findings from the NYHS have shown higher rates of housing stability (Tsemberis & Eisenberg, 2000; Tsemberis, Gulcur, & Nakae, 2004) and cost savings (Gulcur, Stefancic, Shinn, Tsemberis, & Fischer, 2003) for the PTH model. In addition to housing stability, the NYHS also assessed outcomes related to mental health symptoms, quality of life, drug and alcohol use, and utilization of substance abuse treatment. Analyses of the 24-month data showed no significant group differences in these outcomes with the exception of

higher use of substance abuse treatment services by the control group (Tsemberis et al., 2004). The NYHS maintained a remarkable 87% retention rate of participation for 4 years (Stefancic, Shaefer-McDaniel, Davis, & Tsemberis, 2004).

In summary, the NYHS found that "a person's mental health diagnosis is not related to his or her ability to obtain or to maintain independent housing" (Tsemberis et al., 2004, p. 654). Moreover, housing such persons without requiring abstinence and sobriety did not increase their use of substances during a 2-year period despite comparatively lower levels of use of substance abuse treatment services. The control group's higher use of substance abuse services did not produce comparatively lower rates of drug or alcohol use, thus indicating that residence in "sober housing" did not produce the desired results in terms of abstinence.

In this report, we assessed substance-related and treatment-related outcomes from the full 48 months of data to determine if the previous findings are sustained or change during a much longer period of observation (4 years vs. 2 years). Thus, we address the following research questions:

Research Question 1: Are there group differences in alcohol and drug use at 48 months?

Research Question 2: Are there group differences in participation in substance abuse and mental health treatment at 48 months?

Method

Sampling and Recruitment

Individuals were eligible to participate in the NYHS if they signed an informed consent form (approved by federal and university Human Subjects Committees) and met three inclusion criteria. These were that the person (a) spent 15 of the last 30 days on the street or in other public places, (b) exhibited a history of homelessness during the past 6 months, and (c) had an Axis I diagnosis of severe mental illness. Although substance abuse was not a criterion for eligibility, 90% of the study participants had a diagnosis or history of alcohol or drug disorders according to clinical records. Psychiatric diagnoses were obtained from clinical records and interviews with referring providers.

Respondents were recruited from outreach teams, drop-in centers, state psychiatric facilities, psychiatric wards, and the streets. When it was determined that individuals met the inclusion criteria, they were asked if they would be interested in participating in a research study with compensation of US $25 for each interview. It was further explained that based on a randomized lottery system, individuals would be referred to different housing programs in the city. Recruitment lasted from November 1997 to January 1999. The recruited sample was 225 people (99 in the experimental group and 126 in the control group) between ages 18 and 70 years.

Study Design and Description of Experimental and Control Conditions

The housing first model was developed by Pathways to Housing, Inc. (PTH) in 1992 as a consumer-driven approach to providing housing and support services to adults who were homeless with mental illness. PTH gives immediate access to housing in independent scatter-site apartments and offers tenants an array of services through interdisciplinary Assertive Community Treatment (ACT) teams that include social workers, psychiatrists, vocational trainers, and substance abuse counselors. Two modifications of the ACT model initiated by PTH were the addition of a nurse practitioner to address health problems and a housing specialist to coordinate housing needs. As part of its vision of consumer choice, PTH does not make housing contingent on sobriety or treatment compliance. The single contingency in this model is a money management program for PTH clients who are unable

to meet landlord requirements for leases (e.g., credit histories) or who are not ready to conserve resources necessary to make monthly rent payments. Because it does not refuse clients with histories of violence or incarceration, PTH has accepted and housed the most problematic among persons who are homeless with mental illness; that is, those other programs would not take or had ejected (Tsemberis, 1999).

PTH tenants who abuse drugs or alcohol are counseled by clinical services staff based on their readiness for change. Those with serious substance abuse problems are urged to accept referrals to residential treatment (and their apartments held for them or another one found when they are discharged). PTH also offers harm reduction support groups at its various branch offices. PTH clients whose substance use causes disruption face the usual consequences of a tenant in a similar situation with the exception that PTH staff will assist them in moving to another apartment if evicted.

Individuals randomly assigned to the control group were referred to usual care programs that offer abstinent-contingent housing and services based on a treatment first model. A typical program would be exemplified by a group home or a single-room occupancy residence in which clients are expected to attend day treatment, 12-step, and other therapeutic groups and follow medication regimens enforced by on-site staff. Sleeping, cooking, and bathing facilities are shared, and house rules strictly prohibit consumption of any substances and overnight guests.

During the research design phase, volunteer tenants at PTH reviewed the proposal and provided feedback. Tenants also served on the PTH Institutional Review Board (IRB) and had a voting role as to whether the project and the randomization process was fair and not harmful. Fidelity to the ACT model in the experimental condition was assessed using the Dartmouth fidelity model (Teague, Bond, & Drake, 1998) and was found to be satisfactory (Shinn, Tsemberis, & Moran, 2005).

Data Collection and Measures

A structured interview was administered at 6-month intervals for 48 months. To reduce attrition and maintain contacts, monthly 5-minute call-in interviews were conducted. Participants were paid $25 for in-person interviews (9 in all) and $5 for the monthly calls. These repeated contacts are one of the reasons for the study's high retention rate (Stefancic et al., 2004).

Because the NYHS was one of eight sites participating in a federally funded demonstration project, standardized cross-site measures were used to assess key variables.

Use of alcohol and illegal drugs. Use of alcohol and illegal drugs was assessed with the Six-Month Follow-Back Calendar (Sobell, Sobell, Leo, & Cancella, 1988). Participants reported the number of days drinks were consumed, and the number of days that certain illicit drugs were used during the 6-month period. Four summary variables were defined by the cross-site team: any use of alcohol, any use of illegal substances, heavy use of alcohol (more than 28 days in 6 months), and heavy use of drugs (more than 4 days in 6 months). Of these four variables, two (heavy use of alcohol and heavy use of drugs) were utilized in analyses for the current study.

It is possible that individuals in the treatment first programs underreport substance use differentially because these programs typically require abstinence or at least the promise of sobriety. Although such a bias would work against finding effects favoring the experimental condition, we considered this possibility of differential self-report in interpreting the findings.

Participation in substance abuse treatment. Participation in substance abuse treatment was collected through the use of a modified Treatment Services Review (McLellan, Alterman, Woody, & Metzer, 1992). Service use was computed as the average of a seven-item measure consisting of questions such as whether the participant had received treatment in a detox program or consulted with a counselor to talk about substance problems, and attended AA, NA, or any other substance abuse self-help group.

Participation in mental health treatment. Mental health service use was also collected through the modified Treatment Services Review (McLellan et al., 1992). Service use was computed as the average of a five-item measure consisting of questions such as whether the participant had received overnight treatment in a psychiatric hospital, attended a day hospital program or day treatment center, and visited with a doctor or nurse to discuss medication or emotional problems.

For both utilization variables, the average proportion of services used is reported as the outcome of interest. A proportion of .20, for example, means that group members averaged one of a possible five "yes" answers to the mental health services measure.

Data Analyses

Checks on random assignment. A preliminary data analysis question checked on random assignment of the sample retained at each data collection point. One of the best guarantees of random assignment is a strong retention rate, which we successfully attained. We compared respondents who were and were not retained in the sample at several data collection points to see if they differed from baseline and found no differences in key demographic or other baseline variables. Because random assignment produced satisfactory equivalence of the groups, no demographic variables were used as covariates because they were not correlated with the outcomes. For this reason, we reported the demographic characteristics for the total sample rather than by group (see Table 1 (on p. 254)).

Analyses of research questions. Research Question 1 was analyzed graphically and with a growth curve model with group-by-time interactions to formally assess whether differences are changing over time, also known as hierarchical linear modeling (Bryk & Raudenbush, 1992). We created a Level-1 (repeated measures) model for the trajectory of each participant, and a Level-2 (person level) model to examine differences in experimental versus control trajectories for participants. At Level 1 (repeated measures), we estimated a regression equation for alcohol and drug use outcomes as a function of time. At Level 2 (person level), we estimated whether the intercept and growth parameters of the Level-1 models differed by group. Note that with nine points of data collection, we were able to include participants in this analysis even if they missed as many as one half of the assessments; this was an advantage of utilizing SAS Proc Mixed over repeated measures MANOVA.

Research Question 2 was tested using a subsample of participants who were in some type of service-related program, namely, experimental participants who were currently housed by the PTH/ housing first program and control participants who reported living in one of the following places at time of the interview: supportive single-room-occupancy (SRO) hotels, drop-in centers, safe havens, detox facilities, crisis housing, intermediate care, boarding houses, transitional housing, group homes, alcohol- and/or drug-free facilities, or treatment and/or recovery programs. The rationale for using this subsample for Research Question 2 was to "level the playing field" in terms of including only housed study participants—those in shelters, incarcerated, or on the streets were considered less able to avail themselves of such services. Because participants' residential status changed from one time point to the next, the subsamples also changed; we, therefore, had to conduct separate *t* tests for each time point instead of SAS Proc Mixed.

Perhaps it is not surprising to note, sample sizes varied considerably in this analysis across the nine points of data collection (every 6 months for 48 months).

Thus, control group sample sizes ranged from a high of 126 at baseline to a low of 53 at 24 months. Similarly, experimental group sizes ranged from a high of 99 at baseline to a low of 35 at 12 months. In addition to the analysis decision to include only individuals who were housed at each specific time of data collection, samples were reduced because of study dropout, no-shows, incarceration, or other forms of institutionalization. PTH (experimental) participants were not considered "housed" if they were institutionalized even though they had access to housing on discharge. Because of these multiple group comparisons, a more conservative significance level was applied using a Bonferroni-corrected alpha of .006.

Results

Description of the Study Sample

As can be seen in Table 1, the sample consisted of 173 men (76.9%) and 52 women (23.1%) with an average age of 41.5 years. Most of the participants (69.2%) had never been married. Sixty-three (28%) participants identified their race as White, and 90 (40%) identified their race as African American. Twenty-three (10.3%) participants did not go beyond eighth grade in their education. Among Axis I diagnoses, psychotic disorders were dominant (53.8%).

Thirty nine (17.6%) of the participants reported becoming homeless before age 18 years. The average age at which participants reported experiencing homelessness for the first time was 29.5 years (age range was 5 to 64 years). The longest period of time homeless was an average of 4.4 years with a median of 3 years. The majority (50.1%) of the participants lived on the streets or a public place or in a drop-in shelter at time of the baseline interview, and 36% ($n = 81$) were living in a psychiatric hospital. According to their psychosocial histories, 90% had substance use disorders either in the past or currently. At the study's end at

Table 1   Participant Characteristics

Percentage	Variable	Number
Study group: Experimental	99	44
Control	126	56
Gender: Female	52	23.1
Male	173	76.9
Age: 18 to 30 years	43	19.1
31 to 40 years	62	27.6
41 to 50 years	68	30.2
51 to 60 years	41	18.2
61 to 70 years	11	4.9
Race: White	63	28
African American	90	40
Hispanic American[a]	33	14.7
Mixed and/or other[a]	39	17.3
Education: Some high school or less	94	42
High school diploma or GED Equivalent	55	24.6
Postsecondary education	75	33.5
Marital status: Married	8	3.6
Separated[b] Divorced[b]	20	8.9 [1]
Widowed[b]	32	14.3
Never married[b]	155	69.2
Residence at baseline: Streets/subway/drop-in[v]	80	35.6
Shelter and/or safe haven[v] Crisis housing with family and/or friends[d]	5	2.2
Psychiatric hospital Hotel and/or motel[d] Short-term transitional housing[d]	1	.4
Psychiatric Diagnosis: Psychosis	121	53.8
Bipolar Disorder	30	13.3
Major Depression	32	14.2
Other[e]	10	4.4
Missing[e]	32	14.2

NOTE: Some percentages do not add up to 100% due to rounding error. Categories with the same superscripts were combined for analysis of group differences.

48 months, housing first clients were stably housed 75% of the time during the previous 6 months compared to 50% of the time for treatment first clients (L. Gulcur, personal communication, July 25, 2005).

Group Differences in Alcohol and Drug Use

To answer Research Question 1, SAS Proc Mixed was utilized to test whether there were changes in reported drug and alcohol use over time. Because of low reported levels of drug and alcohol use, the "heavy use" variables were analyzed and predicted by time, group assignment, and the Time × Group Assignment interaction. As can be seen in Figures 1 and 2, none of the parameters were significant: Reports of drug use remained constant during the 48 months of the evaluation project, the groups did not differ from each other, nor were there differences in their rates of change over time. The same predictors were used to examine change in alcohol use over time, and again, none of the parameters were significant. However, there was a visual trend indicating that the PTH group used less alcohol than the control group.

Group Differences in Substance Treatment and Psychiatric Services Utilization

Substance treatment utilization showed notable differences at 6 months ($p = .012$), 18 months ($p = .021$), 24 months

($p = .025$), 36 months ($p = .006$) and 48 months ($p = .014$) with the control group members showing higher utilization (see Figure 3). With the Bonferroni correction, these differences were significant only at 36 months. Control groups members were somewhat higher utilizers of mental health treatment though the differences were statistically significant only at 48 months ($p = .003$; see Figure 4).

DISCUSSION

The above results extend those cited earlier (Tsemberis et al., 2004) to an additional 2 years of data collection. We note the continued absence of group differences in alcohol and drug use, though with a nonsignificant trend toward lower alcohol use by the housing first group. The lack of compliance with sobriety requirements by a significant proportion of the

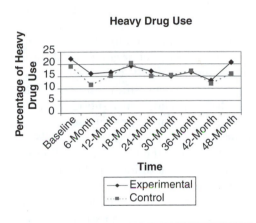

Figure 1 Heavy Drug Use, Baseline to 48 Months

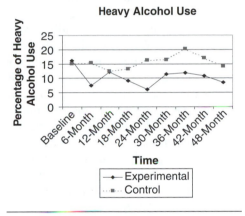

Figure 2 Heavy Alcohol Use, Baseline to 48 Months

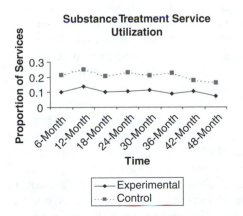

Figure 3 Substance Treatment Service Utilization, Baseline to 48 Months

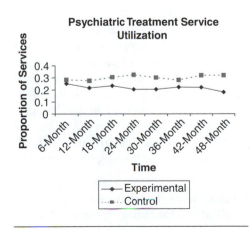

Figure 4 Psychiatric Treatment Service Utilization, Baseline to 48 Months

treatment first group—now extending to 4 years' duration—is an indication that such strictures fall short in bringing about abstinence among consumers whose primary need is for housing (Watkins, Shaner, & Sullivan, 1999). Although substance use was almost certainly underreported by members of both groups, it is likely to be greater among those in treatment first because the adverse consequences of any admission of substance use are greater for them.

The treatment first group's higher use of substance abuse treatment services during the 48 months of the study must be considered in this context in which service use is linked to housing. It is not unusual to see clients continue to use drugs or drink surreptitiously even while attending treatment groups (Wolford et al., 1999). Our findings that treatment first clients did not reduce substance use and had comparably greater use of substance abuse and mental health services underscore this possibility.

Access to and availability of such services might influence these findings aside from program philosophies and requirements. However, it is useful to distinguish between services that are available versus those that are required. Housing first participants had an array of services available to them but were not required to use them. Control participants were required to use certain services (e.g., detox, 12-step groups, day treatment) to maintain their housing and presumably had access to them. Given the systemic factors influencing an individual's ability and willingness to seek help for mental health and substance abuse problems, our findings of "no significant difference" in substance use despite lower treatment service utilization and no program-specific restraints on substance use connotes clinical and programmatic significance favoring the housing first approach.

Limitations of the Study and Implications for Future Research

Despite a rigorous experimental design, low attrition rate and the use of standardized measures known for their reliability among persons who are homeless with mental illness, the current study is subject to concerns about accuracy in recall and social desirability bias. Such concerns are common to studies using self-report measures (Calsyn, Morse, & Klinkenberg, 1997) but are especially pertinent given the complex interplay of mental symptoms, drug effects (illicit and prescribed), and the severe deprivations of homelessness. If a man who is homeless is taken to a hospital emergency room disheveled, incoherent, and violent, he could be psychotic, high, or both. When it comes to substance abuse and psychiatric medication adherence, study participants may have a number of reasons for memory loss, misunderstanding Likert-type questions, or deliberately misleading researchers (Wolford et al., 1999).

In the current study, the thresholds selected as indices of a substance abuse problem do not necessarily square with providers' perceptions (Drake et al., 1991) nor should they be construed as clinically significant. In addition, the lower overall rates of substance use reported in this sample do not conform to estimates from previous sources. It is possible that this discrepancy is because of measurement bias or deliberate underreporting. As well, previous estimates may have been higher because of their reliance on persons who were dually diagnosed and homeless rather than those enrolled in services as in the current study. The absence of verification measures (e.g., urine toxicology tests) makes it impossible to draw definite conclusions about these reported rates.

Concerns about inaccuracies in detecting substance use are widespread in research dealing with problems of persons with severe mental illness. Yet Wolford et al. (1999) were surprised to find that self-report was superior to laboratory tests and clinical exams in a controlled evaluation of detection methods with this population. Although beyond the scope of this article, methodological problems related to accuracy in detecting and diagnosing substance abuse continue to challenge clinicians and researchers alike (Calsyn et al., 1997; Wolford et al., 1999). The current study's reliance on psychosocial histories and clinic records, rather than formal *DSM* diagnoses (Axis I or II) limits our capacity to analyze or compare findings based on *DSM* criteria. However, we are reasonably certain that the Axis I eligibility criteria were met.

Given the unquestionable negative effects of drug and alcohol abuse on rehabilitation of persons with mental illness, it is imperative that researchers pursue a number of avenues for understanding the beginning and ending of substance abuse among individuals in this population (Hohmann & Shear, 2002; Ridgway, 2001). To this end, the NYHS investigators and the first author have embarked on a longitudinal qualitative study designed to address this gap in knowledge by asking consumers about their histories of substance use and experiences in the service delivery system.

Beyond methodological improvements, future research is needed on supported housing in general (and housing first programs in particular) to compare outcomes across different settings and geographic areas (Mares, Kasprow, & Rosenheck, 2004). Currently, the PTH program is being replicated in a number of cities (Anderson, 2005), and plans for formal evaluations of the replicated model are under way.

Implications for Practice and Policy

The results of the current study show that individuals with severe mental illness and substance use problems do not have to undergo mandatory treatment to be able to live independently in the community. Moreover, consumer-driven programs that practice housing first and harm reduction are not linked to increased substance use despite the absence of restrictions. The current study has also revealed consistent (and probably underreported) use of illicit substances by individuals enrolled in treatment first programs despite abstinence requirements.

Our findings have distinct relevance for practitioners charged with engaging and retaining clients who are homeless with mental illness in care. Thus, the one-size-fits-all assumption that mental disorders and homelessness cannot be addressed until a client is clean and sober is no longer valid. Indeed, engagement and retention may be far more effective when clients who are dually diagnosed are able to actively participate in their own treatment decisions.

Yet long-held beliefs are difficult to change. Research has shown that consumers who are dually diagnosed and homeless prefer independent living while clinicians recommend supervised congregate housing (Schutt, Weinstein, & Penk, 2005; Watkins et al., 1999). Although the landscape of mental health and homeless policies is continually changing (McGray, 2004), there is a marked lag in implementation of empirical findings in policy and practice (Tsuang et al., 2003). Even individual components taken separately from housing first "packaging" (e.g., harm reduction and integrated treatment) remain far less common than treatment first and abstinence-oriented approaches. Organizational cultures, funding streams, and a conservative sociopolitical climate present obstacles to change and have the ultimate impact of restricting consumer choice (Tsuang et al., 2003).

As part of a federally funded national demonstration project, the NYHS was intended to inform housing and treatment policies for this deeply vulnerable population. Millions of public and private dollars are spent each year on treatment for persons with mental illness, and services for persons who are homeless have expanded exponentially (McGray, 2004). For example, the New York State Office of Mental Health has an annual budget of $5.6 billion, yet a small fraction (about $6.5 million) is dedicated to supported housing initiatives.

Further support for housing first

approaches comes from comparative cost analyses. A groundbreaking study released in 2001 documented substantial cost savings from community-based care compared to shelters, jails, and hospital beds (Culhane et al., 2001). Because "community-based care" encompasses many noninstitutional approaches, future policy decisions to redirect public funds toward more effective alternatives will invariably also consider costs. Annual per capita costs of the PTH program are $22,500 compared with $40,000 to $50,000 for treatment first congregate housing programs, $85,000 for a jail bed, and $175,000 for a state psychiatric hospital bed (Anderson, 2005).

Social work practitioners, policy makers, and educators can benefit from these findings as some of the strongest support for "evidence-based practice" in housing and services for persons who are homeless with mental illness. As the largest single group of mental health practitioners and a significant part of the substance abuse treatment workforce, social workers play a critical role in implementing best practices for this vulnerable population.

Heartened by results showing that housing first leads to residential stability even for those considered least capable of benefiting, we end on a note of optimism that future research will shed additional light on the complex dynamic surrounding decisions of individuals who are homeless about substance use and the many other dimensions of successful recovery from mental illness. In this context, program philosophies favoring choice over restrictions and empowerment over compliance deserve consideration as not only effective but humane.

References

Anderson, L. (2005, June 20). A reverse approach to homelessness [Electronic version]. *Baltimore Sun*, p. 1 A.

Baumohl, J. (Ed.). (1996). *Homelessness in America*. Phoenix, AZ: Oryx.

Bebout, R. R., Drake, R. E., Xie, H., McHugo, G. J., & Harris, M. (1997). Housing status among formerly homeless dually diagnosed adults. *Psychiatric Services, 48*(7), 936–942.

Bryk, A. S., & Raudenbush, S. W. (1992). *Hierarchical linear models: Applications and data analysis methods*. Newbury Park, CA: Sage.

Butterfield, F. (2003, October 22). Study finds hundreds of thousands of inmates mentally ill. *The New York Times*, p. A1, A7.

Calsyn, R. J., Morse, G. A., & Klinkenberg, W. D. (1997). Reliability and validity of self-report data of homeless mentally ill individuals. *Evaluation and Program Planning, 20*, 47–54.

Carling, P. J. (1990). Major mental illness, housing, and supports: The promise of community integration. *American Psychologist, 45*, 969–975.

Culhane, D. P., Metraux, S., & Hadley, T. (2001). The impact of supportive housing for homeless people with severe mental illness on the utilization of the public health, corrections, and emergency shelter systems: The New York-New York Initiative. *Housing Policy Debate, 5*, 107–140.

Dixon, L. B., Krauss, N., Kernan, E., Lehman, A. F. & DeForge, B. R. (1995). Modifying the PACT model to serve homeless persons with severe mental illness. *Psychiatric Services, 46*, 684–688.

Drake, R. E., McHugo, G. J., Clark, R. E., Teague, G. B., Xie, H., Miles, K., et al. (1998). Assertive community treatment (ACT) for persons with co-occurring severe mental illness and substance use disorder. *American Journal of Orthopsychiatry, 68*, 201–215.

Drake, R. E., Osher, F. C., & Wallach, M. A. (1991). Homelessness and dual diagnosis. *American Psychologist, 36*, 1149–1158.

Drake, R. E., Yovetich, N. A., Bebout, R. R., Harris, M., & McHugo, G. (1997). Integrated treatment for dually diagnosed adults. *Journal of Nervous and Mental Disease, 185*(5), 298–305.

Fakhoury, K. H., Murray, A., Shepherd, G., &

Priebe, S. (2002). Research in supported housing. *Social Psychiatry and Psychiatric Epidemiology, 37*, 301–315.

Gonzalez, G., & Rosenheck, R. A. (2002). Outcomes and service use among homeless persons with serious mental illness and substance abuse. *Psychiatric Services, 43*(4), 437–446.

Gulcur, L., Stefancic, A., Shinn, M., Tsemberis, S., & Fischer, S. (2003). Housing, hospitalization, and cost outcomes for homeless individuals with psychiatric disabilities participating in continuum of care and housing first programmes. *Journal of Community and Applied Social Psychology, 13*, 171–186.

Hohmann, A. H., & Shear, M. K. (2002). Community-based intervention research: Coping with the "noise" of real life in study design. *American Journal of Psychiatry, 159*, 201–207.

Hopper, K., Jost, J., Hay, T., Welber, S., & Haugland, G. (1997). Homelessness, severe mental illness and the institutional circuit. *Psychiatric Services, 48*, 659–665.

Inciardi, J. A., & Harrison, L. D. (2000). *Harm reduction: National and international perspectives.* Thousand Oaks, CA: Sage.

Lipton, F. R., Siegel, C., Hannigan, A., & Samuels, J. B. (2000). Tenure in supportive housing for homeless persons with severe mental illness. *Psychiatric Services, 51*, 479–486.

Lovell, A. M., & Cohn, S. (1998). The elaboration of "choice" in a program for homeless persons labeled psychiatrically disabled. *Human Organization, 57*, 8–20.

Magura, S., Laudet, A., Mahmood, D., Rosenblum A., & Knight, E. (2002). Adherence to medication regimens and participation in dual-focus self-help groups. *Psychiatric Services 53*(3), 310–316.

Mares, A. S., Kasprow, W. J., & Rosenheck, R. A. (2004). Outcomes of supported housing for homeless veterans with psychiatric and substance abuse problems. *Mental Health Services*

Research, 6(4), 199–211.

McGray, D. (2004, June). The abolitionist: Bush's homelessness czar has some new ideas. *Atlantic Monthly, 101*, 36–39.

McHugo, G. J., Bebout, R. R., Harris, M., Cleghorn, S., Herring, G., Xie, H., et al. (2004). A randomized controlled trial of integrated versus parallel housing services for homeless adults with severe mental illness. *Schizophrenia Bulletin, 30*(4), 969–982.

McLellan, A. T., Alterman, A. L., Woody, G. E., & Metzer, D. (1992). *Treatment services review.* Philadelphia: University of Pennsylvania.

Miller, N. S., & Flaherty, J. A. (2000). Effectiveness of coerced addiction treatment (alternative consequences): A review of clinical research. *Journal of Substance Abuse Treatment, 18*, 9–16.

Minkoff, K. (2001). Developing standards of care for individuals with co-occurring psychiatric and substance use disorders. *Psychiatric Services, 52*, 597–599.

Padgett, D. K., & Struening, E. L. (1992). Victimization and traumatic injuries among the homeless: associations with alcohol, drug, and mental problems. *American Journal of Orthopsychiatry, 62*, 525–534.

Ridgeway, P. (2001). Restorying disability: Learning from first-person narratives of recovery. *Psychiatric Rehabilitation, 24*, 335–343.

Ridgeway, P., & Zipple, A. M. (1990). The paradigm shift in residential services: From the linear continuum to supported housing approaches. *Psychosocial Rehabilitation Journal, 13*, 11–31.

Schutt, R. K., Weinstein, B., & Penk, W. E. (2005). Housing preferences of homeless veterans with dual diagnoses. *Psychiatric Services, 56*(3), 350–352.

Shern, D. L., Tsemberis, S., Anthony, W., Lovell, A. M., Richmond, L., Felton, C. J., et al. (2000). Serving street-dwelling individuals with psychiatric disabilities: Outcomes of a psychiatric rehabilitation clinical trial. *American Journal of Public Health, 90*, 1873–1878.

Shinn, M., Tsemberis, S., & Moran, L.

(2005). *Fidelity outcomes for a consumer preference living model of housing.* Manuscript in preparation.

Sobell, L. C., Sobell, M. B., Leo, G. L., & Cancella, A. (1988). Reliability of a timeline method: Assessing normal drinkers' reports of recent drinking and a comparative evaluation across several populations. *British Journal of Addiction, 83,* 393–402.

Srebnik, D., Livingston, J., Gordon, L., & King, D. (1995). Housing choice and community success for individuals with serious and persistent mental illness. *Community Mental Health Journal, 31,* 139–152.

Stefancic, A., Shaefer-McDaniel, N., Davis, A., & Tsemberis, S. (2004). Maximizing follow up of adults with histories of homelessness and disabilities. *Evaluation and Program Planning, 27,* 433–442.

Substance Abuse and Mental Health Services Administration. (2003). *Report to Congress on the prevention and treatment of co-occurring substance use disorders and mental disorders.* Washington, DC: U.S. Department of Health and Human Services.

Teague, G. B., Bond, G. R., & Drake, R. E. (1998). Program fidelity in assertive community treatment: Development and use of a measure. *American Journal*

of *Orthopsychiatry, 68,* 216–232.

Tsemberis, S. (1999). From streets to homes: An innovative approach to supported housing for homeless adults with psychiatric disabilities. *Journal of Community Psychology, 27,* 225–241.

Tsemberis, S., & Eisenberg, R. F. (2000). Pathways to housing: Supported housing for street dwelling homeless individuals with psychiatric disabilities. *Psychiatric Services, 51,* 487–493.

Tsemberis, S., Gulcur, L., & Nakae, M. (2004). Housing first, consumer choice, and harm reduction for homeless individuals with a dual diagnosis. *American Journal of Public Health, 94,* 651–656.

Tsuang, J. W., Fong, T. W., & Ho, A. P. (2003). Dual diagnosis and treatment compliance. *Psychiatric Services, 54*(4), 576.

Watkins, K. E., Shaner, A., & Sullivan, G. (1999). The role of gender in engaging the dually diagnosed in treatment. *Community Mental Health Journal, 35*(2), 115–125.

Wolford, G. L., Rosenberg, S. D., Drake, R. E., Mueser, K. T., Oxman, T. E., Hoffman, D., et al. (1999). Evaluation of methods for detecting substance use disorder in persons with severe mental illness. *Psychology of Addictive Behaviors, 13*(4), 313–326.

16

HARM REDUCTION

A Model for Social Work Practice With Adolescents

KATHERINE VAN WORMER

UNIVERSITY OF NORTHERN IOWA

Abstract. *A practical antidote to the war on drugs, the harm reduction approach seeks to meet clients where they are, establish rapport and help them modify or give up their risk-taking behavior. This article presents the case for harm reduction techniques for work with youth whose risk-taking behavior is problematic. Emphasis is on drinking, drug use, and high-risk sexual activity. [Article copies available for a fee from The Haworth Document Delivery Service: 1-800-HAWORTH. E-mail address: docdelivery@haworthpress.com. Website: http://www.HaworthPress.com. © 2004 by The Haworth Press, Inc. All rights reserved.]*

Keywords: harm reduction approach; client-centered approach; strengths perspective; adolescents; high-risk adolescent behavior

INTRODUCTION

"Meet the client where the client is," the popular slogan of social work practice, sums up harm reduction philosophy in a nutshell. From its origins as a way of addressing the negative consequences of drug use, the harm reduction concept has grown considerably in recent years (Hill,1998). An international public health movement, harm reduction joins client and therapist in the realistic pursuit of reducing the harm in one's life. Typical strategies include: helping clients substitute a less harmful drug for a life-threatening drug; recruitment of clients into methadone maintenance and needle exchange programs; giving women returning to their

Author's Note: Correspondence may be addressed to Katherine van Wormer, MSSW, PhD, Professor of Social Work, University of Northern Iowa, Cedar Falls, Iowa 50614 (e-mail: vanworme@uni.edu).

battering husbands a safety plan for self protection; and an after-school program to help gays and lesbians "talk through" problems of internalized homophobia that might otherwise seek self-destructive channels of expression.

Although social work and the harm reduction approach are a natural fit and widely integrated in Europe (see van Wormer, 2002), the U.S. social work literature is remiss in terms of describing the utilization of this practice/policy perspective. A search of *Social Work Abstracts* online as of August, 2003, reveals ten listings for harm reduction, only four of which are in American social work journals—from *Health and Social Work* are articles by Brocato and Wagner (2003); Reid (2002); and MacMaster, Vail, and Neff (2002); and from *Social Work Research* an article by Burke and Clapp (1999). (Actually, this is a big improvement over one year earlier when only one article from a U.S. journal of social work was listed.) For point of comparison, PsycInfo lists 388 at the time of this writing. In substance abuse texts written by American social workers, as well, the harm reduction model is relatively absent. Exceptions are Abbott (2000) and van Wormer and Davis (2008). Abbott provides a two-page description of the model and includes a chapter by Dunn (2000) that utilizes the stages of change model consistent with harm reduction and strengths-based principles. The van Wormer and Davis volume, similarly, is strengths-based and utilizes a harm reduction conceptualization throughout. One can expect to hear much more about harm reduction and its practice counterpart, motivational interviewing, in the future, however. The prestigious *Journal of Social Work Education* recently published "After the War on Drugs Is Over: Implications for Social Work Education" by McNeece (2003). I believe, indirectly, the empirical research in the federally funded Project Match (1997) which confirmed the effectiveness of a variety of treatment approaches but which showed that motivational strategies worked well and especially well with angry clients, has brought a belated effect to bear on treatment offerings. At the same time, there is a general consensus that prevention is preferable to treatment and that harm reduction strategies, like the public health model, are geared toward preventing the development of addictions problems in the first place.

A further promising development is the endorsement by the National Association of Social Workers (NASW) (2003) in their handbook of policy statements of a comprehensive public health approach for the prevention of alcohol, tobacco, and other drug problems and harm reduction strategies aimed at persons affected by such problems. In this article we will examine the principles of a harm reduction or public health framework, relate these precepts to the strengths perspective of social work practice, and explore work with adolescents as just one of the areas of social work for which the harm reduction model has special relevance. Emphasis will be on adolescent risk taking in the areas of sexuality and substance abuse.

HARM REDUCTION VERSUS TRADITIONAL APPROACHES

What is the harm reduction approach? To define this term, we need to take into account the two aspects of harm reduction that are often poorly differentiated in the literature—these are the policy and practice aspects. As *policy*, harm reduction is an outgrowth of the international public health movement. Its most familiar representation is as a philosophy that opposes the criminalization of drug use and views substance misuse as a public health rather than criminal justice concern. The goal of the harm reduction movement is to reduce the harm to high risk takers and to the communities in which they live, including the harm caused by criminalization of the substances (Jensen and Gerber, 1998). Proponents of this model generally oppose laws against drinking by young adults under age twenty-one and harsh punishments for drug use and possession. The war on drugs, from this viewpoint, exacts a deadly toll. This toll is generated in terms of: use of contaminated, unregulated chemicals; the spread of hepatitis, tuberculosis, and AIDS through the sharing of dirty needles; the social breakdown in America's inner cities; and political corruption elsewhere (van Wormer and Davis, 2002). In Europe, in fact, it was the AIDS epidemic of the 1980s which catapulted harm reduction policies into prominence in several countries, including Britain (Abbott, 2000). Drug use was medicalized, and the behavior of drug use closely monitored at methadone and other clinics where a safe drug supply was provided under medical supervision. Several U.S. cities including Baltimore and Seattle have moved in the direction of such progressive policies.

Because harm reduction measures are diversified and highly pragmatic (as opposed to moralistic), scientific research plays a key role in convincing legislators and other policymakers to sponsor the establishment of such strategies. Proof is essential, moreover, to establish which programs are truly harm reducing, as Canadian public health specialist, Eric Single (2000), reminds us. Fortunately, despite the U.S. federal government's reluctance to publicly endorse non-abstinence based programs for youth, there is much grant money available for experimental treatments, as, for example, the Cannabis Youth Treatment Series described at the National Clearinghouse for Alcohol and Drug Information and unveiled by the Substance Abuse Mental Health Services Administration (SAMSHA, 2000). This series compared traditional with alternative approaches, including motivational therapy, in which clients, in individual sessions, are given the message that the decision to stop smoking marijuana is up to them. Results with a large sample showed that there was substantial reduction in marijuana use with the various methods that were applied. Consistent with the principles of harm reduction, note that in the research literature today, the measure of treatment success relevant to substance misuse is a *reduction* in use and in harmful consequences; the traditional measure was always complete abstinence from the drug (van Wormer and Davis, 2002).

At the *practice* level, harm reduction is an umbrella term for a set of practical strategies based on motivational interviewing and other strengths-based approaches to help people help themselves by moving steadily in the direction of reduction of high-risk practices. As practice, harm reduction entails removing barriers such as lack of childcare or bureaucratic constraints that impede people from getting treatment. Typical advice given to clients is of the order of, "Don't drink on an empty stomach," or "Don't drink and drive." Duncan, Nicholson, Clifford, Hawkins, and Petosa (1994) describe how they confronted an epidemic of paint and solvent "huffing" after two boys died from inhaling paint fumes in plastic bags. Educational presentations to youth groups emphasized the dangers of huffing and warned them if they did do it, to at least use paper bags instead of plastic bags which could be lethal.

In this client-centered approach, use of negative labels such as "antisocial" and "borderline" in mental health, "criminal personality" in criminal justice, and "alcoholic/addict" in substance abuse treatment is avoided; clients provide the definition of the situation as they see it. The traditional message imparted to kids, such as in educational programs, is the total and immediate abstinence from all dangerous, risk-taking activities such as no sex before marriage and don't drink until you're 21. Peterson, Dimeff, Tapert, Stern, and Gorman (1998) warn against the "boomerang" effect of these absolutist approaches as alienating of youths and lessening adult's credibility. An approach stressing choice in decision making, in contrast, empowers youth to make practical decisions about their own lives. Given the obvious reluctance of drug users to volunteer for treatment under the old, police-dominated system, new and very different forms of intervention must be developed (McNeece, 2003).

PUNITIVE TRADITIONS ON THE AMERICAN CONTINENT

Forcing young unwed mothers to carry their babies to term; returning parolees who have relapses to prison; mandatory sentencing; zero tolerance in the schools–such practices commonly supported by the American public and policy makers reflect a punitive ethos that has its roots in Colonial times.

Like the very language that shapes our every thought and deed, the present day American value system is rooted in the New England experience, in the foundation laid down by the colony of religious zealots in Massachusetts Bay. The essence of this foundation was the holy experiment known to the world as Puritanism. In his classic, *Wayward Puritans: A Study in the Sociology of Deviance*, Kai Erikson (1966) provided a colorful portrait of this society and of the dissenters among them. Theirs was a society run by the clergy whose role it was to interpret the scriptures for guidance in all matters of living. Indeed, back in England, the English had found their narrow liberalism and lack of humor baffling. To Puritans who reached Massachusetts, the truth was perfectly clear: God had chosen an elite few to represent Him on earth. It was their responsibility to control the destinies of others.

Influenced by the doctrines of predestination, the Puritans believed that people were either to be saved or condemned—this was their destiny. Sooner or later persons would give evidence of the category to which they belonged. Those who had reason to fear the worst would inevitably sink to the lowest echelons of society. In accordance with the will of God, punishment for offenders was harsh.

We find the peculiar ethos of Puritanism in evidence in American society today. Despite the modern secularism, the Puritan ethic manifests itself in the severity of punishment, the moralism pertaining to "welfare cheats," common criminals, and users of illegal substances. The uniqueness of this history is important because many of the differences between Old and New World attitudes concerning drug use and work ethic have their origins in these humble beginnings. Sexual prudery and enforced abstinence from drink, however, were not a part of the Puritan scene. The Puritans regarded drinking intoxicants as conducive to good health. The restrictions against consumption of alcohol were added later after the impact of hard liquor had become a cause for concern (Bryson, 1994). The spirit of Puritanism, the rigidity and punitiveness, however, survived in these later developments, and are evidenced in many of the policies of today.

The war on drugs is taking a double toll on children, first in taking their parents away and subjecting them to the tragedy of premature separation. The stigma of having one or both parents incarcerated weighs heavily upon a growing child. The second toll on children occurs when their own reactive, acting-out behavior brings harsh consequences. Half of the 1.5 million kids with a parent in jail or prison, in fact, will commit a crime before they turn 18 (Drummond, 2000).

Youths who get into trouble with drugs and who are sent to juvenile facilities have high rates of recidivism (Noble and Reed, 2000). Yet more and more youths are being dealt with harshly in juvenile court for minor crimes and tried as adults for major crimes. An innovative and carefully orchestrated development, the Drug Courts movement, provides mandatory alcohol and drug treatment and a continuum of community services to ensure compliance with its two-year program. Education, vocational experiences, and life skills training are provided. Results from the over 300 programs nationwide indicate that Drug Courts have been highly effective in saving taxpayers money ("Study Shows Drug Courts Reduce Substance Abuse, Crimes," 1998). Addiction treatment costs between $2,000 to $3,000 per person. Compare that to the $25,000 or so required to incarcerate someone. Today, there are treatment strategies, moreover, that are specifically geared to a person's maturity level or, in other words, to his or her readiness to address the substance use issues.

Harm reduction philosophy is built on pragmatism and compromise. It operates on the belief that between moderate use (as of a drug) and life threatening behavior, moderation is better. It does not always gel well with American moralism, therefore. As Marlatt (1998) explains:

> Consistent with a policy of total abstinence, the principle of zero tolerance establishes an absolute dichotomy between no (zero) use and any use whatsoever. This all-or-none dichotomy labels all drug use as equally criminal (or sick), and fails to distinguish between lighter and heavier drug use or degrees of harmful use. (p. 51)

Philosophically, harm reduction has its roots in European pragmatism; the focus is on maintaining good health rather than punishing bad behavior. From this perspective, all potentially risk-taking behavior such as sexuality is viewed along a continuum ranging from no involvement or abstinence at one end to extremely harmful activities at the end, with casual practices in the middle.

Harm Reduction and Adolescent Risk Taking

Society's moralism is especially pronounced with regard to risk-taking behavior of youth. Drinking, drug experimentation, sexual expression—all are behaviors, the consequences of which are feared and even resented when engaged in by youth. In the 1990s, in fact, U.S. Surgeon General Joycelyn Elders took a realistic stance toward adolescent sexuality. She advocated teaching young people in school sex education classes about the risks of unprotected sex and giving them ways to reduce these risks. A public uproar ensued, and Elder's remarks ultimately resulted in her dismissal (Peterson et al., 1998). Official government policy has largely supported abstinence-only sex education. Yet, as Peterson et al. indicate, scientifically controlled studies show that discussion of safe sex practices with youth does not lead them to initiate sexual activity earlier than they would have otherwise.

Harm reduction, the preferred European approach, emphasizes abstinence as an important option, but also provides information to reduce the risk of AIDS, venereal disease, and unplanned pregnancy. In Amsterdam on weekends, peer counselors seek out rave dancers, provide them with glow-in-the-dark pamphlet racks and cushions, and inform them about uppers and downers and keeping safe. "Just Say Know" as opposed to "Just Say No" is the group's motto (Power, Johnson, and Theil, 1999). "Knowledge is power" as the saying goes. It, knowledge, is also empowering.

Prevention as Harm Reduction

Harm reduction strategies with youth apply at various levels ranging from community-based educational programs to individual guidance. Some methods of reducing harm are indirect; for example, reducing the size of schools and classes to create a more personal learning environment and to keep an eye on children in need of help. The situation regarding drinking and drug use parallels the high-risk sex situations. Often, inevitably, intoxication and unhealthy sexual behavior go together. Unlike law enforcement strategies which focus on reducing the supply side of drugs, harm reduction is geared to reducing the demand for drugs. This form of prevention is sometimes termed *primary* prevention and includes early childhood education, treatment programs, and community interventions to reduce indirect risk factors such as parental alcohol abuse and child mistreatment.

The public health approach to preventing harm is multidimensional and ideally operates across systems. Knowledge of the developmental progression of substance use is important for the focus and timing of preventive interventions (Botvin and Botvin, 1997). Knowledge of the typical pathways that lead into reckless behavior is also instrumental in alleviating or treating underlying psychological problems that can increase the risks for harmful experimentation. Prevention of early childhood abuse and trauma is key to prevention of the development of the kind of substance misuse that relates to affect-use of chemicals to counteract low feelings resulting from early childhood trauma. Social policy initiatives must include a coordination of services to protect children from the earliest age onward. Parenting courses, periodic public health nurse visits to all homes where there are babies, a well-funded child welfare system to ensure the safety of children are the first priority—these are among the initiatives that are sorely needed. In the United Kingdom, the Labour government has introduced new strategies that are based on a coordination of efforts across national and local bodies; these bodies include education, health, and prevention services to reduce the demand for drugs (Howard, 1998). The message to the British "drug tsar," according to this report, is that treatment is a cornerstone to reducing demand; harm reduction gets the seal of approval.

The aim of all these efforts is to help children get through adolescence relatively unscathed, and to prevent experimentation with substances, the use of which carries the potential for personal destructiveness down the road. Many of the developmental changes that are necessary prerequisites for becoming healthy adults unfortunately increase an adolescent's risk of smoking, drinking heavily, or using drugs (Botvin and Botvin, 1997).

Primary prevention efforts can be divided into seven general strategies:

- Child protection aimed at the cycle of violence and substance misuse;

- School-based prevention programs directed toward social influences prompting youths to smoke;

- Information dissemination approaches focusing on immediate consequences of smoking (bad breath, breathing problems);

- School programs based on dialoguing with youth to answer questions honestly and provide information about which drugs are the most dangerous and to promote moderate drinking over bingeing;

- Mass media campaigns showing the negative side of alcohol, tobacco, and other drug misuse;

- Social resistance and personal competence skills approaches (e.g., anxiety management skills, assertiveness training);

- Campaigns to reduce or eliminate TV beer ads, student newspaper local bar and national beer ads;

- Advocacy for the hiring of more school counselors and social workers to work with high-risk students (bullies, victims, children who suffer from mental disorders, children of alcoholic/addicts).

Because of the extremely addictive properties of nicotine, an all-out effort should be made to keep youths from ever starting to smoke; this effort should be bolstered by community and media support. A clever strategy to get youths to quit smoking is to involve them in strenuous exercise programs. According to an article in the *Washington Post* health section (Krucoff, 1999), a study of male runners showed that 70 percent of those who smoked subsequently quit. Almost half of the women in an exercise group quit smoking as well.

Alcohol, in contrast with tobacco, has positive, health-benefiting properties. Many families enjoy moderate drinking while condemning intoxication; cultural traditions come into play here. Moderate drinking and abstinence should therefore be presented in health education classes as equally acceptable choices. Since practically all youths will at least sample alcohol, a focus on safe and unsafe practices associated with its use would seem to be the only practical course to take. Expecting youngsters not to drink until they reach 21, then suddenly to become responsible drinkers is unrealistic (Boroson, 1993). Information based on ideology rather than fact, furthermore, will be given little credibility by teens. The whole strategy of demonizing alcohol for youth and reserving its pleasures for adults over a certain age merely increases its attractiveness.

Given the high rates of pregnancy, sexually transmitted diseases, growing rates of HIV infection, and risk of lethal overdose among teens, and especially marginalized teens, harm reduction holds the maximum potential for protection (de Miranda, 1999). Leshner (1999) describes two paths to drug use; these pathways have significance for treatment. The first path involves the group of kids who are seeking novelty or excitement, who are striving to be "cool." These youth are most likely to be responsive to prevention education about the harmful effects of drugs on their bodies; for example, the side effects of steroids on the testicles and complexion. The second path to substance use involves dynamics of another sort. Using drugs to escape emotional pain, youths in this category are bent on self-medication. Their problem is getting through the day; messages about long-term damage are apt, therefore, to have little impact. Teenage

girls tend to fall in this category, drinking heavily to ward off depression and relieve stress while boys tend to do it for thrills or heightened social standing in the group (Alex, 2003, October 24). Girls thus require gender-specific educational efforts. Fear arousing messages beamed at adolescents, paradoxically, are irrelevant to emotionally troubled youth and apt to attract rather than deter the risk takers among them. Leshner recommends professional help for youth with problems. Sadly, only one in five of every adolescents in need of treatment services actually receives such treatment (U.S. Department of Health and Human Services, 2001).

In a survey of research effectiveness studies, Botvin and Botvin (1997) found that social life skills training either alone or in combination with other approaches emerged as having the most effective impact on substance use behavior. These approaches, as Botvin and Botvin indicate, utilize well-tested behavioral intervention techniques; they also help prepare adolescents to deal with strong feelings without resorting to use of alcohol and other drugs. The coping mechanisms acquired here should be invaluable in later life as well. Marlatt (2003), a professor of psychology at the University of Washington, who is noted for his empirical research with first-year college students in helping them moderate their drinking through brief motivational counseling sessions, reported excellent results in small group work with high school seniors as well. The goal was to move students from where they were into taking small, manageable steps toward healthy living. School officials reportedly were pleased with the results and requested that more workshops be offered.

MOTIVATIONAL INTERVIEWING

As a practice technique, harm reduction strives to get the client motivated to make a health-seeking choice. The focus thus becomes the client's motivation.

Motivational interviewing (MI) is a non-confrontational model based on the fundamental truth from social psychology that decisions to move toward change are more powerful if they come from within. Derived from the teachings of psychologists Miller and Roll-nick (1991), MI, in its basic formulation and precepts, closely parallels the strengths perspective of social work practice (van Wormer and Davis, 2003).

The strengths approach, as Saleebey (2002) suggests, is "a versatile practice approach, relying heavily on ingenuity and creativity, the courage and common sense of both clients and their social workers. It is a collaborative process" (p. 1). Traditionally, work in the substance abuse field has focused on *breaking* client resistance and denial (Rapp, 1998). According to this more positive framework which builds on client's strengths and resources, however, client resistance and denial are often viewed as healthy, intelligent responses to a situation that might involve unwelcome court mandates and other intrusive practices.

As in the strengths formulation, the focus of MI is on collaboration of counselor and client as well as on personal choice (see Saleebey, 2002). When the focus on the professional relationship is on promoting healthy lifestyles and on reducing the problems that the client defines as important rather than on the substance use per se, many clients can be reached who would otherwise stay away (Denning, 2000; and Graham, Brett, and Baron, 1994). Central to this approach is the building of a relationship between therapist and client. In working with youth, this relationship is crucial in terms of promoting self-esteem and the confidence to try on new roles. In the MI orientation, the strategy is to help develop and support the client's belief that he or she can change; this is the principle of self-efficacy (SAMHSA, 2000).

The motivational, like the strengths approach, meets the client where he or she is at that point in time. The harm reduction practitioner assesses the level of the client's motivation for change and, instead of engaging in a tug of war with the client, "rolls with resistance." MI techniques are geared to help people find their own path to change. The therapist provides feedback through additive paraphrasing, a technique that involves selectively reflecting back to the client what he or she seems to be saying about the need to reduce or eliminate self-destructive behaviors (van Wormer and Davis, 2003).

Ideally suited for work with troubled and rebellious teens, harm reduction meets the youth where the youth is and is disarmingly nonthreatening. There is no moralizing tone here, no forcing teens to sit in a circle and label themselves as alcoholics or addicts. A certain amount of ambivalence is expected and, in fact, deemed healthy. Central to the whole framework is the belief that clients are amenable to change. This optimism closely parallels Saleebey's notions of "promise and possibility" (2002, p. 15).

MI therapists draw on the stages of change model, originally formulated by Prochaska and DiClemente (1992). This model is built on the assumption that treatment interventions can be matched to the client's readiness to change. Taking an adolescent who is ambivalent about drug taking, we can conceive of him or her as progressing through the following stages of change:

- Precontemplation: (for example, "My parents can't tell me what to do; so what if I get high now and then?")

- Contemplation: ("When I'm high, I'm high but being down is a drag.")

- Preparation: ("I know the things I'm doing will have to stop sometime in the future.")

- Action: ("The date I've set is my birthday; I'm going with a friend to one of those groups, just to try it out.")

- Maintenance: ("It's been a few months, a few dull months. But my mind seems much clearer. I've made some new friends.")

Patricia Dunn (2000) finds that the stages of change model is appropriate for social work because it is compatible with the mission and concepts of the profession, is an integrative (transtheoretical) model, and is grounded in empirical research. Through building a close therapeutic relationship, the counselor can help the client develop a commitment to change. The way motivational theory goes is this: if the therapist can get the client to do something, anything, to get better, this client will have a chance at success. This is a basic principle of social psychology. Examples of tasks that William Miller (1998) pinpoints as predictors of recovery are: going to AA meetings, coming to sessions, completing homework assignments, and taking medication (even if a placebo pill). The question, according to Miller, then becomes, "How can I help my clients do something to take action on their own behalf?" A related principle of social psychology is that in defending a position aloud, as in a debate, we become committed to it. One would predict, from motivational enhancement perspective, that if the therapist elicits defensive statements in the client, the client will become more committed to the status quo and less willing to change. For this reason, explains Miller, confrontational approaches have a poor track record. Research has shown that people are more likely to grow and change in a positive direction on their own than if they get caught up in a battle of wills.

The starting point for the therapist is to determine where the client is, at what level of change. As Boyle (2000) indicates, it is not unusual for involuntary clients to enter treatment at the *precontemplative* stage. At this preliminary stage, the goals for the therapist are to establish rapport, to ask rather than to tell, and to build trust. Eliciting the young person's definition of the situation, the counselor can reinforce discrepancies between the client's and other's perceptions of the problem. During the *contemplation* stage, while helping to tip the decision toward reduced drug/alcohol use, the counselor emphasizes the client's freedom of choice. "No one can make this decision for you" is a typical way to phrase this sentiment. Information is presented in a neutral, "take-it-or-leave-it" manner. Typical questions are, "What do you get out of drinking?" "What is the down side?" And to elicit strengths, "What makes your sister believe in your ability to do this?" At the *preparation* for change and *action* stages questions like, "What do you think will work for you?" help guide the youth forward without pushing him or her too far too fast.

(For more on motivational enhancement strategies for social workers see Dunn (2000) and van Wormer and Davis (2003). The seven-part professional training videotape series presented by Miller and Rollnick (1998) provides guidance in both the art and science of motivational enhancement. The role-plays provide a highly useful didactic technique.)

INNOVATIVE PROGRAMMING

The difficulty in offering true harm reduction programs for teens in the United States relates to the potential conflict between agency policy and political legislation. Harm reduction policies for adults such as needle exchange programs, are controversial and underfunded. Programs for teens such as DanceSafe, which tests Ecstasy pills for toxic substances for youths attending raves to ensure their safety before youths consume them, are privately funded and operated by volunteers. Recently passed legislation, however, threatens persons helping in any capacity at raves with arrest.

In Canada, Youthlink Inner City serves the hard-to-reach and alienated youth who frequent downtown Toronto. Since the harm reduction model is widely accepted in Canada, this agency appears to be widely respected despite a shortage of funds (Youthlink, 1999). Alan Simpson, BSW, (June 12, 2002), in private correspondence with the author, describes this progressive program:

> Youthlink Inner City runs a drop-in center for street-involved youth aged 16-24 and utilizes a harm reduction approach with all aspects of youth. This ranges from a needle exchange program, access to health care, providing food for many youth who haven't eaten in several days, and mainly accepting the youth where they are at now.
>
> This process can be very hard to imagine, let alone put into practice. Many agencies use an abstinence-based objective and the only success is that which can be measured on a scale. The use of harm reduction, especially with this population, is empowering and gives a voice to those who have been marginalized in so many ways. In our eyes and opinion, youth who have started to become aware of what is affecting them and have started to make changes that improve their decisions and lives are a success to us. Once you give a person the information and the ability to utilize the decision-making process for his or her gain, improvements will be made. InnerCity works extremely well in helping youth make this transition.

InnerCity is committed to the reduction of the transmission of HIV. A needle exchange program and free condoms are provided in the hope of curbing the spread of this disease, according to the web site. Some of the other services available at this drop-in center range from medical care, welfare and housing services, legal advice by volunteer lawyers, recreational activities, and job referrals.

IMPLEMENTATION OF HARM REDUCTION STRATEGIES FOR TEENS

We have talked about what social workers can do as practitioners, drawing on their best listening skills and using motivational strategies to engage youth to choose a sober lifestyle. Schools of social work should require coursework related to substance use, teach empirically-based interventions, and encourage field placements in substance abuse treatment programs that use motivational and other harm reduction strategies (Brocato and Wagner, 2003). Policy courses, as Brocato and Wagner further suggest, should include drug policy with the other policies covered.

In Iowa, we have had an interesting experience due to our exchange with the University of Hull, England. Each summer several visiting British students do their field practicum at substance abuse treatment centers to learn about 12-step approaches. In so doing, they have broadened the horizons of counselors and medical staff with whom they have worked. This is one way of introducing new ways of doing things, through the introduction of international perspectives: same problem, different solutions. American students, meanwhile, have learned firsthand of harm reduction in their coursework in addictions at the University of Hull.

Once social workers have grasped the essentials of harm reduction, and more specifically, of motivational techniques, and are equipped with research on treatment effectiveness, they can shape policies through their influence in the course of school social work or substance abuse counseling. They can speak to parent's groups and conduct workshops for teachers and counselors. Insurance companies today are amenable to motivational strategies, probably because of their cost-saving qualities and this has opened the door in many states to a stronger focus on prevention and treatment before the problems have grown severe. One program in Iowa that has been well received is the Strengthening Families Program. This program, when introduced in Iowa, has significantly delayed initiation of alcohol use by improving parenting skills and family bonding (National Institute on Alcohol Abuse and Alcoholism, 2003).

Making oneself known to legislators, progressive and otherwise, is a crucial first step in influencing state policy. While punitive policies persist at the federal level, social workers can take advantage of devolution (or the turning over of responsibility for social welfare functions to the states) to work through state representatives. This can be done through informative Fact Sheets (sent by e-mail or personally delivered) at the time a relevant bill is introduced in Congress and legislators are anxious to learn of cost-benefits ratios and of treatment effectiveness research findings. Social workers can advocate by attending county-level public forums with their legislators to produce their evidence and keep the issues of concern alive. Letters to the editor in the local newspapers can argue that funding (especially from gambling and tobacco settlements) be targeted to antismoking initiatives and other media prevention campaigns. From a harm reduction perspective, social workers should lobby legislators to advocate for neighborhood drop-in centers where teens can drop in or their parents can bring them for immediate and informal counseling sessions.

In summary, programs can be implemented in collaboration with teachers in the schools and substance abuse counselors, who are colleagues working within the system, for strategies to help our youth reduce the harm to themselves. Another option is working at the broader policy level for the funding that is needed for public health policies aimed at the prevention of risk-taking behavior.

CONCLUSION

A common misconception of harm reduction is to see its ultimate goals as incompatible with the 12-step approach. Sustaining a healthy lifestyle is probably the goal of all treatment models. Harm reduction can be distinguished from traditional approaches in that it is individualized and low key. Through showing a great deal of patience while the young person gropes for his or her way to sobriety and safe living, the harm reduction practitioner helps the client move from high levels of risk-taking toward progressively safer behaviors. Harm reduction seeks, above all else, to save lives. Clients, accordingly, are reinforced in whatever moves toward sobriety, abstinence, and safe sex practices they are able and willing to make.

The harm reduction framework differs from that of many traditional counselors of the 12-step school; in short, in its flexibility, client centeredness, strengths perspective, and orientation toward public health. This approach is especially relevant to acting-out youth, youth who above all, need someone to talk to, someone older and wiser who will listen. Society's proclaimed zero-tolerance approach, all the metaphors of war used in connection with the war on drugs, the one-size-fits-all treatment schemes—these off-putting policies are harm inducing rather than harm reducing. They cause harm to the young who tune out the message that drug use and unsafe sex can have consequences; to families, especially African American and Latino families, who lose their loved ones to the criminal justice system; and to society through providing punishment rather than care. Money invested in the drug war could be far better spent on prevention and the demand side of drugs.

Under an expanded harm reduction model, social work and counseling intervention would be geared toward community prevention work and early treatment of drug users to monitor their use and lifestyle. Because the "abstinence-only" model emphasizes treatment *after* the drug dependent person has "hit his or her bottom," an opportunity to introduce life-saving measures at early stages of drug use and/or problem drinking is lost. Forcing young people to attach a label to themselves is inconsistent with social work's value of self-determination. In the words of a visiting British addictions worker who was speaking before an Iowa student audience, "You are failing to meet the needs of a very significant number of people out there. I'm thinking especially of adolescents who do not identify with a label such as alcoholic or addict but who could benefit from help on their own terms" (Hobby, 1996).

REFERENCES

Abbott, A. (2000). Values, ethics and ethical dilemmas in ATOD practice. In A. Abbott (Ed.), *Alcohol, tobacco, and other drugs: Challenging myths, assessing theories, individualizing interventions.* (pp. 44–73). Washington, DC: NASW Press.

Alex, T. (2003, October 24). Should reform be gender specific? *Des Moines Register,* B1.

Boroson, W. (1993, August 8). Drinking age: Abstinence vs. moderation. *The Record,* 17–20.

Botvin, G. and Botvin, E. (1997). School-based programs. In J. H. Lowinson, P. Ruiz, R. Mulliman, and J. G. Langrod (Eds.), *Substance abuse: A comprehensive textbook* (pp. 764–775). Baltimore: Williams and Wilkins.

Boyle, C. (2000). Engagement: An ongoing process. In A. Abbott (Ed.), *Alcohol, tobacco, and other drugs* (pp. 144–158). Washington, DC: NASW Press.

Brocato, J. and Wagner, E. F. (2003). Harm reduction: A social work practice model and social justice agenda. *Health & Social Work, 28*(2), 117–125.

Bryson, B. (1994). *Made in America.* London: Minerva.

Burke, A. C. and Clapp, J. D. (1999). Ideology and social work practice in substance abuse settings. *Social Work, 42* (6), 552–562.

de Miranda, J. (1999, June 7). Harm reduction holds potential to reach marginalized youth. *Alcoholism & Drug Abuse Weekly 11*(23), 5.

Denning, P. (2000). *Practicing harm reduction psychotherapy.* New York: Guilford Press.

Drummond, T. (2000, November 6). Mothers in prison. *Time,* 105–107.

Duncan, D. F., Nicholson, T., Clifford, P., Hawkins, W. and Petosa, R. (1994). Harm reduction: An emerging new paradigm. *Journal of Drug Education, 24* (4), 281–290.

Dunn, P. (2000). The stages and processes of change model: Implications for social work ATOD practice. In A. Abbott (Ed.), *Alcohol, tobacco, and other drugs.* (pp. 111–143). Washington, DC: NASW Press.

Erikson, K. (1966). *Wayward Puritans: A study in the sociology of deviance.* New York: Wiley and Sons.

Graham, K., Brett, P. J., and Baron, J. (1994). *A harm reduction approach to treating older adults. The clients speak.* Paper presented at the 5th International Conference on the Reduction of Drug Related Harm. Toronto, Ontario, March 7–10.

Hill, A. (1998, Spring). Applying harm reduction to services for substance using women in violent relationships. *Harm Reduction Coalition,* 7.

Hobby, J. (October 22, 1996). *The harm reduction model.* Talk presented at Covenant Medical Center, Waterloo, Iowa.

Howard, R. (1998, October 8–14). Labour in power. *Community Care,* 17–29.

Jensen, E. L. & Gerber, J. (1998). The social construction of drug problems: An historical overview. In E. L. Jensen & J. Gerber (Ed.), *The new war on drugs: Symbolic and criminal justice policy.* (pp. 1–23). Cincinnati, Ohio: Anderson.

Krucoff, C. (1999, March 23). Smoke and mirrors. *Washington Post,* 20.

Leshner, A. I. (1999). Science-based views of drug addiction and its treatment. *Journal of the American Medical Association 282*(14), 1314–1316.

MacMaster, S. A., Vail, K. A., and Neff, J. A. (2002). The Xchange point: A drop-in center for African American active injection drug users. *Health and Social Work, 27*(3), 227–229.

Marlatt, G. A. (1998). Basic principles and strategies of harm reduction.

In G. A. Marlatt (Ed.), *Harm reduction: Pragmatic strategies for managing high-risk behaviors* (pp. 49–66). New York: Guilford.

Marlatt, G.A. (undated). Expert opinion: Harm reduction works. *Alcohol information.* Retrieved on August 13, 2003, from www2.potsdam.edu/alcohol-info/

McNeece, C. A. (2003). After the war on drugs is over: Implications for social work education. *Journal of Social Work Education, 39*(2), 193–212.

Miller, W. (1998). Enhancing motivation for change. In W. Miller and N. Heather (Eds.), *Treating addictive behaviors* (2nd ed., pp.121–132). New York: Plenum Press.

Miller, W. R. and Rollnick, S. (1991). *Motivational interviewing: Preparing people to change addictive behavior.* New York: Guilford.

Miller, W. R. and Rollnick, S. (1998). *Motivational interviewing: Professional training videotape series.*

National Association of Social Workers (NASW) (2003). Alcohol, tobacco, and other substance abuse. In *NASW, Social work speaks: NASW policy statements* (6th ed., pp. 20–27). Washington, DC: NASW Press.

National Institute on Alcohol Abuse and Alcoholism (2003, April). Underage drinking: A major public health challenge. *Alcohol Alert,* no. 59. Rockville, MD: U.S. Department of Health and Human Services.

Noble, M. C. and Reed, C. (2000, January). Kentucky drug courts. *Bench & Bar 64,* 6–10.

Peterson, P., Dimeff, L., Tapert, S., Stern, M., and Gorman, M. (1998). Harm reduction and HIV/AIDS prevention. In G. A. Marlatt (Ed.), *Harm reduction: Pragmatic strategies for managing high-risk behaviors.* (pp. 218–297). New York: Guilford.

Power, C., Johnson, S., and Theil, S. (1999, November 1). Europe just says maybe: Authorities abandon faith in prohibition and enhance "harm reduction." *Newsweek,* 20.

Prochaska, J. and DiClemente, C. (1992). In search of how people change: Applications to addictive behaviors. *American Psychologist 47,* 1102–1114.

Project MATCH Research Group (1997, January). Matching alcoholism treatment to client heterogeneity: Project MATCH post treatment outcomes. *Journal of Studies on Alcohol 58,* 7–28.

Rapp, C. A. (1998). *The strengths model: Case management with people suffering from severe and persistent mental illness.* New York: Oxford University Press.

Reid, R.J. (2002). Harm reduction and injection drug use: Pragmatic lessons from a public health model. *Health and Social Work, 27*(3), 223–226.

Saleebey, D. (2002). Introduction: Power to the People. In D. Saleebey (Ed.). *The strengths perspective in social work practice* (3rd ed., pp.1–22). Boston: Allyn & Bacon.

Single, E. (2000). *The effectiveness of harm reduction and its role in a new framework for drug policy in British Columbia.* Presented to the National Federal/ Provincial/ Territorial Meeting on Injection Drug use. Vancouver, January 31.

Study Shows Drug Courts Reduce Substance Abuse, Crime (1998, November 11). Available online at www.jointogether.org.

Substance Abuse and Mental Health Services (SAMHSA) (2000). Motivational enhancement therapy and cognitive behavioral therapy for adolescent cannabis users: 5 sessions. *Cannabis Youth Treatment Series.* Online at: www.health.org/govpubs/.

U.S. Department of Health and Human Services (2001). *National Drug Control Strategy: 2001 Annual Report.*

Washington, DC: Office of the
National Drug Control Policy.

van Wormer, K. (2002). Harm induction vs.
harm reduction: Comparing American
and British approaches to drug use.
Journal of Offender Rehabilitation,
29 (1/2), 35–48.

van Wormer, K. and Davis, D. (2008).
Addiction treatment: A strengths
perspective. Belmont, CA: Wadsworth.

Youthlink (2009). What is youthlink-
Innercity? Retrieved on September 21,
2009 from http://www.youthlink.ca/
innercity.html.

17

SECONDARY PREVENTION SERVICES FOR CLIENTS WHO ARE LOW RISK IN DRUG COURT

A Conceptual Model

DAVID S. DeMATTEO

DOUGLAS B. MARLOWE

DAVID S. FESTINGER

TREATMENT RESEARCH INSTITUTE AT THE UNIVERSITY OF PENNSYLVANIA

The drug court model assumes that most drug offenders are addicts, and that drug use fuels other criminal activity. As a result, drug court clients must satisfy an intensive regimen of treatment and supervisory obligations. However, research suggests that roughly one third of drug court clients do not have a clinically significant substance use disorder. For these clients, standard drug court services may be ineffective or even contraindicated. Instead, these clients may be best suited for a secondary prevention approach directed at interrupting the acquisition of addictive behaviors. Unfortunately, there are no established secondary prevention packages for adults in criminal justice settings. This article presents a conceptual framework for developing and administering secondary prevention services in drug courts and proposes a platform of prevention techniques that can

Author's Note: This article was supported by Grants #R01-DA-13096 and #R01-DA-14566 from the National Institute on Drug Abuse (NIDA). The views expressed are ours and do not reflect the views of NIDA. Address correspondence concerning this article to David DeMatteo, JD, PhD, Treatment Research Institute at the University of Pennsylvania, 600 Public Ledger Bldg., 150 S. Independence Mall West, Philadelphia, PA 19106-3475; e-mail: ddematteo@tresearch.org

SOURCE: "Secondary Prevention Services for Clients Who Are Low Risk in Drug Court: A Conceptual Model" by David S. DeMatteo, Douglas B. Marlowe, and David S. Festinger. In the 2006 issue of *Crime and Delinquency, 19*(1), 114–134. Used with permission.

be tailored in a clinically relevant manner for the sizeable population of drug court clients who are low risk.

Keywords: *drug court; prevention; drug abuse; risk assessment*

A range of programs has been developed to provide substance abuse treatment to drug offenders in lieu of criminal prosecution or incarceration. These vary in intensity from pretrial diversion programs (sometimes called "probation without verdict"), to intensive supervised probation programs, to judicially supervised drug courts. The underlying assumption of these programs is that drug use fuels or exacerbates other criminal activity, and the offender has a clinically significant syndrome that could be expected to respond to treatment.

Yet research suggests that 30% to 40% of drug offenders do not have a diagnosable or clinically significant substance use disorder (Kleiman et al., 2003). In our studies, nearly one half of misdemeanor drug court clients (Marlowe, Festinger, & Lee, 2003), one third of felony drug court clients (Marlowe, Festinger, & Lee, 2004), and two thirds of pretrial clients in a drug treatment and monitoring program (Lee et al., 2001) produced "sub-thresh-old" drug composite scores on the Addiction Severity Index (ASI; McLellan et al., 1992), similar to a community sample of individuals who were not abusing substances. Despite having been screened-in as requiring drug treatment, more in-depth and confidential assessments revealed that these individuals did not have a minimally identifiable disorder. Furthermore, in one study, roughly one third of clients in misdemeanor drug court provided a virtually unbroken string of drug-negative urine specimens over nearly a 4-month period following intake (DeMatteo, Festinger, Lee, & Marlowe, 2005). If these individuals could readily abstain from drug use over such an extended interval of time, there may be little clinical justification for labeling their use as compulsive or assuming they need formal treatment.

There are several possible explanations for these findings. First, some offenders may feign substance abuse symptoms to avoid a more serious criminal disposition. It is possible, for example, that drug dealers who are not addicted might end up in diversion programs simply because they were charged with a drug possession offense and reported having a drug-use problem to avoid mandatory incarceration.

Second, many commonly used screening measures may inflate the prevalence of substance use disorders because they assume most addicts to be in "denial" or "precontemplation" about their problem, and thus likely to be underreporting drug use. Few such screening measures were normed on criminal justice clients, who could be expected to overreport symptoms. For example, research on the Substance Abuse Subtle Screening Inventory, 3rd edition (SASSI-3; Miller, Roberts, Brooks, & Lazowski, 1997) suggests it may overestimate the need for drug abuse treatment among offenders. The SASSI-3 was designed to discriminate between groups with and without drug-use problems using "subtle" items that do not inquire explicitly about substance use but are believed to reflect behavioral correlates of addiction. Although initial validation studies found that the SASSI-3 reliably identified those in need of drug abuse treatment (e.g., Lazowski, Miller, Boye, & Miller, 1998), subsequent studies revealed poor specificity (i.e., high false-positive rates) (e.g., Peters et al., 2000). For example, in one study involving juvenile offenders, the SASSI-3 misclassified nearly two thirds of individuals who were not abusing substances as being substance dependent (Rogers, Cashel, Johansen, Sewell, & Gonzalez, 1997), which suggests the SASSI-3 may substantially overestimate the need for substance abuse treatment among offenders.

Finally, the diagnostic criteria for substance abuse and substance dependence contained in the fourth edition of the *Diagnostic and Statistical Manual of Mental Disorders* (*DSM-IV*; American Psychiatric Association [APA], 1994) have become so generic and overinclusive that they may have lost clinical relevance for purposes of treatment planning. For example, to receive a diagnosis of substance abuse, a client only needs one symptom recurring in a 12-month period. Legal entanglement is one such symptom, which is not difficult to satisfy for individuals involved in the criminal justice system. This can lead practitioners to the tautological conclusion that anyone arrested for drug possession is, by definition, a drug abuser.

Moreover, according to the *DSM-IV*, a client can be diagnosed with substance dependence without exhibiting any features ordinarily associated with addiction, such as compulsive use, cravings, or withdrawal symptoms. To be diagnosed as substance dependent, a client must have three symptoms recurring at any time during a 12-month period, with no requirement that the symptoms occur at the same time. Moreover, several diagnostic criteria are written imprecisely to the point of losing their original meaning. For example, one criterion is that "the substance is often taken in larger amounts or over a longer period than was intended" (APA, 1994, p. 181). This criterion is intended to gauge "binges" and "loss of control" but is not typically applied that way. It is often erroneously interpreted to mean the client simply failed to plan his or her usage in advance, which is a common occurrence and certainly not pathognomonic of addiction.

Another criterion is "a persistent desire or unsuccessful efforts to cut down or control substance use" (APA, 1994, p. 181). This is meant to gauge compulsivity of use, yet clients can technically meet this criterion simply by expressing a continued desire to stop using drugs or indicating that prior efforts to cut down have been unsuccessful. Neither of these patterns necessarily conveys compulsivity of use. Finally, a further criterion is "a great deal of time is spent in activities necessary to obtain the substance" (APA, 1994, p. 181). Needless to say, this is not difficult to satisfy for individuals who are engaged in drug dealing or manufacturing activities, or who simply associate with other drug abusers in their day-to-day lives.

The result of employing these overly broad inclusion criteria is that clinical programming may not be appropriately suited to the needs of many clients in drug diversion programs, and the programs may end up providing unnecessary and costly clinical services. For the roughly one third of clients in diversion programs who do not have a diagnosable or clinically significant substance use disorder, best-practice standards in the substance abuse field suggest that a "secondary prevention" approach is most appropriate. Whereas standard drug abuse treatment is designed to ameliorate the clinical symptoms of addiction, secondary prevention strategies seek to interrupt the acquisition of addictive behaviors. Secondary prevention strategies are ideally targeted to individuals who have been exposed to known risk factors for a problematic behavior, or who have engaged to some degree in that behavior, but who have not yet developed a clinical syndrome (e.g., DeMatteo & Marczyk, 2005; Institute of Medicine, 1994; National Institute on Drug Abuse [NIDA], 2003).

Unfortunately, many drug diversion programs provide the same slate of services to all clients, regardless of drug-use severity. For example, all clients in drug courts typically must satisfy an intensive regimen of treatment and supervisory obligations, including several hours per week of drug abuse counseling, regularly scheduled status hearings in court, case management meetings, and random weekly urine testing (National Association of Drug Court Professionals [NADCP],

278 PART V. POLICY CONSIDERATIONS

1997). According to a national survey of drug courts, the large majority of drug court programs reported using a standard menu of clinical services, such as psychoeducational peer groups (82% of responding programs), 12-step groups (93%), and motivational interviewing and relapse prevention (93%) (Peyton & Gossweiler, 2001). Although research suggests that some drug court programs may actually provide a low dose of these services (Taxman & Bouffard, 2003), these treatments are nonetheless typically applied to all clients. One might question whether it is clinically effective or cost-efficient to provide such high-intensity services to offenders who are subthreshold as assessed by standardized clinical assessment instruments and premorbid in the sense that they have not, as yet, exhibited clinically significant symptoms or functional impairments related to their drug use.

In this article, we provide a conceptual framework for developing and administering secondary prevention services in a drug court setting. We begin by reviewing why current practices may be clinically contraindicated for some clients, and then propose a platform of prevention interventions that can be tailored in a more clinically relevant and cost-efficient manner for low-risk drug court clients. Throughout this article, we use the term *low risk* to refer to clients who are subthreshold and premorbid for a drug-use disorder. We recognize, however, that being low risk for substance abuse is not necessarily equivalent to being low risk for criminal offending. As is discussed, clients with certain criminogenic risk factors, such as antisocial personality disorder (APD), would not be appropriate for a prevention program, even if premorbid for a drug problem. Finally, we focus here on drug courts because they represent one of the most intensive drug diversion initiatives; however, the principles and techniques we discuss could be expected to apply with equal force to other forms of diversion programs.

SUITABILITY OF STANDARD DRUG COURT PRACTICES

Research on substance abuse treatment has generally failed to identify reliable principles for matching clients to suitable treatment regimens. In nearly all studies, equivalent outcomes have been obtained using a variety of counseling methods (e.g., Project MATCH Research Group, 1997) and a range of therapeutic modalities (e.g., McKay, Cacciola, McLellan, Alterman, & Wirtz, 1997; McKay et al., 2002). Outcomes rarely diverged as a consequence of detectable interactions between the treatment regimens and various client characteristics such as demographics, motivation for change, or drug-use severity. Still, recent findings do raise serious concerns about whether a "one-size-fits-all" approach is justified among drug-using offenders.

Scheduling Considerations

By design, drug court participation takes up a considerable amount of time. Clients must attend counseling sessions several times per week, meet regularly with a case manager, attend status hearings, and deliver random weekly urine samples. This may be beneficial for many clients because it fills their days with drug-incompatible activities and limits exposure to drug-related stimuli. However, these requirements may compete with clients' legitimate responsibilities, such as work, which puts them in a tough spot. On one hand, drug courts may require clients to be employed; on the other hand, program requirements may hinder their ability to maintain employment. This may be particularly true for clients who are subthreshold or premorbid, who are higher functioning and thus more likely to be employed. This suggests that interventions for these clients should, perhaps, limit requirements for on-site attendance and instead use more home-based strategies, such as brief telephone contacts.

Group Counseling

Group counseling is the most widely used format for delivering drug treatment services in drug courts (Peyton & Gossweiler, 2001; Taxman & Bouffard, 2002). The underlying philosophy is that groups create a safe and supportive environment that promotes abstinence by helping clients resist commonly encountered pressures to use drugs (e.g., Panas, Caspi, Fournier, & McCarty, 2003). Moreover, groups provide a forum for sharing ideas and coping strategies. For programs providing services to large numbers of clients, group treatment is quite cost-efficient. Unfortunately, we know surprisingly little about the effective components or parameters of group treatment. The mechanism(s) of action of groups and their potential side effects, dose-response effects, and contraindications are largely unproven (Marlowe, Kirby, et al., 2003).

Importantly, what we do know about group treatment is that it may be contraindicated for certain populations because it can paradoxically function as "deviancy training" (e.g., Dishion & Andrews, 1995; Rice, Harris, & Cormier, 1992). Research suggests that aggregating certain offenders who are high risk in groups can produce short-term and long-term negative effects. For example, Rice et al. (1992) found that violent recidivism increased for offenders who were psychopaths receiving group treatment versus those receiving individual treatment. Some studies also found that aggregating adolescents who were high risk in group treatment led to increases in delinquency, drug use, and violence at 1-year and 3-year follow-ups (Dishion & Andrews, 1995; Poulin, Dishion, & Burraston, 2001). In particular, research suggests that mixing offenders who are high risk and offenders who are low risk has a more pronounced negative effect on offenders who are low risk. For example, Petrosino, Turpin-Petrosino, and Finckenauer (2000) found that adolescents who were low risk

in Scared Straight programs often performed worse than their counterparts who were high risk. These results may be attributable to the socialization of clients who are low risk into an antisocial milieu, in which they adopt the values and attitudes of deviant peers who have relatively greater influence in the group. This suggests that clients who are low risk should either be treated on an individual basis or in separately stratified groups.

12-Step Groups

According to Peyton and Gossweiler's (2001) national survey of drug court programs, more than 90% of drug courts required or strongly encouraged participation in 12-step groups. These self-help recovery groups typically emphasize abstinence as opposed to reduced or controlled drinking. Addiction is conceptualized as being a medical and spiritual disease, and progress toward recovery is gauged by measuring one's progression through the "12 steps" that form the philosophical foundation of these groups (Alcoholics Anonymous [AA], 1976). Clients receive group support, repeated reminders about the consequences of drug use, and straightforward advice about methods for maintaining abstinence.

Step 1 to recovery in 12-step groups is to acknowledge one's "powerlessness" over addiction, which is believed to open addicts up to the possibility of turning their lives over to a higher spiritual power that can relieve their suffering (AA, 1976). Arguably, however, it makes little sense to require individuals who are not addicts to admit they are powerless over their drug use when, in fact, they may not be. Such a program might feel irrelevant to these individuals, or start them on a path of paying lip service to what others want to hear. Another common practice in 12-step groups is to confront individuals as being in "denial" if they do not admit to having an addiction. Because it is assumed that clients who participate in 12-step groups are, indeed, addicted to drugs, and because denial is a common feature of addiction, the failure to acknowledge one's addiction is viewed as further evidence of an addiction. However, this sentiment may seem sorely misplaced to one who is not, in fact, an addict. For these individuals, the failure to admit to having an addiction may reflect an accurate self-appraisal.

Motivational Interviewing

Motivational interviewing (MI; Miller & Rollnick, 2002) and motivational enhancement therapy (MET; Miller, Zweben, DiClemente, & Rychtarik, 1992) are also commonly used in drug courts (Peyton & Gossweiler, 2001). These interventions seek to enhance motivation for change by creating cognitive discrepancies between clients' current level of functioning and their desired goals (Rollnick, Heather, & Bell, 1992). The aim is to have clients realize they have not accomplished their goals because of their drug use, and to renew their efforts to attain those goals. Through open-ended questioning, clients are led to verbalize the negative effects that drugs have had on their lives. In this way, it is believed they will come to realize how drugs have created a multitude of problems for them, such as broken relationships, loss of employment, and health problems. However, for those who have not experienced serious problems related to drugs, these techniques may not be clinically effective. In fact, having such individuals verbalize the effects of drugs on their lives could highlight the fact that drugs have not had much negative effect yet, possibly leading the intervention to fall flat or even backfire.

A related strategy often used in MET is showing clients their own test results related to their biopsychosocial functioning. An example is the Drinker's Checkup (Miller, Sovereign, & Krege, 1988), which involves reviewing with clients the results of their liver-enzyme tests and other biological markers. It is important to note, however, if the test results are, in fact, relatively normal, there is a risk the client could conclude that drugs are not a problem for him or her. This could have the paradoxical effect of delaying consideration about stopping drug use.

For such clients, a better strategy might be to show anonymous test results of other clients who were not so fortunate as to stop their drug use in time. One could display examples of test results at various stages in the addictive process, from early use, to acceleration of use, to addiction, to medical and psychiatric decline. Then, the client could see that his or her own "normal" results are thankfully premorbid; however, more serious illness could await. Paradoxically, for clients who are already addicted, this latter approach tends not to work because it is often perceived as confrontational and preachy, and it raises clients' anxiety and defensiveness.

Relapse Prevention

Relapse prevention is another commonly administered intervention in drug courts (Peyton & Gossweiler, 2001). Relapse prevention strategies are designed to help drug abusers identify the antecedents and consequences of their drug use. One important goal is to assist clients to recognize the "people, places, and things" that precipitate their drug use. The belief is they will be more able to avoid using drugs if they sidestep the precipitants of drug use.

According to relapse prevention theory, these precipitants are referred to as "triggers." For addicts, triggers are conceptualized as the automatic thoughts or autonomic hyper-arousal engendered by exposure to classically conditioned stimuli for drug use (Marlatt & Gordon, 1985). These triggers may include the people with whom they use drugs, the places in which they use drugs, or emotional states (e.g., depression) that lead to drug use. For addicts, encountering these triggers leads to visceral and autonomic responses, such as sweating, increased heart rate and blood pressure, and cravings. The indicated interventions for such classically conditioned responses include extinction, desensitization, response stopping, and escape planning (e.g., Martin & Pear, 1999). For example, clients may be taught to use progressive muscle relaxation, meditation, or mental imagery to interfere with their cravings.

Although it may also be prudent to help clients who are low severity avoid the people, places, and things that occasion their drug use, these precipitants are not properly conceptualized as "triggers" in the classical sense. This is not merely semantics because if the stimuli do not precipitate hyper-arousal or cravings, then the interventions commonly used in relapse prevention approaches would not be indicated. For example, it would make little sense to teach a client skills for managing cravings when he or she does not experience cravings. Rather, the indicated intervention would be to help the client plan his or her day in advance to avoid situations that make drug use more likely to occur, and to arrange for the client's day to be taken up with drug-incompatible activities that are, themselves, naturally reinforcing. These goals may be accomplished by using the technique of daily activity scheduling (e.g., Beck, Wright, Newman, & Liese, 1993), in which clients are assisted to schedule drug-incompatible and prosocial activities ahead of time on a weekly basis. Then, brief checkup phone calls are used to gauge their compliance with the scheduled activities and troubleshoot unanticipated deviations.

A related aim of relapse prevention is to assist clients to identify the negative consequences of drug use. Typically, clients are asked to discuss how drugs have negatively affected their relationships, employment, health, and so on. The belief is that increasing clients' awareness of the damaging effects of drugs will make them more likely to think about those effects before using. As with MI and MET, having individuals who are low severity verbalize the effects of drugs in this way may highlight the fact that drugs have not had much negative effects. Accordingly, the indicated strategy would be to assist clients to imagine the types of negative effects that could develop in the future, and to bring those effects to consciousness before engaging in new drug use.

Judicial Status Hearings

One of the "key components" of drug court is to have clients attend regularly scheduled status hearings in court (NADCP, 1997). At these hearings, the judge reviews each client's progress in the program and applies sanctions for infractions and rewards for achievements. In most drug courts, status hearings are held on a biweekly or monthly basis.

There is a debate in the drug policy field regarding the importance of judicial status hearings in drug courts (e.g., Marlowe et al., 2004). On one hand, some commentators have argued that status hearings are among the most costly elements of drug court (e.g., Cooper, 1997), which means less money is available for counselors' salaries. Some commentators also have argued that the intrusion of the judge into the treatment process may be disruptive or harmful because clients may be hesitant to convey clinically relevant information to their counselors for fear the information will be disclosed to the judge and used against them (e.g., Schottenfeld, 1989). On the other hand, proponents of drug court have argued that offenders who abuse drugs often fail to meet their obligations and pose a continuing threat to public safety if they are not closely monitored and do not receive immediate and consistent sanctions for their noncompliance in treatment (e.g., Hora, Schma, & Rosenthal, 1999). In fact, status hearings may be equally therapeutic, or more therapeutic than treatment, because they instill a sense of accountability and apply basic principles of behavior modification in the most effective manner (Marlowe & Kirby, 1999).

Research suggests that both of these positions may be correct, but with reference to different clients. Our own program of experimental research in several adult drug courts found that high-dose, biweekly status hearings were most effective for drug court clients who were high risk (i.e., had Antisocial Personality Discorder (APD) or a history of failed experiences in drug treatment) (Marlowe, Festinger, & Lee, 2003, 2004). In contrast, fewer status hearings produced similar or superior results for drug court clients who were low risk and did not have these characteristics. In these studies, the clients who were low risk performed equally well, or better, when they were not scheduled in advance to attend status hearings, but rather only attended hearings if their case managers determined there was a need because of serious noncompliance in treatment or rule violations (we termed these "as-needed" hearings). Based on these experimental findings, it would appear that as-needed status hearings might be most appropriately suited to the needs of many clients who are subthreshold or premorbid and are naïve to treatment and to the criminal justice system.

SECONDARY PREVENTION STRATEGIES FOR LOW-RISK DRUG OFFENDERS

As the foregoing suggests, many interventions that are typically used in drug courts may be ineffective or contraindicated for clients who are subthreshold or premorbid. The dominant service model assumes it is desirable to place substantial time demands on all clients, immerse them in a milieu populated by other drug abusers, require their verbal commitment to the self-label of "addict," and require them to commit to interventions targeted at symptoms they might not, in fact, have. Instead, these clients may require a diametrically opposed intervention scheme. Best-practice standards in the substance abuse field dictate they would be better suited to

a secondary prevention approach directed at interrupting the initial acquisition of addictive behaviors.

Prevention strategies are typically classified into three categories according to how the target group is selected and the anticipated impact of the intervention (DeMatteo & Marczyk, 2005; Institute of Medicine, 1994; NIDA, 2003).

- Primary (or universal) prevention strategies target the general population with the goal of preventing substance involvement from emerging in the first place.

- Secondary (or selective) prevention strategies target individuals who have an elevated risk for developing a substance use problem with the goal of forestalling the development of a clinical substance use disorder.

- Tertiary (or indicated) prevention strategies target individuals who are high risk and already experiencing a substance-use disorder with the goal of reducing further harm from drug use.

Drug court clients who are low risk are an example of a population for which secondary prevention strategies would be most appropriate. These clients have engaged in problematic behavior (i.e., drug use) but have not yet developed a clinical syndrome. Compared to clients who are addicted, these clients have engaged in minimal drug use and are, therefore, less likely to experience the problems associated with drug dependence. Unfortunately, the existing secondary prevention literature is not particularly instructive for intervening with adult drug court clients. Virtually all of the research on secondary prevention of drug use has focused on children or adolescents and evaluated interventions delivered at the school, family, or community level. These interventions are not suited for adult offenders in drug court. Few clients in drug court are enrolled in school, and many come from unstable families or are estranged from their family and friends (Belenko, 2002). This makes school-based or family-based interventions impractical to implement.

To our knowledge, the only published studies of secondary prevention strategies for adult substance abusers have been conducted with college binge drinkers (e.g., Baer, Kivlahan, Blume, McKnight, & Marlatt, 2001; Marlatt et al., 1998; Marlatt & Witkiewitz, 2002). Baer et al. (2001) reported on a 4-year follow-up study of 2,041 college freshman who received the Brief Alcohol Screening and Intervention for College Students (BASICS; Dimeff, Baer, Kivlahan, & Marlatt, 1999). The BASICS protocol consisted of education about social norms, education about the effects of alcohol on physical health and social behavior, drug-refusal skills training, self-monitoring, and motivational interviewing. The results indicated that the BASICS intervention brought about a significant reduction in the quantity of alcohol consumed and negative consequences of alcohol over 4 years compared to an at-risk college control sample.

Needless to say, the context of a college campus is substantially different from that of a drug court. Individuals in these two environments could be expected to differ substantially in terms of educational attainment, socioeconomic status, and degree of functional success or impairment. In addition, one of the most effective elements of the BASICS package was the use of "social norming," in which college students were shown that they significantly overestimated how much drugs and alcohol their peers typically consume. For clients in drug court, there is a serious concern that many of their peers do, in fact, abuse a lot of drugs and alcohol (e.g., Belenko & Peugh, 1998), which could cause a social-norming intervention to backfire or fall flat.

Finally, many secondary prevention packages for adolescents and college students utilize a harm reduction approach, which may include explicit goals for controlled alcohol use, as opposed to a zero-tolerance policy (e.g., Marlatt & Witkiewitz, 2002). Bearing in mind that clients in drug court are under the jurisdiction of judges and other criminal justice authorities, it would not be acceptable to make controlled use of illicit substances an explicit goal of the program. The public and policy makers would not tolerate allowing criminal offenders—who are only out on the street because of a diversionary opportunity—to continue to use intoxicating substances.

A Conceptual Model for Providing Secondary Prevention Services in Drug Court

There are many ways to conceptualize the onset of drug use and its subsequent progression to abuse and addiction, and we present one such conceptual model in Figure 1. This model is not intended to serve as a universal framework for explaining the process of addiction. Rather, the purpose is to suggest, in broad strokes, how prevention strategies should vary according to where a client is in the process of acquiring addictive behaviors. Moreover, this conceptual model points to concrete strategies that may be used to interrupt the development of addictive behavior at various stages in the acquisition process.

The onset of drug use is, of course, determined by multiple factors, including genetic predisposition, learning history, situational variables, and the environment. For example, individuals who have a first-degree relative with a history of drug dependence may have a genetic predisposition to prefer the effects of drugs, tolerate relatively higher doses, and withstand hangover symptoms. Moreover, those who have a genetic propensity toward experiencing symptoms of anxiety or depression may be more likely to experiment with drugs in an effort to "self-medicate" these symptoms. The availability of drugs and norms of social behavior in one's environment will also influence initial experimentation with drugs. Individuals will be more likely to experiment

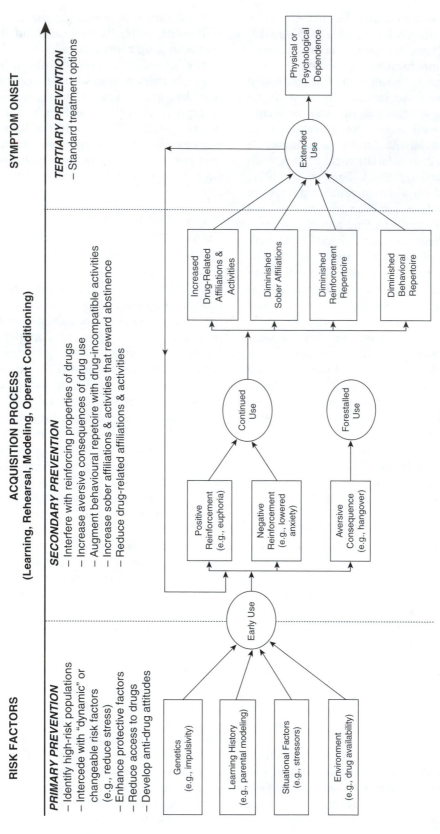

Figure 1 A Conceptual Model of Drug Addiction and Relevant Prevention Strategies

with drugs if drugs are readily obtainable in their community or if drug use has become an accepted activity in their immediate subculture.

Whether an individual continues to use drugs after initial experimentation is contingent, in part, on his or her subjective experiences. For example, if the initial drug use results in euphoria or decreased anxiety, it is more likely that drug use will escalate. This is a straightforward application of the laws of operant conditioning, in which pleasurable events are known to be repeated with greater frequency (i.e., "positive reinforcement"), as are events that lead to reductions in negative affects (i.e., "negative reinforcement"; e.g., Skinner, 1938). Euphoria is a prime example of positive reinforcement, and decreased anxiety is a prime example of negative reinforcement. Of course, for some individuals, initial drug use will lead to aversive consequences, such as a hangover or "bad trip." However, they may still continue to use drugs if these aversive effects are "outflanked" or "outnumbered" by the sheer density of social rewards that ensue, such as fitting in with peers, becoming popular, or receiving secondary gains such as sex.

Over time, as individuals continue using drugs, they begin to augment their involvement with drug-related peers and activities and attenuate their involvement in constructive activities. They may, for example, associate more with the "druggies" at school and spend less time in the classroom or in recreational activities or hobbies. As a result, they decrease their involvement in pleasurable activities that could compete naturally with drug use. Continued drug use may also diminish the enjoyment they previously derived from nondrug activities and behaviors. This is because, relatively speaking, the "dopamine surge" from drugs often outpaces anything comparable that is obtained from the exhilaration of a job or project well done. In the last stages, drug use progresses to drug dependence, which is characterized by compulsivity and withdrawal.

The choice of prevention strategies differs according to where an individual is in the process of acquiring an addiction. Primary prevention strategies are directed at individuals who are in the left-most sections of the model. These strategies seek to interrupt initial access to and experimentation with drugs. Common strategies at this juncture include restricting the availability of drugs (i.e., supply-side interventions), developing antidrug attitudes (e.g., "Just Say No"), and altering dynamic risk factors for drug use (e.g., reducing stress, improving parenting practices). At the other end of the continuum, tertiary prevention strategies are aimed at individuals who are already experiencing the addictive effects of drugs, and the goal is to ameliorate the clinical symptoms of addiction through standard treatment services.

Secondary prevention strategies are targeted to individuals in the midsections of the model. These individuals have engaged in some drug use but are not yet exhibiting clinically significant symptoms. Nevertheless, they may already be steeped in the process of acquiring an addictive behavioral pattern. It, therefore, follows that secondary prevention strategies at these junctures should focus on interrupting further acquisition of addictive behaviors.

Interfering with the reinforcing properties of drugs. As noted previously, repetitively experiencing the reinforcing properties of drugs will lead to escalated use. It follows that interventions should be directed at interfering with these reinforcing reactions. Helping clients to avoid the "people, places, and things" that occasion their drug use is one obvious method to accomplish this task. If they do not use drugs, they cannot experience drugs' reinforcing effects. One technique is to assist clients to plan their days in advance to minimize the likelihood they will encounter circumstances that historically led to drug use.

More to the point, however, pharmacological blockades can be very helpful in preventing positive reinforcement from occurring. For example, naltrexone is a nonaddictive, nonintoxicating medication that is capable of completely blocking the pleasurable effects of opiates and partially blocking the pleasurable effects of alcohol. It has been used quite successfully in reducing drug use among probationers with minimal side effects (Cornish et al., 1997). Medications such as these, which are inexpensive, safe, and effective, are grossly underutilized in the criminal justice system (e.g., Cornish & Marlowe, 2003; Marlowe, 2003).

We recognize that suggesting the use of a pharmacological blockade for drug users who are low severity runs counter to traditional thinking. Pharmacological treatments have typically been reserved for the individuals who are most seriously drug addicted. However, we believe these medications are, perhaps, best suited for drug users who are low severity. These medications were not designed to treat the features of addiction, such as withdrawal or compulsions. Instead, they were designed to interfere with drugs' pleasure-inducing properties, which is a critical aspect of any prevention approach.

Increasing the aversive consequences of drug use. Logically, drug use should decrease if it is followed by aversive consequences. As noted, however, aversive effects can be "outnumbered" by the large density of social rewards that may follow drug use. In drug courts, clients receive graduated sanctions for positive urine specimens, which offers a powerful opportunity to reliably pair drug use with discomfort. Moreover, drugs like disulfiram (Antabuse) can provoke uncomfortable feelings in response to substance use that can compete in magnitude against the pleasurable effects. These pharmacological effects may be "too little, too late" for clients who are already addicted but may be quite potent for those who are early in the addictive process. Clients can also be taught to anticipate the negative effects that may ensue as a consequence of continued drug use (e.g., declining health, employment difficulties, criminal arrests), which may serve to augment the magnitude of aversive cognitions paired with drug use.

Increasing involvement with drug-incompatible peers and activities. The more time clients spend with drug-incompatible peers and activities, the less likely it is they will use drugs. This is an important consideration, because in a "vicious cycle," continued drug use results in decreased involvement in adaptive activities that would normally compete with drug use. Assisting clients to "pencil-in" prosocial, drug-incompatible activities to their daily schedules is a promising and inexpensive technique for clients who are low risk, and it is consistent with the restorative justice concepts of building prosocial attachments, increasing commitment to the community through prosocial activities and involvement, and helping individuals to be better citizens (e.g., Bazemore, 1998, 2001). Through daily activity scheduling, clients can be assisted to increase their involvement with non-drug-using peers and non-drug-related activities. This is consistent with the community reinforcement approach (CRA), which rearranges the drug user's environment such that healthy, nondrug behaviors are naturally reinforced and unhealthy, drug-related behaviors are not reinforced (e.g., Sisson & Azrin, 1989). Importantly, CRA has achieved favorable long-term results in several empirical studies (e.g., Higgins et al., 1995).

The techniques of daily activity scheduling and self-monitoring would appear to serve as a promising platform for a secondary prevention regimen. Activity schedules are blank grids containing the 7 days of the week divided into 1-hour blocks. Either in person or on the telephone, clients are assisted to plan their weekly activities, focusing on avoiding drug-related peers and events and increasing involvement in drug-incompatible activities. Counselors may need to help some clients distinguish between acceptable and unacceptable social behaviors. Research suggests that delivering such services by telephone can be effective at reducing substance use in a variety of populations while avoiding the expense and time of in-person sessions (e.g., McKay, Lynch, Shepard, & Pettinati, 2005). During the week, clients keep a "real-time" record of their compliance with the schedules and identify antecedents and consequences of noncompliance (e.g., thoughts, affects, situational events). During each phone session, clients and their counselors review the previous week's events to assess compliance with their schedule, determine which strategies were successful, "troubleshoot" deviations from their planned routine, and craft new strategies to avoid a recurrence of problems in the future.

IMPORTANT CAVEATS

As noted earlier, we recognize that a low risk for drug use is not necessarily equivalent to a low risk for criminal reoffending or absconding from treatment. This can have significant implications for public safety. For example, it is possible that offenders who are seriously antisocial may be erroneously assigned to drug court despite being premorbid for a drug problem. Placing such individuals into a low-intensity prevention regimen would not be appropriate and could present a serious threat to program integrity and public safety. Of course, such individuals do not belong in drug court at all. On being identified, they should be transferred out of any drug diversion program. Similarly, drug dealers who are not addicted, who may end up in drug court as a result of being charged with a drug-possession offense and "admitting" to having a drug problem, would not be appropriate for a secondary prevention approach designed to forestall continued drug use. Given the mandatory sentencing that results from a conviction on drug trafficking charges, drug dealers may have a strong incentive to

"end up" in a drug court. Ideally, these individuals should be identified prior to being admitted to the drug court program.

In addition, some premorbid clients who are drug involved may still be unsuited to a prevention package because they have other risk factors that require greater supervision. For example, as noted previously, research reveals that clients with APD require a greater intensity of judicial supervision than most drug court clients (Marlowe et al., 2004). Other risk factors in drug court may include a younger age during treatment (typically younger than age 25 years), an earlier age of involvement in crime (especially violent crime prior to age 16 years), an earlier age of beginning drug use (typically prior to age 14 years), previous failed efforts in drug treatment, and having first-degree relatives with drug-use problems or criminal histories (Marlowe, Patapis, & DeMatteo, 2003). Individuals with these risk factors could, perhaps, be excused from certain interventions, such as 12-step groups, if they do not exhibit clinical features of addiction; however, they ought not be excused from other on-site requirements at the courthouse or treatment program. If reasonable attention is paid to these risk factors for criminality, in conjunction with drug-use severity, there should be sufficient safeguards against threats to public safety.

CONCLUSION

In summary, the services provided in many drug court programs may be clinically contraindicated for a sizeable proportion of clients who do not have a diagnosable or clinically significant substance use disorder. Our review of the literature suggests the following hypotheses about how best to intervene with clients who are low risk:

- They should not have time-consuming requirements for on-site attendance at the program (with the obvious exception of on-site delivery of urine specimens).

- They should not be treated in heterogeneous groups and, instead, should be treated either on an individual basis or in separately stratified groups.

- They should not be required to attend traditional 12-step groups that follow the disease model of addiction.

- They should not be required to admit or verbalize the negative effects of drugs on their lives but rather should receive psychoeducation about the potential impacts from drugs they might experience in the future.

- They should not be exposed to classical conditioning exercises aimed at desensitizing craving responses.

- They should attend status hearings on a reduced or as-needed schedule.

- They should engage in a carefully crafted regimen of daily or weekly activity scheduling combined with self-monitoring of compliance with the schedules, which is overseen at a distance by clinical counselors through such means as phone-based or Internet-based counseling.

We recognize that these are merely educated hypotheses that need to be confirmed in a controlled manner. An empirical test of these hypotheses would reveal what benefits, if any, may accrue from matching clients who are low severity in drug court to a program of prevention services based on their service needs. This has the potential to lend important guidance to drug courts about how to tailor services in the most effective and cost-efficient manner.

REFERENCES

Alcoholics Anonymous. (1976). *Alcoholics anonymous* (3rd ed.). New York: Alcoholics Anonymous World Services.

American Psychiatric Association. (1994). *Diagnostic and statistical manual of mental disorders* (4th ed.). Washington, DC: Author.

Baer, J. S., Kivlahan, D. R., Blume, A. W., McKnight, P., & Marlatt, G. A. (2001). Brief intervention for heavy-drinking college students: 4-year follow-up and natural history. *American Journal of Public Health, 91*, 1310–1316.

Bazemore, G. (1998). Restorative justice and earned redemption: Communities, victims, and offender reintegration. *American Behavioral Scientist, 41*, 768–813.

Bazemore, G. (2001). Young people, trouble, and crime: Restorative justice as a normative theory of informal social control and social support. *Youth & Society, 33*, 199–226.

Beck, A. T., Wright, F. D., Newman, C. F., & Liese, B. S. (1993). *Cognitive therapy of substance abuse.* New York: Guilford.

Belenko, S. (2002). Drug courts. In C. G. Leukefeld, F. Tims, & D. Farabee (Eds.), *Treatment of drug offenders: Policies and issues* (pp. 301–318). New York: Springer.

Belenko, S., & Peugh, J. (1998). *Behind bars: Substance abuse and America's prison population.* New York: National Center on Addiction and Substance Abuse at Columbia University.

Cooper, C. S. (1997). *1997 drug court survey report: Executive summary.* Drug Court Clearinghouse and Technical Assistance Project, Office of Justice Programs, U.S. Department of Justice.

Cornish, J., & Marlowe, D. B. (2003). Alcohol treatment in the criminal justice system. In B. Johnson, P. Ruiz, & M. Galanter (Eds.), *Handbook of clinical alcoholism treatment* (pp. 197–207). Baltimore: Lippincott, Williams & Wilkins.

Cornish, J. W., Metzger, D., Woody, G. E., Wilson, D., McLellan, A. T., Vandergrift, B., et al. (1997). Naltrexone pharmacotherapy for opioid dependent federal probationers. *Journal of Substance Abuse Treatment, 14*, 529–534.

DeMatteo, D., & Marczyk, G. (2005). Risk factors, protective factors, and the prevention of antisocial behavior among juveniles. In K. Heilbrun, N. E. S. Goldstein, & R. E. Redding (Eds.), *Juvenile delinquency: Prevention, assessment, and intervention* (pp. 19–44). New York: Oxford University Press.

DeMatteo, D. S., Festinger, D. S., Lee, P. A., & Marlowe, D. B. (2005, June). *Substance use patterns in drug court: No problem?* Paper presented at the 67th Annual Scientific Meeting of the College on Problems of Drug Dependence, Orlando, FL.

Dimeff, L. A., Baer, J. S., Kivlahan, D. R., & Marlatt, G. A. (1999). *Brief Alcohol Screening and Intervention for College Students (BASICS): A harm reduction approach.* New York: Guilford.

Dishion, T. J., & Andrews, D. W. (1995). Preventing escalation in problem behaviors with high-risk young adolescents: Immediate and 1-year outcomes. *Journal of Consulting and Clinical Psychology, 63,* 538–548.

Higgins, S. T., Budney, A. J., Bickel, W. K., Badger, G. J., Florian, E., & Foerg, D. O. (1995). Outpatient behavioral treatment for cocaine dependence: One-year outcomes. *Experimental and Clinical Psychopharmacology, 3,* 205–212.

Hora, P. F., Schma, W. G., & Rosenthal, J. T. A. (1999). Therapeutic jurisprudence and the drug treatment court movement: Revolutionalizing the criminal justice system's response to drug abuse and crime in America. *Notre Dame Law Review, 74,* 439–538.

Institute of Medicine. (1994). *Reducing risks for mental disorders: Frontiers for preventive intervention research.* Washington, DC: National Academy Press.

Kleiman, M. A. R., Tran, T. H., Fishbein, P., Magula, M. T., Allen, W., & Lacy, G. (2003). *Opportunities and barriers in probation reform: A case study of drug testing and sanctions.* Berkeley: University of California, California Policy Research Center.

Lazowski, L. E., Miller, F. G., Boye, M. W., & Miller, G. A. (1998). Efficacy of the Substance Abuse Subtle Screening Inventory-3 (SASSI-3) in identifying substance dependence disorders in clinical settings. *Journal of Personality Assessment, 71,* 114–128.

Lee, P. A., Marlowe, D. B., Festinger, D. S., Cacciola, J. S., McNellis, J., Schepise, N. M., et al. (2001). Did "Breaking the Cycle" (BTC) clients receive appropriate services? [Abstract]. *Drug and Alcohol Dependence, 63*(Supp. 1), S89. Presentation at the 63rd Annual Scientific Meeting of the College on Problems of Drug Dependence, Scottsdale, AZ.

Marlatt, G. A., Baer, J. S., Kivlahan, D. R., Larimer, M. E., Quigley, L. A., Somers, J. M., et al. (1998). Screening and brief intervention for high-risk college student drinkers: Results from a 2-year follow-up assessment. *Journal of Consulting and Clinical Psychology, 66,* 604–615.

Marlatt, G. A., & Gordon, J. R. (Eds.). (1985). *Relapse prevention: Maintenance strategies in the treatment of addictive behaviors.* New York: Guilford.

Marlatt, G. A., & Witkiewitz, K. (2002). Harm reduction approaches to alcohol use: Health promotion, prevention, and treatment. *Addictive Behaviors, 27,* 867–886.

Marlowe, D. B. (2003). Integrating substance abuse treatment and criminal justice supervision. *NIDA Science and Practice Perspectives, 2,* 4–14.

Marlowe, D. B., Festinger, D. S., & Lee, P. A. (2003). The role of judicial status hearings in drug court. *Offender Substance Abuse Report, 3,* 33–46.

Marlowe, D. B., Festinger, D. S., & Lee, P. A. (2004). The judge is a key component of drug court. *Drug Court Review, 4*(2), 1–34.

Marlowe, D. B., & Kirby, K. C. (1999). Effective use of sanctions in drug courts: Lessons from behavioral research. *National Drug Court Institute Review, 2,* 1–31.

Marlowe, D. B., Kirby, K. C., Festinger, D. S., Merikle, E. P., Tran, G., & Platt, J. J. (2003). Day treatment for cocaine dependence: Incremental utility over outpatient counseling and voucher incentives. *Addictive Behaviors, 28,* 387–398.

Marlowe, D. B., Patapis, N. S., & DeMatteo, D. S. (2003). Amenability to treatment of drug offenders. *Federal Probation, 67*, 40–46.

Martin, G., & Pear, J. (1999). *Behavior modification: What it is and how to do it* (6th ed.). Upper Saddle River, NJ: Prentice Hall.

McKay, J. R., Cacciola, J. S., McLellan, A. T., Alterman, A. I., & Wirtz, P. W. (1997). An initial evaluation of the psychosocial dimensions of the American Society of Addiction Medicine criteria for inpatient vs. intensive outpatient substance abuse rehabilitation. *Journal of Studies on Alcohol, 58*, 239–252.

McKay, J. R., Donovan, D. M., McLellan, T., Krupski, A., Hansten, M., Stark, K. D., et al. (2002). Evaluation of full vs. partial continuum of care in the treatment of publicly funded substance abusers in Washington State. *American Journal of Drug and Alcohol Abuse, 28*, 307–338.

McKay, J. R., Lynch, K. G., Shepard, D. S., & Pettinati, H. M. (2005). The effectiveness of tele-phone-based continuing care for alcohol and cocaine dependence: 24 month outcomes. *Archives of General Psychiatry, 62*, 199–207.

McLellan, A. T., Cacciola, J., Kushner, H., Peters, R., Smith, I., & Pettinati, H. (1992). The fifth edition of the Addiction Severity Index: Cautions, additions and normative data. *Journal of Substance Abuse Treatment, 9*, 461–480.

Miller, F. G., Roberts, J., Brooks, M. K., & Lazowski, L. E. (1997). *SASSI-3 user's guide.* Bloomington, IN: Baugh Enterprises.

Miller, W. R., & Rollnick, S. (2002). *Motivational interviewing: Preparing people to change addictive behavior* (2nd ed.). New York: Guilford.

Miller, W. R., Sovereign, R. G., & Krege, B. (1988). Motivational interviewing with problem drinkers II: The Drinker's Checkup as a preventive intervention. *Behavioural Psychotherapy, 16*, 251–268.

Miller, W. R., Zweben, A., DiClemente, C. C., & Rychtarik, R. G. (1992). *Motivational enhancement therapy manual: A clinical research guide for therapists treating individuals with alcohol abuse and dependence.* Rockville, MD: National Institute on Alcohol Abuse and Alcoholism.

National Association of Drug Court Professionals. (1997). *Defining drug courts: The key components.* Washington, DC: Office of Justice Programs, U.S. Department of Justice.

National Institute on Drug Abuse. (2003). *Preventing drug use among children and adolescents: A research-based guide for parents, educators, and community leaders* (2nd ed.). Washington, DC: U.S. Department of Health and Human Services.

Panas, L., Caspi, Y., Fournier, E., & McCarty, D. (2003). Performance measures for outpatient substance abuse services: Group versus individual counseling. *Journal of Substance Abuse Treatment, 25*, 271–278.

Peters, R. H., Greenbaum, P. E., Steinberg, M. L., Carter, C. R., Ortiz, M. M., Fry, B. C., et al. (2000). Effectiveness of screening instruments in detecting substance use disorders among prisoners. *Journal of Substance Abuse Treatment, 18*, 349–358.

Petrosino, A., Turpin-Petrosino, C., & Finckenauer, J. O. (2000). Well-meaning programs can have harmful effects! Lessons from experiments of programs such as Scared Straight. *Crime & Delinquency, 46*, 354–379.

Peyton, E. A., & Gossweiler, R. (2001). *Treatment services in adult drug courts: Report on the 1999 National Drug Court Treatment Survey, executive summary.* Washington, DC: U.S. Department of Justice.

Poulin, F., Dishion, T. J., & Burraston, B. (2001). 3-year iatrogenic effects associated with aggregating high-risk adolescents in cognitive-behavioral preventive interventions. *Applied Developmental Science, 5*, 214–224.

Project MATCH Research Group. (1997). Matching alcoholism treatments to client heterogeneity: Project MATCH posttreatment drinking outcomes. *Journal of Studies on Alcohol, 58*, 7–29.

Rice, M. E., Harris, G. T., & Cormier, C. A. (1992). An evaluation of a maximum security therapeutic community for psychopaths and other mentally disordered offenders. *Law and Human Behavior, 16,* 399–412.

Rogers, R., Cashel, M. L., Johansen, J., Sewell, K. W., & Gonzalez, C. (1997). Evaluation of adolescent offenders with substance abuse: Validation of the SASSI with conduct-disordered youth. *Criminal Justice and Behavior, 24,* 114–128.

Rollnick, S., Heather, N., & Bell, A. (1992). Negotiating behavior change in medical settings: The development of brief motivational interviewing. *Journal of Mental Health, 1,* 25–37.

Schottenfeld, R. S. (1989). Involuntary treatment of substance abuse disorders: Impediments to success. *Psychiatry, 52,* 164–176.

Sisson, R. W., & Azrin, N. H. (1989). The community reinforcement approach. In R. K. Hester & W. R. Miller (Eds.), *Handbook of alcoholism treatment approaches: Effective alternatives* (pp. 242–258). Elmsford, NY: Pergamon.

Skinner, B. F. (1938). *Behavior of organisms.* Englewood Cliffs, NJ: Prentice Hall.

Taxman, F. S., & Bouffard, J. A. (2002). Treatment inside the drug treatment court: The who, what, where, and how of treatment services. *Substance Use and Misuse, 37,* 1665–1689.

Taxman, F. S., & Bouffard, J. A. (2003). Substance abuse counselors' treatment philosophy and the content of treatment services provided to offenders in drug court programs. *Journal of Substance Abuse Treatment, 25,* 75–84.

David S. Dematteo, JD, PhD, is a research scientist in the Section on Law & Ethics Research at the Treatment Research Institute at the University of Pennsylvania. Douglas B. Marlowe, JD, PhD, is the director of Law & Ethics Research at the Treatment Research Institute, and an adjunct associate professor of psychiatry at the University of Pennsylvania School of Medicine. David S. Festinger, PhD, is a senior scientist in the section on Law & Ethics Research at the Treatment Research Institute.

CRITICAL THINKING QUESTIONS

Reading 15

1. Differentiate between housing first and treatment first programs.

2. Considering various interest groups, explain how deinstitutionalization came about.

3. Based on what you know of evidence-based practice, evaluate the research methodology utilized by Padgett and her colleagues.

4. Discuss the implications of the research findings for funding sources and policy makers.

5. Discuss the reasons for resistance to the housing first model.

Reading 16

1 How are the basic concepts of human rights delineated in this reading consistent with those of Housing First in Reading 15?

2. Compare human rights with traditional approaches. What are advantages and disadvantages of each?

3. Note how the author contrasts European and United States approaches to illicit drug use in terms of American religious history.

4. Based on the principles of motivational interviewing, consider how a counselor might approach a binge-drinking youth who is not yet contemplating change.

5. Consider some other uses for the human rights approach related to social problems.

Reading 17

1. Do you think the author's criticism of the DSM-IV's criteria for substance dependence is valid? Why or why not? Relate these criteria to some college students you know.

2. Drug courts are a progressive resource to provide people with treatment instead of prison. In light of this fact, discuss whether or not DeMatteo et al. are being overly critical of these programs.

3. A basic assumption of this reading is that many drug users participating in drug court are not addicts. If the offender is an addict, however, would these same arguments apply?

4. How do statements in this article contradict teachings from harm reduction? Argue whether or not harm reduction principles could have some relevance to drug court programs.

The Way Forward: From Research to Practice

KATHERINE VAN WORMER

UNIVERSITY OF NORTHERN IOWA

BRUCE A. THYER

FLORIDA STATE UNIVERSITY

A myth that is widely believed and reinforced by the mass media is that the success rate of substance abuse treatment is extremely low. This broad indictment of the system may be a carry-over from a time when treatment was extremely rigid and confrontational. This indictment fails to account for the many recent advances that have been made in the areas of assessment, individualized, stage-based treatment, and the discovery of medications to reduce drug cravings and prevent relapse.

As will now be clear from this collection of readings, the profession of substance abuse treatment has made considerable advances; the research on treatment effectiveness is solid. Treatment providers, after years of reluctance to pursue new avenues of investigation and change are now moving forward cautiously but with some deliberation to replace interventions of little demonstrable value with interventions that draw on principles of science. The focus must be on outcome rather than to loyalty to "the way it has always been done."

This is not to say there are not powerful forces aligned against the promotion of evidenced-based practice in this field. Practitioners who are of the old school, with incredible life experience but little formal education, stand to see their status reduced as the field professionalizes and hires professionally educated therapists who lack a personal background in addiction and recovery. The trend today is toward offering integrated treatment for persons who have both mental and addiction disorders; specialized training is a necessity for at least a majority of the treatment personnel to meet today's treatment needs. And there is no room for inflicting interventions on clients that are of no proven value. A blending of the new with the old may be the most efficacious way to go.

Our point of departure for the present volume was Eileen Gambrill's essay on evidence-based practice and policy. Evidence-based practice, as Gambrill informs us, was developed to help lessen the gap between research and practice and to critically evaluate treatment interventions to ensure their validity and applicability to clients. Gambrill issues a strong warning, however, that much of what passes for evidenced-based practice in the literature is not the result of rigorous appraisals of the practices or even a presentation of an objective evaluation of a certain intervention. In other words, there is much lip service today to evidence-based research, but high standards are often lacking. In our quest for what works, we must be careful not to enhance a narrow view of evidence-based practice but to develop knowledge from a wide range of resources and through a collaborative effort that includes feedback from front line workers and clients.

The Defining of Outcomes

Empirically-based practices have as their purpose to improve the outcomes of treatment. A major challenge, according to Eliason (2007). is to determine how the outcomes are defined and for which populations the effective outcomes apply. Advances have been made in terms of measuring outcomes for addicted clients, in general, but the evidence-based practices movement has been slow to address issues of diversity as demonstrated in large scale, national studies. In this collection, we have chosen studies, for example, those based on incarcerated populations, Latino families, women receiving domestic violence services, and gender-based treatments in the interests of determining the impact of diversity; however, more studies are needed in this regard.

So how are outcomes defined to determine treatment success? In the past, follow-up surveys of former clients were conducted and the question asked, "When did you have your last drink? Or last use drugs?" Rigid adherence to the traditional, total abstinence standard in the past is one reason that the myth of treatment in effectiveness persists. More recently, the impact of treatment strategies is being measured in terms of retention in treatment (a short-term measure) and self-reported improvement in drinking

and drug use (a long-term measure) (Eliason). Similarly, harm reduction models, commonly used in Europe, measure the extent to which harm has been reduced (van Wormer & Davis, 2008). Significantly, Reading 9 by Bennett and O'Brien used the criterion of a reduction in drinking in a one month period rather than a standard of total abstinence as a measure of program effectiveness.

Once a certain practice has been demonstrated to have a high level of effectiveness, for example, getting clients to quit or reduce their smoking in conjunction with their other substance use, the challenge facing the evidence-based practices movement is how to convince treatment providers to implement the practice nationwide. Because front line staff and some administrators trained in traditional approaches may reject the new approach, Eliason recommends having the stakeholders, the treatment personnel, be involved in the decision making. Additionally, staff attendance at educational workshops and conferences can help spread the word. An effective strategy is to conduct training role-plays to give counselors confidence in applying the new principles. The surest way of all to institute new programming or even a complete paradigm shift in treatment, as Eliason informs us, occurs through a change in financing. When insurance companies no longer paid for 28 days of inpatient treatment, for example, treatment centers shifted their focus to outpatient treatment.

Third-Party Payment Reimbursement

Federal funding is available for pilot projects based on sound research principles and for other related evidence initiatives as well—for example, programs to eradicate homelessness among extremely troubled individuals who have serious mental disorders, and drug courts to provide treatment and intensive supervision in the community (see van Wormer & Davis, 2008). Advocates for a particular form of treatment, however, will be successful in obtaining funding only to the extent that evidence can be presented of its economic advantages over less expensive forms or no treatment at all. Third party payers are far more willing to reimburse treatment providers for the selection of treatment interventions that are of demonstrated effectiveness than for treatments that are based more on tradition than on science.

There are many treatment innovations in the substance abuse field. Included in the innovations are treatment protocols, scientific studies on the brain related to craving and other aspects of addiction, and pharmaceutical discoveries. When multiple practices are shown to be equally effective, managed care puts its support behind the one that is the most cost-effective, for example, outpatient over inpatient treatment, motivational enhancement strategies over traditional 12-step-based programming (van Wormer & Davis, 2008). Traditional methodologies have a place, of course, but their use must be based on standards of science and objectivity and tailored to the needs of the individual. One-size-fits-all, group-based programming, unfortunately, is still the standard treatment offering in most treatment centers even while research recommends that treatment options be provided. As stated in the National Institute of Drug Abuse (NIDA) (2008) "Principles of Effective Treatment":

> No single treatment is appropriate for all individuals. Matching treatment settings, interventions, and services to each individual's particular problems and needs is critical to his or her ultimate success in returning to productive functioning in the family, workplace, and society. (p. 1)

IMPLEMENTING CHANGE

The gap between the treatment approaches or practices that research has shown to be efficacious and what is actually done in substance abuse treatment agencies remains a concern (Iowa Consortium, 2003). To help bridge the gap, the Iowa Consortium offers *An Implementation Guide for Community-Based Substance Abuse Treatment Agencies.* This handbook offers general guidelines for assessing and promoting organizational readiness for change. Useful resources for implementing new strategies of treatment also are available through Substance Abuse and Mental Health Services Administration (SAMHSA). SAMHSA offers a public service training manual to impart the principles of motivational enhancement of clients as one example of an approach that is being widely introduced today.

Evidence of treatment effectiveness and cost effectiveness are areas to which psychologists, social workers, and treatment providers increasingly are attuned. Because of political and legal considerations, however, a lag between research documentation and practice protocols can be expected to occur. Policy makers, concerned with short-term realities, often fail to take either long-term costs of untreated addiction or the documented evidence of treatment effectiveness into account. And yet, progressive policies are being applied in Canada and in some of the cities and states across the United States, policies developed to keep drug addicts out of prison and formerly homeless alcoholics in supportive housing. And the state of Oregon leads the way in their mandating that evidence-based practices be used in substance abuse treatment clinics or funding will be withdrawn.

In conclusion, we agree with Gambrill on the importance of basing professional decisions on sound research evidence. The standards of academic rigor, ethics, and unbiased data-gathering that Gambrill recommends are those that have shaped this special collection of papers on the topic of substance abuse intervention.

REFERENCES

Eliason, M. (2007). *Improving substance abuse treatment: An introduction to the evidence-based practices movement.* Thousand Oaks, CA: Sage.

Gambrill, E. (2006). Evidence-based practice and policy: Choices ahead. *Research on Social Work Practice, 16*, 338–357.

Iowa Consortium (2003). *Evidence-based practices: An implementation guide for community- based substance abuse treatment agencies.* Iowa City: University of Iowa. Retrieved February 2009, from http://www .uiowa .edu/~iowapic/files/ EBP% 20Guide% 20-%20Revised% 205–03.pdf.

National Institute of Drug Abuse (NIDA) (2008, March) *Principles of effective treatment: A research-based guide.* Washington, DC: NIDA. Retrieved February 2009, from http://www .drugabuse.gov/PODAT/PODAT1.html.

van Wormer, K. & Davis, D. R. (2008). *Addiction treatment: A strengths perspective* (2nd ed.). Belmont, CA: Cengage.

A large and diversified set of web-based resources are available pertaining to alcohol and other substance abuse interventions. The outstanding resource for current research in the field is the easy-to-use www.jointogether.org. The following list is divided into websites with a primary focus on alcohol and alcoholism and those including other addictions as well.

WEBSITES WITH A FOCUS ON ALCOHOL ADDICTION

These listings specialize in research concerning alcohol abuse and alcoholism. The government source, NIAAA is the most prominent among the following.

American Council on Alcoholism

http://www.aca-usa.org
Describes new treatment initiatives in treatment for the effects of alcohol abuse and alcoholism.

Amethyst Initiative

http://www.amethystinitiative.org
The website created by university presidents concerned about drinking problems on their university campuses. The purpose is to open up a debate on the feasibility of lowering the drinking age in the U.S. from 21 to 18. Consists mainly of newspaper articles on the initiative; academic research is not provided.

Center for Alcohol & Addiction Studies

http://www.caas.brown.edu
This center which operates at Brown University strives to promote the identification, prevention, and effective evidence-based treatment of alcohol and other drug use problems.

Center on Alcohol Studies

http://alcoholstudies.rutgers.edu/
This multidisciplinary institute is dedicated to acquisition and dissemination of knowledge on substance use and related phenomena with primary emphasis on alcohol use and consequences and alcoholism treatment and prevention.

Institute of Alcohol Studies

http://www.ias.org.uk
This British resource contains up-to-date news stories and references to research findings. The core aim of the Institute is to serve the public interest on public policy issues linked to alcohol.

Mothers Against Drunk Driving (MADD)

http://www.madd.org
The mission of this organization is to stop drunk driving. Information to bolster the case against lowering the drinking age is provided.

National Institute on Alcohol Abuse and Alcoholism (NIAAA)

http://www.niaaa.nih.gov
This is the pre-eminent national agency for alcoholism research on causes, consequences, treatment and prevention of alcoholism and alcohol related problems.

WEBSITES CONCERNED WITH SUBSTANCE ABUSE TREATMENT

The following resources are relevant to treatment interventions. The World Health

Organization and SAMSHA are especially useful for doing research on this topic.

National Addictions Technology Transfer Center Program (NATTC)

http://www.attcnetwork.org/index.asp

National network of centers improving skill levels of treatment practitioners. The Network undertakes a broad range of initiatives that respond to emerging needs and issues in the treatment field. The Network is funded by SAMHSA.

Addiction Treatment Forum

http://www.atforum.com/related-websites/ index.php#research

A very extensive website for research for professionals in the field. *Addiction Treatment Forum* keeps the references updated and weeds out commercial entries.

Downtown Emergency Service Center

www.desc.org

Information here pertains to housing for the addicted homeless. This organization is at the forefront of the Housing First movement.

Drug Policy Alliance Network

www.drugpolicy.org

Progressive organization concerned with facts pertaining to the war on drugs.

Harm Reduction Coalition

www.harmreduction.org

An advocacy group that holds conferences and gives press releases on relevant issues.

Indiana Prevention Resource Center

http://www.drugs.indiana.edu

This clearinghouse for prevention offers technical assistance and information about alcohol, tobacco, and other drugs. The focus is on efforts directed toward youth.

Join Together Online

www.jointogether.org

National resource center on alcohol and other substance use. Great source for news clippings and references to brief reports on current academic research related to AOD issues. The e-mail alert service is invaluable for researchers.

National Center on Addiction and Substance Abuse (CASA)

Columbia University (CASA) Treatment and Recovery Resources

http://www.casacolumbia.org/templates/Resources.aspx?articleid=389& zoneid=11

An excellent research site that reports on its own investigations.

National Families in Action

http://www.nationalfamilies.org

This website has a prevention resource for parents and others to submit questions, etc. Another section contains links to four multicultural groups which share a desire to educate parents and kids about drugs.

Office of National Drug Control Policy (ONDCP)

http://www.whitehousedrugpolicy.gov/treat/index.html

Much material here on treatment and screening.

Signs of Homelessness

www.signsofhomelessness.org

The website is concerned with discrimination against homeless persons with substance use problems.

The Substance Abuse and Mental Health Services Administration (SAMHSA)

http://www.samhsa.gov

A government-funded website that is one of the most comprehensive available for treatment guidelines and knowledge. Check out the TIPS which provide extensive guidelines for work with people at risk for mental or substance use disorders.

World Health Organization. Lexicon of Alcohol and Drug Terms Published by the WHO.

http://www.who.int/substance_abuse/terminology/who_lexicon/en/index.html

A highly useful and extensive reference to terms related to alcohol use and misuse, with a strong emphasis on the biology and pharmacology of alcohol use.

World Health Organization (WHO)

http://www.who.int/substance_abuse/en

This website contains information pertaining to psychoactive substance use and abuse, and also information about the World Health Organization's projects and activities in the areas of substance use and substance dependence.

ABOUT THE EDITORS

Katherine van Wormer, PhD, MSSW, is Professor of Social Work at the University of Northern Iowa and coordinator of the substance abuse certificate. She worked extensively in the field of substance abuse counseling in Washington State and Norway. Dr. van Wormer has authored or co-authored 14 books. Her most recent contributions are two volumes of *Human Behavior and the Social Environment, Micro and Macro Levels Addiction Treatment: A Strengths Perspective, Women and The Criminal Justice System,* and *Death by Domestic Violence: Preventing the Murders and the Murder-Suicides.*

Bruce A. Thyer, PhD, LCSW, has a background in evidence-based practice, evaluation research, and behavior analysis. He served as an enlisted drug and alcohol abuse counselor in the United States Army, stationed in Okinawa, Japan. He has held the advanced rank of Distinguished Research Professor at the University of Georgia and is the former Dean of the College of Social Work at Florida State University where he is currently professor. Dr. Thyer is also the editor of the Sage journal *Research on Social Work Practice,* from which many of the articles comprising this edited collection are drawn.

Supporting researchers for more than 40 years

Research methods have always been at the core of SAGE's publishing program. Founder Sara Miller McCune published SAGE's first methods book, *Public Policy Evaluation*, in 1970. Soon after, she launched the *Quantitative Applications in the Social Sciences* series—affectionately known as the "little green books."

Always at the forefront of developing and supporting new approaches in methods, SAGE published early groundbreaking texts and journals in the fields of qualitative methods and evaluation.

Today, more than 40 years and two million little green books later, SAGE continues to push the boundaries with a growing list of more than 1,200 research methods books, journals, and reference works across the social, behavioral, and health sciences. Its imprints—Pine Forge Press, home of innovative textbooks in sociology, and Corwin, publisher of PreK–12 resources for teachers and administrators—broaden SAGE's range of offerings in methods. SAGE further extended its impact in 2008 when it acquired CQ Press and its best-selling and highly respected political science research methods list.

From qualitative, quantitative, and mixed methods to evaluation, SAGE is the essential resource for academics and practitioners looking for the latest methods by leading scholars.

For more information, visit **www.sagepub.com**.